Routledge Revivals

Arthur Schopenhauer's English Schooling

Originally published in 1988 *Arthur Schopenhauer's English Schooling* examines the famous German philosopher Arthur Schopenhauer, and his image of England and the influences and experiences which formed that image, notably his visit to England in 1803. His philosophy, when he came to formulate it, showed the pervasive influence of his English reading, was riddled with allusions to his three months at Wimbledon School, and was indeed in the 'English' style; above all it was a philosophy designed as a refutation of 'Christianity' as understood and practised by his English headmaster, who is the invisible bête noire behind it. In the course of the book two major figures who have hitherto been known only by name are identified and their lives related. The book also examines many background figures in Schopenhauer's English diary and the letters addressed to him in 1803. This book, which is based on a wide variety of hitherto unknown material from many different sources, will permanently modify our view of his philosophy; it also has important implications for educationalists and for all interest in the history of ideas.

Arthur Schopenhauer's English Schooling

by Patrick Bridgwater

Routledge
Taylor & Francis Group

First published in 1988
by Routledge

This edition first published in 2019 by Routledge
2 Park Square, Milton Park, Abingdon, Oxon, OX14 4RN
and by Routledge
711 Third Avenue, New York, NY 10017

Routledge is an imprint of the Taylor & Francis Group, an informa business

© 1988 Patrick Bridgwater

All rights reserved. No part of this book may be reprinted or reproduced or utilised in any form or by any electronic, mechanical, or other means, now known or hereafter invented, including photocopying and recording, or in any information storage or retrieval system, without permission in writing from the publishers.

Publisher's Note
The publisher has gone to great lengths to ensure the quality of this reprint but points out that some imperfections in the original copies may be apparent.

Disclaimer
The publisher has made every effort to trace copyright holders and welcomes correspondence from those they have been unable to contact.

A Library of Congress record exists under LCCN: 89101888

ISBN 13: 978-0-367-44077-0 (hbk)
ISBN 13: 978-0-367-44079-4 (pbk)
ISBN 13: 978-1-003-00741-8 (ebk)

ARTHUR SCHOPENHAUER'S ENGLISH SCHOOLING

PATRICK BRIDGWATER

ROUTLEDGE
London and New York

First published 1988
by Routledge
11 New Fetter Lane, London EC4P 4EE
29 West 35th Street, New York, NY 10001

© 1988 Patrick Bridgwater

Printed and bound in Great Britain by Mackays of Chatham PLC, Kent

All rights reserved. No part of this book may be reprinted or reproduced or utilized in any form or by any electronic, mechanical, or other means, now known or hereafter invented, including photocopying and recording, or in any information storage or retrieval system, without permission in writing from the publishers.

British Library Cataloguing in Publication Data

Arthur Schopenhauer's English schooling.
1. Schopenhauer, Arthur 2. Philosophers,
Modern — Germany — Biography
I. Title
193   B3151
ISBN 0-415-00743-7

Library of Congress Cataloging-in-Publication Data

ISBN 0-415-00743-7

Contents

Preface
Acknowledgements
Abbreviations
I The Schopenhauers and England 1
    Danzig 1
    Hamburg 13
II Richard Jameson 29
    Background 29
    Divinity Student 32
    Governor 50
    Episcopal Minister 56
    Chaplain in Danzig 66
    Last Years 84
III Arthur Schopenhauer's English Diary 95
    Introduction 95
    Diary 97
IV Arthur Schopenhauer's English Headmaster 140
    Background 140
    Village Schoolmaster 146
    Parson 152
    Parson's Green 159
V Parson Lancaster at Wimbledon 170
    The Eligibility of Wimbledon 170
    The Symposiacks of Wimbledon 177
    Anti-Jacobin and Volunteer 186
    Thomas Lancaster and Lord Nelson 200
    Later Life 215
VI Letters to Schopenhauer at Wimbledon 233
    Introduction 233
    Letters 234
VII Wimbledon School 271
    Mr Lancaster's and Other Academies 271
    Dr Runge and Parson Lancaster 280
    Mr Lancaster's Plan of Education, 1: Theory . 285
    Mr Lancaster's Plan of Education, 2: Practice . 300
    Pulpit Terrorism 306
    Education or Brainwashing? 316

VIII	After-Effects	322
	English Language	322
	English Ways	345
	English Literature	348
	English Bigotry	360
	Schopenhauer and England: Conclusions	368
Bibliography		378
Index		383

Wimbledon School

Preface

My subject is Schopenhauer's image of England and the influences and experiences which formed that image, notably his visit to England in 1803 and the term which he then spent at an English boarding school. His philosophy, when he came to formulate it, showed the pervasive influence of his English reading, was riddled with allusions to his three months at Wimbledon School, and was indeed in many ways an 'English' philosophy written in an 'English' style; above all it was a philosophy designed as a refutation of 'Christianity' as understood and practised by his English headmaster, who is the invisible *bête noire* behind it. The young Schopenhauer's reaction against his English headmaster, an old-fashioned Georgian cleric, radically changed his attitude to religion; his subsequent work would have been quite different but for his traumatic Wimbledon experience, the significance of which can scarcely be exaggerated, for perhaps no other writer has been so profoundly influenced by the experiences of a single term or been so much the product of such rapidly acquired youthful likes and dislikes. In the course of the book two major figures who have hitherto been known only by name (Johanna Schopenhauer's childhood mentor and her son's English headmaster) are identified and their lives related; many background figures are also identified in the course of editing (for the first time) Schopenhauer's English diary and the letters addressed to him in 1803.

All this has entailed countless lines of enquiry of many different kinds; but if the book has demanded research of a peculiarly exacting kind, forcing me to venture into many fields beyond my own, the experience has been a most rewarding one.

Everything originally written in German is translated into English; unless otherwise stated all translations are my own.

P.B.

Acknowledgements

For permission to quote unpublished or copyright material I wish to make grateful acknowledgement to the following for the material concerned: Stadt- und Universitätsbibliothek Frankfurt am Main (Schopenhauer-Archiv: letters addressed to Schopenhauer in 1803-4; the early portrait of Schopenhauer); Staats- und Universitätsbibliothek Hamburg (extract from Lorenz Meyer's unpublished 1802 travel diary); the Trustees of the British Library (unpublished letter from Thomas Lancaster to Earl Spencer dated 27 January 1810, Althorp Papers G.84); the Trustees of the National Maritime Museum (unpublished letter from Thomas Lancaster to Lord Nelson dated 18 November 1803, ref. CRK/8, L/87; and Lieutenant Henry Lancaster's notes on his naval career); the Bishop of Carlisle and Cumbria Record Office (Thomas Lancaster's licence to teach, recorded in the Bishop's Register for 1769, ref. DRC1/8); Hampshire Record Office (unpublished letter from Charles Bond to Thomas Lancaster dated 29 May 1811, Hampshire Record Office, Diocesan Records F/9/B); John Evelyn Society Museum, Wimbledon (R. B. Schnebbelie's 1810 sketch of 'The Rev. Mr. Lancaster's Academy'); University of Durham, Department of Palaeography and Diplomatic (unpublished documents from among the ordination papers of Richard Jameson, 1753, and Gilfrid Gates, 1780); Frau Kathrin Leip (passage from Hans Leip's *Die Lady und der Admiral*).

This brings me to other debts, which are considerable. In the first place I am grateful to all those scholars of whose expertise I have availed myself. Their works loom large in the notes, almost every one of which involves a debt of some kind. I am sensible, too, of how much the book owes to the kindness of colleagues, particularly local historians and local history librarians. I am grateful to all those institutions and individuals who have helped so patiently and generously, often on a number of occasions. It is impossible to list them all, but I am particularly conscious of my indebtedness to the following bodies: Baltic Exchange; Bank of England; Bar Library, Royal Courts of Justice; Berkshire Record Office; Biggar Museum Trust; Bodleian Library, Oxford; Borthwick Institute of Historical Research, York; British Library (Lending Division); British Library (Reference Division); British Museum; Bromley Central Library; Christie Manson and Woods Ltd; Church of Jesus

Acknowledgements

Christ and Latter-Day Saints, Genealogy Library (Sunderland); Cumbria Record Office; Dumfries Museum; Durham Chapter Library; Durham University, Department of Palaeography and Diplomatic; Durham University Library; Edinburgh Central Library; Edinburgh University Library; Ewart Library, Dumfries; General Register House, Edinburgh; General Register Office (St Catherine's House); Gloucestershire Record Office; Guildhall Library; Hammersmith and Fulham Archives Department; Hampshire Record Office; Handelskammer Hamburg (Commerzbibliothek); History of Parliament Trust; House of Lords Record Office; Instytut Baltycki, Gdańsk; John Evelyn Society, Wimbledon; Lambeth Palace Library; Merton Borough Library; National Benevolent Institution; National Library of Scotland; National Maritime Museum; Newcastle Central Library; Newcastle Literary and Philosophical Society; Niedersächsisches Hauptstaatsarchiv in Hannover; Norfolk Record Office; Oriel College, Oxford; Oxfordshire Archives Department; Peterhouse College, Cambridge; Public Record Office (Chancery Lane and Kew); Queen's College, Oxford; St John's College, Cambridge; Schopenhauer-Archiv, Frankfurt a.M.; Scottish Record Office; Scottish Record Society; Society of Genealogists; Southwark Libraries; Staatsarchiv Hamburg; Sunderland Reference Library; Surrey Record Office; Taylorian Library, Oxford; Tyne and Wear Archives Department; Vestry House Museum, Walthamstow; Wimbledon Village Museum. Individuals to whom I am particularly indebted include: Mrs Lyn Arlotte; Anthony Attwood; Dr Iain Bain; E.G.W. Bill; Dr Jeremy Black; the Duke of Buccleuch and Queensbury, KT; Mrs Rosemary Clarkson; J.W.G. Cocke; C. Cooper; Mrs Lorna Cowell; Mrs Mollie Hardwick; Professor Joyce Hemlow; Roy Huddleston, FSA; Chris Jeanes; Mrs Barbara Kosielny; Brian Lambie; Mrs Elizabeth Lancaster; Mrs Kathleen Lowson; Margaret McCollum; Anne McCormack; the Earl of Mar and Kellie; Richard Milward; W. Myson; Roger Norris; Dr Stanislav Potocki; Dr F.J.G. Robinson; Michael Saich; L.J. Schwarz; Rev. Gordon Scott; Rev. Dr Duncan Shaw; Mrs J. Skidmore; Professor Frank Spooner; Dr A.M. Stewart; Rev. Canon J.M. Taylor; A.E. Truckell, FSA, FMA; Mrs Gervaise Vaz; Leslie P. Wenham, FSA; Karen Wilkinson.

There remain two particular debts. To the University of Durham I owe not only several generous grants from the Staff Travel Fund and a subvention from the Publications Board, but also a Foundation Fellowship of Durham University Research Foundation

Acknowledgements

(Society of Fellows), which enabled me to have a year of full-time research at a time when it was most needed and therefore most appreciated. To my wife I owe more than I can say, particularly for her patience in listening to so many accounts of so many 'discoveries', and for the care with which she read such a long manuscript.

Abbreviations

The following abbreviations are used in the text:

Ges. Br.	Arthur Schopenhauer's *Gesammelte Briefe*
P&P	*Parerga und Paralipomena*
SW	Arthur Schopenhauer's *Sämtliche Werke*, ed. Deussen
WWI	*The World as Will and Idea*, trans. Haldane and Kemp

In addition these abbreviations are used in the notes:

A.S.	Arthur Schopenhauer
H.F.S.	Heinrich Floris Schopenhauer
HN	Arthur Schopenhauer's *Handschriftlicher Nachlass*
J.S.	Johanna Schopenhauer
CWAAS	*Transactions of the Cumberland and Westmorland Antiquarian and Archaeological Society*
DNB	*Dictionary of National Biography*
GM	*Gentleman's Magazine*
PR	Parish Register
PRO	Public Record Office
RO	Record office
S-Jb	*Schopenhauer-Jahrbuch*
SS	Johanna Schopenhauer's *Sämtliche Schriften*
VCH	*Victoria County History*

1
The Schopenhauers and England

Danzig

Arthur Schopenhauer was born in the then free city of Danzig on 22 February 1788 (Byron had been born in London on 22 January). If his father had had his way, and his mother had not felt homesick, he would have been born in London and would have enjoyed British natonality. As it was, he regarded himself — with some justification — as a kind of honorary Englishman.

His father, Heinrich Floris Schopenhauer, the 'noble, beneficent spirit' to whom Arthur Schopenhauer dedicated the second edition of his main work, was a wealthy merchant and, at the time of his son's birth, one of the foremost citizens of Danzig. He was also a positive anglomaniac who, even in those days of continental anglophilia, stood out as taking his cult of England further than most; it was the great love of his life. At this time there was, of course, a strong British presence in Danzig. At the beginning of the fourteenth century there was already a colony of 'English' merchants (who were in fact mostly Scottish) in Danzig, and the city soon became the centre of British trade with the Baltic (or the 'Eastland', as it was still known in Pepys's time), which on the British side involved the Muscovy Company, the Eastland Company and the Merchant Adventurers in the North Sea, all of them with their fleets of ships bringing in timber, grain, resin and other Baltic exports. Baltic-based ships were also involved in the trade. The main emigration of Scots to Danzig and West Prussia, and to a lesser extent to East Prussia, only took place from the second half of the sixteenth to the end of the seventeenth century, but long before that the Scottish colony was flourishing and indeed in a privileged position, for 'Upon Account of a signal Service, which one of the Douglass Family did to this City . . . the Scots were allowed to be free Burghers of the Town, and had several other Immunities granted them above other Foreigners'.[1] By the early eighteenth century the Scots, 'excepting the Successors of those who were so incorporated', had 'no Distinction of Privileges', perhaps because by this time 'a better half of the Families or Inhabitants are of Scotch Extraction'. The fact that in 1577 Danzig was able to field (against the King of Poland) 700 Scottish mercenaries under Colonel William Stewart gives confirmation of the early size of the Scottish presence in the city, the largest suburbs of which (those south of the Douglas Gate) were called Schotland. The British colony included a much smaller number of Englishmen. A treaty between Queen Anne and the city of Danzig, giving great privileges to British merchants, was signed in 1707, and was confirmed by the Treaty of Utrecht in 1713. In 1707, the year which also saw the union of England and Scotland, the Anglo-Scottish community acquired its own chapel in the Heilige Geistgasse beside the so-called Long Bridge (in reality a wooden quay) on which, tradition has it, Sir William Douglas, Lord of Nithsdale, 'Prince of Danesvick' and head of the Scots contingent attached to the Teutonic Order, was murdered by English assassins *c.* 1392. The fact that Johanna Schopenhauer's childhood mentor, the Rev. Richard Jameson, came to Danzig from Nithsdale (Dumfries), and that one of the signatories to his call there was a descendant of Sir William Douglas, is typical of the coincidences in which this whole story abounds.

The Anglo-Scottish colony flourished in the eighteenth century, but was hit hard when prohibitive duties were placed on British goods following the Second Partition of Poland and Prussian seizure of Danzig in 1793. Until then, however, during the time when the Schopenhauers and Richard Jameson were living there, Danzig was a place with a flourishing British colony whose members were prominent in the open-air 'Exchange of Merchants' which took place daily from eleven to one. The British were popular, not only because of the earlier military exploits of the Scots, but because they kept a low profile and allowed themselves to be absorbed into the local community. In the earlier eighteenth century the British merchants had their own ordinary, Widow Sheldon's, where they got 'good Victuals dress'd after our Manner' for 24 grosch (about a shilling).[2] Visiting 'Englishmen' were accommodated by William and Lucy Anderson at the 'English House' in the Brotbänkengasse, overlooking the granaries on Speicherinsel, the two largest of which were built by Sir William Brown. The 'Corner House', used occasionally for the reception of the King of Poland, included among its many fine paintings 'portraited Actions to the Memory of our Glorious King William, and the brave Duke of Marlborough'.[3] It is therefore not surprising that when Captain Thomas Fremantle was at Danzig in HMS *Ganges* in June 1801 he wrote to his wife Betsey:

> The manners of these Germans I think more congenial with the English than any I have seen in Europe. I am much pleased at what I have seen but I don't think there is anything that can induce me to come again . . . we have a very good society at the tavern on shore when we can get there . . . I have lived generally on shore and if I could have spoke German should have been well amused.[4]

Heinrich Floris Schopenhauer was born in Danzig in 1747, younger son of Andreas Schopenhauer and his wife Anna Renata Soermans (daughter of the Dutch merchant and shipowner Hendrik Soermans, who settled in Danzig and from 1754 to 1775 acted as Dutch resident for the region).[5] Andreas Schopenhauer was a maritime merchant and banker; it is known that in 1757 he owned one vessel of 120 tons skippered by Christoffel Jansz; he no doubt traded with London and probably acted as shipper for Isaac Solly I and John William Anderson, both of them Baltic merchants known to his son. Whether he came to own other vessels is not recorded. His functions as banker are confirmed by a notarial entry of 14 May 1776 in connection with an outstanding loan of 400 ducats granted to Granowski, *voivode* of Rawa, in 1774. He also invested and dealt in works of art; this is the ultimate source of the interest in art which Arthur Schopenhauer evinced when in London in 1803. Andreas Schopenhauer ended his days on the estate which he had bought at Ohra (Orun), a southern suburb of Danzig. When he died in 1794 his son Heinrich Floris had long since made his own very successful way as a businessman.

Like so many young men of the time, Floris Schopenhauer was sent out into the world to gain knowledge and practical experience. For many years he lived in France and England. In France he served as clerk in the firm of Bethmann, merchants, of Bordeaux, and was so impressed with M. Bethmann's conduct of business and family affairs that in after years he would clinch an argument with the words 'That is what M. Bethmann used to do.' His greatest debt to France was, however, his reverence for the work of Voltaire, which his son was to share. He also read widely in the lighter literature of France and England, and acquired a taste for the novel. Appropriately enough he was in England in 1773, the year which saw both the publication of Mackenzie's sentimental novel *The Man of the World* and much indignation in the press about the First Partition of Poland the previous year and the danger it posed to the lucrative Danzig trade. Shortly after the occupation of Danzig by Prussian troops the English consul, Trevor Corry, sent the Foreign Secretary (Lord Suffolk), on 22 September 1772, a detailed report on the situation. On 11 December 1772 Mr Murray (a leading Danzig merchant of the time) went to the Foreign Office to discuss the growing threat.

One wonders whether Floris Schopenhauer's journey was prompted by the Partition and whether, arrived in London, he made representations on the subject; certainly he will have lost no time in giving an up-to-date report on the situation to his old friend John William Anderson, the Danzig agent in London. Floris Schopenhauer was in a position to confirm the information about the Danzig trade which is contained in the extant 'Minutes of Mr Murray's Conversation', dated 11 December 1772.[6] Mr Murray must have been well known to him. From these minutes one gathers that Danzig at this time was 'a place which is chiefly occupied by Trade and where the Conversation runs only on that subject'. The 'City and Suburbs of Danzig' are said to contain 'each about 70,000 Inhabitants', which is surprising, and the view is expressed that 'There are not many Men of Abilities in the Senate' (Floris Schopenhauer was to be one of the few). Three or four 'Danzig Houses' are said to have 'great Connections in London':

> There are at Dantzig 8 or 9 English Houses, & 24 or 25 Individuals, who are merely Factors; but their Trade is carried on chiefly in the articles sent *to* England. — Those sent *from* Great Britain are managed in great measure by the Dantzickers.
>
> The Exports conducted by the English Factory consist of Grain to Holland, & Timber to England. — The Imports are from the Norwich, Leeds, Sheffield, Manchester and Birmingham Manufactories; & Tobacco, Sugar, Rice, English Beer & Burton Ale, Lead, Tin, Pepper [and Salt] . . .
>
> The Value of the Imports may be estimated at nearly £350,000. That of the Exports at rather more than £250,000.

Britain was concerned to preserve that favourable trade balance, a commercial point of view which Floris Schopenhauer would have understood.

Following the preliminary discussion with Mr Murray, the events in Danzig were discussed at a Cabinet meeting in London on 22 December 1772. John William Anderson, having been to see Lord Suffolk, then wrote to the *Bürgermeister* of Danzig outlining Britain's attitude:

> He reported that the King, on being apprized by Lord Suffolk of the danger facing the City of Danzig, had immediately made representations to the Court at Vienna. An answer having been obtained to the effect that the Court was ready to espouse the cause of the City with the Prussian Government, provided that the Russian Court agreed and was prepared to undertake the necessary negotiations, Mr. Gunning had been ordered to make overtures at St. Petersburg. These were, however, coldly received by Count Panin, who merely said that the Empress was willing to maintain the City in its guaranteed privileges and possessions, insofar as no third power had a claim to them. Now since England was not on good terms with the King of Prussia, and any negotiations could not therefore be expected to succeed, but were, on the contrary, more likely to lead to a rebuff or even to Prussian reprisals in Hanover . . . it had been decided in Cabinet to advise the City of Danzig to negotiate with the Prussian Government an agreement according to which the City would pay the Prussian Government for the harbour [its own claim to which was not entirely sound], in return for the renunciation by the Prussian Government of all other claims, this agreement being guaranteed by London, Vienna and St. Petersburg. When, on being informed of this decision by Lord Suffolk, he [John William Anderson] had remarked that it would be very difficult to find the sort of sum which the King of Prussia would presumably demand, he was told that in such an eventuality the British Government would not fail to advance the City the necessary moneys.[7]

By April 1773 relations between England and Prussia were near breaking point; Frederick II called George III the 'Don Quixote of Danzig', but British reactions far from being quixotic, were — as they too often are — purely mercenary. Eventually a Prussian edict of 11 May 1774 restored the commercial *status quo*. It was to be a different story twenty years later, at the time of the Second Partition of Poland.

How long Floris Schopenhauer stayed in London in 1773 is not known, but it was a long visit (perhaps until 1780), long enough for him to acquire a deep love of the country, its free government and constitution and its liberal institutions. Indeed, he was so taken with family life in England that he seriously contemplated making it his home. Little is known about his English contacts at this stage, but they will have centred on the Baltick Coffee House in Threadneedle Street, the rendezvous of merchants and brokers connected with the 'Russian' trade; he met Isaac Solly I and John William Anderson and his wife Dorothy (who was the first person upon whom the Schopenhauers called thirty years later). He was in England again in 1787 and 1797. When he returned to Danzig he will have found what Nathaniel Wraxall found in 1774:

> the republic . . . is at present diminished on every side, and invested by hussars and grenadiers of an absolute prince . . . The city . . . which no king of Poland ever dared to enslave . . . now awaits in trembling expectation the hour of its destruction . . . Most or all the suburbs, which are very populous and extensive, are already occupied by Prussian soldiery . . . Public diversions of every nature are prohibited by the magistrates, and the German comedy is in one of those suburbs which has been taken from them . . . A langour and decay is . . . visible, at this time, through every department . . . on the ministry of Britain they repose their grand reliance . . .[8]

On his return from his travels he acquired, on 19 November 1780, the full civil and commercial rights which entitled him to conclude business transactions in his own right. He thereupon went into business with his elder brother, Karl Gottfried (1746-95), who had studied at Göttingen, had a thorough knowledge of English, and often visited England, but must also have been something of a liability as a partner, for he is said to have left behind him a character for foolish and discreditable prodigality. Heinrich Floris and Karl Gottfried, who traded under the name of 'Reederei und Kommissionen — Gebrüder Schopenhauer', were shippers and agents, but also maritime merchants, bankers and brokers, and were involved in the trade whereby British manufactured goods were exchanged for grain and raw materials from the Baltic area; Heinrich Floris is usually described as a grain merchant. By 1793, the year in which Heinrich Floris Schopenhauer and his family left Danzig for Hamburg, Gebrüder Schopenhauer owned four vessels.[9]

On 16 May 1785, at the age of 39, Floris Schopenhauer married Johanna Henrietta, the 18-year-old daughter of a fellow merchant, Christian Heinrich Trosiener. Johanna Trosiener (1766–1838) had grown up with Richard Jameson, chaplain to the British colony in Danzig and the Trosieners' next-door neighbour, as her unofficial tutor, guide and counsellor; she, for her part, was (in her own words) his pet. Jameson has never been more than a name in Schopenhauer studies; his life, which is related in the next chapter, reveals him as a fascinating, genial and indeed romantic figure. Nor was he the only 'English' influence in Johanna's childhood, for the family physician, Dr Wolf, came from England bearing letters of introduction to the Rev. Jameson,[10] and she had a close friend of her own age in the person of one Sally Cramp.

Dr Nathanael Matthäus von Wolf is an interesting and distinguished figure. Born at Conitz (West Prussia) on 28 January 1724, and therefore a contemporary of Richard Jameson, he travelled widely in England and elsewhere before coming to Danzig in 1776 to succeed Dr Johann Wilhelm John, who died in that year. He was a member of the Royal Society. His two most important works were published after he had settled in Danzig: *Concordantia botanica* (1780) and *Genera et species plantarum vocabulis characteristicis definita* (1781). How he came to have letters of introduction to Richard Jameson is not known, but we may surmise that one of the letters was from Professor Matthew Stewart (FRS, 1764), under whom Jameson had studied and whom Dr Wolf will have met at the Royal Society. When Nathaniel Wraxall visited Danzig in August 1774, one of those who informed him about local antiquities was Dr Wolf, whom he described as being 'animated with a spirit of independence worthy [*sic*] Hampden or Sidney':

> He resided some years since at Warsaw, but quitted it on account of the troubles and anarchy which foreign ambition has introduced into that capital. He retired to Dirschaw, about twenty miles from hence, built himself an observatory for his astronomical studies, and remained there till the king of Prussia seized on the town and surrounding territory. Unable to bear a yoke so galling, he . . . removed to this city; and

he now declares, that when it is no longer free, he will embark for England, where he has already been, and where every fugitive may find an asylum.[11]

Dr Wolf became the Schopenhauer family doctor and was one of the friends whose death — he died on 15 December 1784, at Danzig — was a source of sorrow to Jameson,[12] who shared many of his interests, including his interest in astronomy. Dr Wolf was also a man after Floris Schopenhauer's own heart; when the latter resolved to leave Danzig in 1793, rather than live under the Prussian yoke, he was only doing what his old friend had said he would do, and if Johanna Schopenhauer had agreed the Schopenhauers might well have gone all the way to England.

That Johanna learned to speak fluent English goes without saying. Given these English influences in her childhood, it was appropriate that she came to marry such a pronounced anglophile. Leaving the story of her childhood to be elaborated in the next chapter, let us at this stage note the description in Anselm Feuerbach's *Memoirs* of the sort of person she became:

> Madame Schopenhauer, a rich widow. Makes profession of erudition. Authoress. Prattles much, and intelligently; without heart and soul. Self-complacent, eager after approbation, and constantly smiling to herself. God preserve us from women whose minds have shot up into mere intellect.[13]

It is not difficult to recognise in this description the person who wrote a series of rather heartless letters to her son while he was languishing at Mr Lancaster's academy;[14] nor is it difficult to sympathise with her son, who, when he heard the description, conceded with a grin that it was fatally accurate. She professed erudition merely; she was not even remotely in Lady Mary Wortley Montagu's league as a bluestocking or character, but was, on the contrary, facile and superficial beneath the self-centredness that comes across so clearly in her diary and letters alike.

Following their marriage this somewhat bizarre and ill sorted couple took up residence on the estate of Polanki (Pelonken, 3. Hof), near Oliva, about four miles to the north-west of Danzig, which Floris Schopenhauer had bought in 1786. Oliva was memorably described by an eighteenth-century English resident of Danzig, who said:

[Oliva] would justly be called a Terrestrial Paradise, if the Inhabitants were but possessed of a Simplicity of Manners, suitable for such a Station. The whole consists of Merchants Country-Seats, and Gardens which Nature, by her Profuseness, at a small Expence, has finish'd to their Hands, abounding with Woods, Springs and Ponds; and before them, all, is a rich champagne open Plain, diversified here and there with pleasant Groves of Pine and Fir-Trees; and beyond them is an enlarged Prospect of the great Arm of the Sea, called the Road, together with a view of the Munde, all Ships at Anchor, coming in and going out.[15]

'Pelonken, 3. Hof' was to be the Schopenhauers' summer home until 1793, or, rather, it was where Johanna lived, being joined by her husband at weekends, for there was only one occasion when he visited his wife during the week, and that was when he rode out to tell her of the fall of the Bastille. Their house, which Heinrich Floris furnished elegantly, after the English manner and (in his wife's phrase) 'with every English comfort', reflected his love of England and English ways. The walls were hung with engravings after the old masters, casts of antique sculptures ornamented the rooms, and there was a library stocked with French and English literature which was particularly strong in novels. Outside was a garden laid out in the English style; partly terraced, it included a small lake with a boat, eight pet lambs whose bells — brought back from England — rang an octave, as well as spaniels and a pair of horses (Floris Schopenhauer also had a fine stud of horses which he kept on his father's estate at Ohra). Such were the elegant, affluent and very 'English' surroundings in which young Arthur Schopenhauer passed his first five summers. His father, who read daily an English and a French newspaper, encouraged his son from early boyhood to read *The Times*, from which, he always said, 'one could learn everything'. The son followed his father's advice so assiduously that the ritual daily reading of *The Times* became a fixed pole of his existence.

It was, however, only after the birth of their son that they settled into this routine. Within two years of their marriage and honeymoon at Oliva, Floris Schopenhauer was seized with one of his periodic urges to travel, a passion which his young wife shared. At the back of his mind was the idea that political changes following the death of Frederick the Great in August 1786 might oblige them to move (as they did), and that they might do worse than settle in

England. He therefore resolved to take his wife to 'observe more nearly the domestic family life in this "land of liberty", as he called it'.[16] In midsummer 1787 they accordingly set out on a long journey which took them, via Berlin, Frankfurt, Antwerp, Brussels and Paris, to London. If they had come to England a matter of months later, they could have brought with them the advance copy of Frederick the Great's works which Thomas Holcroft needed in order to put his translation of them in hand; as it was, Holcroft obtained an early copy through the Prussian ambassador. The Schopenhauers travelled in their own carriage, which they left at Calais, in M. Dessein's *remise* (immortalised in Sterne's *Sentimental Journey*, published almost twenty years earlier), knowing that in England they could do without it; at Dessein's Hotel they too must have felt 'the satisfaction of treading classic ground', must have seen 'Yorick, his interesting French widow, and his incomparable monk, gliding about in every appartment'.[17] They proceeded from Dover to London by stage-coach, the only time that Johanna travelled in such a conveyance, familiar to her from English novels. In 1803 they brought their carriage over with them, and either that carriage was an English one or they bought a new one in England, for when they left they had an English carriage and were carrying English books (we shall see later what some of these books were) and — essential equipment for the English gentleman of the day — a handsome telescope by Dolland, which they had purchased in London.

Johanna was content with what she saw of England in 1787 (years later she had a passing pipe-dream of living in a cottage in Yorkshire), but preferred to return home for the birth of the child she was expecting:

> I was expecting presently to become a mother, and Schopenhauer naturally desired a son to inherit his name; a child born in England, or on board an English vessel, though of foreign parents, becomes thereby an Englishman, and as such is entitled to all the unpurchasable immunities of a true-born son of Albion.
>
> My husband naturally wished that our hoped-for son should possess these rights so valuable to a merchant, but as my desire was to return to Danzig, we left England again in November. During the two months that I passed in this country, I received the greatest kindness from all the families to whom I was introduced, and the readiness with which I spoke the language, rendered me a welcome guest.[18]

They arrived back in Danzig at the end of December. For the anxious parents-to-be it must have been an appalling journey. Nothing is known for certain about their stay in London except that they met a young corn factor named Claude Scott; their other contacts will have included the Andersons and the Sollys.

Floris Schopenhauer's other reason for going to England at this time was none other than his wish that his child should be born there. His wife's sudden but predictable homesickness was probably quite a serious blow to him. Be that as it may, Arthur Schopenhauer was duly born in Danzig (Heilige Geistgasse 117) on 22 February 1788. When the happy father entered his counting house and laconically announced 'a son', there was general amusement when the book-keeper, taking advantage of his employer's deafness, remarked *sotto voce*, 'A pretty baboon he will be if he's like his father.' The child was supposedly named Arthur because the father wished to endow the future head of his firm with a cosmopolitan Christian name; but the name also bears witness to Heinrich Floris Schopenhauer's innate romanticism.

When Floris Schopenhauer came home for the weekend he often brought a friend or two with him, and on Sundays additional guests would come out to dine. These visitors frequently included members of the British colony, with whom they maintained close contacts: Johanna Schopenhauer's old friend and unofficial tutor, the Rev. Richard Jameson; Jameson's successor as British chaplain, Dr William Gardner; the British consuls from Danzig (Alexander Gibsone) and Memel (James Durno); Andrew Scott and his wife Lucy (a sister of John William Anderson, principal of Anderson Drewe and Co., Heinrich Floris Schopenhauer's English bankers) and their son Gilbert; Richard Cowle, one of the most prominent of the British merchants; Mr Murray; members of the Bendlowes family; the elders of the British chapel, particularly Archibald Gibsone (1751–90);[19] and no doubt many others, including visiting English merchants like Isaac Solly I. Alexander Gibsone, who came from a family of Scottish merchants settled in Danzig since the beginning of the seventeenth century, was, like his father before him, British consul; presumably the Schopenhauers heard the complicated story of the *Freiherrn-Titel* for which Alexander Gibsone applied on 23 December 1776, only to refuse to pay for the diploma, with the odd result that Frederick the Great addressed him as Freiherr von Gibsone but the West Prussian provincial government did not! To the 20-year-old Johanna, who liked people and saw little of them during the week, English visitors were particularly welcome, none more so than Richard Jameson; it will have been a sad loss to her when ill health forced him to return to England in summer 1789.

Schopenhauer *père* was a remarkable man, an open-minded and passionate idealist with a resolute tenacity of purpose and a passion for independence. He was known for his cosmopolitanism and for his 'advanced' or 'enlightened' views. It was no accident that he became a disciple of Voltaire. Frederick the Great, whom he had met, had as it were set the fashion for Voltaire by his long entertainment of the Frenchman at the Prussian court. So much of Voltaire rubbed off on Frederick the Great that the king's prose was 'cursed stuff', for 'He writes just as you would suppose Voltaire's footboy to do.' Boswell, reporting this in his London Journal on 19 July 1763, commented, 'How much less parts is required to make a king than to make an author.' Floris Schopenhauer caught some of his unbridled enthusiasm for England from Voltaire, whose own fondness for the country was derived very largely from the extraordinary kindness he met with from Everard Falkener, who befriended him when Voltaire came over as a disgruntled exile from his own country, and who entertained him at his house at Wandsworth for a considerable time. It has even been suggested that his knowledge of this may have caused Floris Schopenhauer to place his son at a school in nearby Wimbledon. I am sure that this idea is fanciful. What is true is that Voltaire's appreciation of England kindled the flame of Schopenhauer *père*'s enthusiasm, and that the father's enthusiasm for Voltaire in turn rubbed off on the son, who, in *The World as Will and Idea*, makes frequent reference to Voltaire, whose detestation of 'l'infâme' he shared from summer 1803 onwards.

Nor was his father's influence restricted to devotion to Voltaire, for, if it is true that Arthur was influenced by his mother's intellectual and literary tastes, he was undoubtedly influenced by his father's cultural cosmopolitanism; indeed, his very anglophilia was a tribute to the father whose death was the darkest day of his life. Floris Schopenhauer belonged in his cultural views to the age of Frederick the Great (whose eye he caught in 1773 and who tried to make him settle in Prussia, which he absolutely refused to do) and the sentimental German travellers to England. In other words, having lived long abroad and had his tastes formed there, he was unaware of the stirrings of German literature and believed in the superior cosmopolitan value of French and English. Unlike Frederick the Great, he did not use German only when addressing his horses; but he did have a fluent knowledge of English and French, as did his wife and, presently, his son. So if Arthur was attracted towards his mother's particular cultural interests, his overall view of culture was strongly coloured by his father. In later life Arthur never tired of contrasting Voltaire, Helvetius, Locke and Hume with Leibnitz, Fichte, Schelling and Hegel; as a philosopher he has more in common with Hume, Locke and Voltaire than with any German philosopher other than the Scoto-German Kant. His philosophical work is peppered with references to literary works, most of them non-German and many of them English, and is written in a style which owes more to the clarity of Locke, the vigour of Bentham and the elegance of Hume than to any German philosophical writings.

Hamburg

It was typical of Floris Schopenhauer that, when Danzig was about to be annexed to Prussia in March 1793, he decided on the spot to leave his native town rather than live under Prussian rule. This decision, the product of his idealism, independence and obstinacy, was a serious one in view of his Danzig-based business and the amount of property he owned in the free city; it caused him to lose one-tenth of his fortune in tax. With his family he crossed Swedish Pomerania and made his way to Hamburg, a sister Hanseatic town with a not dissimilar pattern of trade with England. On the English side this involved the Hamburg Company, successor to the Company of Merchant Adventurers, which, founded in 1296 and incorporated in 1553, was a company of English merchants trading with the Netherlands and north-west Germany. The Merchant Adventurers were also known as the 'Hamburgh Company' once they had established their court there in 1569 and Hamburg had become their chief port of traffic in 1578. By 1803 the company had come to be little more than a trading association; it was dissolved in 1808. But if Hamburg was the obvious choice for Heinrich Floris Schopenhauer, it was not to prove an adequate substitute for Danzig. The Napoleonic Wars severely disrupted trade patterns, and Hamburg in any case lacked something of the sturdy independence and cosmopolitanism of Danzig. Heinrich Floris Schopenhauer's business affairs never prospered there to the extent to which they had formerly done in Danzig. That said, Hamburg was as good a choice as he could have made, short of settling in London or Bordeaux, although his wife found in Hamburg a purely mercantile spirit which was not to her taste and which perhaps helps to account for the way in which both William Wordsworth and Thomas Holcroft were fleeced by Hamburg tradesmen. This is a point to which we shall return, for they are among the English visitors who have left descriptions of Hamburg as it was in and around 1803.

If London had its German church on Ludgate Hill, with Dr Wendeborn as pastor, Hamburg had its English church, with the Rev. John Knipe as chaplain; there was also the English library run by Mr Remnant, and so on. Above all, however, Hamburg had the English House and 'Bowling Green'.[20] The English Episcopal church in Hamburg was established in 1612 as a guild chapel of the Merchant Adventurers of England, who had returned to Hamburg in 1611. The chapel was long housed in a large room in the 'Englisches Haus' in the Gröningerstrasse. According to the contract concluded between Hamburg and the Merchant Adventurers in 1569, the latter were to be allowed the rent-free use of a house; for this purpose the State of Hamburg in 1570 acquired a house belonging to the von Zeven family, built in 1418, on the site of what became Neue Gröningerstrasse 42. Here the English merchants held their courts and transacted their business from 1569 to 1578 and again from 1611 until the company was wound up by Napoleon in 1808.

Heinrich Floris Schopenhauer will have been a frequent visitor to the English House, which was reputedly a fair specimen of Gothic domestic architecture. From the hall a winding staircase ascended to the first storey, where the chapel, which is said to have been very pretty, was constructed in 1612. An organ was added in the eighteenth century, when the Puritan influence waned. In the largest room the Merchant Adventurers' court held its meetings; several merchants had offices in the building, and the courtmaster, the secretary and the chaplain lived there, together with their servants and the housekeeper. The house also contained a refectory, where the bachelors were obliged to take their meals, and English beer, wines, etc., were on sale duty-free. In the cellar was a pump fed by pipes from the Grindel, the English having assured themselves of a pure water supply when they returned in 1611; it was known as the Englisches Wasser. By the eighteenth century the house had grown ramshackle; the refectory had been discontinued, and instead of company officials residing in the building it was inhabited by clerks and bankrupts, although the chaplain appears to have retained his apartments there at least until 1780 (and maybe until 1806). When the court was wound up in 1806/7 the building was in a bad state. In 1821 it was demolished to make way for the Neue Gröningerstrasse. But if the Englisches Haus had lost its former glory by the end of the eighteenth century, the Bosselhof remained *the* fashionable rendezvous of Hamburg.

Being addicted to the ever-popular English pastime of bowls, the Merchant Adventurers rented from the State of Hamburg a piece of land lying between Böhmkenstrasse and the Englische Planke, and turned it into a bowling green; the Englische Planke derived its name from the fence which bordered it on that side. The Merchant Adventurers acquired this piece of land, which amounted to 3,500 square metres, in 1643. Attached to it in the Böhmkenstrasse was a sort of clubhouse where refreshments could be obtained and at which national festivals were celebrated. This clubhouse proving too small for a festival that was to be held on 22 September 1761, it was pulled down and a large wooden hall built in its place, with a scaffolding behind for fireworks. In 1770 this temporary structure was replaced by a massive new building, to which the Senate initially objected. Once grudgingly accepted by the Senate, the building became the fashionable rendezvous of Hamburg until 1800. Even after that date the English continued to use it for their national festivals. Among the important commemorative festivals which took place there were those for the coronation of George II (1727), the marriage of George III (1761), the visit of Lord Nelson (1800), the battle of Copenhagen (1801) and the Peace of Amiens (1801). Of most interest in the present context is Nelson's visit to Hamburg in 1800. On the dissolution of the Hamburg Company in 1808 the Bosselhof was purchased by the State of Hamburg.

The extant list of the English chaplains in Hamburg from 1612 to 1806 shows that there were some interesting and distinguished figures among them. Chaplains before the Schopenhauers' time included Thomas Young (1620-27), who from 1618 to 1620 was Milton's tutor. It was to Thomas Young that Milton owed the material for his Fourth Elegy, in which he describes the advance of Wallenstein's army on Hamburg. A century later there was Dr William Murray (1738-60), mentioned by Lessing, and a friend of the poet Hagedorn, who was secretary to the court from 1733. A later chaplain, Allan Bracken (1780-94), will have known Klopstock and, briefly, the Schopenhauers. From 1794 to 1806, that is, throughout most of the Schopenhauers' time in Hamburg, the chaplain was the Rev. John Knipe.

Son of the Rev. Isaac Knipe (1717/18-86) of Ambleside, Westmorland (schoolmaster and curate of Ambleside, 1753-86), John Knipe (1765-1845) was educated at Ambleside and Heversham Grammar School. He matriculated at Queen's College, Oxford, on 24 September 1781, aged 15; he took his BA in 1785 and his MA in 1789. He was schoolmaster at Windermere from 26 September 1791 and curate of Ambleside from 17 May 1792. In late 1794 he was appointed English chaplain at Hamburg; he took up the post in the following spring, resigning his Ambleside curacy on 21 March 1795. The records of the English chapel say, intriguingly, that 'This young bachelor continued to sow his wild oats after he was appointed to Hamburg.' He remained chaplain until 1806, although he was in Hamburg after that.[21] What makes him an interesting figure in the present context is the fact that the Schopenhauers will inevitably have known him; in 1804, as we shall see, Knipe accompanied a friend of Arthur Schopenhauer's to England. Most interesting of all is the fact that at Queen's he was an exact contemporary of a young cousin and namesake of Schopenhauer's English headmaster, the Rev. Thomas Lancaster. It is therefore likely that John Knipe knew of the English school which Schopenhauer was to attend, and recommended it to his parents.

At the end of the eighteenth century Hamburg not only mediated between England and Germany, the English House being the centre of such mediation; it was a very English sort of place, a place indeed with more ostensibly 'English' features than Danzig. This is emphasised in the Wynne Diaries:

> Hamburg — 5th [May 1798] . . . My feelings were of a most delicious nature when I got on shore, I saw everything almost in the English style, the language of the inhabitants sounding so much like ours (it is a patois of the German, English and Dutch) struck at once my ears and my heart; nay I heard English well spoken from many mouths. I was inexpressibly happy, my whole soul swam in delight . . . The Ladies dress very elegantly, the men ape the English fashion.[22]

Eugenia Wynne adds that 'This is a commercial town and following very flourishing, the merchants are possessors of immense fortunes, the wealth heightens luxury, and makes living at this place very dear.'

There was a world of difference between the conditions under which the Wynnes and the Wordsworths travelled, but their impressions of the Hamburg of 1798 were not so different. William Wordsworth and his sister Dorothy arrived at Altona on 18 September, intending to spend two years acquiring the German language; in the event they stayed something over six months, the first two and a half weeks of which were spent in Hamburg. They were carrying letters of introduction from Mr Wedgwood to 'some Hamburgh merchants'. The chief of these 'Hamburgh merchants' was evidently Ralph Chatterly, business partner of Viktor Klopstock and a correspondent of the Wedgwoods. The Wordsworths, impecunious as they were, did not move in the same circles as more affluent visitors; they lodged at a fairly vile inn, Der wilde Mann. William moved out after a couple of weeks to stay with his Cambridge friend John Baldwin at another inn, in Speersort, and the two were consequently exposed to constant cheating by tradesmen because they were foreigners and obviously impecunious. William wrote to Coleridge from Nordhausen on 27 February 1799 that 'we are every hour more convinced that we are not rich enough to be introduced into high or even literary German society. We should be perfectly contented if we could find a house where there were several young people . . . to converse with us'; his remarks apply to Hamburg too. They would have been no better placed 'in the Pferde Markt, at the house of young men who had lately begun business', where Thomas Holcroft lodged at about this time and was infuriated to find himself cheated by his landlord. Holcroft's comment, 'The Senators of the free imperial city of Hamburg are exceedingly anxious that no stranger, at leaving their Republic, shall defraud the least citizen. It becomes them to be equally watchful that no citizen shall defraud the stranger,'[23] would have been echoed by the Wordsworths, who were continually cheated by tradesmen during their stay. It was this which caused William, on 3 October 1798, to describe Hamburg as 'a *sad* place' where 'money is . . . the god of universal worship'. Dorothy, for her part, wrote in her Journal that 'avarice . . . is the moving spring of the Hamburgher's mind!'

The Wordsworths' account of Hamburg is coloured by their experiences in this respect, but it also includes much other interesting detail. Brother and sister alike were struck, first of all, by seeing 'Some gentlemen's seats after the English fashion' on the banks of the Elbe: 'The banks of the Elbe are thickly sown with houses, built by the merchants for Saturday and Sunday retirement. The English merchants have set the example, the style is in imitation of the English garden.'[24] 'Some gentlemen's houses are of white stone and built after the English fashion.'[25] The people also had an English look, as Dorothy relates:

> The men little differing from the English, except that they have generally a pipe in their mouths . . . The landlord . . . looked like an English landlord living on the good things of the house . . . Many young men . . . dressed in the English fashion and so like Englishmen that we could have imagined ourselves only three miles from London.

These familiar aspects of the place notwithstanding, the Wordsworths tended to retire to Mr Remnant's English library, to which they had their mail directed.

Crabb Robinson passed through Hamburg two years later, in April 1800. His impressions were remarkably similar to the Wordsworths', though his account is more sophisticated. He puts the 'English' features of Hamburg in truer perspective:

> The houses of . . . Hambro and the Adjacent Country . . . perpetually suggest the Idea that you are looking at England as it was a Century ago . . . The Dress of the Lower Classes confirms . . . that Germany is now what England was — Many a poor woman bears . . . a tight black velvet bonnet like that in which Mary Q. of Scots is painted — the Lutheran clergy appear to wear the cast-off ruffs of Queen Elizabeth . . . The higher orders dress differently. All the Gentlemen imitate the English, all the Ladies, the ffrench.[26]

He also comments on the fact that when, on his first Sunday in Hamburg, he was invited to dine, cards were introduced as a matter of course; on another Sunday he was invited to a ball. Such facts do much to explain German visitors' horrified reactions to British sabbatarian misery.

Crabb Robinson also found himself paying through the nose, which caused him to remark that:

> London we have been in the habit of considering as the seat of refined knavery and imposition of every kind — Hambro' will at least stand trial with it — The War has thrown so much temporary business into it that the manners of the people are thoroughly impregnated with every thing that partakes of the

insolence & prodigality of newly acquired wealth.[27]

Clearly it was not only the British national character that had deteriorated. The turmoil occasioned by the war probably also accounts for Cornelia Knight's impression, in 1800, that 'the magistrates of Hamburg must have exercised great vigilance and good sense to keep their city in such good order, for it was filled with such strange characters that I could compare it to nothing but the banks of Lethe'.[28]

Another British man of letters who was in Hamburg in 1800 was the poet Thomas Campbell. He crossed in a 'Hamburgh trader' at the beginning of June, and was made welcome by the British residents, who vied with one another in showing him every mark of respect and hospitality. He stayed in Hamburg until late July; on his return from Ratisbon he lived in Altona from November 1800 to March 1801. He found Hamburg 'dull' and Altona, 'the Montpelier of Germany', 'the pleasantest place of all Germany'. His time at Hamburg/Altona was chiefly employed in reading German and ('I am almost ashamed to confess it') in the study of Kant's philosophy. While there he also made acquaintance with some of the refugee Irishmen who had fled to Altona following the crushing of the 1798 rebellion; in particular he became friendly with Anthony MacCann, the hero of his 'The Exile of Erin'. It is unlikely that the Schopenhauers came across Thomas Campbell or his Irish friends; when Arthur Schopenhauer wrote to Campbell in 1831, he wrote as to a stranger. When Campbell returned to Hamburg later in life, in 1825, the English residents there gave him a public dinner; but by then the Schopenhauers' connection with Hamburg was long since over.

Enough has been said to show that young Arthur Schopenhauer, on leaving Danzig for Hamburg, did not cease to be exposed to English influences. There remains the question of Lord Nelson's visit to Hamburg in 1800 and, more generally, the question of the extent of the Schopenhauers' acquaintance with Nelson.

In July 1800 Nelson set out from Leghorn on an overland journey which brought him, on 21 October, to Hamburg, whence he embarked for Yarmouth on 31 October. At Hamburg everyone wanted to entertain the victor of the Nile and his party. The English merchants arranged a Grand Gala, consisting of dinner, concert, supper and ball, which was held at the Bowling Green. At this gala, to which the Schopenhauers were evidently invited, Nelson proposed a toast to the Hamburgers in the words 'May the Hamburghers, who shut their gates against their friends, be more careful to shut them against their enemies'.[29] It was there that Nelson lost a large diamond from the hilt of a sword given to him by the King of Naples; the English merchants offered to replace it at a cost of £800, but Nelson would not hear of it. Many other anecdotes are said to have been 'related as proceeding from persons in private life at Hamburg',[30] but few have been recorded. Among those who received Nelson and Lady Hamilton were the poet Klopstock, then seventy-six, who was so struck by the beauty of the Englishwoman that he included a reference to Emma Hamilton as 'die Siegerin' in the ode which he composed on this occasion, 'Die Unschuldigen'; the last stanza, in which the reference appears, was omitted from the final version of the poem. Accounts of Nelson's week-long stay at Hamburg contain interesting accounts of the old poet, to whom English visitors were frequently presented. While at Hamburg the Nelson party witnessed a performance at the Deutsches Theater.

In her outline of the projected continuation of her memoirs Johanna Schopenhauer included the names of Lord Nelson and Lady Hamilton among her distinguished acquaintance in Hamburg. Unfortunately she never continued her memoirs, so that we do not know the circumstances of the Schopenhauers' meeting with Nelson or the extent to which Johanna allowed herself to stray into the realms of fiction and self-magnification in this connection. One who published an interesting fictional account of the occasion was the twentieth-century novelist Hans Leip. In his novel *Die Lady und der Admiral* (1933) Leip describes the gala reception in some detail and even reports what the twelve-year-old Arthur Schopenhauer said to Lord Nelson and Lady Hamilton:

Johanna Schopenhauer was present at the Gala too. She loved everything English; the chaplain to the English colony in Danzig had been her childhood friend. She had married a merchant who was a passionate admirer of England and would have liked his son to be born there. In the event he was born in Danzig. They called him Arthur because the name is the same in all languages, an important consideration from the point of view of business correspondence. He was to become a merchant and as much a citizen of the world as any Englishman. They had had to flee Danzig to escape the invading Prussians. That was seven years ago. And now old man Schopenhauer had his granary on the Wandrahm. He had had young Arthur educated at Le Havre together with the son of a business friend there. The boy came home a year ago, speaking French better than German, had travelled home by himself, by ship, twelve years old but already quite grown-up. Recently he had travelled round Germany with his parents. Just three months ago, like Lord Nelson's party, he had been in Prague and Dresden, and had arrived back in Hamburg just four days before the English party arrived there. With his blue eyes and straight brown hair, he was now standing before the Admiral and the celebrated Lady, looking bright and self-confident. Beside him stood his friends of the same age, Charles Godeffroy and Karl Sieveking, together with young Curzon, son of Lord Scarsdale, who attended Abbé Guyot's school in the Close and was amazed to see the cool and self-possessed way in which 'Schopi' was talking to the famous guests.

Had they seen the beast-baiting at Prague? he was asking. Or the King falling off his horse on parade in Berlin? Or Schloss Herrenhausen? Or the Grünes Gewölbe at Dresden? And the Golden Egg with its yellow enamel yoke containing a chicken, which in turn contained a little crown of precious stones? Yes, they had seen that. And the replica of Solomon's Temple, ordered by a Hamburg senator, and, on his bankruptcy, sold to the Elector? And the Jewish instruments for marriage, circumcision and divorce? — No, they had *not* seen those!

Lady Hamilton was astonished at the way in which the boy got on to such unsuitable subjects, and took his mother aside. Johanna Schopenhauer was in her mid-thirties at the time, pleasant-looking rather than pretty, with a slightly malformed hip, still attractive and with a positive greed for life. How jealous she was of Lady Hamilton. And of her own son, who even at his age knew more than she did and was doing things which she had never been allowed to do.

The boy saw, to his annoyance, that Lady Hamilton was talking to his mother about him. A strange pique overcame him. He remembered some grisly things he had seen at Dresden. Had they seen the 'Virgin' in Brühl's Garden? he asked. No? It was, he explained, a ruinous building in which noted criminals had once been made to embrace the figure of a Virgin, whereupon the ground opened up and the malefactor fell on to a collection of spears, wheels and swords, by which he was promptly cut to shreds.

'Dear boy,' Sir William smiled somewhat equivocally, 'may your experience of life be pleasanter than that!'

'Frederick the Great had the terrible thing destroyed!' young Arthur rejoined with a vague feeling that there was more to it than that. The old knight expressed the child's misgivings as he stroked his cheek and joked: 'it's not for nothing that he despised women. But what was it he destroyed, young lion? A symbol, nothing but a symbol.'

Lady Hamilton, shocked at the frivolous tone he was adopting towards a child, dragged her husband away; in any case she was not feeling well. She had had too much to drink, and did not wish to continue to be exposed to the intemperate demands of the Hamburg knights of the dance, which she could only refuse. She fished her Nelson out of the crowd and drove with him and Sir William to their hotel, leaving the Gala to go on into the early hours.[31]

The trouble with this splendid and partly plausible account is that it is unsupported by evidence. Arthur Schopenhauer may conceivably have been at the gala reception, even at the age of twelve, but there is no evidence that he was, and the conversation attributed to him is wholly imaginary. It is, however one of the stranger features of the present story that Lord Nelson should feature in it not once but twice, and on each occasion be involved in a purely apocryphal encounter with the young Schopenhauer. This is a point to which we shall return in connection with Mr Lancaster's academy.

In Hamburg the Schopenhauers lived first in a rented apartment at Altstädter Neuer Weg 76. It was not until three years later that they moved into the more appropriately affluent surroundings of a house at Neuer Wandrahm 92. Quite apart from finding a suitable house, they had had to wait for Heinrich Floris's affairs in Danzig to be wound up and for him to re-establish himself as a merchant in Hamburg. This involved much hard work and much worry, both of which took their toll, so that the man who wrote those extraordinarily fussy letters to his son in 1803 (see Chapter VI) was but a shadow of his former self, although we must also remember that Schopenhauer's father, for all his own attachment to cultural values, was convinced that there was no money in literature, and that his son had to be weaned away from it for his own good. One of his many worries at this time was that Arthur might fail to make his way in the world. Having bribed him away from an academic/literary career, as he thought, his letters to his son were no doubt meant well. Ironically, less is known about the commercial activities of Gebrüder Schopenhauer in Hamburg than in Danzig. Following the outbreak of war between France and Prussia in 1792, Hamburg became the chief *entrepôt* where British goods were exchanged for corn and timber; the clearing house for all bills of exchange was the Hamburg Bank. Speculation flourished, fortunes were made and lost, and inflation set in. In 1799 many business houses became bankrupt. Latterly these losses touched Heinrich Floris Schopenhauer (his brother and partner had died in 1795), who was involved in the exchange of British manufactured goods for grain, a long-established trade which gave rise to the Corn laws. He had known the English corn factor Claude Scott since at least 1787, and no doubt helped Scott to make his fortune by increasing his trade with him at this time. He will also have had dealings with young Edward Solly.

The house at Neuer Wandrahm 92, with its marble floors, picture gallery, library and works of art, was the scene not only of Heinrich Floris Schopenhauer's business worries but of the Schopenhauers' attempts to rebuild their social life; it was also the setting in which Arthur Schopenhauer lived, on and off, between the ages of five and 17. As before, English residents and English visitors were among the guests, for Hamburg at this time was an *entrepôt* for cultural as well as commercial exchange between England and 'Germany'. The Schopenhauers' English contacts there included the British diplomatic representatives of the time,[32] the British chaplain (the Rev. John Knipe) and Mr Remnant of the English library.[33]

The Schopenhauers almost certainly knew the philologist and translator Hannibal Evans Lloyd (1771–1847), who settled at Hamburg in 1800 and suffered severely from the hardships to which the city was exposed during its occupation by the French army. He joined the inhabitants in the defence of their city and eventually escaped with the loss of all his property. It was at the suggestion of the Foreign Secretary, Lord Bathurst, that he published his *Hamburgh, or a particular account of the Transactions which took place in that City during the first six months of 1813* (1813). He married a Fräulein von Schwarzkopff of Hamburg, and was a friend of Klopstock. In addition to numerous translations, he published a *Theoretisch-praktische Englische Sprachlehre für Deutsche* (1833), long a standard grammar at some German universities.[34] Of British émigré families the Schopenhauers will certainly have known the Slomans.

William Sloman was an English ship's captain who in 1793 settled in Hamburg, where he founded the firm which, under the management of his son and grandson, became the Reederei Robert M. Sloman and eventually the Slomanlinien. When William Sloman died at Hamburg in 1800 his firm was taken over by his younger son, Robert Miles Sloman (born at Yarmouth in 1783), who was only five years older than Arthur Schopenhauer and must in some ways have been the son Heinrich Floris Schopenhauer would have preferred. As a fellow shipowner Heinrich Floris Schopenhauer must have known the Slomans and invited them to Neuer Wandrahm.[35]

There is no evidence that the Schopenhauers met or entertained the itinerant English writers passing through Hamburg at this time, or that they entertained Lord Nelson and Emma Hamilton at Neuer Wandrahm 92. They will, however, have known some natives of Hamburg normally resident in England (D.H. Rücker) or until recently resident there (J.W. von Archenholz, Dr Wendeborn); and so on. Gebhard Friedrich August Wendeborn(1742–1811) was an almost exact contemporary of Heinrich Floris Schopenhauer. He lived in England from 1767 to 1793, and from 1770 to 1790 was pastor of the German Lutheran church on Ludgate Hill. He was one of the main interpreters of England to Germany in the later eighteenth century; from 1779 to 1792 he was London correspondent of the *Hamburgischer Correspondent*. While the Schopenhauers, who were living in Danzig at the time, may not have known his articles on England, they will certainly have known his celebrated guide book *Beiträge zur Kenntnis Grossbritanniens vom Jahr 1779* (Lemgo, 1780). This book, of which an expanded version appeared in 1785–88 (under the title *Der Zustand des Staats, der Religion, der Gelehrsamkeit und der Kunst in Grossbritannien gegen das Ende des achtzehnten Jahrhunderts*), to say nothing of an abridged English translation of this by Wendeborn himself (*A View of England towards the Close of the Eighteenth Century*, 1791), became the standard guidebook of the time. Carl Philipp Moritz travelled with it in his pocket in 1782. When Johanna Schopenhauer, in her travel diary, refers to the work of her predecessors, Dr Wendeborn will inevitably have been one of those to whom she is alluding. He retired to Hamburg in 1793, disillusioned by what he saw as a sudden change for the worse in the English national character following the French Revolution. The Schopenhauers must have known this 'scholarly, subtle-minded man' whom Sophie von La Roche describes as 'very pleasant company'.

They will also have known Johann Wilhelm von Archenholz

(1741-1812), another contemporary of Floris Schopenhauer and a Danziger by birth. Having served in the army of Frederick the Great and taken part in the siege of Danzig and the final campaign of the Seven Years War, Archenholz spent much of his life in travel. From 1769 to 1779 he lived mostly in England. The outcome of this stay was two essays published in his journal *Litteratur und Völkerkunde* in October and November 1783; much expanded, they formed the English part of his *England and Italien* (2 vols, Leipzig, 1785), which was in turn expanded and translated as *A Picture of England* (2 vols in 1, 1789 and 1791; new edn, 1797). This is a book which Johanna Schopenhauer is certain to have known. His anthology *English Lyceum, or Choice of Pieces in Prose and Verse, selected from the best Periodical Papers, Magazines and Pamphlets and other British Publications* appeared in Hamburg in 1787; some years earlier a similar anthology had been published (*The English Magazine*, Hamburg, 1779), though not under his editorship. The *English Lyceum* was followed by *The British Mercury*, a weekly journal published in English at Hamburg from 1787 to 1791 (anthologised as *The British Mercury*, or *Englishche Lesefrüchte*, ed. T. Brand, 1-13, Hamburg [1818]). Archenholz's most important work in the present context, however, is his *Annalen der brittischen Geschichte*, 1788[-96] (20 vols, Hamburg, 1790-1800). He too retired to Hamburg, in 1792, and by 1799 had come to share Dr Wendeborn's disillusionment.

Given such a family background, one would have thought young Arthur Schopenhauer bound to be either extremely anglophile or no less anglophobe. In fact he became the former, although it was a near thing because of the unpropitious nature of his first (and only) personal experience of England, in 1803. It was in this year that Heinrich Floris Schopenhauer decided to bribe his son into abandoning his predilection for a scholarly career in favour of a mercantile one, by offering to take him on a long journey to France (where his best friend lived) and England, provided he gave up all that nonsense about studying literature and the classics, which could end only in penury.[36] The then 15-year-old boy agreed, and what followed was *the* formative experience of his life.

In London he will have found plenty of evidence of the strength of the 'German' or, better, Hanoverian, connection. There was not only the royal family; there were some 30,000 Germans resident in London, many of them — like the Anglo-Scots in Danzig — in the process of going native. The Steelyard (on the site long since occupied by Cannon Street Station), depot for steel imports from Germany, had been used by the 'Merchants of Alamaine' since 1250. The armorial bearings of the Hanseatic towns, carved in stone by Cibber, were to be seen on the main entrance in Upper Thames Street, while on the riverside gate piers there were German eagles. The Hanseatic merchants had their own pews at All Hallows. There was a German Hotel in Suffolk Street and in the Old Savoy there were two German churches: the German Lutheran church at the back of the wing connecting the north and south fronts, and the German Calvinist church in the south front.

However, before we come to Arthur Schopenhauer's English journey and school, there remains the most interesting aspect of the 'English' background to his early life: the formative influence on his mother (whose tastes and interests young Arthur shared) of the Rev. Richard Jameson.

Notes

1. *A Particular Description of the City of Dantzick, By an English Merchant, lately Resident there* (1734), 3.
2. Ibid.
3. Ibid., 16.
4. *The Wynne Diaries*, ed. Anne Fremantle, III (1940), 57f.
5. Details from the Instytut Baltycki, Gdansk.
6. These minutes are preserved among the State Papers (Poland) at the PRO (ref. SP 88/177).
7. A summary of John William Anderson's letter is to be found in the *Zeitschrift des Westprussischen Geschichtsvereins*, XX, Danzig (1887), 180f. See also *Diaries and Correspondence of James Harris, First Earl of Malmesbury*, I (1844), 89–109.
8. Nathaniel Wraxall, *A Tour through some of the Northern Parts of Europe* (1775), 344–9.
9. Details, kindly provided by the Instytut Baltycki: *Agatha Philipina* (660 tons), skipper George Mickley; *De oudste Wogter* (520 tons), skipper Johann Gottlieb Joost; *Susanna Henrietta* (312 tons), skipper Paul Gottlieb Jacks; and *La Favorita* (200 tons) skipper Fr. Hans Pieters.
10. See J.S., *My Youthful Life*, I (1847), 124.
11. Wraxall, *Tour*, 350f.
12. For further details of Dr Wolf, see Philipp Adolph Lampe, *Gedächtnisrede auf den Herrn D. Nathanael Matthaeus von Wolf*, Danzig [1785]; for Dr Wolf's publications, see the BL catalogue.
13. Quoted from W. Wallace, *Life of Arthur Schopenhauer* (1890), 81.
14. See Chapter VI below.
15. *A Particular Description*, 45.
16. J.S., *My Youthful Life*, II, 24.
17. Mrs Melesina St George, in her *Journal*.
18. J.S., *My Youthful Life*, II (1847), 90.

19. The elders at this time were J. Dan Clerck, 1763-86; Gilbert Smithson, 1774-97; Michael Barton, 1785-94; Adam Elliott, 1785-1804; Henry Simpson, 1789-1803; John Atkinson, 1790-1826; Archibald Maclean, senior, 1791-1810.

20. Most of the details concerning the English House, English chapel (church), and Bowling Green, are taken from Lambeth Palace Library MS 1859, fols. 14-24.

21. On 10 December 1805 John Knipe was appointed rector of Charlton-upon-Otmoor (Oxon). He drew his stipend as English chaplain in Hamburg for the last time on 27 June 1806. In August that year he fled to England in order to escape arrest by the Danes, who had declared war on England; in November he was back in Hamburg (sowing a final wild oat?), for when the French entered the city on 19 November 1806 he fled into Holstein. Until 9 August 1807, although no longer resident in Hamburg, he returned there occasionally, ministering to the English families on such occasions. He again returned to Hamburg in 1815; according to the chapel register he occasionally officiated as chaplain in December 1815/January 1816 and again in 1817, after which there is no further word of him in Hamburg. Living in Charlton-upon-Otmoor, he probably knew the Rev. T.W. Lancaster (eldest son of Schopenhauer's English headmaster), who was vicar of Banbury at much the same time. From 1834 John Knipe was also sequestrator of St Michael's in the Mount, Lincoln.

22. *The Wynne Diaries*, II, 224f.
23. Thomas Holcroft, *Travels from Hamburg*, I (1804), 2.
24. William Wordsworth, letter of 3 October 1798.
25. Dorothy Wordsworth, in her Journal.
26. *Crabb Robinson in Germany 1800-1805*, ed. E.J. Morley (1929), 18.
27. Ibid., 17.
28. *The Autobiography of Miss Knight*, ed. R. Fulford (1960), 76.
29. In *Life and Letters of Thomas Campbell*, ed. W. Beattie, I (1849), 345.
30. T.J. Pettigrew, *Memorials of the Life of Lord Nelson*, I (1849), 390.
31. Hans Leip, *Die Lady und der Admiral* (1933), 322-4.
32. Charles Henry Fraser, resident to the Hanse towns, 1791-8; James Craufurd, resident to the Hanse towns, 1798-1801; Sir George Berriman Rumbold, Bart, chargé d'affaires, 1801-4; E. Nicholas, vice-consul at Hamburg; Mr [Alexander] Cockburne, consul at Altona.
33. Other likely contacts include the Parish family, who feature in Lorenz Meyer's letters; Hodgkinson Morewood (mentioned by Lorenz Meyer) and other British merchants, including Edward James Smith (mentioned in Sir John William Anderson's will), the Robinson family (mentioned by Crabb Robinson; cf. the Mr Robinson whom they met in London in 1803), Ralph Chatterley (the business partner of Viktor Klopstock, the poet's brother), and possibly including the Mr Thornton mentioned by Hans Leip in his novel *Die Lady und der Admiral* (who may be Richard Thornton, 1776-1865, known as 'Richard Duke of Dantzic'), as well as the peripatetic 'Sir' Levett Hansom (1754-1814), who was at school with Nelson and who wrote to him from Hamburg in 1802.
34. On Hannibal Evans Lloyd, see *DNB* (includes a list of his translations) and *GM*, 1847/II, 324-6.
35. I have found no evidence that the Schopenhauers knew Nathaniel

Curzon (cr. Baron Scarsdale, 1804), who married for the second time in Hamburg in 1798, although they could have known him and his son Nathaniel Curzon (b. 1781), whom Hans Leip made out to be a friend of Arthur Schopenhauer, which is unlikely in view of the disparity in their ages.

36. In John Galt's *Annals of the Parish* (1821) Colin Mavis is told, in 1801 (Chapter XLII), that 'poem-making was a profane and unprofitable trade, and he would do well to turn his talent to something of more solidity'.

II
Richard Jameson

Background

It has long been known that a Scottish clergyman acted as mentor to Johanna Trosiener throughout her childhood:

> In her early years the fair Johanna attracted the notice of her father's neighbour in town, Dr. Jameson, an Edinburgh minister, who looked after the spiritual needs of the British colony there. Under his friendly lead her reading was ampler in range, and more stimulating in quality, than could be expected from the cut-and-dried themes of the schoolroom.[1]

In her long since forgotten account of her early life Johanna Schopenhauer elaborated on the reading in question, but nothing more has ever been known of this 'Dr. Jameson'. He has remained unidentified, the story of his life untold. It is time this was made good, for he had a strong indirect influence on the young Arthur Schopenhauer's literary interests and tastes.

Johanna Trosiener's guide, counsellor, friend and unofficial tutor was Richard Jameson, born in 1724 (the same year as Kant and Klopstock), son of Richard Jameson in Stane (Biggar, Lanarkshire) and his wife Anna (*née* Mitchel). He was baptised in nearby Biggar on 17 December 1724 by Robert Livingstone (minister of Biggar Kirk from 1690 to 1732); by birth he was therefore a Presbyterian. But for the fact that he was subsequently ordained, it would almost certainly have proved impossible to identify him. As it is, a certificate of his birth exists among his ordination papers.[2] It reads as follows:

Richard Jameson

Testificate from Biggar in favours of Mr. Richd. Jamieson 1753:

> Biggar 26th May 1753.
> That Richard Jamieson, Son to Richard Jamieson in Stane and Anna Mitchel his spouse was Baptized at Biggar the Seventeenth of December Seventeenth [*sic*] hundred and Twenty four Years, is attested (there being at present No Minister in the Parish) by
>
> Ja: Gladstones Eldr.

Stane, where he lived until about 1747, is a long, single-storey stone-built cottage steading (really a butt-and-ben cottage plus byre) standing about a mile east of Biggar on the Biggar-Broughton road (the B7016).[3] In the mid-nineteenth century the centre section of the cottage was raised by a storey and given a typical mid-Victorian frontage; the original nature of the building is, however, clearly visible. The view from the farm is over fields and marshland to Cardon Hill and Culter Fell in the background. The countryside all around is characterised by successive ranges of bare-topped hills with rich pasturage on their lower slopes.

Stane is known to Scottish local historians as the residence, from 1656 to 1659, of the Covenanter Andrew Hay. The Greenhill Covenanters' House museum at Biggar has a reconstruction of Andrew Hay's study at Stane. Originally the Stane lands belonged to the Knights Templar. From the mid-seventeenth century the property belonged to the Dickson family of Hartree, but was tenanted and farmed by the Jameson family, at least from the time of Richard Jameson's great-grandfather, Richard Jameson, who started as tenant of the next farm, Heavyside, but later took over the tenancy of Stane. In Andrew Hay's diary there is a passing reference to this Richard Jameson, who married one Helen Kello and died *c.* 1685. Otherwise nothing is known of our Richard Jameson's forebears. He seems to have been an only son, maybe an only child; in his will[4] he remembered two cousins who were evidently sons of his father's sisters; there were other members of the Jameson family farming in nearby Culterallers, Wandel and Lamington. The Jamesons of Culterallers seem to have been particularly closely related, for the name Richard occurs regularly, as it does in Richard Jameson's own branch of the family. The Richard Jamieson, tenant in Culterallers, who died in May 1761 was most likely his uncle.[5]

His father was, then, a poor tenant farmer. No doubt he

expected his son to help on the farm and eventually to take over the tenancy; he will have been disappointed when his son turned his back not only on the family farm, but also on the family religion.

At this time boys in Richard Jameson's position normally studied Latin, English, writing, arithmetic, book-keeping, geography and the first four books of Euclid. As often as not they were taught in a butt-and-ben two-room cottage, the outer room serving as the schoolroom, the inner as the schoolmaster's accommodation. For his services the dominie was paid about £12 per annum with grass for a cow. These details are taken from the *Personal Memoirs* of P.L. Gordon, who commented:

> Here was a man who was capable of filling with credit a chair of rhetoric or belles lettres, fagging from morning to night to earn the wages of a ploughman, and . . . living in a damp and dark kennel, on the vilest food, which a pauper in England would have spurned.[6]

The conditions which Schopenhauer's English schoolmaster enjoyed in his early years in the north of England will have been very similar, for he began teaching at precisely the time described by Gordon.

In fact Richard Jameson attended school in Biggar not in a cottage but in a tower. Biggar Kirk Session agreed in 1659 to the use of 'James Brown's tower' as a school. Richard Jameson clearly obeyed the injunction carved on the lintel of the school in the 1690s: 'Ora et labora ut floreant studia'. His time at the school corresponded with the period of office as schoolmaster of John Girdwood, who was presented to the office in 1730 and still held it in 1737. Son of Daniel Girdwood, schoolmaster, of Carnwath, John Girdwood studied at Edinburgh University, where he matriculated in 1725. He will have been a keen and well educated young man, for he not only came from a schoolmastering family but had also been educated at what was the best university in the country, if not in Europe, at that time. Nothing is known about him except that he refused to accept appointment as schoolmaster unless he were excused from acting as precentor in the parish kirk (it was normal practice for the schoolmaster to act as precentor). It was a brave step for a young man, as well as showing that it was possible to have moral principles independent of the Kirk Session, a point that was to be important to Jameson. Jameson will also have been taught by Mr Girdwood's successor, James Philips, but only for a year or two.[7]

We now come to the first of two gaps in his life, for there is no record of what he did between 1739 and 1747. It may be that he was helping his father on the farm, if, that is, his father was able to support him. The fact that he did not go straight on to Edinburgh University points to poverty, and probably also means that he was either not free or not ready to work his way through university. It may have taken him some time to pluck up the courage to do this. If he had to support himself — either because he was unwilling to work on the farm, or because the farm could no longer support him now that he had finished his schooling — then he probably acted as amanuensis or tutor to a bonnet laird such as James Murray of Broughton (a Jacobite and an Episcopalian), or as assistant to a local schoolmaster (possibly Mr John Scott, a private schoomaster in Biggar, who was a noted mathematician). These obvious possibilities are suggested by the fact that Jameson went on to become an Episcopalian minister after working as tutor in a famous Jacobite family, and by the fact that he studied mathematics at Edinburgh and retained a lifelong interest in the natural sciences. The other question is whether he was 'out in '45' (though the phrase is really too grand to be applied to the son of a tenant farmer) or in some way involved in the events of that year, the most momentous of his early life. While there is no evidence that he was in any way involved, it is a fact that immediately after university he became tutor in the family of a notorious Jacobite who would have been most unlikely to appoint someone who did not share his own views, and that he apparently enjoyed his subsequent preferment to the Jacobite old-boy network. The possibility that he owed his tutorship to a character provided by the Murray family of Broughton in return for some kind of help to the Jacobite cause cannot be excluded. The fact that he spoke fluent French raises the intriguing possibility that he may have been involved in the '45 by working in France, although a more obvious explanation is the fact that in later life one of his closest friends was French. It is unlikely that the truth will ever be known.

Divinity Student

In 1747/8 Richard Jameson made his way — like so many poor but ambitious young Scots of the time — to the Divinity Hall in the University of Edinburgh. He must have done so with many misgivings, for he could not afford to pay the fees, and probably took a good deal of persuading by people like the Rev. Livingstone, James Murray of Broughton, James Philips and John Scott. By 1747 he may well have heard reports from one or two schoolfriends who had already been to Edinburgh of the brilliance of John Stevenson, Professor of Logic and Metaphysics (1730-74), for it was under John Stevenson — among others — that he proceeded to study.

If Jameson had gone up at the normal age of 14, he would have been a younger contemporary of Alexander Carlyle, Sir Gilbert Elliott and John Home (all of whom matriculated about 1735). If he had stayed in Edinburgh until 1753, he would have met Oliver Goldsmith (matric. 1752) and James Boswell (matric. 1753). As it is, he left Edinburgh in 1751, the year in which David Hume moved there. However, his period of residence corresponds exactly with the two courses of lectures on literature and literary criticism which Adam Smith gave — outside the university — in 1748-51. In his 1793 edition of Adam Smith's *The Theory of Moral Sentiments* (1759) Schopenhauer wrote, in English, that the root of Smith's system of morality is 'the sentiment of honour, i.e. anxiety for the approbation of others: & this is, properly speaking, what he grounds all morals upon'. He added, 'His is therefore a very gentlemanly system of morals, placing us on the footing of good company as is obvious in all his developments. But that's not the thing, my good Sir' (*HN*, V, 165 f.). By the time *The Theory of Moral Sentiments* appeared, Jameson had left Edinburgh.

Richard Jameson appears to have gone up to Edinburgh University in 1747/8 and to have completed his course in 1751. According to Edinburgh University records he neither matriculated nor took his degree, as was not uncommon at the time. That he attended university is, however, attested by the following certificate found among his ordination papers:[8]

> Edim 12th March 1753
> That the Bearer Richard Jameson in the Course of his Studies at this University attended our severale Colleges for the Greek Logick and Mathematicks with Application and Success, and behaved himself with Discretion and to our Satifaction in his morale Character is attested by
>
> Jon Stevenson, P.R.P.
> Robert Hunter Gr.P.
> Matth: Stewart Matk.P.

Another document makes it clear that he had completed his studies two years earlier. The fact that he studied under John Stevenson, Robert Hunter (Professor of Greek, 1741–72) and Matthew Stewart (Professor of Mathematics, 1747–75) means both that, like other divinity students of his time, he followed the normal MA course, and that his course is well documented. That the name of George Stuart (Professor of Humanity) does not appear on Jameson's reference probably means that his Latin was good enough for him to bypass the thinly attended Latin class, and that he began his course with Greek. Logic was most often taken in the penultimate year, and natural philosophy in the final year; Jameson evidently took the mathematics option. Before examining his course in detail, however, let us first note what sort of place Edinburgh was in 1748 and what life was like for a student in those days, particularly one suffering from dire poverty.

In 1748 the University of Edinburgh had about 500 students, half of them studying medicine; at the time the population of the Scottish capital was some 50,000. Edinburgh, that 'most picturesque (at a distance) and nastiest (when near) of all capital cities',[9] was a 'hot-bed of genius',[10] but it was not for nothing that the justly famed Athens of the North was popularly known as 'Auld Reekie', for the truth is that it stank to high heaven:

> *Edinburgh* is certainly a fine City, and, I believe, can boast of the highest Houses in *Europe*; notwithstanding, it has its Faults, and those very great, meaning its Nastiness, which is composed of Excrements in all Parts of the Town; and in a Morning, about seven o'clock, before the Excrements are swept away from the Doors, it stinks intolerably, for which, I believe, it exceeds all parts of the World: For after ten o'clock in the Evening, it is Fortune favors you if a Chamberpot, with Excrements, &c. is not thrown on your Head, if you are walking the Streets; it is then not a little Diversion to a Stranger, to hear all Passers-by cry out with a loud Voice, sufficient to reach the Tops of Houses (which are generally six or seven Stories high, in the Front of the High-Street), *Hoad yare Hoand*, i.e. hold your Hand, and means, do not throw till I am past.[11]

Edinburgh may have been 'the true Scene for a man of Letters',[12] but he needed a strong nose in those days before the building of the New Town, when 'Edinburgh' meant the Old Town (familiar to most readers from Scott's novels, but more systematically described in Pococke's *Tours in Scotland*).

Hotbed of genius Edinburgh may have been, but being trained up to genius was no laughing matter in 1748, especially if one was as poor as Richard Jameson — and many of the students were. The regulations of the university had been revised in 1733, with the result that classes now began at eight o'clock (instead of seven, at Edinburgh; at other Scottish universities they used to begin at six), but the students still assembled in dark lecture rooms, dimly lit by smoky tallow candles, and ill heated by the newly kindled fire on bitter winter mornings.[13] Students were no longer required to speak to one another in Latin, and corporal punishment had been abolished, as had the wretched regent system. Instruction was no longer 'given by starveling dotards, lecturing in Latin on scholastic philosophy',[14] but Latin was still used as the language of some formal lectures. The uncommonly enlightened John Stevenson, for instance, lectured on logic in Latin (but on *belles-lettres* in English). There was only one undergraduate college, and that had no dormitories or refectory. Students not normally resident in Edinburgh had to find lodgings. They lived in mean garrets in the wynds, having been given a few pence by the Kirk Session to help them on their way. When they went up to university in October they often took with them a supply of oat and barley meal, which had to last until the end of the session in May. So dependent were they on such supplies that a bad harvest might cause the membership of a class to drop by half. They had the greatest difficulty in buying books. Instead they read books in the college library (in Edinburgh books were chained and padlocked to their shelves until 1730, and were not unlocked for students) and — occasionally — borrowed them from an easy-going professor. The result was that 'Many [a] lad starved his body to feed his mind . . . clad in threadbare hodden gray, too poor to buy candles, . . . studying by the fire-light in the unfurnished garret.'[15] That hardly any students paid to graduate in Jameson's time is hardly surprising.

Many of the students were therefore a good deal worse off than Oliver Goldsmith, who considered himself unfortunate to find a leg of mutton, dished up in various ways by the ingenuity of his landlady, served for the better part of dinner during a week, a dish of broth being made on the seventh day from the bones. In a letter to Daniel Hodson, written from Edinburgh in the winter of 1752/3, Goldsmith gave, briefly, a more general account of his life as an undergraduate: '[during the] day I am obliged to attend the Publick L[ectures. At night] I am in my Lodging. I have hardly an[y other s]ociety but a Folio book a skeleton my cat and my meagre landlady.'[16]

Richard Jameson's experiences must have been similar, though not the same. He will not have had a skeleton, although he may have had a cat (as he later did in Danzig). The main difference is that he probably lodged with one of his two Edinburgh aunts, maybe with Mrs Mason at the foot of Monteith's Close. How much difference that may have made to his life is impossible to tell, but there is no reason to doubt that his lot, like Goldsmith's, was 'poverty, hopeless poverty';[17] indeed, it may be that Melancholy was beginning to make him her own too. Johanna Schopenhauer later compared him to Sterne's Yorick, but at this stage of his life the obvious parallel is with Scott's Reuben Butler, who was:

> decidedly the best scholar at the little parish school . . . every advance that Reuben made in learning . . . rendered him less capable of attending to the domestic duties of his grandmother's farm. He read Virgil's Georgics till he did not know bear from barley.[18]

In due course Reuben:

> pursued his studies at the university, supplying his wants by teaching the younger lads the knowledge he himself acquired, and thus at once gaining the means of maintaining himself at the seat of learning and fixing in his mind the elements of what he had already obtained. In this manner, as is usual among the poorer students of divinity at Scottish universities, he contrived . . . to maintain himself according to his simple wants.[19]

Scott might almost have had Jameson as his model, though there were many others in the same position. That Jameson failed to matriculate with the professors whose classes he attended, and whose goodwill he enjoyed, is explicable in terms of poverty. As the son of a small tenant farmer he will have had to work his way through university in the usual ways, by acting as tutor to other, younger students (particularly easy for him, given his age and ideal temperament for tutoring), and by writing lecture notes for his fellow students. He will not have paid the matriculation fee, simply because he could not afford to do so, even though non-payment presumably deprived him of the use of the university library. It seems likely that Professor Stevenson lent him books, and that he was one of those to whom Professor Hunter occasionally gave money for necessities. It is time we devoted our attention to these good men, taking them in reverse order of significance.

Matthew Stewart was elected Professor of Mathematics on 2 September 1747, in succession to Colin M'Laurin, who died in June 1746. The electors had wished to appoint James Stirling to succeed M'Laurin, but his Jacobite principles led him to decline the chair. Matthew Stewart was a geometrician. His work was assessed in these terms by one of his successors, John Playfair:

> If it be confessed that Dr. Stewart rated . . . too high the merit of the ancient Geometry, this may well be excused in the man whom it had conducted to the discovery of the *General Theorems*, to the *solution of Kepler's Problem*, and to an accurate determination of the *sun's disturbing force*. His great modesty made him ascribe to the method he used that success which he owed to his own abilities.[20]

More important, however, than the discoveries which Professor Stewart was able to make the ancient geometry yield are his personal qualities. Thomas Somerville (1741-1830), who entered the University of Edinburgh a few years later than Jameson, in November 1756, wrote that:

> Even in his own department, Dr. Matthew Stewart, though perhaps the first mathematician of his age, as appears from his publications, was unfortunately found deficient in the qualifications of a teacher. He could not deviate from the standards of consummate science, or accommodate himself to the capacity of his scholars. Besides, he was of a disposition so bashful and sensitive, that the slightest irregularity, or approach to rudeness, in the behaviour of the students, disconcerted him. The misconduct of any of these boys, for such most of his pupils were, instead of meeting with a reproof from the Professor, made him blush like a child.[21]

Alexander Carlyle, for his part, wrote that Matthew Stewart was 'of an amiable disposition and of a most ingenuous mind' but that:

> when he was preferred to a chair in Edinburgh, being of diminutive stature and of an ordinary appearance, and having

withal an embarrassed elocution, he was not able to bring himself into good company . . . and fell into company of an inferior sort.[22]

The upshot appears to have been that Matthew Stewart 'died bankrupt after embezzling University funds'.[23] I am sure that Richard Jameson, who was a sensitive and civilised person, will have 'seen through the shell, and put a due value on the kernal'[24] and that, more especially, he will have respected Matthew Stewart's scholarship; otherwise, he will no doubt have learned from the mathematical professor's difficulties.

There remains a further point. Matthew Stewart was succeeded by his son, Dugald Stewart, who ten years later (in 1785) moved to the chair of moral philosophy. One of the Scottish 'commonsense' school of philosophers, Dugald Stewart was more an expositor than an original thinker; by and large he followed Thomas Reid. He becomes relevant in the present context because he had the temerity to condemn Reid's essays on the powers of the human mind, of which Schopenhauer thoroughly approved. No doubt Schopenhauer disapproved of Dugald Stewart's Whiggery; at all events he wrote of him that 'Dugald Stewart . . . belongs to that large class who have obtained an undeserved reputation through favour and friends, and therefore I can only advise that not an hour should be wasted over the scribbling of this shallow writer' (*WWI*, II, 240).

Robert Hunter was elected to the chair of Greek, having already 'given proof of his qualifications by teaching Greek privately within this city with great applause'.[25] He is said to have taken particular care that the students should be well grounded in the elements, the generality of young men who entered the first Greek class, including Richard Jameson, possessing no previous knowledge of the language.[26] However, before beginning to teach the elements of the Greek language, which is what the public Greek class essentially involved, Hunter used to spend some six weeks reading Latin with his students, probably because Latin was his forte. A. Dalzel, who attended his classes, found that Professor Hunter, 'with a familiar and less dignified manner, discovered a much more accurate and profound skill, even of Latin grammar, and of all the niceties of that language' than the Professor of Latin, George Stuart.[27] The books normally used for this preliminary course in Latin were Livy's *Roman History* and Lucan's *Pharsalia*.

Richard Jameson certainly attended the public class in elementary Greek grammar, which involved readings from the New

Testament, as well as some of Aesop's *Fables*, some of Lucian's *Dialogues* and some books of the *Iliad*. However, in addition to this class Professor Hunter also ran a private class for those who wished to apply their knowledge of Greek to their philosophical studies. Given that Jameson was a highly conscientious student, and that Professor Stevenson used to read the *Iliad* with his students, we may be sure that he attended the private class in Greek, which involved the study of the *Odyssey*, one or two tragedies (possibly those taught by Hunter's predecessor: Euripides' *Hippolytus* and *Iphigenia in Aulis*) and passages from Xenophon or Herodian.

Professor Hunter generally lectured on Mondays, Tuesdays and Wednesdays. On Thursdays he examined the students on the subject of his lectures, and on Fridays he heard their discourses. The way in which he criticised his students' work was admirable, for:

> Whatever was worthy of commendation, was always noticed by him, in such terms as were very agreeable to the author; and when he either differed in sentiment, or had any observations to make on the manner of delivery, he stated them in so conciliating a way, that it was impossible to take offence. The liberality of his views, and his Christian temper, were on such occasions most exemplary.[28]

If Robert Hunter's gentle and familiar manner made him a great favourite with the students, to Jameson he must have been an inspiring figure: his great virtues are Jameson's own. Thomas Somerville described Hunter as one of the best classical scholars in Scotland, but added that 'His method of teaching . . . did not differ materially from that of most country schoolmasters.'[29] Others frequently remark on how little difference there was at this time, in terms of scholarship, between professors and schoolmasters. A more amusing anecdote about Professor Hunter comes from Henry Mackenzie:

> So little was Greek taught when I went to College, that at the Logic Class, where Aristotle and Longinus were used as text-books, only another lad [and I] were able to read them in the original. I had an advantage over the other lads, having had a good private master for Greek for several months before I entered to the class. That class was taught by Mr. Hunter, himself a keen scholar both in Greek and Latin, but indolent and indulgent, and inspired no zeal or spirit in his pupils.

He was a great man for politics and news. When I attended him, it was at that brilliant period of the Seven Years War, during the elder Mr. Pitt's administration, when every day brought us accounts of a victory, for which the guns of the Castle were fired. At the end of the class-room, opposite to and farthest from the professor's chair, was a wall so loosely wainscotted that a blow on it sounded like the report of a distant cannon. When the lads, many of whom were from the indolent inattention of the professor idle enough, wished to get out ten or twelve minutes before the end of the hour, one of them struck his back against this wainscot, which the professor taking for the report of a gun, and anxious to hear the news, made some apology for adjourning the class, that he might hurry to the Cross to know the cause of the firing of the Castle guns.[30]

By the time Henry Mackenzie heard him lecture, in the 1760s, he may have become 'indolent and indulgent', although this is not confirmed by others; but in Richard Jameson's time he was 'exceedingly attentive to the students, and was always ready to exert himself in their behalf in any way'.[31] More particularly:

The sums of money that he gave to poor students to assist them in the prosecution of their studies were very considerable. There were bestowed as if by stealth, and done in such a way as not to hurt the feelings of those upon whom they were conferred.[32]

Richard Jameson will, inevitably, have been a beneficiary of the good professor's charity, and he will have benefited in many other ways from attendance at his classes. Quite apart from the knowledge of Greek as such, invaluable to a scholarly cleric, he will have been enabled by these classes to benefit more profoundly from John Stevenson's classes. Robert Hunter's homely manner and broad Scots pronunciation, scorned by James Boswell and his friend William Temple as an epitome of all that was provincial in Scottish education, will have had a totally different effect on the farmer's son, who will have been encouraged by them in his own ambition to rise above the poverty of his origins. More generally the gentleness of Hunter's manner, added to John Stevenson's easy-going attitude, will have had a formative effect on the young man in his mid-20s who, 20 years later, was to be compared to Sterne's Yorick.

The evidence of other students of the time, and indeed of Johanna Schopenhauer, leaves one in no doubt that the most important of those whose 'colleges' Richard Jameson attended was Professor John Stevenson. Little is known about Stevenson. He is not in *DNB*, though many lesser men are. According to Bower, he received his education at Edinburgh; he may therefore be the son of the John Stevenson who laureated MA on 4 September 1694. He was born about then, for we are told that he was 'upwards of seventy' when Reid's *Inquiry into the Human Mind* appeared in 1764. He is almost certainly the John Stevenson who was a classmate of David Hume in Colin Drummond's logic class in 1723/4. He did not serve as a regent in Edinburgh; at the time of his election to the chair of logic and metaphysics he was governor in the family of Hamilton of Bargeny, which must mean that he was tutor to James Hamilton, fourth Lord Bargeny (born 29 November 1710; succeeded in 1711 on the death of his father; his mother died in 1717). Bargeny travelled abroad for a time, if one can believe William Hamilton of Bangour's epitaph on the companion of his travels:

With kind Bargeny, faithful to his word,
Whom heaven made good and social, though a lord,
The cities view'd of many languaged men.[33]

Whether John Stevenson travelled with them is not known. James Hamilton, Lord Bargeny, died in 1736.

The fact that the Hamiltons were a Jacobite family is a reminder that it can only have been to Stevenson that Richard Jameson owed his appointment as tutor in a notorious Jacobite household. Perhaps as a result of travelling abroad, John Stevenson was possessed by the modern spirit; he was not an original thinker, but he was receptive and appreciative of what was new (Locke, literary criticism). The fact that he published no books, but had such a deep impact on those who heard his lectures, gives one a good idea of the sort of man he was. As befits a philosopher, he was an easy-going character:

J. Stevenson is in the west at some other well or bottle, I suppose, and with a calmness becomes a philosopher lets matters go on as they will. After all if they do more than they say they will, the harm will not be great perhaps. How many are busy in doing what would be better undone.[34]

No doubt this was one reason why he was regarded by his students with such affection.

Stevenson was the senior of the three professors under whom Jameson studied and the one with an established reputation. He had been appointed Professor of Logic and Metaphysics back in 1730, at a time when 'philosophy' meant the medieval philosophy of the schoolmen, conjoined with 'pneumatics' (a part not of 'mechanicks' but of the doctrine of the soul). This was, however, a time when philosophers were 'beginning to become disgusted with the school logic',[35] the downfall of which was to be accomplished by the writings of Locke, notably the *Essay on Human Understanding*, which John Stevenson was the first Scottish professor of philosophy to take seriously, although the *Essay* was in use at Cambridge by this time. On his appointment he at once instituted changes, with the result that 'the Logic of Aristotle has scarcely been a subject of lecture in Edinburgh since the year 1730'.[36] It was presumably to distance himself from what was understood as logic in 1730 that Stevenson took to referring to himself as Professor of Rational Philosophy. He also taught, with conspicuous success, rhetoric or what would now be known as literary criticism.

Professor Stevenson lectured daily at eight o'clock (on *belles-lettres*) and eleven o'clock (on logic and metaphysics); three times a week he also lectured at two o'clock (on the history of philosophy); he also examined his students, read their essays, and listened to their discourses. Since these classes constituted the better part of Richard Jameson's education, let us examine them briefly to see what they involved.

Although he was no admirer of the old school logic, Stevenson considered it essential to give a clear account of the history and nature of what had for so long been considered the only valid approach to knowledge and therefore the only way to truth. In doing so, he strongly impressed upon his pupils his own conviction that truth was not to be discovered in such a way. He used the *Elementa philosophiae rationalis* of Heineccius as a textbook, correcting Heineccius' doctrines where necessary, and then went on to what was more to his taste, the philosophy of Locke, which he taught by means of a work which he greatly admired: Bishop John Wynne's *Abridgement of Locke's Essay on the Human Understanding* (1696). We are told that:

> With uncommon pains, and great patience, [he] developed the doctrines of the 'Essay', to render them more intelligible

to his youthful hearers. Such speculations were altogether new to them; and it required the earnestness of his address, and familiarity of his illustrations, to enable them to comprehend such abstractions, and, consequently, to relish inquiries that explained the operations of the human mind.[37]

I shall come presently to the effects of Stevenson's classes on his pupils, but the significance of his course on Locke, the philosopher whose glory it was to 'free the world from the lumber of a thousand vulgar errors',[38] is self-evident. Stevenson was ahead of his time in annexing a proper value to 'the speculations of that illustrious philosopher, which have created a new era in the history of human knowledge'.[39] That this part of the course had an often profound, and therefore unsettling, effect on his youthful hearers' minds is well attested. The third part of this eleven o'clock course consisted of lectures on what used to be called ontology. In these he spoke of *being* in general, and its most general qualities, using as his text Devries's *Ontologia*. The lectures in this course were given in Latin.

On alternate afternoons Stevenson lectured on the history of philosophy, giving an account of the lives of the most famous philosophers, ancient and modern, and the several opinions by which the different schools were distinguished. His text was the *Historia philosophica* of Heineccius; he also made much use of Diogenes Laertius, of Thomas Stanley's *History of Philosophy* (1655–62), and of the more recent *Historia critica philosophiae* (6 vols, Leipzig, 1742–67) of Johann Jacob Brucker on the same subject. Stevenson's approach to the history of philosophy was, like Stanley's, essentially biographical.

His students were required to compose a discourse on a subject which was assigned to them, and to impugn and defend a philosophical thesis, in the presence of the principal and whoever chose to attend. A volume of prize essays by Stevenson's students has been preserved; the essays, half of which are in Latin and half in English, do not include one by Jameson.

Generally recognised as the most valuable part of Stevenson's teaching were his eight o'clock lectures on the grounds of criticism. At the beginning of the session the students normally read a book of the *Iliad*, both to test their proficiency in Greek, and for the sake of beginning with 'an easy author'. On either score Homer was intended to prepare them for the study of the rhetorical and critical works of writers such as Cicero, Quintilian and Horace. Stevenson commented on the beauty of Homeric poetry and referred to the imitations of Homer by Virgil, Milton and other poets. The class then moved on to Aristotle's *Poetics* and Longinus *On the Sublime*, to the discussion of which Stevenson added copious extracts from the critical works then known, including the writings of Sir William Temple, the prose discourses and prefaces of Dryden, Addison's papers in the *Spectator*, Le Bossu, Dacier, and Pope's notes on Homer. Using the anthology of such extracts which he had assembled (but unfortunately never published), Stevenson lectured on the principles of criticism, to the great delight and instruction of his audience. This class was the centrepiece of Richard Jameson's education, so that we are fortunate in having descriptions of the lecturer and his course. A former student, John Ramsay of Ochtertyre, describes Stevenson:

> Mr. Stevenson was a man of much learning and good plain understanding, without any pretension to genius. Though regarded as a dull man, he had the merit of converting a class, which had for ages been esteemed a very dry one, into a school of criticism and *belles lettres*, whilst logic and metaphysics were by no means neglected. He was . . . among the first of his brethren that gave lectures in English, which he found absolutely necessary in pointing out the beauties of the English classics, and comparing them with those of the ancients. Till then Latin was so much the language of colleges, that most of the professors spoke and wrote it with more fluency and elegance than English. And his lectures on logic were still in that language. In a word, if Mr. Stevenson's lectures on critical subjects were less elegant and scientific than those of Dr. Blair, he was certainly one of the first professors in Scotland who called the attention of their pupils to matters of taste, and connected the compositions of Greece and Rome with those of modern times. Incomplete as his rules might be, he had the good fortune to breed up some of the most eminent orators and authors that Scotland has produced. It was, I remember, alleged, that by setting young men's heads agog with the lighter parts of literature, he diverted their attention from branches of science which, though seemingly dry and uninteresting in the first stages of them, are indispensable in the learned professions. This was, I confess, too much the case with myself; for no part of his prelections made so deep an impression on my mind as those in which he treated

of the *belles lettres*. He was a pleasant, good-humoured man, of much courtesy and good-breeding, rich in literary anecdotes of all kinds, and abundantly communicative when he found young people disposed to listen to him.[40]

The *belles lettres* course as such is more fully described in A. Bower's *History of the University of Edinburgh*,[41] and Thomas Somerville, who attended these lectures just a few years after Jameson, explained that:

> His [Stevenson's] usual method was, to call upon the students to read [and translate] a prescribed portion of Aristotle's *Ars Poetica*, or Longinus on the Sublime, and then himself to add a copious exposition of the passage, often accompanied with critical remarks, which were both instructive and amusing. He also occasionally read lectures on the cardinal points of criticism suggested by the text-books now mentioned; and although not written with much attention to elegance or arrangement, his lectures included some judicious philological discussions, as well as many excellent examples and useful practical rules of composition.[42]

Somerville added, 'I derived more substantial benefit from these exercises and lectures than from all the public classes which I attended at the University.'[43] Alexander Carlyle, who attended the course almost twenty years earlier, was of the same mind ('our minds were more enlarged, and . . . we received greater benefit from that class than from any other').[44] So was Principal William Robertson, whose fellow student Jameson would have been had he gone up on time. Robertson later said that he owed more to this course 'than to any other circumstances in [my] Academical studies'.[45] Even in his own student days Stevenson seems to have had the gift of firing his friends' enthusiasm. This brings us to Schopenhauer's favourite philosopher, David Hume.

In *My Own Life* David Hume wrote:

> I passed through the ordinary Course of Education with Success; and was seized very early with a passion for Literature which has been the ruling Passion of my Life, and the great Source of my Enjoyments. My studious Disposition, my Sobriety, and my Industry gave my Family a Notion that the Law was a proper Profession for me: But I found an

insurmountable Aversion to every thing but the pursuits of Philosophy and general Learning; and while they fancyed I was poring over Voet and Vinnius, Cicero and Virgil were the Authors which I was secretly devouring.[46]

Given that Hume was a student at Edinburgh from 1723 to 1725 or 1726, it seems likely that his passion for literature was connected with his study of philosophy there. This in turn means that it must have been indebted either to the then professor of logic and metaphysics, Colin Drummond, or — more likely — to a fellow student, John Stevenson. In a letter to Michael Ramsay dated 4 July 1727 Hume not only quotes from Virgil and Cicero but also refers to Longinus and Milton. This combination points to Stevenson and must, I think, mean that Hume derived his passion for literature from him, unless both he and Stevenson were indebted to Colin Drummond, which seems unlikely. In the early 1730s Hume would have had ample opportunity to talk with Stevenson. It is therefore the case that Schopenhauer, who had the highest opinion of David Hume, owed his own passion for literature — via his mother and Richard Jameson — to the person to whom Hume owed his own enthusiasm: John Stevenson. Schopenhauer would, I think, have been well pleased to be linked with Hume in this way. Be that as it may, there can be no doubt that the 'slight tincture of letters' which Smollett ascribes to his fellow Scots at this time[47] owed more to Stevenson than to any other person, for 'his lectures on Rhetoric and Literary Criticism . . . made the deepest impression on his students and contributed most to the intellectual Renaissance of eighteenth-century Edinburgh'.[48]

That Richard Jameson was similarly affected cannot be doubted, for Stevenson's course is reflected in the works which Jameson later read with Johanna Schopenhauer. In general terms the benefit he derived from his years in Edinburgh will have been similar to that described by Alexander Carlyle, who wrote:

> It was not long before I . . . felt the superiority of an education in the College of Edinburgh; not in point of knowledge, or acquirements in the languages or sciences, but in knowledge of the world, and a certain manner and address that can only be attained in the capital.[49]

If, however, Jameson emerged from Edinburgh a civilised and well educated young man, it would have been wholly contrary to his nature to preen himself on the fact. Johanna Schopenhauer stressed this in her description of this honest, modest gentle man, to whom affectation alone was anathema. By the time Johanna enjoyed his friendship some twenty years had elapsed since he had left Edinburgh, and his self-education had continued under the friendly influence of another benign soul, Dr George Chapman. But one comes back to the fact that what Jameson derived from Edinburgh University is identical with what he derived from John Stevenson, and that is incalculable, for it is a matter not of knowledge of any kind (unless it be that of *savoir vivre*) but of less tangible and more significant things (intellectual curiosity, honesty and enthusiasm; critical foundation and approach; a sense of balance; the power of personal example). There can be no doubt that Richard Jameson received a good general education at Edinburgh, particularly from Stevenson's classes, for 'The lectures which he gave were more miscellaneous, and included a greater number of different subjects, than were taught at any class in the college'.[50] This left its mark in the way in which he was able to enlighten Johanna Trosiener on such a wide variety of subjects, and in his later membership of the Newcastle Literary and Philosophical Society.

Everything that Johanna Schopenhauer writes about him suggests that Richard Jameson too acquired, if not a passion for literature, then certainly a love of letters from Stevenson's literature class. It was precisely for this that the class was so famous:

> It is universally known in this part of the country, that no man ever held a professor's chair in the university of Edinburgh, who had the honour of training up so many young men to a love of letters, and who afterwards made so distinguished a figure in the literary world, as Dr. Stevenson. He was beloved and respected by them all; and they ever afterwards retained the most affectionate regard for him.[51]

One of Stevenson's former students who went on to cut a distinguished figure in the world of letters was James Boswell, whose biographer has rightly said that 'Stevenson not only introduced him to some of the greatest works of literature, ancient and modern, but also gave him a more coherent and comprehensive foundation for criticism than he is commonly supposed to have had'.[52] Richard Jameson's mind and horizons must have been similarly enlarged by it, and indeed by Stevenson's logic class, of which Alexander Carlyle (who probably knew Jameson in his Dumfries

days) wrote that 'the knowledge I had acquired at the Logic class
. . . cured me of many prejudices about ghosts and hobgoblins and
witches, of which till that time I stood not a little in awe'.[53]

There is often a price to be paid for this opening of the mind,
and peace of mind can easily fly out of the window with the
hobgoblins. David Hume lost his religious faith while studying at
Edinburgh, and James Boswell — under the impact of Stevenson's
logic class — became melancholy. F.A. Pottle was clearly right when
he wrote:

> In the autumn of 1756, he [Boswell] began studying logic and
> metaphysics under John Stevenson, and promptly fell prey
> to a horrible melancholy. The study of metaphysics forced
> him to think about the problem of determinism . . . The suspi-
> cion that Necessity governed all his actions filled him with
> . . . anxiety.[54]

I am not suggesting that Richard Jameson became melancholy, but
we do have Johanna Schopenhauer's word for it that there was about
him an abiding sadness, and it may well be that it was partly
Stevenson's lectures that caused him to abandon the Calvinistic
Presbyterianism of his childhood in favour of Episcopalianism, in
which Necessity plays a less dire role. In other words, he may have
been affected by the same idea as James Boswell, responding to it in
much the same way. In his London Journal Boswell wrote, in
December 1762, of 'dreary Tolbooth Kirk ideas, than which nothing
has given me more gloomy feelings'. He went on: 'I shall never
forget the Dismal hours of apprehension that I have endured in my
youth from narrow notions of religion while my tender mind was
lacerated wth infernal horror.' What caused him finally to turn his
back on Presbyterianism was Stevenson's lectures on metaphysics.
It is highly likely that Richard Jameson's experiences were similar.

James Boswell and his friend William Temple took to slipping
off to the old-world, aristocratic, Jacobitical precincts of Carrubber's
Close on a Sunday afternoon, to attend the Rev. James Grant's
English chapel in Skinner's Close. In a letter to John Johnston of
Grange, dated 27 October 1762, Boswell wrote of what Edinburgh
had meant to his friends and himself in their student days:

> You also think of the Church of England chapels, the decent
> form of prayer, a well-drest Clergyman and the grand sound
> of the Organ which lifts the soul to the celestial Regions. O

what elevated what delightfull Notions of a future state have
I sometimes had! Have not you and I of a Sunday afternoon
in Grants been full of chearing views of the immortality of
the Soul and the state of bliss in the world above?[55]

Boswell is romanticising here, for in fact the Episcopal chapels
founded in 1746 in Skinner's Close and Carrubber's Close were
'mean and inconvenient apartments'.[56] In a slightly earlier letter,
dated 13 September 1762, Boswell had written to Johnson of:

Your mind . . . filled . . . with curious ideas of France —
churches lighted with wax Candles — gilded prayer Books
— Prince Charles with a white feather in his hat, — Old
Jacobite Ladies drinking tea in an old carved room down a
north closs, in the month of January.[57]

By this time Robertson's *History of Scotland* (1759) had appeared to
fuel these young Romantics' enthusiasm, but before that their
enthusiasm had been fired — as, surely, was Jameson's — by the
romantic associations of Carrubber's Close, the centre of
Episcopalianism and Jacobitism in Edinburgh, and by the more
romantic services to be experienced at the Rev. Grant's English
Chapel. It was only at such chapels, for instance, that organ music
could be heard in Scotland.

In attending James Grant's English Chapel Boswell and Johnston
were probably following in Jameson's footsteps. In the years
between the '45 and Jameson's entering university such chapels
had been springing up in Edinburgh. Two were opened in 1746
and a third, Grant's, in January 1747. Jameson was probably one
of the earliest members of Grant's congregation. He must have
known the author of the pamphlet *A Letter to the Reverend Mr. James
Grant at his Chapel in Skinner's-Close*, by 'Philalethes', dated 21
December 1748, which purports to be written by a student of
languages and mathematics, recently arrived in Edinburgh, who
hopes to become a member of an English congregation but is beset
with doubts about what he sees as the schismatical nature of the
Church of England.[58] 'Philalethes' is the *nom-de-plume* of Robert
Forbes (1708-75), an inveterate Jacobite who was Episcopal minister
at Leith from 1735 and Episcopal Bishop of Ross and Caithness from
1769. Unlike Jameson, who presumably knew him, 'Philalethes'
was born and bred an Episcopalian. We know from an extant
character reference in which the minister of the Episcopal chapel

at Haddington, writing in March 1753, says that he has known Jameson for three years, that Jameson attended William Ritchie's Episcopal chapel at Haddington in his student days. He will have read logic, let us remember, in either the 1748-9 or the 1749-50 session. It is unlikely that he became a member of the 'true (though suffering) Episcopal Church of Scotland'[59] before he went up to university. He almost certainly became an Episcopalian because of his own basic romanticism, which very likely involved him in some way in the events of 1745, and because of Stevenson's lectures, which will have taught him to back his own romanticism against the dreary determinism of the Tolbooth Kirk. Grant's English Chapel will have played its part, for not only was it the nearest such chapel, but its situation off Carrubber's Close points straight to Jameson's future employer, David Erskine (Lord Dun), who was precisely the sort of person who was at home in Carrubber's Close. It is even possible that Jameson was introduced to David Erskine there.

This brings us to Jameson's final debt to Stevenson, for, as Dalzel writes:

> It is usual for young men of narrow circumstances, at the Scottish Universities, to embrace the earliest opportunity of being employed, either as private tutors in families, or in giving private assistance to other students, younger than themselves: and the professors have great pleasure in recommending to such situations young men of that description, who have distinguished themselves in the classes.[60]

This John Stevenson did for Richard Jameson by recommending him to David Erskine, Lord Dun, as tutor to his grandson.

Governor

From May 1751 to March 1753 Richard Jameson was governor (tutor) to the grandson of David Erskine of Dun. This is attested by three certificates found among his ordination papers.[61] The first is headed 'Certificate by Lord Dun in favours of Mr. Richd. Jameson, 1753'. In it 'David Erskine of Dun Esq., one of the Senators of the College of Justice in Scotland', certifies that Richard Jameson has been 'some years in my family, attending upon my Grandson and Heir in aiding and assisting him in some proper parts of his education' and that 'his Conduct . . . dureing his residence with me was unexceptionable pious and Religious, of a good Temper and Christian Disposition'. Lord Dun accordingly recommends Richard Jameson as a suitable candidate for ordination. The certificate was made out in Edinburgh and is dated 15 March 1753. The other two certificates are testimonials or characters by the ministers of the Episcopal chapels at Brechin and Montrose, which Jameson attended during his time at Dun House. The first certifies that the minister of the Episcopal chapel at 'Brechin, North Britain' has been acquainted with 'Mr Richard Jamison, late Governor to Mr. Erskine his Children in this neighbourhood for the space of about two Years last past', and that to the best of the Minister's knowledge he 'hath . . . behaved himself soberly, virtuously & piously, & as a loyal Subject to His Majesty King George'. It is dated 17 March 1753 and is signed Nor: Sievwright'. Norman Sievwright took his MA at Marischal College, Aberdeen, and was ordained deacon at Gloucester in 1749 (priest 1750); he was roughly Jameson's age. The second character, dated 20 May 1753, is signed 'Richard Fleming Minr. of the licensed Chapel at Montrose'. Richard Fleming was a young man of Jameson's own age; he was the son of John Fleming of Ulverston and his wife Ann, and was baptised on 2 December 1721 at Ulverston. As Richard Jameson may well have done, Richard Fleming took up schoolmastering (Millom, 1743; Old Hutton, 1743–7) before, in his case, going up to Oxford. He matriculated at Queen's College on 2 August 1747, aged 25, having been ordained deacon at Chester on 9 June 1745. He was curate of Ulpha (1745–6) and of Irthington (1749) before becoming minister of the Episcopal chapel at Montrose (1750–6), where he will have provided Richard Jameson with the sort of company, conversation and stimulus that he needed. He went on to become vicar of Bywell St Andrew (1757–78), and died in 1807.

Jameson probably owed his appointment at Dun to Stevenson, although the Rev. William Ritchie, minister of the Episcopal chapel at Haddington, may also have been involved. It seems likely that Jameson became an Episcopalian about 1750; in a character dated March 1753 the Rev. William Ritchie said that he had known Jameson for three years. Whatever the precise reasons for Jameson's move to the Episcopal Church, it led first to his appointment at Dun and then to his call to Dumfries.

David Erskine of Dun, to whose grandson Richard Jameson acted as tutor, was at this time 'a venerable old man, of very great experience, and greatly distinguished for piety'.[62] He was born in 1670, son of David Erskine of Dun, near Montrose, Forfarshire. He studied at the Universities of St Andrews and Paris, became a member of the Scottish bar in 1698, and soon rose to eminence. He represented Forfarshire in the parliaments of the 1690s, and opposed the Union. In 1710 he took his seat as an ordinary lord by the title of Lord Dun, and in 1714 was also appointed a lord of justiciary. He resigned as an ordinary lord in 1753, his place as judge of session being taken by James Boswell's father;[63] he died on 26 May 1758, aged 85.

In *The Expedition of Humphry Clinker* Smollett wrote, 'I have known a member of the House of Commons speak with great energy and precision, without being able to engage attention, because his observations were made in the Scotch dialect.' Whether Smollett was thinking of Lord Dun I do not know, but Henry Home reported of a speech by Lord Dun before the House of Lords in 1737 that 'Deil ae word, from beginning to end, did the English understand of his speech.'[64] It is John Ramsay of Ochtertyre who has left us the fullest description of Jameson's venerable but idiosyncratic employer:

> If not a first-rate lawyer, he had sufficient learning to make him a useful judge. As he spared no pains in discharging the duties of his laborious office, so he was accounted a man of honour and integrity, both on and off the bench. His piety and zeal for religion were conspicuous, even in times when all men prided themselves upon being decent in these matters. The pedantry of his talk and the starchiness of his manners made him the subject of ridicule among people who had neither his worth nor innocence of heart and life. He was likewise overrun with prejudice, which sometimes warps the judgement of able, well-intentioned men; but for that, one would be at a loss to account for his Toryism which approached very near to Jacobitism. How this could be reconciled to the oaths he had taken, is not the question here; but sometimes we see people wonderfully ingenious in grossly deceiving themselves. Be this as it may, it could not escape observation that, for a number of years Lord Dun hardly ever voted on the side of the Crown, even when the decision was wellnigh unanimous. This never appeared more glaring than after the Rebellion of 1745. Had he been a chancellor it was wrong; but circumstanced as the Bench then was, his single

vote was of little avail. In his notions of Church government he was decidedly Episcopal, which was nowise inconsistent with his solemn obligations. His conversing much with that species of clergy gave, probably, a tinge to his principles, of which he himself was not aware. He was, I have been told, prolix and diffuse in his speaking, both in public and in private. It did not serve to set off what he said to greater advantage, that he spoke a language peculiar to himself which he called English. Upon the whole he was assuredly a good, if not a great and shining character. His foibles were either venial, or occasioned by prejudices which it was impossible for him to shake off. In one point he carried his notions of duty much too far. He thought when a judge could not constantly do his duty he ought to retire; for which reason he resigned his Justiciary gown in 1744, because he was not longer able to ride the circuit — for in those days it was literally performed on horseback. And in 1753, when his health and strength were much impaired, he quitted the bench entirely, without asking a pension, to which his long and faithful services well entitled him; and he was by no means rich. He ought therefore to have retained the emoluments of his office, though not able to discharge the duty. His 'Advices', which were published not long after his death, convey no very high idea of his teaching and judgments, or of the beauty of his diction. He hardly lived two years after quitting the bench.[65]

David Erskine Lord Dun lived at Dun, half way between Brechin and Montrose in what was then known as Forfarshire. Bishop Pococke, writing from Glamis on 7 August 1760, referred to Dun House:

> I left Montrose in the afternoon and crossing a skirt of the strand came into a most beautifull Country, and passed by a fine grove of Firr trees belonging to Colonel Scott whose house is happily situated on the Eminence. We then rode by Mr. Erskine's of Dun[,] much the same situation.[66]

By 1760 Lord Dun was dead and Dun House belonged to his son, John Erskine (1712-87). Violet Jacob's *The Lairds of Dun* (1931) reproduces as its frontispiece a most attractive old print of the 'House of Dun'. Designed by the elder Adam, it was built by Lord Dun in 1730 and was set in an idyllic park.

The boy to whom Richard Jameson acted as tutor was John Erskine (b. 11 December 1742, d. 1812), son of David Erskine's only son, John. Tutoring him must have been a thoroughly thankless task, for he was a boy almost totally lacking in parts, who turned into a 'slow witted man',[67] of whom the Rev. John Waugh (minister of Menmuir) wrote, on 14 March 1781:

> He does not read, not for want of opportunity, but from want of inclination; indeed he was, as his father has informed me, much foundered in his education, and it was no wonder, for he has had not less than five tutors, one of whom was your worthy *gallant* Mr Main.[68]

The no less worthy Mr Jameson must have found tutoring young John Erksine an irksome task, particularly since David Erskine was at this time a tetchy, eccentric character and the tutor's lot was in any case frequently a wretched one. James Boswell — one of whose university friends, known to him as 'the Horse', was John Francis Erskine (1741–1825), restored Earl of Mar, a cousin of Jameson's cloddish pupil — wrote of his own governors that they were both 'men without manners, men of the meanest sort of education. They were like my father's servants. They ate at table, but they hardly dared open their mouths. I saw them treated with contempt.'[69] When visiting friends in Scotland in 1762 Boswell found that their tutor, Mr McCartney, had formerly been in the same class at the University of Edinburgh, which prompted him to write:

> I cannot help censuring the method of most Families to their Children's Tutor, who is treated as a sort of cringing Animal little better than a livery servant and who sits at table like a condemned Criminal two days before his Execution. Here indeed my old acquaintance was fed above stairs in his own Garret, which I think a preferable scheme as it must be easier both for himself and other people. For my own part I have often felt very sensibly for them while in Company. How can it be expected that men of tolerable Genius and Spirit will undertake the ungracious Office? How can it be expected that Boys can have a proper reverence for a Being whom they considered as an Insect, or how can they help despising learning and knowledge when their teacher is so shamefully used?[70]

Whether Jameson was treated as badly as this is, of course, not known; but he may well have sat at table 'like a condemned Criminal' when Lord Dun's neighbours (Colonel Scott of Hedderwick House; Sir David Carnegie, Bart, of Kinnaird; Lord Panmure of Brechin Castle) dined. He is unlikely to have spent very much time sitting in the elegantly formal drawing-room at Dun House (such a far cry from Stane farmhouse). Maybe things were a little different when Lord Dun's guests were the local Episcopal clergymen (the Rev. Sievwright of Brechin and the Rev. Richard Fleming of Montrose), whose company Lord Dun over-cultivated and whose friendship Richard Jameson enjoyed.

When Jameson was employed as tutor in his household Lord Dun was preparing for publication a curious little volume entitled *Lord Dun's Friendly and Familiar Advices adapted to the various Stations and Conditions of Life*, which came out in Edinburgh in 1754. The volume is of interest partly because of its timing, which makes it likely that Jameson was in some way involved. While Lord Dun was not the sort of person to take advice from a person a third his age, except possibly on matters of composition, he is likely to have recruited Jameson as scribe and proof reader. The main significance of the volume, however, is that it perpetuates particular 'advices' which Lord Dun must have given Richard Jameson in plenty. In the book he makes clear his views on education. We can be sure that when he engaged Jameson as tutor to his nine-year-old grandson he will have emphasised that a tutor's prime responsibility was the religious instruction and catechism of his charge, and that teaching children to read was to be seen as a means to that end.[71] Jameson will have been enjoined to make young Erskine read every day 'some portion of the holy Scriptures' and to put into his hands 'proper books, for improving both [his] knowledge in, and practice of, true piety and devotion'. Instruction in any other 'human arts and sciences' will have taken second place. It does not sound as though Jameson's charge will have been very responsive, assuming that he could read by the age of nine; he evidently did not care for reading. It was probably not until he took young Johanna Trosiener's reading in hand that Jameson was able to put into practice the ideas of John Stevenson and George Chapman.

Among the 'friendly and familiar advices' which he offered to all and sundry Lord Dun included some advice for those intending to offer themselves for ordination. We may therefore be sure that he did not fail to give Richard Jameson plenty of advice on this score. Indeed, we can hear what he will have said:

> I beg leave to offer this caution . . . that none do presume to take on him holy orders without finding in himself a call and disposition thereto; by which I mean, without, after a strict and narrow examination of his own heart and inward disposition, he find in himself such a state of mind, such a heavenly spiritual temper of soul, as makes him both able and willing to renounce this world, with all its vanities, and sinful customs, and with it all temptations of both flesh and devil.[72]

After a good deal more advice on the same lines, Lord Dun went on to say 'what a doom' the man must expect 'whose chief motive in seeking after the office of the holy ministry is wordly interest, of getting himself settled in a good benefice and living'. Jameson must have been quizzed thoroughly as to his motives, but once his sincerity was confirmed (he was a completely unworldly person) I have no doubt that Lord Dun — a well known Episcopalian — will have helped him.

Episcopal Minister

In February 1753, while at Dun House, Jameson received a call to be minister of the Episcopal chapel in Dumfries. The Erskine family had a number of links with the Dumfries area and with such prominent local lairds as Charles Stewart of Shambellie, Sir William Grierson of Lag (son of the notorious 'Bluidy Lagg', the inveterate Jacobite preserved in Scott's *Redgauntlet* under another well known Dumfries name, that of Robert Herries), and Sir John Douglas of Kellhead. Sir John (*c.* 1708-78) had been sent to the Tower of London after the 'late rebellion', for rebellious practices, finally being released for want of evidence. No less important, he was (through his mother, Helen Erskine, daughter of Lieutenant-Colonel John Erskine, 1660-1737, by his first wife) a distant relative of David Erskine of Dun. David Erskine wrote Jameson a testimonial in March 1753 in support of his application for ordination; it seems more than likely that, before then, he was instrumental in getting him called to Dumfries.

Jameson's ordination title, then, was a call from the Episcopal Society in Dumfries, dated 7 February 1753, inviting him to succeed the Rev. Alexander Howie, who had been obliged to resign at the beginning of 1752 because of ill health. The living was worth a relatively generous £40-52 per annum. The call was signed by Charles Stewart of Shambellie, John Story (writer), William Carruthers (merchant) and a number of other well known Dumfries names (Robert Herries, Thomas Nicholson, Thomas Hudelston, John Wilson, Will McCornock, etc.). Richard Jameson accepted the call, which was flattering and an opportunity not to be missed, and proceeded to apply to the Bishop of Durham for admission to Holy Orders. He had apparently tried the Bishop of London first, only to be referred to Durham. His application, in March 1753, was initially unsuccessful because it was incomplete, lacking two of the necessary certificates. On 7 June Jameson, who was then in Edinburgh, addressed to 'Mr —— Secretary to the Lord Bishop of Durham' a letter which has survived.[73] It reads as follows:

Edinburgh June 7th 1753.

Sir,

I presume you'll remember that in March last I applyed to the Bishop of Durham for Orders, but was disappointed, partly on account of my wanting a certificate of my Age, and partly because I was too late in my Application. I left my Title with you in Expectation of Orders when the Bishop came to Durham, and as the Congregation to which I am called have been destitute of a Minister for eighteen Months and upwards, and are at present unsupplyed, waiting on me, I beg you'll do me the Favour to let me know when the Bp. will be down, and what Time I may expect Orders at Durham; and if you please to write, be so good as [to] let me know when I should send you up my Certificates. I have every thing ready you desired me to get, and if any thing else be requisite, I hope you'll please to inform me that I be not disappointed a second time which will prove extremely hard on me. I should not have troubled you with this had not the People of Dumfries pressed me to it. If you please to return me a speedy Answer to this, you'll very much oblige

Sir, you most obedient
and most humble Servant
Rich. Jameson

Please direct for me
to the care of Mr. James Brown
Bookseller in the Parliament closs
Edinburgh

Compared with similar compositions by Georgian clergymen, the letter is a remarkably fluent and civilised document. Reading it, one must agree with his later friends who remarked that he 'composed with great elegance' in his native language. No doubt some of the credit is due to John Stevenson's 'unaffected plainness' of style.

This time Jameson's application was successful. He was ordained deacon in Durham on 7 June 1753 (there is no record of any subsequent ordination as priest) and took up his position as minister of the Episcopal chapel (or 'English chapel', as it was generally known) in Dumfries shortly afterwards.

'In the religious life of Scotland of the eighteenth century', wrote H.G. Graham, 'Episcopacy plays an inconspicuous part, though in its social life it formed a picturesque element.'[74] On the whole, Episcopacy began north of the Forth. There were scattered pockets of its adherents in the Lowlands but they were few and far between, and in the south-west there was only one Episcopal congregation at the time, that in Dumfries. Episcopacy was so closely linked with Jacobitism that the two were often regarded as synonymous. It was essentially the religion of the Jacobite lairds, who relished claret more than dogma. Thus in Dumfries, which was essentially Presbyterian, Episcopacy was mainly restricted to some of the landed gentry and wealthy merchants, although Jameson's congregation also included farmers, tanners, hatters, wrights and labourers, as well as members of the English regiments quartered in the town.

The great majority of Episcopalian ministers were Non-jurors, which means that they were on the side of Prince Charles in 1745. Such non-juring, non-qualified clergymen led an appalling life. Some became chaplains in Jacobite families, where for £5 per annum, with board and washing, they 'tutorised the children, said grace at meat, read the prayers, and went the household errands'.[75] Richard Jameson's life at Dun cannot have been very different. However, the life of many non-qualified clergymen was far worse than this. H.G. Graham reports that 'A wretched cottage, with walls of turf and clay, covered with heather, containing two . . . little ill-lighted rooms, from whose rafters hung the family wardrobe, utensils and provisions furnished with a scanty "plenishing"'' was the usual dwelling of an Episcopal minister in rural Forfarshire at the time when Jameson was at Dun. A salary of some £10 per annum enabled the minister to buy 'oatmeal, a little meat [and] some rough clothing'; to supplement his pittance he might try to farm a few acres of land. Others lived an itinerant existence, skulking in the woods while their hole-in-the-corner chapels were sacked by the English soldiery. Jameson will have known all this, and will therefore not have needed Lord Dun to advise him against entering the ministry from any worldly motive.

The law-abiding clergy who took the oath of allegiance, as Richard Jameson did, lived more comfortably; Jameson was paid four times as much as his counterpart in rural Forfarshire. They officiated in 'chapels of mean adornment' but were spared most of the persecution which the oppressed non-qualified clergy suffered, although they might, it is true, have to listen to the rude rhyme 'Pisky, Pisky, Amen, / Down on your knees and up again,' called after them by the little horrors of their day. By and large 'Their doctrine was sensible if their teaching was dull; their character was genial, and they were free from . . . political and sacerdotal fanaticism.'[76] Such was the body of men joined by Richard Jameson in 1753. In several ways he will have stood out. Dumfries was more civilised than any other town in Scotland after Edinburgh. His congregation included a number of wealthy merchants, so that he was relatively well paid. He was also better and more liberally educated than many of his fellows. According to John Ramsay of Ochtertyre, the Episcopal clergy of the time, though 'very learned and assiduous', had little 'proficiency in polite literature, or pretended to write elegant English'.[77] Jameson had no pretensions of any kind, but thanks to John Stevenson (and presently to a newfound friend in Dumfries, George Chapman) he had some proficiency in polite literature and was not inattentive to the graces of diction.

At the time of Jameson's appointment the Episcopal Society in Dumfries had been without a minister for more than a year, and the society's meeting house was 'very unfit and uncommodious'.[78] Nothing more is known of this meeting house, which had replaced the 'privy kirk' of the early years of the century, but within a matter of months of Jameson's arrival in Dumfries the members of the Episcopal Society, who had been steadily increasing in number since 1746, had decided to build a more appropriate and more centrally situated place of worship:

> A scheme for erecting a suitable fabric was laid before a meeting of 'the Episcopal Society in Dumfries', held on the 22nd of March, 1754 . . . The proposal . . . was, that a chapel should be built, at a cost (including site) of £250, to accomodate from

150 to 200 persons — £100 of the sum to be raised by subscription, the rest to be borrowed; that the minister's stipend should be restricted to £50, 'paid out of the profits of the chappell' ... This scheme, on being read to the meeting, was signed by all present, numbering twenty-seven ... and a committee — consisting of Mr. Richard Jameson, minister; Mr. Charles Stewart of Shambelly ... ; Mr. John Story, writer [to the signet] there — was named to carry it into effect. In due time the chapel was built on a site in Lochmaben-gate; but though Sir William Grierson of Rockhall furnished building materials without charge, in the shape of 10,000 bricks, and Sir John Douglas of Kelhead supplied twenty cartloads of lime on the same free terms, and though others of the neighbouring gentry gave liberal subscriptions, the committee found that the expenditure exceeded the fund at their disposal by more than £200 ... The papers relating to its early history show that the revival and reorganisation of Episcopalianism in Dumfries were mainly due to the exertions of Mr. Charles Stewart of Shambelly. The chapel in Lochmaben-gate was a plain building, octagonal in form, with a pavilion roof.[79]

This chapel was known as the 'English Chapel' and its congregation as the 'English Congregation'. Clearly Charles Stewart of Shambellie received energetic support from Richard Jameson, who even helped with some of the actual building. One of the subscribers to the chapel building fund was the Jacobite 'Painter McGhie'. The subscription was topped up by a loan from Dumfries's wealthiest citizen, Richard Lowthian, a prominent non-juror and owner of the house occupied by Prince Charles Edward in 1745. The Jacobite (or Erskinite) connection was evidently very real.

Since services were confined to Sundays, Jameson can hardly have been overworked, although he no doubt spent a good deal of time outside Dumfries visiting members of his scattered congregatoin. They included Boswell's friend John Johnston of Grange (a sentimental Jacobite particularly attracted to Episcopal devotions) and his cousin Captain William Douglas of Kellhead, son of Sir John Douglas, whom Boswell describes as 'a lively man but hurried away by fancifull project'.[80] When he got to Kellhead in October 1762 Boswell found himself 'surrounded with Cousins' and Sir John's estate lumbered with 'princely improvements' in the best eighteenth-century manner. Jameson's congregation may also have included Sir William Maxwell of Springkell and Boswell's other cousins, Captain William Maxwell of Dalswinton and his brother George. It was largely thanks to Jameson that the attitude of Presbyterian Dumfries towards its 'English Congregation' changed. As it became clear that there was no danger of a third Jacobite uprising attitudes relaxed, but Jameson's industry and palpable honesty also did much to commend him to the citizens of Dumfries, for on 10 July 1758 the magistrates admitted him an honorary burgess, thereby formally recognising the respectability of his congregation.

Dumfries, 'always a good town, and full of . . . merchant-adventurers' (Daniel Defoe, writing in the year of Jameson's birth), was at this time 'a very elegant trading town', so much so that Smollett, describing it thus in *Humphry Clinker*, added, 'If I was confined to Scotland for life, I would choose Dumfries as the place of my residence.' Bishop Pococke, visiting the town in 1750, found it 'pleasantly situated', while Alexander Carlyle, who had relatives there, whom he often visited, wrote of passing eight days at Dumfries in 1748, 'with such a variety of amusement as would fill half a volume of a novel'.[81] Clearly there was no lack of polite society, although Jameson will have been on the fringes of it until he had become accepted outside his own congregation. No doubt some Dumfriesians were as bigoted as ever against Episcopalianism, which they identified with 'Black Prelacy', but Jameson will have found a fair measure of acceptance, for he was very much that *rara avis* among the clergy of the lower order, described by Alexander Carlyle — who may well have met him — as 'accomplished and agreeable, a man of the world without licentiousness, of learning without pedantry, and pious without sanctimony'.[82]

Lord Kames used to declare that in no place which his official duties as assize-court judge called him to visit was he more delighted with the manners and conversation of the ladies than in Dumfries. This brings us to Richard Jameson's closest friend there, George Chapman, who was responsible for the politeness of the manners of the fair Dumfriesians.

George Chapman (1723-1806), a 'very eminent and successful teacher, not perhaps surpassed by any of his time',[83] comes into this story because he was rector of the grammar school in Dumfries from 1751 to 1774, and because it is clear both from Jameson's will and from George Chapman's tribute to his memory that the two men enjoyed a close friendship. Chapman was doubtless one of the first people outside the English congregation to make Jameson welcome on his arrival, while Jameson, for his part, will have been delighted to find in Dumfries a person of exactly his own age and background (Chapman's father was a tenant farmer in Alva), with a similar temperament and similar interests. What evidence there is suggests that Richard Jameson, like George Chapman, was distinguished by placidity of temper, correctness of manners, benevolence and liberality of disposition.[84] They had similar educational and literary interests. Chapman, who attended the parish school at Alva under George Robertson, proceeded to university (Aberdeen in his case) at the normal age, in 1737. He took his MA in 1741, having spent his long vacations working as tutor in a gentleman's family and then teaching in his old school. After graduating he became assistant teacher in the grammar school of Dalkeith. He went on to produce a number of publications, four of which deserve mention: *A Treatise on Education* (1773), *Hints on the Education of the Lower Ranks of the People, and the Appointment of Parochial Schoolmasters* (n.d.), *Advantages of a Classical Education; the Importance of the Latin, and its Usefulness for the Attainment of the English Language* (1804) and *An Abridgement of Mr. Ruddiman's Rudiments and Latin Grammar* (n.d.). Further details of his life will be found in the *Sketch of the Life of the late George Chapman* (1808). His 'plan of education' is discussed in a later chapter, where his aims and methods are compared with those of Arthur Schopenhauer's English schoolmaster. We are told that:

> A few years after he had formed and experienced the success of the Plan of Education he had adopted for the Institution, he committed it to writing, and occasionally submitted it, in the various stages of progression, to the inspection and observations of his particular friends.[85]

Although the Rev. Richard Jameson, as an Episcopal clergyman, was not a member of the Presbytery of Dumfries (a body of 18 clergymen of the Established Kirk charged by law with the inspection of schools within their parish), which from 1757 onwards inspected Chapman's school annually, he will surely have been one of those to whom George Chapman submitted early drafts of his later *Treatise on Education*. He probably also attended Chapman's school, for it was no uncommon circumstance to see a whole class of parish schoolteachers attending the school in order to gain a more critical knowledge of the Latin and Greek languages and of the method of inculcating them. The author of the *Sketch* speaks of the liberality of Chapman's attentions to such people and the gratitude with which they were ever afterwards acknowledged. Nor were Chapman's educational activities confined to the grammar school, as the *Sketch* again indicates:

> Dumfries was . . . one of the neatest small towns in Scotland; the manners of the people remarkably polite and dignified, and the conversation in general more interesting than perhaps any where out of the metropolis. But the means of improving the female mind, were not equal to those of the other sex. Dr. Chapman [as he later was] was . . . therefore often consulted on that subject; and at the hours of interval in the public teaching, or after them, was prevailed upon to receive a limited number of young ladies into his house for instruction in English grammar, geography, French, the principles of natural philosophy . . . and the elements of belles lettres. This gradually diffused so general a taste for reading and literary conversation, that the gentlemen were said to study in order to qualify them for conversation with the ladies.[86]

It is likely that Richard Jameson was recruited by his friend to help with the literary conversation; indeed, this even helps to explain his sudden departure from Dumfries in January 1762. No doubt Jameson met Lord Kames, who not only visited George Chapman frequently from 1752 onwards but, as an Episcopalian, will have been an occasional member of Jameson's congregation. Indeed, Kames probably discussed with Chapman and Jameson some of the fundamental ideas of his *The Elements of Criticism* (1762), and the three may also have discussed the 'culture of the heart', which was to be the subject of Kames's *Loose Hints upon Education* (1781). Jameson will also have known the local physician, Dr Evan (Ebenezer) Gilchrist (1707-74), who had graduated at Rheims and in 1756 published his *Use of Sea Voyages in Medicine*. One thinks of Jameson's repeated journeys from Danzig to Newcastle in the 1780s, when his health was deteriorating, and of his fluent knowledge of French, to which Chapman later attested. Jameson obviously knew Provost George Bell, and probably met his nephew, Alexander Carlyle, on one of his flying visits to Dumfries, perhaps in early 1757 on the occasion of Provost Bell's death, or in 1760. He no doubt witnessed the riots in Dumfries at Michaelmas 1760, caused by the inflammatory oratory of the clever young Andrew Crosbie (1736-85) on the occasion of the election of a new provost. He most likely knew Andrew Crosbie, who is said to have been the prototype of Pleydell in *Guy Mannering* and was a friend of James Boswell. Another friend of Boswell's whom Jameson will have known is Collector Gordon, described by Boswell as 'a lively little man of a constant flow of vivacity and not so much feeling or depth of Sentiment as to render him susceptible of unhappiness'. He wrote verses sometimes, and had an epistle in Donaldson's *Collection of Original Poems by Scotch Gentlemen* (1762). His wife was (in Boswell's words) 'a smart, comely, gay girl'.[87] No doubt Jameson also knew, and counted among his congregation, some at least of the masters of the 'English [non-Latin] school' of the time (James Turnbull, Alexander Shand, Hugh Branderith, William Auld and William Talbert), particularly William Talbert, who was an exact contemporary of his, coming to Dumfries as he did in 1753 and leaving it (in death) in 1762.

During the summer months, when Chapman usually walked along the banks of the Nith, from soon after four until six in the morning (those were heroic days), Jameson no doubt sometimes accompanied him[88] on his walks past the picturesque ruins of twelfth-century Lincluden Abbey (in the shadows of which Burns was to compose several poems) or, on the other bank, Holywood Abbey, the two of them discussing literary subjects or Chapman's educational ideas. Jameson will also have been one of those who used to meet Chapman in the coffee house at twelve o'clock on Saturdays. It was only in the evening that George Chapman had any time for relaxation, and that he generally devoted to reading and an extensive correspondence. From 1762 to 1796 that correspondence will have included Jameson, whose friendship with the like-minded Chapman tells us a good deal about how he spent his time in Dumfries. Chapman was the ideal person to continue the inspiration previously provided by John Stevenson. On Jameson's death Chapman wrote an affectionate tribute to his memory.

Jameson's time in Dumfries came to an abrupt and mysterious end in 1762, when he resigned, being replaced by the Rev. Joseph Wilson (1734–78) before 31 January. One of his last acts in Dumfries was to pay the dues of 2s 6d for his 'Burges Ticket' in best gilt, which he did on 3 December 1761. It is possible that he timed his resignation to coincide with an important date in the Episcopal church year, the commemoration of the martyrdom of Charles I on 30 January, by way of reasserting his Romanticism of a decade earlier. This is, however, pure speculation. Why he resigned is not known. It is a surprising decision, for he had had a successful nine years in Dumfries, which was as elegant and agreeable a place as any in which he was likely to find himself, had built a new chapel, had become a burgess, and had made a lifelong friend. One would have thought that he was set for a longer stay, for there could have been few better positions open to him. Something clearly happened to make him decide to move on, something which had little to do with logic or reason. Much the most likely explanation is that he had become attached to one of the gentle Dumfries ladies whose polite conversation so delighted Lord Kames, and had suffered some kind of emotional loss or setback. This is the most likely explanation of that abiding sadness which he is said to have carried around with him. Otherwise it may simply be that, after the death of his uncle in May 1761, there were no longer any family ties standing in the way of his desire to see more of the world.

Following his resignation in January 1762, Jameson disappears from sight for two years. He presumably left Dumfries and probably returned to Edinburgh for a while. The chances are that he worked as governor in Edinburgh or London, or as travelling governor in France, which would help to account for the fact that he spoke fluent French. He surfaces in London in 1764 and may, of course, have gone there straight away in 1762. If so, he could not have chosen a worse time, for Scots (from the Prime Minister, the Earl of Bute, downwards) were extremely unpopular. English merchants resented the fact that the Union meant sharing their privileges with the Scots; in 1763 Charles Churchill was to attack the Scots in *The Prophecy of Famine*, and in 1762 it was only 17 years since Prince Charles Edward had led a Jacobite army to within 127 miles of London. When he was in London, Jameson will have seen the heads of two officers of Prince Charles's army mouldering on pikes over Temple Bar, and if he had felt that there was no reason to remain in Scotland he will certainly have felt disinclined to stay long in London. November 1762 was when James Boswell set out for London to conquer the 'civil nymph with white-thread stockings who . . . will resign her engaging person to your honour for a pint of wine and a shilling'.[89] Although there is no particular reason to suppose that Jameson knew Boswell (whom he had missed at university, and who moved in different circles), he probably knew some of Boswell's friends who were in London at the time, including John Johnston of Grange (who had been an occasional member of Jameson's congregation in Dumfries), Captain William Douglas of Kellhead (a former member of that congregation) and his uncle, Charles Douglas (brother of Jameson's patron, Sir John Douglas of Kellhead), and James Murray of Broughton. He may also have met another friend of Boswell's: that other Scottish ex-tutor and clergyman-in-waiting, James Macpherson, then in London and at the height of his fame following the publication of his *Fingal* in 1761. He may, for that matter, have met Boswell himself.

Chaplain in Danzig

One day in summer 1764 Jameson met Joshua Kenworthy, a respected Danzig merchant who was on a business visit to London and had been charged by the English Factory in Danzig to find a new chaplain to replace the Rev. Johnnie Tucker, who had just resigned. By tradition chaplains were supposed to be Scottish and English alternately. Since he was looking for a suitable Scottish clergyman, Joshua Kenworthy probably began his search with the secretary to the Bishop of London, in whose gift the nomination was supposed to be (and of whom Jameson may well have made enquiries about such a post), only to be referred either to Jameson in person, or to the British Coffee House or Scots Coffee House, both near Charing Cross, where exiled North Britons tended to forgather. Whether this was where Joshua Kenworthy found him or not, Richard Jameson was offered and accepted the post of chaplain to the English Factory at Danzig. According to the register of the chaplaincy, he officiated in Danzig from 26 November 1764 to 19 July 1789; in fact[90] he took up the appointment in October 1764. His time in Danzig therefore closely corresponds to Dr Wendeborn's time in London, and, like Wendeborn, Jameson left his post feeling that things were not what they had been.

In 1734 an 'English Merchant, lately Resident there' published *A Particular Description of the City of Dantzick*. In it he described his first impression of the city:

> When I first came to Dantzick, having seen no other City before I travell'd, but my native One in the North of England, and coming at once into the Gross Hoff, or Great Court, without any previous Notice of its Grandeur, the Surprize of its Spatiousness, and elevated noble Houses, struck me on a sudden with such an Impression of Surprize, as I shall never be able to forget.[91]

The merchant in question was almost certainly George Mallabar of Newcastle-upon-Tyne. No doubt Richard Jameson's first impression was similar, but, being familiar with Edinburgh, his 'Surprize' will not have quite been so great. Though arguably 'neither elegant or handsome',[92] Danzig was, Jameson will have found:

> a very considerable city, well situated on the mouth of the Vistula, with a very advantageous harbour for all but the largest ships. It very much resembles Hamburgh, both in the loftiness of the houses, the manner of building them, and in the narrowness of the streets.[93]

With its English House and English Chapel, and the large number of North Britons among its residents, Danzig will also have seemed a reassuring place. We have seen that at the beginning of the fourteenth century there was already a community of British merchants in the city, which soon became the centre of the Baltic trade. Many of them were Scots, and indeed Aberdonians. By 1475 they already had their own chapel in the Schwarzmönchenkirche, and from that time the Anglo-Scottish community grew continually; eventually the community was allowed to hold its own services, in English, in the Nikolaikirche and the Brigittenkirche. A further landmark in its prosperity came in 1577, when a Scottish force of 700 men, under Colonel William Stewart, fought for Danzig against the Polish King Stephen Bathory, an action in which Captain Robert Gurlay distinguished himself. However, the story of the 'English Chapel' as such begins in 1639, when Dr William Guild of Aberdeen preached to a 'Worshipfull and religious societie' in the presence of the British ambassador, Francis Gordon. The following year Francis Gordon sought permission for a suitable public room to be assigned to the community, in which such services could be held. The council, unwilling to concede such a privilege at that time, urged the merchants to find a suitable room in a private house, and it is likely that a makeshift private chapel was soon after established in the Englisches Haus. This arrangement did not last, however, presumably because the Englisches Haus was not really suitable for the purpose, so that in Danzig (as opposed to Hamburg) the English House and the English Chapel were separate establishments.

The house in the Brotbänkengasse long known as the Englisches Haus was built for Dietrich Lilie by Hans Kramer of Dresden in 1565-70. If it was known as the Englisches Haus before *c*. 1640 — and it may well have been — then it would have been because of a passionate love affair between a well-to-do English merchant, James Fluelin (Fluellyn), and Lilie's sister-in-law, Barbara Rosenberg. The story of their love and the difficulties which James Fluellyn had to overcome is worthy of a novel.[94] In 1622 the Baltic Company of London sent a deputation (Thomas Ofley, William Culpepper and Theophilus Eaton)[95] to try to establish an English House on the model of that established in Hamburg a generation earlier. As a result the Englisches Haus was apparently established *c.* 1640, although it only comes into our ken when William Anderson bought it from David Kade in 1738. The house remained in the possession of the Anderson family until 1794, when it was sold to Anna Luise and Elisabeth Ross, the daughters of another British merchant, Jacob Ross. In Jameson's time the English House was run first by William Anderson's widow, Lucy (*née* Sheldon), and then, after her death in 1772/3, by her daughter Lucy, who was by then the widow of Andrew Scott. The famous painter and engraver Daniel Chodowiecki (1726–1801), who came from Danzig, left a vivid description of a visit he paid to the English House in 1773 in the company of the Rev. Boquet, Mrs Scott's son-in-law.[96] The merchant Karl Gottfried Grischow had a shop within the English House in which all sorts of English goods and furniture were for sale, including 'newly discovered, restored and newly varnished' paintings; no doubt Floris Schopenhauer was a good customer of Grischow's establishment. In Jameson's time the English House also had the reputation of being the most respectable hostelry in the city.

As I have said, the idea of establishing a chapel in the English House proved unsatisfactory. Later in the seventeenth century services were held in the chaplain's residence, which means in the Sandgrube, in the Frauengasse (Rev. Thomas Burnet) and in the Hintergasse (Rev. Alexander Beck). Two other chaplains are known to have been active in Danzig and the surrounding district in the later seventeenth century: the Rev. Jakob Brown and the Rev. Samuel Hammond.

The English Chapel proper dated from 1707 and owed its existence to the treaty between Queen Anne and the City of Danzig negotiated by the British ambassador, John Robinson (1650–1723; later Bishop of London), in 1706 and signed in 1707.[97] This treaty, confirmed by the Treaty of Utrecht in 1713, gave the British merchants a privileged position which lasted until the Second Partition of Poland in 1793, when Frederick the Great, following the seizure of Danzig, placed prohibitive duties on British goods, thus justifying all the fears which had been expressed in 1772/3 at the time of the First Partition. The treaty of 1706 had another result, for 'Mr. Robinson our Envoy to Sweden, afterwards made Bishop of London, procur'd Permission for the Publick Exercise of the English Liturgy for the Use of our Factory'.[98] In the words of the council record, the British community received permission 'sich einen Prediger zu bestellen, der in einem Privathause den Gottesdienst zu versehen hat. Die Stadt wird demselben freie Accise geben, auch andere Vorteile zuwenden'.[99] What was new was that the community was allowed to buy a house in which to establish an official 'English chapel'. The majority of the members of the community or 'Factory' were Scots, but the union of England and Scotland in 1707 enabled all the British residents to work together and pool their resources. John Robinson called a meeting at which he argued that, since there was hardly a larger British colony anywhere else in Europe, they should take advantage of this new privilege and set about establishing their own chapel. Subscriptions were invited and soon came in; the subscribers included an anonymous donor who sent in 300 Polish guilders accompanied by the following note:

> For the Glory of God, For the Honour of Greatt Anne, first Imperes of greatt Brittan, for the Prosperity of the Nation, For the edifieing and blessing of there soales and unto the bilding of greatt Brittans Chapell, payes with all his Heart three hundred gilders one who is much obliged to kingdoms heretofore named Ingland an Scotland and now the Impire of Greatt Brittan. The 30 Nbr of December Anno 1707, In Dantzigk.[100]

In all, 14,551 Polish guilders were pledged. A committee was formed to find and buy a suitable house. This was quickly done; a house suitable for accommodating both chapel and chaplain was soon found and was bought for 6,200 Polish guilders. Thomas Leslie acted for the committee, and the contract was also signed by George Mallabar of Newcastle, a merchant who died in 1734, reputedly worth £100,000, which makes him a multi-millionaire in modern terms. Despite his wealth, George Mallabar left no money to the English chapel, most likely because of the Jacobitical inveteracy of the chaplain. The house in question, Heilige Geistgasse 80, stood on the south side of the Heilige Geistgasse, between the Trosieners' house and the Schiffergildehaus. As soon as the contract had been signed on 3 December 1706 the alterations necessary to turn a merchant's house into a chaplain's residence, with a chapel upstairs, were begun. They were described by Martha Dunsby, wife of a later chaplain:

> The typical Danzig store-room made the vestry, while the first and second storeys together went to form the actual chapel. The chaplain's quarters were at the side and rear of the house. The front was given four tall, narrow windows, with three little oval ones above them, and the date 1707. The painter Michael Sommer undertook the painting of the outside of the house, which was grey, except that 'all mouldings and embellishments' were painted white, the front door green and white, and the window-frames blue; the date was gilded.
>
> The interior fittings were gradually completed. The organ was placed over the stairs; the pulpit, carved in the English style of the time, still exists; a richly carved gilt table, which probably came with the house (there is no record of it being bought or donated), served as the altar until 1914. For the further embellishment of the church the sculptor Georg Söwert was commissioned, in 1709, to 'carve the arms of Great Britain faithfully, faultlessly, and in accordance with the design provided, for the agreed sum of 45 Gulden.' The painter Johann Jakob Feyerabendt was commissioned to paint two large frescoes, one of Moses and the Tables of the Law, and the other of two Tablets bearing the Lord's Prayer and the Credo, with the rising sun in the background.[101]

The alterations produced what Johanna Schopenhauer, in *My Youthful Life*,[102] described as 'a small, friendly sort of domestic chapel'. Her description of the chapel, which she knew well, agrees with that of an English merchant and former member of the congregation who wrote, in 1734, that 'a House was purchased for the Minister's Residence, which is a very good one, and a neat pretty regular Chappel above Stairs.[103] This early account is worth quoting in full, for it contains information which is available from no other source:

> The nomination is in the Bishop of London, and his Salary a Thousand Gilders a year, which is above Sixty Pounds, besides a Perquisite of a Crown from every *British* Ship that arrives. In short, 'tis a pretty Preferment and Beginning for

a Young Man; who, if he be agreeable in Principle with the Factory, and hearty for the Revolution, may clear a hundred Pounds a Year, possess an excellent House, Rent-free, and have his Maintenance into the Bargain, by the voluntary Kindness of one or other to him. The Minister, when I was there, was called D——son: He was in his Living a Man of good Morality, in his State of Health *Hypocon*: But an open bigotted Jacobite, with whom were joined about half a Dozen more. At the Queen's Death, and during the time of the *Preston* Rebellion, he actually refus'd praying for King *George*, till it was confirmed in whose Favour Affairs succeeded. This Behaviour of his lost him all Respect, and occasion'd a great part of his Congregation to leave him, who chose rather to hold Communion with the *Calvinists*, than join in a Worship where the Priest us'd constant Prevarication in Praying.

The number of *English* and *Scotch Contoirs*, that were not natives, did not exceed half a score: There us'd to be a good Harmony between them, and they met every Evening together at the Widow of Major *Shelden's*, where was a daily Ordinary of good Victuals dress'd after our Manner for twenty *Grosh*, or a Shilling a Man, but now they are divided. The best Traders resorted to John du Mair's, a noted Tavern, where Abundance of Holland and Dutch Merchants daily frequented. The Factory also had a large Country-House, nigh the Olive [a sumptuous and richly endowed Cloister], with a spacious fine Garden belonging to it; but they had quitted that too: So that the good Understanding when I was there, was not so firm amongst them, as it used to be. This I must own is a Digression, but my own Country extorted it from me . . . The best Accommodation for . . . Englishmen [is] at the English House in Brotbancken Gass, the highest in all Dantzick, kept by one Anderson.[104]

This description, which may have been written by George Mallabar shortly before his death, includes a number of facts relevant to our story. There is, first, the matter of the appointment to the chaplaincy being in the Bishop of London's nomination. The situation when Jameson was appointed in 1764 was not as simple as that. The catalogue of manuscripts relating to foreign chaplaincies in the Guildhall Library has this introductory note:

Although the Bishop of London was held to exercise spiritual and canonical jurisdiction over Anglican communities abroad from at least 1686, this was until 1748 by personal commission only, not *ex officio*, and from 1748 to 1813 successive bishops made no claims at all to any such jurisdiction.

The fact that Jameson was not licensed by the Bishop of London is therefore explained; but, as I have said, the bishop or his secretary was no doubt consulted. By 1764 Widow Sheldon's ordinary had presumably passed into other hands, but Jameson would in any case not have been dependent on it, for he had a housekeeper, Jungfer Concordia. (Was she, one wonders, Anna Concordia, fourth daughter of William and Lucy Anderson, born in 1733?) In any case he often dined with members of his congregation and friends of theirs, including the Trosieners and Schopenhauers. In 1734 the English House had been kept by William Anderson (steward to Mr Resident Jeffreys), who in 1721 had married Lucy Sheldon, third daughter of the late Major Thomas Sheldon, merchant and burgess. William Anderson died in 1736, so in 1764 the running of the English House was in the hands of his widow, Lucy, and their eldest son, Andrew. The second son, John William Anderson, business partner of Floris Schopenhauer and later Lord Mayor of London, was probably still living in Danzig in 1764, aged 30. William Anderson's widow survived until the First Partition of Poland; she was dead by the time Floris Schopenhauer returned from London in 1773.

The Jacobitical gentleman whose inveteracy offended his congregation and cost it a bequest from George Mallabar was Alexander Davidson, chaplain from 1713 to 1723. He had been called from St Petersburg to succeed the first chaplain of the new chapel, Alexander Burnet of Aberdeen(1693-1712). Davidson was succeeded by William Bickerton(1723-7), Peter Hay (1727-60), Johnnie Tucker (1761-4) and Richard Jameson (1764-89). Jameson was succeeded by Dr William Gardiner (1790-1806). In accordance with a decision of 1707 the chaplains were chosen in turn by the Scottish and English members of the congregation. While this tended to mean that the chaplains were Scottish and English alternately, such was not always the case. When Richard Jameson resigned in 1789 he was succeeded by another Scot, on the grounds that he could be obtained more cheaply![105]

Richard Jameson arrived in Danzig in October 1764, at the age of 40. He therefore became acquainted with Christian Heinrich Trosiener and his wife Elisabeth before the birth of their daughter

Johanna two years later. Floris Schopenhauer was 17 at the time. Jameson's congregation presently included the English friends of the Schopenhauers mentioned in Chapter I and others whose names are preserved in the extant chapel register. The head of the community, and its greatest ornament, was the British consul, Trevor Corry, who was to be knighted in 1776. Johanna Schopenhauer has left a memorable account of this colourful character:

> The English consul, Sir Trevor Corry, contributed, with his showy equipage and his coal-black negro boy, Pharaoh, to the splendour of the city. The world has never seen a resident, who stood longer and more firmly at his post, for he is still there, though he has been dead these fifty years; he is still unburied in the great parish church; for the noble baronet, during his life, scorned our German earth, and the superstition of the sailors prevented his body being carried to England after his decease.[106]

Sir Trevor Corry was to leave a legacy of £1,000 to the British chapel. The chapel also had friends and benefactors among the local community. The Anglo-Scottish Fund for the Poor, which had been set up in 1707, included among its administrators Jakob Kabrun (his family were originally Scottish Cockburns; he was later Arthur Schopenhauer's principal), and Floris Schopenhauer is known to have lent money to the fund.

As she explained in *My Youthful Life*, Johanna Trosiener grew up in a house next door to the English chapel:

> On our left stood the English church, and to our right was a public house; however, I must beg that no one will call to mind the old proverb about the devil's building by the house of prayer, for this English church is really a small friendly sort of domestic chapel, which was styled church only by courtesy; neither can his satanic majesty have had any authority at the trusty old house belonging to the ship-masters' guild, for the people were very honest and respectable. This edifice was, at least, four times as large as the church, and in appearance it closely resembled a haunted castle . . . The other rooms of the capacious and angular edifice were given up to the landlord [Bergman] who passed, not merely for the best cook in Danzig, but

who even enjoyed a European celebrity.[107]

It was very likely at Herr Bergmann's that Captain Thomas Fremantle enjoyed such good society on his visit to Danzig in summer 1801. Johanna was therefore well placed: on one side was the Scottish clergyman whose pet she became, and on the other the 'haunted castle' to which Floris Schopenhauer was a frequent visitor (though it must be added that he had the appearance less of a Prince Charming than of a toad). She then turns to the house on the left of her parents' and writes:

> In consequence of a contract made in earlier times, which secured privileges, otherwise pertaining to none but native citizens, a company of English merchants had for many years established themselves with their families in Danzig, and having been inhabitants for so long a time, neither they nor we ever regarded each other as foreigners. Their houses ranked with the very first on 'Change, and in manners and customs they deviated as little as possible from the other inhabitants. They spoke German, did not turn night into day, dined, according to the custom of the country, at one o'clock, brought up their children, most of whom were born in our midst, in the manner that was usual among us; in short, they behaved themselves like sensible people, instead of embittering their own lives and those of others by absurd pretensions and arrogant vagaries.
>
> The house which stood on the left of my native home belonged to this English colony: by sacrificing its first and second floors, they made a high, light, and tolerably spacious chapel, furnished with organ, pulpit, and reading-desk, for the due performance of the worship according to the English fashion.
>
> The remaining portion of the house was the residence of their clergyman, whom they themselves elected.[108]

This brings her to Richard Jameson, of whom she proceeds to draw a memorable portrait. From an early age she was devoted to her 'dear friend' Jameson, in whom she had 'the most implicit confidence'; it was to him that she owed the better part of her education, which clearly rubbed off on her son. Her affection for this remarkable and totally sympathetic man is implicit in her description of his appearance and character:

Dr. Richard Jameson had accepted the invitation of the English colony, who called him to become their preacher, on terms as honourable as they were advantageous: his arrival at Danzig was nearly contemporary with the marriage of my parents. Whether there had been any predecessor in the office he held I cannot say, but I think not, as I never heard speak of any one before him.

He had taken his degree of D.D. at Edinburgh, and had undoubtedly brought with him the well-grounded, and extensive fund of learning which his station required; to himself this must have proved a source of refined enjoyment; but never did an expression escape from him which savoured in the slightest degree of pedantry, or which betrayed a feeling that he was better than other people, because more highly educated than they.

On his arrival in Danzig he must have been, as nearly as I can tell by reckoning backwards, about four or five and thirty years old. His countenance was distinguished only by an expression of the purest benevolence; his face was not handsome, though pleasing, and its regular features did not belie his native land; bright blue eyes, blond eyebrows and eyelashes, marked the native of Scotland. His figure was slim, he was of middle stature, not ungraceful in his movements; he wore a round well-curled wig, and from year to year a light grey coat with black buttons, black silk stockings and small-clothes.

Never was there a more quiet and contented mind than his, never a heart more open to every worthy and noiseless pleasure, never a more lively feeling for all that is noble, grand, and beautiful, or a soul more sensitive to every human woe, the alleviation of which seemed the purpose for which he lived. His compassionate nature rendered him the advocate of all who suffered, embracing in its sympathies even the dumb animals, the meanest of which he could not see ill-used without taking its part; but false, artificial, or exaggerated sentimentalism, such as in his day was just coming into vogue, was his extreme aversion, and he mercilessly hunted it to death with gibes and satire whenever he met with it.

His character and appearance reminded one forcibly of Yorick, as he is represented in Tristram Shandy, and in the Sentimental Journey.

With all his peculiar serenity of disposition there betrayed itself occasionally an almost imperceptible tinge of melancholy, as if he felt a pain from some wound received in the earlier part of his life, and long since healed over. He never gave us his past history, for it was not his custom to talk much about himself. A word never escaped him in reference to any such event, and I never heard my parents, acquaintance, or intimate friends hint at it. Far from his beloved native land, in a world altogether foreign to him, there he stood with his warm heart quite alone.[109]

We now know that Jameson was 40 when he took up his appointment, just as we know that, while he studied divinity at Edinburgh, he left without taking his degree; the title which Johanna gives him is both understandable and necessary, though he did not use it himself. The 'imperceptible tinge of melancholy' may have had several causes, and further speculation would be pointless. I would only add that there is no evidence that (unlike David Hume and James Boswell) he was a victim of the 'blue devils'. Indeed, the idea that he might have been can be discounted in view of the fact that he reminded Johanna of Sterne's Yorick, the 'lively, witty, sensible, and heedless parson' who:

> Was . . . as mercurial and sublimated a composition, — as heteroclite a creature in all his declensions; — with as much . . . *gaité de coeur* about him, as the kindliest climate could have engendered and put together . . . Yorick had an invincible dislike and opposition in his nature to gravity; — not to gravity as such; — for where gravity was wanted, he would be the most grave or serious of mortal men . . . but he was an enemy to the affectation of [this] . . . mysterious carriage of the body to cover the defects of the mind . . . in plain truth, he was a man unhackneyed and unpractised in the world [,marked by] . . . honesty of mind . . . innocence of heart [and] integrity of conduct.[110]

It is a description which does credit both to a good man long since forgotten and to a young girl's affection for him. *Tristram Shandy* was to be her son's favourite novel.

To compare Jameson to Yorick was to make an obvious if slightly old-fashioned comparison, for Yorick-Sterne's satirical tolerance had so deeply impressed German writers of Jameson's generation that in the 1760s they had given one another nicknames from Sterne.

Thus Hamann and Herder read *Tristram Shandy* together in Riga in 1764–9 and during temporary separations wrote letters in which Hamann was addressed as Tobias Shandy and Herder as Yorick,[111] while a mutual friend was called Trim. In his correspondence with Hamann and Merck in the late 1760s Herder constantly alluded to Sterne, whose 'system' he adopted; he also possessed *The Sermons of Mr. Yorick* (1760). Johann Georg Jacobi too fell under Sterne's spell to the extent of being called 'Toby' by his literary friends, while Lessing, when he heard of Sterne's death, said that he would gladly have given five years of his own life to keep him writing. Wieland, who read *Tristram Shandy* in late 1767, was no less enthusiastic, and in a letter dated 15 November 1770 defined the 'Evangelium Yoricks' as 'lauter Naturalismus, Deismus und Pelagianismus, ja purer verfeinerter Epikurismus, Philosophie der Grazien und, mit einem Worte, pures Heidenthum'.[112] If we look back to Jameson's education and his rejection of Presbyterianism, there is no reason to think that this definition will not have comprehended his religion too. That said, Sterne's profoundest appreciator in Germany was Goethe, who wrote that Yorick-Sterne discovered man's humanity and was 'der schönste Geist, der je gewirkt hat'.[113] No doubt Johanna Schopenhauer told Goethe of her Yorick-like mentor.

Jameson knew Johanna from her birth in 1766 onwards, and their friendship lasted until he left Danzig the year after her son was born:

> My parents, as his nearest neighbours, soon made his acquaintance; the quiet domestic life of the new-married couple was highly attractive to him; closely connected by the contiguous terraces of the houses, this slight acquaintance speedily ripened into an intimate friendship. The two parties saw each other almost every day; Jameson had so thoroughly mastered the German language that a slightly foreign pronunciation alone showed him not to be a native, and thus one great impediment to intimacy was removed.
>
> When Kasche carried me into the balcony for the first time, one bright sun-shiny day to exhibit the little stranger to the neighbour, he took me up in his arms with pleasure, and it seemed as if at that moment the band were drawn tighter that had already attached him to our family.
>
> As I grew up, Jameson was my tutor, guide, and counsellor; he stood by my side, and watched over my young

soul, never leaving me till the time when another received with my hand the obligation also of caring for me.[114]

She describes Jameson's own establishment, which also included the mahogany writing table and spinet to which he was so attached, as well as the rather starchy library of mainly seventeenth-century theology left to his successors by Alexander Burnet:

> Jameson noticed with what ease and pleasure I comprehended what I was taught, and much was he pleased at it. Rarely did a day pass without his taking me to his house; his whole establishment was then set in motion to contribute to my amusement. His great black tom-cat, Tamerlane, and his snow-white little dog, Frei, performed their best tricks for my diversion: his old house-keeper, Jungfer Concordia, crammed me with bonbons, and peeled oranges for me; Jameson himself often enchanted me by displaying all manner of magical performances with the aid of an excellent electrical machine, and sometimes he told me tales about animals, plants, and foreign lands. Thus I gradually acquired English almost unconsciously to myself; I learnt it as I had my native tongue, prattling it first, and reading and writing it afterwards.
>
> A girl learn English! what good in the world could that do her ? This question was put again and again by friends and relations, for it was a thing unheard of in Danzig. At last I grew almost ashamed of my knowledge of English, and some years later resolutely refused to learn Greek, though I longed to do so in my heart, and Jameson so kindly urged me to begin.[115]

No wonder that she wrote, 'every child has a guardian angel; thanks to mine . . . for entrusting to such men as Jameson . . . the charge of preparing me for the chequered life that awaited me'.[116]

It was to Richard Jameson that Johanna owed her knowledge of English, which she spoke and read as fluently as he spoke German. That she at one time became rather self-conscious about appearing to be the only girl of her age in Danzig (her friend Sally Cramp excepted) who could chatter away in English is a reminder of how the education of women was regarded in all but exceptional families or under the most enlightened tutors. Even more important, Jameson introduced her to the world of English literature, of poetry, towards which her son was to be irresistibly drawn:

The time had not yet arrived for me to penetrate into the wonderful regions of poetry, nor was I to be guided thither by Kuschel, who had been somewhat bowed down himself by the prose of every day life; the task of guiding me into those walks of literature, where he was so thoroughly at home, was reserved for my happier friend, Jameson.[117]

We shall come to her reading of English literature shortly. First she describes the various subjects about which she learned so easily and so happily from her morning and evening meetings with her 'dear friend Jameson':

Jameson drew his pet towards him with redoubled zeal and affection. In what manner he carried on my education, what he taught me, or how I learned, I cannot possibly describe; I might perhaps say it was unconsciously, for he taught and I learned without either of us being fully aware of it.

On a fine summer evening, when the little ones had been put to bed, my father used to smoke his pipe under the chestnut tree that overshadowed our terrace, while my mother sat happily at his side; then Jameson, who never failed to be of the party, would point out to me the stars which our limited horizon allowed us to view. How I hung upon his words as he spoke of the mysterious courses of the myriads of worlds that encircle our planet! He taught me the names of the most remarkable stars; on the next morning I used to find out on the celestial globe the constellations to which they belonged, and again on the following evening I found them in the heavens. I was acquainted with the length and breadth of the different countries in the world, and could tell exactly what o'clock it was at Paris or Archangel when it was three in the afternoon with us. He was able to tell me something about every butterfly and beetle that flew about during the summer. Thus I was always adding to my store of knowledge; I have forgotten much that I learned; but I acquired a habit of observation that remained with me, so that I did not go through the world staring about it without an idea in my head.

My astronomical knowledge has come to a sad end; of the constellations I now know scarcely any but the Great Bear, but I still experience the silent rapture with which I used then to gaze upon the heavens, and should I live to a more advanced age, I shall never forget the emotion.

At the same time I was almost imperceptibly making such progress in English that I could read and speak it as fluently as my native tongue. Jameson carried me on from the Spectator, the Tales of the Genii, and Lady Montagu's Letters, to the Poets, and I found a world full of warm and enchanting life expanding before me.

First of all we read Homer, as translated or rather travestied by Pope; we read only selections from Young's Night Thoughts and Milton's Paradise Lost, and then passed on to Shakespeare.[118]

What is so interesting about this general account is that it means that the unofficial part of her education, that which she received from Jameson, corresponded exactly with the supplementary education which George Chapman offered the young ladies of Dumfries (English, geography, French, the principles of natural philosophy, and the elements of *belles-lettres*). Clearly Jameson was putting quietly into practice the principles which he used to discuss with George Chapman and which were no doubt the subject of correspondence between the two. When we turn to English literature, it is again evident that Jameson had a model, this time in John Stevenson's *belles-lettres* class. We remember how large the *Spectator*, Pope's Homer and Milton loomed in that class. Whether Shakespeare figured largely in Stevenson's course is not recorded; he is much in evidence in Johanna's Jameson-inspired reading and, later, in her son's reading. It is not clear exactly what Johanna Trosiener's age was at this stage, although she was still very young. She herself commented, 'Romans, Greeks, Shakespeare, Homer, what a confused whirl must it all have been in the head of so young a girl as I then was! Doubtless I was in imminent danger of becoming an intolerably precocious little body.'[119] The phrase 'precocious little body' probably reflects Jameson's efforts to counteract this tendency. There were times when 'poetic exaltation threatened to become uncontrollable'.[120] With Jameson she spent the first part of the morning and the last hour before supper. She now acquired a French governess as well, and was soon able to chatter French as fluently as English. No doubt she practised her French with Jameson, too (it was at this time that he was practising French with his friend Jean Robert Bocquet).

Although Johanna presently found herself metamorphosed from a little girl into a grown-up *Mam'selle*, she still enjoyed Jameson's friendship and guidance:

Jameson still continued to be my only comfort; his zeal did not grow cool; my leisure hours, and of them I had only too many, I spent most pleasantly at his house and in his company, in reading Shakespeare.[121]

She was about 14. It was now that she acquired a good friend in the person of Sally Cramp, a pretty, merry, amiable girl of her own age, to whom she was introduced by Jameson, 'who knew what would be good for us both'.[122] She continued to read with him in the morning, though she discontinued going to him in the evening. One wonders whether Tieck's story in 'Das Zauberschloss' ('Ein Professor aus Edinburg lebte lange in unserem Haus, da er aber, noch nicht alt, zu freundschaftlich und zärtlich wurde, musste ich ihn auf ihr dringendes Verlangen wieder enfernen') may be based on Johanna's memoirs, with the professor a conflation of Richard Jameson (from Edinburgh) and Kandidat Kuschel (the one who forgot himself and his station).

Johanna's reading now began to change and she turned to novels, not always well chosen and therefore not always enjoyed:

> I did not get on much better with 'Sir Charles Grandison', which was then praised as a model of superhuman excellence. Jameson never read novels with me, so I was obliged to content myself with a very loose German translation of this voluminous work, and it occasioned me much trouble to strive against the weariness it caused. 'Pamela', another novel of the same author's, which, however, I could not procure, had been lauded in England, even from the pulpit, as a very edifying book for Christian reading; so all the newspapers announced, in praise of English enlightenment . . . we were soon reduced to the necessity of returning to our old library, a collection of some twenty volumes of novels translated from the English, which belonged to [Sally Cramp's] mother.[123]

The loose translation of Richardson's *Sir Charles Grandison* must have been Gellert's. It has been said that 'Richardson was the founder of the German novel, and Gellert was his prophet'.[124] There is some truth in this, but *Pamela* and *Clarissa* were more important. Johanna's taste did not deceive her, for *Grandison* is too much of its time. If Jameson had read it he would have agreed with Hazlitt's view[125] that Sir Charles Grandison is a mixture of automaton, puppet and self-complacent coxcomb, 'ugly all over with affectation', whose propriety of conduct and fine qualities are never for a moment out of sight. Such coxcombical perfection becomes tedious. *Pamela*, for its part, had been twice translated into German, in 1742 and 1743. That it was not available in Danzig is a reminder that Danzig was not Germany. That said, Johanna's reading (Young, Milton, Shakespeare, Richardson) involved precisely those English authors whose reception into Germany was so important at this time. Though Jameson naturally did not read novels with his young protégée, this does not mean that he did not occasionally read them himself. Among the books belonging to the English church was Fielding's *History of Joseph Andrews* (London, 1762), which Jameson probably brought with him in 1764 as part of his reading for the voyage. Another book later found in the English chapel library was *The Pleasing Instructor and Entertaining Moralist* (1770). This Jameson no doubt brought back from a visit to England and Scotland in 1770 to use with Johanna. One wonders whether L.M. Stretch's *The Beauties of History, or: Pictures of Virtue and Vice, drawn from real life, Designed for the Instruction and Entertainment of Youth* (2 vols, 3rd edn, 1777), which Arthur Schopenhauer possessed (*HN*, V, 472), may not originally have been bought by Jameson for the same purpose.

To Johanna Trosiener, Jameson was the pleasing instructor and entertaining moralist *par excellence*. She was his pet, he the favourite 'uncle'. No doubt he spoiled her; the affection he gave, and which she so fully returned, she was, unhappily, to prove unable to give to her son. Jameson imparted to her education a breadth which it would not otherwise have had, a breadth which reflects the educational plans of John Stevenson and George Chapman. He gave her, obviously, a fluency in English which became an important part of the pervasive anglophilia of Arthur Schopenhauer's youth, and it was he who taught her critical awareness and gave her an unusually sound knowledge of English literature in particular. He did so much to make her what she became that he is an important indirect influence on Schopenhauer, despite the fact that he knew him only at the age of one.

Richard Jameson's life in Danzig revolved around his official duties and his friendship with the Trosieners and others. The chaplaincy can hardly have kept him very busy, for the chapel register contains only 41 baptisms and five marriages during his whole period of office (burials are not recorded), and Communion was celebrated only at Easter, Whit, Michaelmas and Christmas. Given the size of the British congregation, visiting must have taken more time. Jameson was a genial soul who felt keenly the inevitable loss of his friends in the course of time. When he got to know Floris Schopenhauer they must have had lengthy discussions on the subject of Voltaire's *Candide*. It was Floris Schopenhauer's favourite book. Jameson had purchased a copy in Edinburgh in 1761 and brought it with him to Danzig. One wonders whether the copy of Locke's *An Essay concerning Human Understanding* (14th edn, 2 vols, London, 1753) which Arthur Schopenhauer later possessed may originally have belonged to Jameson. He had been bred on Locke, and was using James Brown, bookseller in the Parliament Close, Edinburgh, as his accommodation address in June 1753; he was also in London that year.) His other friends probably included Jakob Kabrun (friend of Heinrich Floris Schopenhauer and one-time principal of Arthur Schopenhauer; he signalled his Scottish ancestry by signing an extant document[126] as a member of the joint corporation of English and Scottish residents in Danzig) and certainly included Dr Wolf, physician to the English Factory. No doubt he was on terms of friendship with those of the English merchants who were most involved with the chapel (men like William Joshua Kenworthy, Andrew Scott, Adam Elliot, James Balfour, Henry Simpson and James Boyd).

When he first arrived in Danzig he will have been reminded by the daily Exchange of merchants from eleven o'clock to one o'clock of the equivalent daily meeting in Edinburgh (held at the Cross, at one o'clock). He was not only chaplain to a colony of merchants but was in Danzig at the time of the First Partition of Poland, which so nearly led to a rupture between England and Prussia on account of Prussian interference with the Danzig trade.[127] The papers which he unfortunately destroyed at the end of his life may well have referred to this, among other things. He was uniquely positioned to obtain an objective, insider's view of the whole affair. If the First Partition was the occasional subject of conversation at dinner parties in England — and it was, for the importance of the Danzig trade was widely appreciated — it must have dominated such conversations at Danzig for much of 1772/3. In her memoirs Johanna Schopenhauer appears to confuse the effects of the First and Second Partitions, for it was the Second (in 1793) which destroyed the Danzig trade.

Johanna takes her leave of Jameson in these words:

> Jameson could not see without emotion the growing misery of a place he had known in all the bloom of prosperity; he felt as if he were standing by the death-bed of one incurably

wasting away with a painful malady. In the circle of his intimate friends such sad changes had taken place, and gaps had been made which he could not hope to see filled up again; when at last he saw my parents' house shut up and left desolate, as he threw his window up ten times a day, from mere habit, to walk on to our terrace, and no longer saw a single friendly form, he felt the last bond was snapped that bound him to the place. I, the child of his heart, his earliest pet, who he had instructed and guided with such affection and faithfulness, remained still; but new duties and new relations claimed my attention, so that it was impossible for me to replace what he had lost by the breaking up of the neighbourhood to which he had been accustomed for thirty years and more.

His health began to fail, and nothing but a prompt decision could save him from gradually sinking into feebleness and melancholy; and he had strength enough to make it and to act it out. He gave up his charge and embarked for his native home, — the mountains of Scotland, to which he had become almost a stranger by his lengthened absence, — with what feelings, with what bitter pain at parting, he never tried to express, and I will in this imitate his example.[128]

Last Years

Jameson resigned as chaplain to the English Factory in July 1789. Ill health had made it impossible for him to continue. In the final years he had twice had to return to England for treatment and convalescence. For weeks on end he was unable to carry out the duties of the office which had brought him such keen joy in the past. At such times the Rev. Jean Robert Bocquet, minister of the French congregation in Danzig, presumably deputised for him, as he had done during Jameson's absence in the winter of 1770/1. No doubt the climate had taken its toll. Nelson had found, when off Danzig in 1801, that the keen air of the Baltic cut him to the heart. On his return Jameson settled not in Edinburgh, where he had two distant cousins and a good friend in George Chapman, but at Newcastle-upon-Tyne, lodging at first with John and Mary Leighton and family (Thomas, b. 1762; Jane, b. 1770; Mary, 1771) in Queen's Street, off Quayside. John Leighton was a surgeon (and a Glassite to boot). Jameson had evently been treated by him when he landed at Newcastle on his visits to England for medical reasons in recent years. Either he had been recommended by Dr Wolf in Danzig, or by the master of the ship in which he returned (Captain John Renwick), or he had needed immediate treatment. Whichever was the case, Jameson had been well treated by John Leighton and well cared for by his daughters Jane and Mary, and by their brother Thomas, who was at the beginning of his own distinguished career as a surgeon. It was young Thomas Leighton who identified Jameson's handwriting when his will was proved. He was the same sort of person as Jameson himself, and is said to have been:

> An eminent surgeon . . . highly esteemed and respected not only on account of his skill and experience, but also for his amiable disposition and uniform courtesy of demeanour. At the time of his decease he was Consulting Surgeon to the [Royal Victoria] Infirmary, Surgeon to the Trinity House, and the father of the profession. He died June 28th 1848, aged 86, and was interned in St. John's Churchyard.[129]

Of Thomas Leighton's father — Jameson's doctor — nothing else is known.

After lodging with the Leightons for a time Jameson was fit enough to move out. He took lodgings near by, with Mrs Barbara Alcock, widow of Samuel Alcock, publican, of the Sign of the Cannon, at the foot of the (old) Flesh Market. Mrs Alcock and her daughter Ann (b. 1772) also looked after him well, judging by his bequests to them.[130] Though living in the parish of St John, the Alcocks, like John Leighton and his wife, were dissenters. The heart of old Newcastle was a far cry from the mountains of his native Scotland, to which the romantic Johanna had envisaged Jameson returning. Yet, living not far from the Quayside, in a maritime town with its own guild of merchant adventurers (whose members had included at least one earlier member of the English congregation in Danzig, George Mallabar) and strong trading links with Hamburg and Danzig, Jameson must have felt fairly well at home. The town, then a medieval walled city with gates and towers and tall Tudor buildings, was not a little reminiscent of Danzig.

In these last years in Newcastle he lived a quiet life; he had, after all, retired from a harsh climate at the age of 65. He had no benefice; he is not listed in the Bishop of Durham's visitation of 1792. When he arrived in Newcastle in 1789 Hugh Hornby was mayor, and his son Thomas was lecturer at St John's, the parish in which

Jameson settled. When viewing the somewhat gloomy, rural-looking old church, Jameson will have seen that the silver font spoon had been ' broken to pieces' by his fellow countrymen in 1639. Thomas Hornby (b. 1758), who took his MA at Oxford in 1783 and was appointed to St John's in 1786, was to die only two years after Jameson. How well Jameson knew him is not known, but he was probably too much of an 'intolerant high Churchman' (Thomas Bewick's words) for the notably tolerant man of twice his age.

What is more interesting is the fact that in the mid-1780s Thomas Bewick used to attend meetings at Sam Alcock's inn:

> I got acquainted with a number of genteel young men, of a literary turn, who kept a library of Books & held their meetings in a Room at Sam: Alcocks, at the Sign of the Cannon, at the foot of the old Flesh Market — & I used to frequent this house in the Evenings, to get my pint of ale & a cake & to hear the News & to have a bit of chat or conversation with some of them, when they adjourned from their Book society — I did not join them in this society, but I sometimes dined with them at their annual cheerfull Dinner.[131]

Bewick had been married at St John's, lived in the parish, and wrote of his 'friend', the Rev. Thomas Hornby:

> I was also often attended . . . by my friend the Revd. Thomas Hornby, Lecturer of St. John's — he would not . . . adjourn to a public house & join in a Tankard of Ale but he had it sent for to us at my workplace, — we frequently disagreed in our opinions, as to religious matters — he being[,] as I thought[,] an intolerant high Churchman — but notwithstanding this, he was a warm well wisher and kind friend to me — and was besides of so charitable a disposition in other respects that his purse was ever open to relieve distress.[132]

Bewick had an extensive acquaintance centred on the parish of St John's and the Alcocks' public house; that he and Jameson were acquainted is virtually certain. They could not have failed to meet. Assuming that they did meet, Bewick would have found Jameson more tolerant than Thomas Hornby towards his unorthodox religious views:

> Every Church ought to have its Library of good Books & its

philosophical apparatus, to illustrate, or explain the various Phenomena of Nature & the amazing magnitude & distances, of 'the heavenly bodies' or rather the incalculable number of Suns and Worlds, floating about, with the velocity of light in immeasurable endless space — it is from these that something like the truest conception of the adorable Author of the whole, can be formed.[133]

This view, to which Thomas Bewick was particularly attached, would inevitably have received a more sympathetic hearing from someone as widely educated as Jameson than from someone as narrowly educated as Hornby.

At this time there was much to interest Richard Jameson when he was fit enough to get out. He might not have been able to afford to attend the subscription concerts, but there were many other musical activities. There were circulating libraries, including John Marshall's collection in Flesh Market (was this the library that was kept at the Sign of the Cannon?), and there was St Nicholas's Library. There were the latest engravings by Thomas Bewick and his partner Ralph Beilby (a member of the Literary and Philosophical Society) to be seen, a particular attraction for someone as interested in natural history as Jameson. There was 'Swarley's Club' ('the most rational society or meeting I ever knew', Bewick called it), which used to meet at the Spread Eagle (popularly known as the House of Lords Arms) at the bottom of the Groat Market. There was the Philosophical Society; and there was the Literary and Philosophical Society, which Jameson joined in 1794, the year after it was founded. Though not a founder-member, he was one of the earliest members of the society, and was a friend of Robert Spence (appointed first librarian of the society in 1797, the year after Jameson's death) and of one Dr Blacklock. In 1795, in response to a request to members to donate books for which they had no immediate use, Jameson presented to the society a copy of James Grant's *Essays on the Origin of Society, Language, Property, Government, Jurisdiction, Contracts and Marriage. Interspersed with Illustrations from the Greek and Galic Languages* (London and Edinburgh, 1785), which he most likely bought on a visit to England for medical treatment in 1785; there are no annotations by Jameson in the text. This donation is added confirmation of the breadth of his interests. How much he would have had in common with Herder, had he met him in Danzig in the late 1760s!

Richard Jameson died at Newcastle on Tuesday 26 January

1796[134] His death was reported in the *Newcastle Courant* on 30 January and, more important, in the *Third Year's Report of the Literary and Philosophical Society of Newcastle-upon-Tyne* (1796), which contained the following notice:

> The third of our deceased associates, with whom, as members of this Society, we were much more intimately connected than with either of the other two, was the Rev. *Richard Jamieson*. An affectionate tribute to his memory, by Dr. George Chapman of Libberton near Edinburgh, is inserted in the minutes of the Society, from which it appears that he was the intimate friend of Mr. Spence and Dr. Blacklock; that he had early formed an extensive acquaintance with the Greek and Latin writers, and composed with great elegance in his native language; and that to these acquirements he added, during a long residence abroad, an accurate knowledge of the French and German. It is to be lamented that, during a severe illness which, some years ago, threatened his life, he had destroyed many valuable papers, which otherwise would probably have afforded us much instruction and entertainment: and that, since his residence here, he felt that disinclination to literary composition which is so often experienced by those who are advanced in life: but his conversation was always animated and judicious, and his manners were distinguished by a liberality and simplicity which will be long recollected by his friends with a pleasing regret.[135]

This notice constitutes the only record of Chapman's memorial, which was read or received at the meeting of the society held on 9 March 1796; no letter or other separate document has survived.

This tribute formed the basis of a notice of Richard Jameson in E. Mackenzie's *History of Newcastle* of 1827,[136] but while Jameson's memory is thus preserved in the history of the city in which he came to rest, it has not been realised for almost 200 years what a brilliant and genial man he was, and what distinguished connections he had in the course of an exceptionally interesting life. It is tragic that his characteristic modesty led him to destroy the papers for which the present essay is but a poor substitute. That Arthur Schopenhauer's work would have been totally different if the Anglican clergyman of his experience had been not the Rev. Thomas Lancaster but the Rev. Richard Jameson is indisputable. It is just as indisputable that Jameson left his mark, via Johanna

Schopenhauer, on our philosopher's knowledge of and love of English literature, and therefore on the lucidity and literate nature of his work. Ther are, of course, few things less tangible than indirect influences, but it would, I think, be unwise to underestimate the significance for Arthur Schopenhauer's egregious anglophilia of Richard Jameson's friendship with his mother and father. Indirectly Jameson was responsible for Arthur Schopenhauer becoming what he was, for the literary interests and tastes which Arthur inherited from his mother had been formed by Jameson.

Notes

1. Wallace, *Arthur Schopenhauer*, 27.
2. They are preserved in the Department of Palaeography and Diplomatic, University of Durham).
3. I am grateful to Brian Lambie for showing me Stane.
4. Also preserved in Durham (Chapter Records, in the Department of Palaeography, University of Durham).
5. There is no register of births for Biggar prior to 1730 and no register of deaths for this period, so it is impossible to be more precise.
6. P.L. Gordon, *Personal Memoirs*, I (1830), 3–13.,
7. Details from W. Hunter, *Biggar and the House of Fleming*, 2nd edn (Edinburgh, 1867), 293.
8. Durham Chapter Records.
9. *The Works of Thomas Gray*, ed. E. Gosse, III (1903), 209.
10. T. Smollett, *The Expedition of Humphry Clinker* (1771), Matt. Bramble's letter of 8 August.
11. Anon., *A Journey through part of England and Scotland along with the Army under the Command of His Royal Highness the Duke of Cumberland*, 3rd edn (1747), 93 f.
12. David Hume, in *My Own Life* (quoted from E.C. Mossner, *The Life of David Hume*, 1954, 241).
13. H.G. Graham, *The Social Life of Scotland in the 18th Century* (1928), 460.
14. The phrase comes from N.S. Bushnell, *William Hamilton of Bangour* (Aberdeen, 1957), 9.
15. Graham, *Social Life*, 457.
16. *The Collected Letters of Oliver Goldsmith*, ed. Katharine C. Balderston (Cambridge, 1928), 3.
17. James Prior, *The Life of Oliver Goldsmith, M.B.*, I (1837), 156.
18. Walter Scott, *The Heart of Midlothian* (1818), Chapter IX.
19. Ibid.,
20. Quoted from A. Dalzel, *History of the University of Edinburgh*, II (1862), 343; original in *Transactions of the Royal Society, Edinburgh*, I.
21. Thomas Somerville, *My Own Life and Times, 1741-1814* [1861], 15.
22. *Autobiography of the Rev. Dr. Alexander Carlyle* (1860), 81 f.

23. D.B. Horn, *A Short History of the University of Edinburgh, 1556-1889* (Edinburgh, 1967), 48.
24. Carlyle, *Autobiography*, 81 f.
25. A. Grant, *The Story of the University of Edinburgh*, I (1884), 323.
26. See A. Bower, *The History of the University of Edinburgh*, II (1817), 332.
27. See Dalzel, *History*, I, 264.
28. Bower, *History*, III, 207.
29. Somerville, *My Own Life and Times*, 11.
30. *Anecdotes and Egotisms of Henry Mackenzie, 1745-1831*, ed. H.W. Thompson (1927), 38 f.
31. Bower, *History*, III, 207.
32. Ibid., III, 208.
33. Quoted from *The Scots Peerage*, ed. Sir James Balfour Paul, II (1905), 33.
34. Letter from Colin MacLaurin, Professor of Mathematics at Aberdeen and Edinburgh, to Professor Charles Mackie at Moffat, dated 13 August 1735; in *Report on the Laing Manuscripts*, II (1925), 241.
35. Bower, *History*, II, 270.
36. Principal Lee, in 1826; quoted from Grant, *Story*, I, 328.
37. Bower, *History*, II, 279 f.
38. Sterne, *Tristram Shandy*, Book III (1761), Chapter 20.
39. Bower, *History*, II, 279 f.
40. John Ramsay of Ochtertyre, *Scotland and Scotsmen in the Eighteenth Century*, I (1888), 232 f.
41. 'He never attempted to compose, far less to deliver, a formal system of rhetoric, in which a strict regard should be paid to systematic arrangement, or which, by elegance of composition, and metaphysical subtlety, might dazzle, but could be of little real service, to the youth committed to his care. The observations which he in a manner incidentally made, naturally arose from the authors whose works they were perusing; and though no strict adherence was paid to method, I entertain no doubt that it was this variety which capitivated his pupils, and gave to so many of them that decided love of letters which afterwards distinguished them through life. In his illustrations, during this part of his course, there was no branch of the *Belles Lettres* which he omitted. Such works as had appeared in his time, were carefully analysed by him; and both the doctrines which they contained, and the manner in which they were handled, were stated to the class with the most unaffected plainness and perspicuity of language. Thus, without professedly investigating the nature of the principles of taste, by way of dissertation, or in a set form of lectures, he insensibly conveyed to his young audience just notions of the theory which he exemplified in the numerous extracts which he publicly read. He treated, after the same manner, whatever related to languages, its origin and progress and was particularly attentive to point out the comparative merits of the Greek and Latin languages; and of these again with the English. The philosophy of rhetorical figures was scarcely touched upon by him, as he very justly considered such disquisitions to be far above the comprehension of his hearers. He enumerated, however, the different figures of speech, as they are commonly laid down in systems of rhetoric, but followed the arrangement of no particular author; neither did he always follow his own. The examples

which he brought forward were such as had struck himself in the course of his own private study; or, if familiar to those who were well acquainted with polite literature, might be considered as novel to some of his young friends, and conveyed to them some important or amusing lesson. He was careful to describe the distinct characters of the various kinds of literary composition; and his observations upon history and poetry are represented to have been interesting in a high degree to young minds.' (Bower, *History*, II, 276 f.)

42. Somerville, *My Own Life and Times*, 13.
43. Ibid.
44. *Autobiography*, 43.
45. Quoted from Grant, *Story*, I, 329.
46. Mossner, *The Life of David Hume*, 1954.
47. *Humphry Clinker*, Matt. Bramble's letter of 15 July.
48. Horn, *Short History*, 48.
49. Carlyle, *Autobiography*, 74.
50. Bower, *History*, II, 270.
51. Ibid., II, 280 f.
52. F.A. Pottle, *James Boswell: The Earlier Years, 1740-1769* (1966), 25.
53. *Autobiography*, 46.
54. Pottle, *Boswell*, 32.
55. *The Correspondence of James Boswell and John Johnston of Grange*, ed. R.S. Walker (1966), 17 f.
56. James Grant, *Cassell's Old and New Edinburgh*, II (n.d.), 247.
57. *Correspondence of Boswell and Johnston*, 15.
58. I owe my knowledge of this pamphlet to R.S. Walker (*Correspondence of Boswell and Johnston*, 17). On the opening of Grant's chapel, see *Scots Magazine*, IX (1747), 47.
59. Walter Scott, *Waverley* (Edinburgh, 1814), Chapter 10. Members of the Episcopal Church considered themselves to be imitators of the primitive Christians — see the *Memorial by Rev. W. Harper*, Edinburgh, 18 August 1752, 17 (Edinburgh University Library MS. La. II. 414).
60. Dalzel, History, I, 269.
61. Preserved in the Department of Palaeography, University of Durham.
62. Dr Robert Wallace, minister at Moffat; quoted from *DNB.*,
63. *Boswell Papers (Isham Collection)*, XIII (1932), 97.
64. Ramsay of Ochtertyre, *Scotland and Scotsmen*, II, 543, n. 2.
65. Ibid., I, 84 ff.
66. Richard Pococke, *Tours in Scotland*, ed. D.W. Kemp (Edinburgh, 1887), 214.
67. Violet Jacob, *The Lairds of Dun* (1931), 274.
68. Ibid., 267 f.
69. Quoted from Pottle, *Boswell*, 18.
70. James Boswell, 'Journal of My Jaunt' (1762), in *Boswell Papers (Isham Collection)*, I, *Early papers* (1928).
71. See *Lord Dun's Friendly and Familiar Advices* (Edinburgh, 1754), 194-7.
72. Ibid., 123.
73. In Durham University (Department of Paleography).
74. Graham, *Social Life*, 382.

75. Ibid., 382.
76. Ibid., 391.
77. Ramsay of Ochtertyre, *Scotland and Scotsmen*, I, 306 f.
78. Jean S. Maxwell, *The Centenary Book of St. John's, Dumfries* (Dumfries, 1968), 1–5.
79. W. McDowall, *History of the Burgh of Dumfries* (Dumfries, 1867), 818 f. See also Maxwell, *Centenary Book*.
80. Boswell, 'Journal of My Jaunt', 6 October 1762. Cf. Thomas Holcroft, *Anna St. Ives* (1792), letter II; 'When once a taste for improvement . . . becomes a passion, gaming itself is scarcely more ruinous.'
81. *Autobiography*, 223.
82. Ibid., 441.
83. *GM*, 22 February 1806.
84. Ibid.
85. Anon., *Sketch of the Life of the Late George Chapman* (Edinburgh, 1808), 7.
86. Ibid., 12 f.
87. Boswell, 'Journal of My Jaunt', 5 October 1762.
88. See ibid., 15.
89. *Boswell's London Journal, 1762–1763*, ed. F.A. Pottle (1950), 14 December 1762.
90. See Martha Dunsby, 'Die Englische Kirche in Danzig', *Mitteilungen des Westpreussischen Geschichtsvereins* (31. Jg., 1932), Heft 1, 8.
91. *A Particular Description*, 14.
92. Wraxall, *Tour*, 355.
93. Joseph Marshall, *Travels . . . in the Years 1768, 1769 and 1770*, III (1772), 246.
94. See J. Papritz, 'Dietrich Lilie und das Englische Haus', *Zeitschrift des Westpreussischen Geschichtsvereins*, Heft 68 (Danzig, 1928), 127–84.
95. Theophilus Eaton (1590?–1658), deputy governor of the Eastland Company, acted as agent of Charles I to the court of Denmark. He went on to found the settlement of New Haven (1638), of which he became first Governor (see *DNB*, XVI, 340).
96. See Daniel Chodowiecki, *Von Berlin nach Danzig. Eine Künstlerfahrt im Jahre 1773* (Berlin, [1883]). The whole portfolio (which was reproduced by Insel Verlag of Leipzig in 1937) gives a fascinating glimpse of life in Danzig in those far-off days; see especially drawings No. 29 (Rev. Jean Robert Bocquet, French chaplain from 1755 to 1814; a close friend of Richard Jameson, he married Lucy Scott, the daughter of the proprietress of the English House, in 1771), No. 34 (Chodowiecki drinking coffee at the English House with the proprietress, her daughter and son-in-law), No. 75 (an evening gathering at the Rev. Bocquet's) and No. 84 (an English merchant).
97. The main sources of information on the English chapel in Danzig are Martha Dunsby's article and Lambeth Palace Library MSS 1847 (the chapel register), 1848 and 1857. These MSS contain the names of many eighteenth-century Scottish residents in the Danzig region, important material for any comprehensive history of Scots in the Baltic.
98. From *A Particular Description*, 40.
99. Quoted from Martha Dunsby, 'Die Englische Kirche', 3.

100. Ibid., 4, F.S.N. Dunsby (*Danzig, Marienburg, Oliva, Zoppot,* Danzig [1913], 30 ff.) printed a list of the original subscribers and another of those who subscribed shortly afterwards. The latter list includes the name of Mr W. Kant (presumably from Königsberg) evidence of the fact that Immanuel Kant's family believed themselves to be of Scottish origin. Though more recent genealogical research may dispute this descent, it remains most likely. (Cant is a common name in the Borders region to this day.)
101. Ibid., 6 f.
102. J.S., *My Youthful Life,* I, 33.
103. *A Particular Description,* 40.
104. Ibid., 40 f., 49.
105. Quoted from Martha Dunsby, 'Die Englische Kirche', 8.
106. *My Youthful Life,* I, 201 f.
107. Ibid., I. 33.
108. Ibid., I, 34 f.
109. Ibid., I, 36 ff.
110. *Tristram Shandy,* Chapter 11.
111. See L.M. Price, *The Reception of English Literature in Germany* (1968), 242.
112. Wieland, *Auswahl denkwürdiger Briefe,* ed. L. Wieland (Vienna, 1815), II, 286 f.
113. Quoted from Price, *Reception,* 245.
114. *My Youthful Life,* I, 38 f.
115. Ibid., I, 87. f.
116. Ibid., I. 84.
117. Ibid., I, 114.
118. Ibid., I, 114–17.
119. Ibid., I, 117.
120. Ibid., I, 118.
121. Ibid., I, 193.
122. Ibid., I, 206.
123. Ibid., I, 230 f.
124. Quoted from Price, *Reception,* 196.
125. In *Memoirs of Thomas Holcroft* (1926), 172.
126. Lambeth Palace Library MS 1848.
127. See D.B. Horn, *British Public Opinion and the First Partition of Poland* (1945).
128. *My Youthful Life,* II, 120 f.
129. See *Additional Notices of Old Scholars of Queen Elizabeth's Grammar School, Newcastle upon Tyne* (Newcastle, 1870); to be found in *Newcastle Literary and Philosophical Society Tracts,* vol. 283.
130. He also left (even smaller) sums of money to Mrs Alcock's five sons (John, b. 1773; William, b. 1775; Samuel, b. 1777; Thomas, b. 1778; Ralph, b. 1780).
131. Thomas Bewick, *A Memoir* (Newcastle-upon-Tyne, 1862), Chapter 10.
132. Ibid., Chapter 12.
133. Ibid., Chapter 28.
134. He was interred in St John's churchyard on 2 February 1796. In

an interesting will, beginning, 'I Richard Jameson late Chaplain to the British Factory in Dantzick . . . ' he made the following bequests. (1) To his cousins Ebenezer Mason and John Thomson, merchants, in Edinburgh, £20 each. (2) To Miss Jane Leighton and Miss Mary Leighton, daughters of Mr John Leighton, surgeon, of Queen's Street, Newcastle, £10 each. (3) To his landlady, Mrs Alcock, £20 and all his 'linnen'. (4) To her daughter, Miss Ann Alcock, £10 'together with my Spinet, music, and mahogany writing Desk'. (5) To her five sons, John, William, Samuel, Thomas and Ralph, £5 each. (6) To 'my most worthy and most esteemed Friend Doctor George Chapman, Master of the Academy at Liberton Kirk near Edinburgh', £20. (7) All the residue to Mr John Leighton, surgeon, whom he also made his executor. The will (preserved in Durham, Department of Palaeography) was witnessed by John Renwick of the chapelry of St John, master mariner and Thomas Leighton of the chapelry of St John, who, in being described as 'aforesaid Surgeon', is mistaken for his father. Jameson's cousins were Ebenezer Mason, who lived at the foot of Monteith's Close, and John Thomson, who lived in Constitution Street, Leith; they worked together as woollen drapers, their linen warehouse being situated at 35 North Bridge. They presumably had trading connections with Poland. John Thomson was acting Prussian consul in Edinburgh in the 1790s.

135. *Third Year's Report of the Literary and Philosophical Society of Newcastle-upon-Tyne* (1796), 9.,

136. E. Mackenzie, *A Descriptive and Historical Account . . . of Newcastle upon Tyne* (Newcastle-upon-Tyne, 1827), 465.

III
Arthur Schopenhauer's English Diary

Introduction

The Schopenhauers arrived at Dover on 24 May 1803 and left England via Harwich on 8 November of the same year. On arrival in London they stayed first at the York Hotel near Blackfriars Bridge, and then in rooms at 43 Norfolk Street, Strand. They spent the first month in and around London, seeing the sights, and it is immediately clear that young Arthur enjoyed most aspects of his first month in England, which exceeded his probably somewhat guarded expectations, except for the rain, for 1803 was a wet summer. For three months (30 June to 20 September) Arthur was at Mr Lancaster's academy at Wimbledon while his parents went on a tour which took in much of England and Scotland. From 20 September to 8 November the family were together again, seeing more of their English friends and acquaintances and more of the sights of London. During his months in England Arthur Schopenhauer kept a diary which is in many ways exceptionally interesting. It shows that he saw all the obvious sights, responding to a number of them (e.g. Westminster Abbey) in a surprisingly profound way for a 15-year-old; he saw the famous actors of the time and has judicious comments on them, and saw some things which are now little known (e.g. Weeks's Museum). His diary and the letters he received from his parents while at Wimbledon reveal for the first time the nature of Heinrich Floris Schopenhauer's business contacts, who included a baronet and former Lord Mayor of London, a millionaire baronet-to-be, three one-time MPs, a future Governor of the Bank of England, and so on; the nature of these contacts, together with the fact that he was at one time the owner of four ships, shows Schopenhauer *père* to have been a bigger businessman than has been realised.

It is interesting to contrast Arthur Schopenhauer's English diary with his mother's. Both are very much in the tradition of the 'sentimental' anglophile travel diary *à la* Moritz of the late eighteenth century, but their interests and reactions are naturally different. Johanna Schopenhauer, who was a socialite and a snob, is mainly interested in people. Her son is more curious and more idiosyncratic. He is a typical schoolboy: more interested in a ventriloquist than in a public hanging (which he had seen before); he is interested in the unusual, the large, the intricate, etc. He is particularly interested in art and literature; he has no time for 'sloppy' plays. He is well brought up, civilised, sophisticated (cf. the picture of him dancing a minuet at a girls' boarding-school open day). His favourite word is 'extraordinary'. He has no time for religion. His punctuation is erratic.

As with the correspondence, we find an extraordinary gap: his three months at Mr Lancaster's are a complete blank in his diary. He mentions setting out for Wimbledon and departing from it. The rest is silence. Whether he kept a diary while at Mr Lancaster's is not known. It is possible that he did, and that it too was destroyed by his mother. What is much more likely, however, is that he kept no diary because the monotony of his existence made diary-keeping pointless. A remark after leaving Wimbledon about only keeping a diary in respect of those days when there was something to write about supports this opinion. If he had kept a diary, it would doubtless have recorded some facts which are almost certainly lost for ever, such as the names of the ushers at Mr Lancaster's establishment, and would have greatly simplified my task. Fortunately, however, much of the necessary information is obtainable from other sources. The account of Mr Lancaster's in his mother's diary can safely be regarded as tantamount to his own account of the establishment. There is nothing in his English diary about the horrors of English Sundays, simply because it was only at Wimbledon that he was confronted with them. Before that he had been taken out every Sunday (on 29 May they dined at Mr Robinson's; on 5 June they dined with Mr van der Hufen; on 12 June they spent the day with the Percivals, near Sydenham; on 19 June they went to Greenwich with Sir James Durno; and on 26 June they drove out to Salthill, Slough and Windsor). He will, however, have been expecting the worst (from current views of *Engländerei* and previous travellers' accounts of the horrors of English Sundays); but the combined onslaught of Thomas

Lancaster and Herbert Randolph was evidently traumatic.

In fairness to Mr Lancaster one should add that after his stay at Wimbledon Schopenhauer's English diary becomes better punctuated and better written. It also becomes more sophisticated.

Diary

Monday, 23 and Tuesday 24 May. We left Dunkirk early this morning and were in Calais by eleven, but on account of the contrary wind we were unable to embark all day, and it was not until two o'clock at night that we set forth. After a quarter of an hour I became excessively sick, and with several others had to go on deck for fresh air, where I remained the whole time. I was one of those most afflicted and passed a wretched night. At four o'clock Calais was still in sight and three boats were being rowed out towards us as hard as they could. It turned out to be the passengers from the French packet-boat, which had not been able to set out because just after we had got under weigh, news of the war had reached Calais. These unfortunate passengers had not even been able to take their baggage with them. With great trepidation and difficulty the women and children had to scramble aboard our tossing ship. I saw how each of them had to give two guineas to the sailors who had rowed them over, and in addition they had to pay for their passage on our boat and, I imagine, on the French packet-boat as well. In France one is for the most part grossly overcharged in every possible way. There were now about 100 people on board our ship. We eventually arrived at Dover at about one o'clock. We dined there, set out at six o'clock and lodged at Canterbury.

Wednesday 25 May. We set forth from Canterbury this morning, breakfasted in Rochester and dined at Shooting Hill.[1] From there there was a splendid view of London and the surrounding country, which we could not see, however, because of thick fog.

We arrived in London in the afternoon.[2]

Thursday 26 May. We walked through some of the liveliest streets of the city today. I found that London surpassed my expectations; I really had not imagined it to be *like this*, and was astonished to see the magnificent houses, the wide streets and the rich shops which one finds in front of every house in every street in all their colourful variety.

Friday 27 May. We drove this morning to Lady Anderson's,[3] but did not find her at home. As we were about to go out in the afternoon, we met Mr Drewe,[4] who was on his way to see us and who caused us to miss our walk.

Saturday 28 May. This evening we went to Astley's,[5] one of the many small theatres in London. They put on nothing but pantomimes. The first was very undistinguished, but the second and last, in which Harlequin had the leading role, was amusing on account of the quick succession of scenes. In the interval between the plays horse-riding stunts were performed, these being the real *raison d'être* of this establishment.

Sunday 29 May. Today we dined at Mr Robinson's,[6] in the garden.

Monday 30 May. In the morning we accompanied Mr Jourdan to Somerset House [Gallery],[7] where we saw an exhibition of paintings by English artists, in which there were, however, few good things.

Mr Jourdan dined with us today and went with us to Drury Lane[8] this evening. The playhouse exceeded my expectations: I was amazed at the many stairs we had to climb and the antechambers we had to pass through before reaching our box. It was very full. *Much Ado about Nothing* was on, and after that a pantomime in which, as usual, Harlequin played the main role. His part and all the other parts were played so well, and the settings and props were so outstanding, that the piece pleased everyone.

Tuesday 31 May. Although London is one of the biggest cities in the world, foreigners do not find it difficult to find their way about, the main reason for this being the fact that the streets are all fairly straight, so that one can see one's way far ahead. Today I found my way to St James's Park without having to ask, after I had first seen it on the map of London. The park was not as I had imagined it. I thought it would be a sort of English *Bosquet*, and was surprised to see a large meadow on which horses were grazing, surrounded by walks and elegant buildings.[9]

This evening we went to the Italian Opera[10] with Mr Jourdan. The theatre is even bigger than Drury Lane, but by no means so elegantly decorated. There are seven tiers of boxes. The boxes are all taken by the aristocracy: anyone who does not have a box goes into the pit, which costs half a guinea. One has to appear 'in full dress', that is to say, the ladies in white dresses, preferably without a hat, and the gentlemen in silk stockings, three-cornered hats, and usually all powdered. Mrs Billington is the prima donna, beside whom all others are greatly inferior, and she is certainly unequalled in skill and power, although she does not have much expression.

She is no longer beautiful, and her voice is beginning to age too, for she has been famous for over 30 years now. In the interval there was dancing. M. and Mme Laborie and Mlle Perisot enchanted the entire audience. When the opera, *Calypso*, was over, they danced again in a *ballet pantomime* in which, among other things, Laborie executed a minuet with his wife. It was the first time that I had watched a minuet without being bored.

During the opera — apart from when Mrs Billington was singing — very few people listen to what is going on, and often a general conversation takes place; for although one can listen to *one* beautiful aria with the greatest of interest and admiration, a whole grand opera can be boring, particularly if one does not understand the language, and it becomes wearisome in the long run. The performance, which began at half past seven, did not end till one o'clock.

Wednesday 1 June. We dined this day at Mr Harris's; he lives just outside the City of London and has a very fine view from his house. This evening we drove with him to a boarding school for young girls, where Mr Harris has two daughters. They learn dancing there too and had a sort of ball today where they all danced in front of their parents and others who had come as spectators. It was a delightful sight to see 40 young girls of between 8 and 16 and all dressed alike dancing together with great grace. Afterwards there were a couple of dances in which gentlemen took part and in which I myself danced.[11]

Thursday 2 June. As my mother was ill today, and it was raining very heavily, we stayed indoors in the morning. In the afternoon I went out with my father; we saw the Stock Exchange, the Bank of England, the Tower of London, the Monument and other remarkable and, for the most part, very fine buildings.

Friday 3 June. This morning we called upon Mrs Percival. She has a son of exactly my age, whose acquaintance I made.[12]

Towards nightfall I walked to St James's Park. The fine weather had tempted out crowds of people and it was very full. The full moon, which was rising over the Gothic outline of Westminster Abbey, and which was reflected in the canal, lit up the park so beautifully that it was much pleasanter to walk through than by day.

Saturday 4 June. Today was the King's birthday. Sir James Durno[13] conducted us to St James's Park, where a salute of cannon was fired, and thence we walked to St James's Street, where we obtained seats on the balcony of a coffee-house in order to watch the nobility being driven to court. There was a procession of more than a thousand splendid state carriages. Behind each stood servants in rich gold liveries, and on the box sat old-fashioned coachmen with gold coats, short wigs and little long-cornered hats trimmed with gold. We saw the Duke of Gloucester and the Duke of York being driven past in glass-sided coaches with servants, and accompanied by the Household Cavalry. In the coaches sat the gentlemen in embroidered clothes and huge wigs, and their ladies with dresses with pocket hoops. Sir James Durno promised to obtain for us tickets to the King's antechamber, where we should be able to see them all in their court dress.

We dined this day at Mr Percival's. In the evening all public buildings and the shops that serve the King were illuminated.

Sunday 5 June. We dined today in the garden of Mynheer van der Hufen, an unmarried Dutchman. On the way there we made a detour and passed by the Grand Junction Canal. Because of the very fine view from there a very high wooden bridge was only last week built alongside the big stone bridge. I mounted the bridge: the view really is most attractive, only the rain, which fell all day, prevented me from seeing the whole extent of it.

Monday 6 June. Percival junior called for me today, and together with him and a young person of his acquaintance interested in military matters I went for a walk which was, however, interrupted by a violent thunderstorm. Afterwards we watched a boat race from Westminster Bridge, in which a number of boats were competing for a prize.

[Later] in the morning Mr Jourdan took me to see a kind of panorama [at the Lyceum].[14] It depicted the battle of Lodi, which took place between the French, the Austrians and the Neapolitans in the late war. It is very realistic and very well painted, and is really worth seeing.

Mr Jourdan dined with us and went to the Haymarket [Theatre][15] with us in the evening. They were representing *The Mountaineers*, a play whose subject is taken from *Don Quixote*. Mr Elliston, a very good tragic actor, played the part of a madman and won wholehearted applause. He had made a deep study of his part, in which he was greatly assisted by his fine figure and expressive face. He portrayed with the greatest skill the contradictions and the unstable character of a half-crazy person, right down to the physical symptoms of the disease, the spasmodic movements and the feverish trembling. This was followed by a farce, in which Mr Matthews, a comic actor, particularly excelled.

During the interval between the two pieces a sailor in the gallery started singing in a loud voice. At first people hissed him, but then, when he did not stop, they quietened down. He sang really well, everyone listened to him and he received general applause at the end of the first verse. In the second he ran away with himself somewhat, which made people laugh, but he was applauded all the same.

Tuesday 7 June. This afternoon we drank tea in a public garden in Chelsea which turned out to be not very attractive. From there we went on to the Royal Circus,[16] where we saw the end of a pantomime, some horse-riding stunts and the beginning of an opera with first-rate scenery, in which Harlequin as usual played the principal part.

Wednesday 8 June. This day morning I was present at a sad spectacle: I saw three people hanged. It is one of the most shocking of sights to see people coming to a violent end. That said, an English hanging of this kind is by no means as gruesome as executions otherwise are.[17] The unfortunate victim certainly suffers for no more than thirty seconds; as soon as he drops he is still; one does not even see his face, over which a white hood is pulled. I think that the reason why this is a speedy end comes from the fact that they do not die of strangulation, but rather have their necks broken by a hitch in the rope as they fall. The fact that their heads all hang to one side confirms this. In England the spectacle is less shocking in that the whole thing is not so ceremonious. Here there are no death knells, no execution shirt, etc.; the scaffold stands just outside the prison door, and the crowd of spectators is not so large because here they have regular hangings every six weeks. I was standing at a window, opposite the prison, near enough to be able to see the expressions of the criminals quite clearly.[18] They did not seem particularly pale. I shuddered when the rope was placed around their necks. This was the awful moment. Their souls seemed to be already in the next world, and it was as though they did not notice what was going on. A clergyman was with them on the scaffold; to one of them in particular he talked continuously. The fear which prompted these people to use their very last moment for prayer was a sorry spectacle. One of them who moved his hands up and down as he prayed, made the same movement a couple more times after he had fallen . . .

This evening I went to see a ventriloquist whose performance had been advertised daily in the newspapers.[19] The performance began at nine o'clock. I have never watched anything with so much astonishment and admiration as this ventriloquist. He is a Frenchman and is called Fitz-James. On his own he acted whole plays in which the other characters were in part supposed to be hiding beneath a bedspread, on the cellar floor, under the table, outside the door or in the street. One heard a post boy blowing his horn in the street and the watchman calling the hours. Beneath a bedspread he mimicked the whole Assemblée Nationale, in the course of which a dozen different voices came from different directions in turn. He made all this seem so real that he drew astonishment and applause from all present. He himself declared his talent to be a gift of nature, hardly one person in a million being born a true ventriloquist. He said too that it is quite wrong to suppose that he and his fellow ventriloquists speak from the stomach. He merely spoke, he said, in a hollow voice from down in his chest, and even moved his mouth, but for the sake of the illusion was normally able to conceal this by a trick of the trade. His rare talent affords this man a good living: he only gives three performances a week (each lasting a little under two hours), but asks 7s per ticket. In addition he is a great mimic. He did a number of skits at which even the most serious-minded members of the audience could not help laughing freely. Then he sat down and put on faces expressive of divers characters, moods and passions — for instance, thoughtfulness, fear, terror, surprise, joy, desire, etc. In each case he seemed to change, his features became quite different. He kept up each character for a couple of minutes and seemed stuck in it, and every time he would have made the most impressive character portrait. It was with the greatest admiration that I left the presence of this really extraordinary man.

Thursday 9 June. This day there was a great Drawing Room at court. Sir James Durno had gained us an *entrée* to the antechamber, and from there we were able to see the whole court walk past in old-fashioned but splendid court dress. It was noticeable with how little decorum and grace the ladies of the court walked in their dresses with enormous pocket hoops and long gold trains: they looked like dressed-up country girls. When all were assembled the King and Queen came with their family.

This day we had been invited to dine at Mr Solly's,[20] but there was such monstrous heavy rain that we had to wait two hours before we could obtain a hackney coach (which normally stand around in every street), despite sending messenger boys in every possible direction, and we only arrived at Mr Solly's at half past six, by which time dinner was half over.

Friday 10 June. This morning I went to see the menagerie at Exeter 'Change.[21] It contained an extraordinarily large collection of wild animals.

Sir James Durno dined with us and in the evening went to Covent-Garden[22] with us. The theatre is not quite as large as Drury Lane, but the actors are altogether better. They were performing *The Stranger*, a very good translation of Kotzebue's *Menschenhass und Reue*, in which on the whole every part was well played. This was followed by *A Tale of Mystery*, a tragedy, which could not have been better performed. In the interval between these two pieces one actor sang a patriotic song, another danced a hornpipe, a third sang a comic song, and another essayed the 'Illusions of Imitation' [as he called them], that is to say, he mimicked a number of famous tragic and comic actors, and those who had seen these actors assured us that the imitations were extraordinarily good.

Saturday 11 June. We dined this day in Hampstead, whence one has a very striking view of the surrounding countryside, which we could not see for the heavy rain.

Sunday 12 June. I spent this day at Mr Percival's house. In the afternoon I went with Percival Junior to see the Quaker Meeting House.[23] It is a very simple building. The men and women sit separately. As we entered, a Quaker was standing behind a partition and speaking, but so indistinctly that I understood but little. He sat down again and there was silence for a while. Then someone else came forward to say 'a common prayer', for which all had to take off their hats (which had not happened earlier) and stand. He spoke as though his voice were choked by sighs, swallowed half of every word and then left a minute-long interval until the next word, so that, particularly for a foreigner, it was impossible to understand him. When he had done, someone else stood up after a short while who spoke more clearly; we left before he had finished.

Monday 13 June. This morning I climbed the Monument. It was of course erected to commemorate the Great Fire which incinerated a large part of the City of London 150 years ago. The Monument consists of a gigantic Doric column, 202ft high. The pedestal is almost as high as the four-storey buildings by which it is surrounded, and indeed serves as the custodian's residence. On top of the column is an iron-railed balcony which is reached by a turnpike stair with 345 steps. From the top there is a very extensive view, and one would be able to see almost the whole of the City if it were not for the smoke rising from every chimney, which restricts the view to the nearby streets and the tips of spires.

From the Monument I went to the Ceverian [*sic*] Museum.[24] It is really just a natural history collection, but the most complete and proper natural history collection I ever saw, those in Göttingen,

Kassel and Dresden not excluded. It consists of twelve rooms and a great rotunda. In each room are to be found, in their proper classes, every kind of animal, so well stuffed and preserved that they are as good as alive; every kind of mineral; the best-known kinds of wood. In a word, all Nature's works in their gradations, series and varieties are there, arranged in the most easily understandable way, in glass cases; and beside each one the name, normally in English, French and Latin. In every room the light comes from overhead. In the great rotunda are the birds. Downstairs are the bigger birds, together with an extraordinarily well preserved and complete collection of butterflies. Upstairs, in the dome, supported by Ionic columns of red marble, is a gallery with an immense variety of birds in glass cases. Gathered together from every climate, and so expertly stuffed that it is impossible to tell them from live ones, they stand side by side, colours and sizes contrasting vividly.

In addition this museum also has some art objects: for instance, a vase painted by Raphael, some ancient Roman vases, some things which are remarkable because of their age, e.g. a calendar for the year 1432 and many similar things. One example of oriental art, remarkable for its intricate and really beautiful workmanship and because of its value, is the tomb of Confucius, reproduced in gold and precious stones. The figures on it are very well done and so minute that they are best seen magnified in the concave mirror standing beside it. Particularly remarkable are the weapons, clothes, utensils and figures of deities of almost all the uncivilised peoples. One cannot help admiring the artistry of some of these: they were mostly collected by [Captain] Cook. A nice thing about this museum is the fact that here, unlike in other museums, one is not escorted round and obliged to leave at the end of the circuit. One can stay as long as one wishes; I stayed two and a half hours. In most rooms there is an open fire, and in front of each fire stand two sofas. Most appropriately, in one of the largest rooms are to be seen Pope's beautiful lines, the truth of which one really feels on being compelled to admire Nature in all her infinite variety:

See through this air, this ocean and this earth!
All matter quick and bursting into birth:
Above how high progressive life may go!
Around how wide, how deep extend below!
Vast Chain of Beings, which from God began:
Natures ethereal, Human, Angel, Man:

Beast, Bird, Fish, Insect, what no eye can see!
No glass can reach from Infinite to thee!
From thee to nothing. —

This evening I went to see Metlin's [sic] Museum.[25] It contains only mechanical artefacts: toys, really, but good for an hour's entertainment, e.g. swings, roundabouts, a pair of chairs which make a terrible noise when one sits on them, a pair of curious pianos, a blackamoor who opens and closes his mouth while you try to pop a coin in and who rolls his eyes in a terrifying way; a little gentleman who walks up and down all the time eyeing spectators through his monocle and saluting them, and a host of suchlike things.

Tuesday 14 June. This morning we went to see Westminster Abbey,[26] where the immortality of England's great men was made doubly sure by means of a marble statue. Milton's, Garrick's, Handel's and Shakespeare's tombs are what one first sees on entering. Serious of mien, Shakespeare stands on his tomb, life-size, holding in his hand his beautiful lines on the transience of life:

> The cloud-capp'd towers, the gorgeous palaces,
> The solemn temples, the great globe itself,
> Yea, all which it inherit, shall dissolve
> And, like this insubstantial pageant faded,
> Leave not a rack behind. We are such stuff
> As dreams are made on, and our little life
> Is rounded with a sleep.
>
> Shakespeare, Tempest, IV, 1

Garrick is represented coming from behind a curtain which he is pushing aside, apparently entering a better world. Beneath Gay's bust are his famous lines:

> Life is a jest, and all things show it:
> I thought so once, and now I know it.[27]

We were conducted down every aisle of this great Gothic building, which contains mostly very old tombs, many of them, however, displaying excellent workmanship. In every corner and every little side chapel we saw ancient tombs on which the hero whom they contain is lying, carved in wood, in full armour and with his hands folded in prayer. We were shown the tomb of Queen Elizabeth, with the Queen herself, finished in wax, wearing the clothes she wore in life. The other kings have no monuments as such; their coffins are in a vault beneath the Abbey. We also saw the tomb and the statue of the unhappy Mary Queen of Scots, and many tombs of men who made their names in older English history. In one particular aisle are the tombs of famous men of more recent times: well known writers, and scholars in every branch of learning, but above all many admirals. We were also shown the room in which are hung the arms, helmets and swords of all the Knights of the Bath.

Westminster Abbey certainly provides endless food for thought. Seeing within these Gothic walls the remains and monuments of all these poets, heroes and kings, seeing how they, coming from so many different centuries, here stand side by side — or rather, how their bones lie side by side — it is a pretty thought to wonder whether perhaps they *themselves* are now together somewhere where neither centuries nor social barriers nor space nor time separate them any longer; and to wonder what any of them took with them of their temporal glory and greatness. The kings will have left behind their weapons, and the poets their reputations; but the great men among them, whose distinction came from their very being and not from anything outside of them, will have taken their greatness with them, will have taken with them everything that they had.

Wednesday 15 June. Today we drove to Richmond Hill.[28] Although it rained, as it has done throughout the whole of our stay in London, the air was at least reasonably clear, so that we were able to see the very fine views which one has both from Richmond Hill and on the way there. On the way there we halted at the Royal Garden in Kew.[29] We saw the Botanical Garden, which has some very remarkable hot houses and is altogether very handsome, but we could not gain admittance to the Pleasure Ground.

The view from one of the principal rooms in the inn (the Star and Garter), in Richmond Hill, is prodigious fine. It is not too extensive, just the right size for the eye to take it all in. In great diversity one sees meadows bounded by rolling downs, and with the Thames winding its way through the landscape, wide pale green meadows covered with grazing horses and cows and occasional groups of dark trees. Little villages and isolated houses are dotted about and serve to animate the secne. The first thing on which one's eye comes to rest is [Alexander] Pope's house, in which he wrote many of his poems.[30] He has been dead for sixty years. After dinner we went to see the house, but it is no longer open to the public. Thence we drove to Hampton Court, a royal palace which the King has not been in for twenty years. The Dutch *Stadtholder* has been living there for the past seven years. This palace is very old, one part of it is still Gothic in style. It is monstrous large; we only walked through the main rooms, which contain many paintings, some of them (including the portraits of most of the kings of England) very striking. The garden is not in the modern taste, but is quite nice and large; the orangerie is very handsome.[31]

Thursday 16 June. This day noon we dined with Mr Solly's brother, whose house we had visited a week ago; he lives just outside the City.[32] In the morning, before we drove out there, Mr Jourdan called for us. Since it was a fine day he took us through the most beautiful streets and squares of London. We went to the Roman Gallery,[33] a collection of paintings. It is not very large and contains mostly Italian paintings, some of them outstandingly good. Then we went on to the Shakespeare Gallery.[34] It is well worth seeing, being an extensive collection of oil paintings illustrating Shakespeare's plays. Many of them are masterpieces, and the passages for illustration have also been very well chosen.

Friday 17 June. This morning we went with the Percivals to see the Tower of London.[35] We were shown around by a member of the Yeomen of the Guard, founded by Henry VII. First he showed us a room in which old Spanish weapons, booty from the Armada in Queen Elizabeth's time, are kept. Our guide's uniform was exactly the same as that given to the Yeomen of the Guard by Henry VII: red, with puffed decoration in blue velvet and gold, a flat round hat with the crown and the English royal arms with the words 'Dieu et mon droit' embroidered on the back, and a long halberd. This uniform went very well with the old weapons which he showed us. The room with the Spanish weapons also contained a wax model of Queen Elizabeth wearing the suit of armour which she wore when she addressed her army in 1588. Then we were taken into the armoury in which there are all sorts of old weapons and armour and helmets (for men and horses) hanging on the walls. All the kings of England are there too, carved in wood from original portraits, wearing their own armour, and mounted on horseback. Thence we were taken into the arsenal as such, where in one room there are weapons for 2,000 men hanging on the walls; before the outbreak of the current war with France there were weapons for 3,000 men there. All the muskets, pistols and swords are so tastefully displayed and are in such good condition that they form a delightful spectacle. Then we were shown the Crown Jewels: crowns for every member of the royal family, the sceptre, the orb, the sword of peace, the ampulla, and many similar things. I find it strange and repugnant that these things are displayed in a cellar lit by two paltry candles and are kept behind a grill; all the more so because earlier I had seen the much more valuable jewels in the Green Room in Dresden, which everyone is allowed to handle. We then saw the Tower of the Lions. It contains many lions and tigers, wild cats, eagles, etc.

We dined at Mr Percival's.

Saturday 18 June. Since it rained incessantly and we had not planned to go anywhere, we stayed in all day. The Misses Percival dined with us.

Sunday 19 June. Today we drove to Greenwich[36] with Sir James Durno. We dined there and in the afternoon saw the famous hospital for naval pensioners. It looks more like a palace than a hospital. It consists of a number of massively built, elegant buildings separated by large courtyards. It is situated beside the Thames, so that the retired sailors have the pleasure of seeing ships every day. The pensioners are all very neatly dressed; each one has his own bedroom. In some of the hallways and rooms of the establishment there are very good paintings, nearly all of them paintings of ships or battles at sea, or else portraits of some of the benefactors of this great institution. The chapel is extraordinarily handsome.

Monday 20 June. It rained unceasingly today. I did not go anywhere and spent the evening writing letters home to Hamburg.[37]

Tuesday 21 June. I spent the whole day at Mr Percival's.

Wednesday 22 June. We dined with old Mrs Solly.[38]

Thursday 23 June. This evening we went to Covent Garden.[39] They were performing *John Bull*, a patriotic play in which all the characters are typically English. It was followed by a farce, *The Lying Valet*, which was acted very well.

Friday 24 June. This morning we visited the warehouse of one of the main furniture dealers here.[40] We were conducted through many large rooms filled with furniture of all kinds. I was astonished at the state of perfection which has been attained here in the satisfaction of every little need, and at the artistry with which the highest degree of comfort, taste and opulence is combined in every item of furniture. It being a very fine day, we had gone there on foot, and on the way back we passed Bedlam.[41] It is no longer shown to the public, because it is considered cruel to make the misery of lunatics into a spectacle to satisfy people's idle curiosity. But we stood outside Bedlam for a few minutes to examine the two very handsome statues over the archway, the madman and the melancholic, which are considered masterpieces of art.

This evening we went to Vauxhall with Herr and Frau Schmidt from Danzig, who used to live in the same house as us,[42] Herr Paleske, Sir James Durno, and Captain Barnby[43] from Hull. The illuminations are very splendid and very elegant, albeit not quite as startling as I had expected. From eight o'clock to eleven o'clock there is a concert. The musicians are housed in a superbly illuminated temple in the middle of the gardens. The concert was very good: Miss Bland sang most attractively, and a musician whose name I have forgotten played a trumpet concerto, and very well done it was too. At eleven o'clock the water is turned on, in other words, the curtain of the little theatre rises, on the stage of which are to be seen a bridge with sundry artificial but most realistic waterfalls. Across the bridge walk all sorts of puppets — a huntsman who proceeds to shoot a wild duck, a farm cart, the mail coach, etc. — all of them extraordinarily realistic. At midnight there was a superb firework display. After the fireworks everyone makes for the boxes and tables in order to sup.

After supper the company becomes more boisterous and more mixed. Musicians take up their positions in various parts of the gardens and play dances which are danced by women of very questionable appearance.

Vauxhall is open every evening. When it rains people remain in the indoor part of the establishment, which consists of a number of large, elegant, well lit rooms. It was after two o'clock in the morning when we left.[44]

Saturday 25 June. With the same company which accompanied us to Vauxhall yesterday we made a long excursion which had been agreed on the previous evening.

First we drove to Kew Gardens, which we managed to see this time, since we had an entrance ticket. A German gardener who is working there to perfect his skills showed us round. Though the gardens are monstrous large, they are but little cultivated. We did not have time to see the palace and the Chinese pagoda because they were too far away. One very strange whimsy is a herd of 27 kangaroos hopping about in a grass enclosure, which afford the most comic spectacle. It was seven o'clock when we got to Salthill, where we straightway dined and also lodged.

Sunday 26 June. In Salthill[45] there is nothing of interest except an extraordinarily good inn, the Castle Inn. But in a nearby village lives Herschel, whom we visited this morning.[46] He showed us his telescopes, which are enormous and are mounted on proportionate — that is to say, house-high — platforms in his garden.

This afternoon we drove to Windsor, which is only two English miles distant from here. On arrival we went straight to the terrace, from where one has a quite superb view. An hour later the King came out. It was now very crowded, and his subjects formed two lines between which the King walked up and down with his family. He had the Queen's arm, and was followed by his son, the Duke of Cambridge, with two princesses; behind these were two other princesses, and several ladies of the court brought up the rear of the procession. And every Sunday, provided it is not raining, the King, with his family, walks in this homely way between his subjects. He is not accompanied by any soldiers, etc.; a constable merely walks in front of him to clear the way. The King is a very good-looking old man. The Queen is ugly and not at all ladylike. The princesses are not pretty and beginning to get long in the tooth.[47]

Towards evening we returned to Salthill.

Monday 27 June. Today we left Salthill and drove to Oatland,[48] where the castle and gardens of the Duchess of York are, which we saw. The castle is quite undistinguished, but the gardens are handsome. They contain an extraordinarily beautiful grotto, very tastefully lined with shells and stones; most of the stones were brought from the great cave in Derbyshire. In one part of the grotto is the clearest pool I have ever seen: the water drips slowly all the time and really is so clear that it is almost impossible to tell whether the pool is full or empty. Then we drove to Wimbledon, where we dined with Mr Lancaster at what is to be my abode.[49] Mr Percival and his family were also present.[50] In the evening we returned to London.

Tuesday 28 June. We dined at Herr Paleske's. Herr and Frau Schmidt from Danzig were also there.

Wednesday 29 June. This evening we went to Vauxhall with Herr and Frau Schmidt and Herr Paleske. It was exactly the same as last time.

Thursday 30 June. Today I took leave of my parents and in the evening drove out to Wimbledon to Mr Lancaster's.[51]

Tuesday 20 September. Today I left Mr Lancaster's establishment and Wimbledon, after a stay of twelve weeks, and returned to my parents in London, they having got back a fortnight ago. It rained incessantly; going out in despite of it, I returned soaked to the skin.

Wednesday 21 September. The rain, which did not stop today either, prevented us from going to the horse races at Enfield as planned.

Saturday 24 September. [*Note*: In this part of my journal I have not included every day, because we saw nearly all the sights of London during the first part of our stay; now we are staying on because there is no traffic between England and France, so that we cannot travel via Calais, rather than from choice.] This evening we went with Messrs von Hess, Mathiessen and Wieler,[52] and Sir James Durno, to Covent Garden, where we saw *Hamlet*. [Charles] Kemble, who appeared in this theatre for the first time today, played Hamlet, his *tour de force*, in an unsurpassable way;[53] the other roles were played equally well. But in my view the great comic actor Munden played Polonius in too comic a manner. However, in the afterpiece, *The Rival Soldiers*,[54] a farce in which as always he had the main part, he was most genial. Before we set forth for Covent Garden I witnessed, through a window, a strange street comedy which would have given Hogarth a good subject for an engraving. Right outside our window a mountebank set up his Punch and Judy show. A crowd of low types immediately gathered round and blocked the street, their laughter at the beatings dealt out by Punch filling the air. After the first act had ended, to general applause, our artiste took off his hat in order to harvest the reward of his labours, leaving it to the generosity of the delighted spectators to decide how much his labours were worth. But as soon as he so much as touched his hat, the ungrateful and, unfortunately, greater half of the spectators turned their backs on him and went their way, some of them with a look and attitude which implied that they had had enough of such foolish stuff and were taking their fine tastes off to indulge them elsewhere. As soon as our artiste had been paid by the loyal part of his audience he proceeded to the second act, whereupon those who had just left him so disdainfully came creeping back to see the end of the performance. But now a spoilsport appeared. A man in a black coat and tricorn hat and with a face on which was written sly, sardonic pleasure at the airs he was about to give himself, pushed his way through the crowd with a pompous, self-important step, until he was standing in front of the box of tricks, on which he banged twice with a white truncheon which he drew from a pocket. As soon as this magician touched the box with his wand Punch and his opponent on stage froze as though turned to stone, and the Punch-and-Judy man stuck his head out of the box. The man in black, who was a constable, rebuked him with a majestic look for the public nuisance he was committing. And watched triumphantly as the poor mountebank was obliged to pack up, and the disappointed crowd slowly dispersed. A few rascally urchins couldn't resist the temptation to raise the lid of the box and expose the heroes of the piece, who were now lying with their legs bound together, to public laughter. The constable, wishing to show his impartiality, came to the aid of the unfortunate street entertainer, took the walking stick out of the hand of one of the spectators and with it aimed at the urchins who, avoiding his blows, skipped along in front of him, laughing and pulling faces. [*Note*: It is only because when I wrote it I didn't know what else to do with it that I have allowed this trivial story to take up so much room in my diary.[55]]

Sunday 25 September. This morning we drove out to see Mr Scott, who has a superb country house near Bromley which he had built recently in the latest style.[56] It is situated in the middle of his estate (park), which is very large and laid out most tastefully. We stayed the night there.

Monday 26 September. After again walking through Mr Scott's park with him this morning, we took leave of him and his wife, and drove to Sevenoaks, where we dined. Here we saw the Duke of Dorset's residence and park.[57] The house is a very large old Gothic building, but contains many paintings, some of them very good. They are mostly portraits of famous men, most of the English kings, Mary Queen of Scots, O[liver] Cromwell, Luther and Melanchton, Thomas More, Louis XIV, Pope, Locke, Baile [*sic*], Addison, Newton, Shakespeare, Swift and most of the famous English writers; also the [Earls and] Dukes of Dorset. Some rooms are still in use and are furnished in the modern style. In one room we were shown a landscape which we took for an engraving, but which was in fact an embroidery and so very finely worked that one could not tell that it was embroidered unless one knew this to be the case. In the afternoon we drove from Sevenoaks to Tunbridge [Wells], where we were late arriving and spent the night.

Tuesday 27 September. Tunbridge is a little spa town which is probably visited more for the sake of fashion than of health. The water is cold and has a very faint mineral taste. This morning we walked on the Promenade, but found it deserted, the Season being almost over.[58] At eleven o'clock we departed, drove for 37 English miles without alighting, and at five o'clock were in London, where we dined and then went to Covent Garden with Sir James Durno. *Isabella* was being performed, a very old and grisly tragedy. Mrs Siddons, who is reckoned to be the greatest tragic actress, and who has quitted Drury Lane together with her brother Kemble, made her début here in the part of Isabella.

In the afterpiece, *The Irishman in London*, Munden as usual made everyone laugh.[59]

Thursday 29 September. This day we dined with Herr Mathiessen and Herr von Hess, the deputies from Hamburg. The company was more numerous than is normally the case in England, and, with two or three exceptions, consisted entirely of Germans.

Saturday 1 October. Today we dined at Mr Drewe's in Kensington. Before going there we made a long excursion via Kingston to Richmond Hill, where we again saw the fine view and walked through the park. From there we drove to Kew, where we saw the Botanical Garden again. This time the autumn colouring of some of the trees made it even more impressive.

Sunday 2 October. This day we dined at Mr Court's in Maryland Point.[60] [*Note*. Here I made the acquaintance of a young Dutchman, Suirmand, who works in Mr Court's counting house and whom I saw a good deal of subsequently.[61]]

Monday 3 October. Today I accompanied my father to Enfield, where we saw Mr Mellish's park, which is very handsome.[62]

This evening we went to see *King Richard the Third* at Covent Garden. The beautiful tragedy by Shakespeare had been altered so much as to be barely recognisable. Not only had a great deal been cut, but whole parts had been added and others omitted. Cook played King Richard[63] and surpassed all the English acting I have seen. I much prefer him to Kemble. His only mistake lay in not disfiguring himself sufficiently in view of the fact that in the play there is continual allusion to his ugliness and deformity.

Wednesday 5 October. This evening I went to the Royal Circus.

Thursday 6 October. This morning we went to see the 'invisible girl'. This unaccountable trick, which has won widespread applause, remained inexplicable to me, as it does to everyone else who has witnessed it. Out of a metal sphere, which is only suspended from thin cords, a woman's voice can be heard speaking through four speaking tubes. The invisible girl speaks English, German and French, sings, and plays the piano. One can quite clearly hear the sounds coming out of the sphere and can even feel her breath. As soon as one gets within a couple of feet from the sphere, nothing more can be heard.[64] Herr Mathiessen and Herr Paleske visited us this evening.

Friday 7 October. Today we went to see the Ceverian [*sic*] Museum again. Although I had seen it during the first part of our stay in London, everything seemed unfamiliar, and I stayed there a very long time.

In the morning Mynheer Apostool from Rotterdam called on us, and in the afternoon Herr Schwalbe from Hamburg paid us a visit.

Saturday 8 October. Today we once again went to see the menagerie at Exeter 'Change.

Sunday 9 October. We drove out to Epping Forest today. The way there is very pleasant . In Epping Forest itself there is nothing to see. We met Mynheer van der Huven and dined with him.

Wednesday 12 October. Mynheer Apostool, Herr Schwalbe, Mr Percival and his daughter, and Master Suirmand dined with us this day and accompanied us to Covent Garden in the evening.[65] They were performing *The Provoked Husband*, which I did not enjoy very much. But the afterpiece, *The Padlock*, an operetta, was very nice. Miss Mortimer sang delightfully.

Thursday 13 October. We dined with Mr Rich.

Saturday 15 October. This morning we visited the Lyceum: a kind of panorama which differs from the Panorama proper in that the spectacle only occupies a semicircle. On an earlier occasion [6th June] I saw the battle of Lodi here. Today we saw the storming of Seringapatam,[66] which I found more enjoyable and which gives one a vivid impression of the terrors of a battle.

Afterwards we drove with Herr Mathiessen to Kensington Gardens, which, although they are so close to the city, I had not seen before. It was a nice warm autumn day. The gardens looked very well because the autumn had turned the leaves of the trees so many different colours. We walked through the whole of the gardens, which are quite extensive.

Sunday 16 October. We again dined with Mr Court in Maryland Point. I stayed the night.

Monday 17 October. This morning I went into the City again with young Suirmand. In the evening we went to Covent Garden. *Pizarro* was being performed at this theatre for the first time,[67] and the house was packed, as all the great actors were to appear. Cook was playing Pizarro, Kemble was Rollo, and Mrs Siddons Elvira. Cook was greeted with general applause, but no sooner had he spoken a few words than his voice failed him; he could not manage another word, and was obliged to leave the theatre. This is said to have happened to Cook on one or two previous occasions when he was drunk the previous evening. He is famous for often being only half sober when he comes on stage. When Cook departed, the greatest consternation registered on the faces of the other actors. They tried to leave out that scene and go on with the rest of the play, but the hissing of the disappointed audience put an end to that, and the curtain fell. The orchestra promptly struck up the overture and went on playing it again and again when the curtain failed to rise, until they could no longer make themselves heard for the whistling and hissing. An actor in one of the minor parts came on stage to say something, but he was not allowed to make himself heard, and people started calling for Kemble. Kemble appeared at once, but even he found it difficult to obtain a hearing. When he began by saying, 'Mr Cook is taken ill,' the pit retorted, 'No, he's not, he's drunk!' — and the noise began again.[68] Only with the greatest difficulty was Kemble able to announce that, by the audience's leave, the play would be begun again with Siddons junior reading Cook's part. This is what happened, and, leaving this incident aside, the play was very well done. The costumes and the settings too were indescribably brilliant [*Note*. The American settlers, for instance, had real Indian head-dresses.] By way of afterpiece they performed *The Rival Soldiers*, which we had seen before.

Tuesday 18 October. This morning we visited the British Museum[69] with Mynheer Apostool and Herr Schwalbe. First we were shown [Sir William] Hamilton's collection of antiquities. So far as the Etruscan vases were concerned, I found my expectations disappointed. I had imagined these world-famous vases to be made of marble, with glorious low-relief decoration, and was astonished to find only black earthenware vases with red figures painted on them. Their shapes, however, are very beautiful; the only reason why we do not find them particularly striking is that we are accustomed to seeing these shapes imitated in all modern vases. The figures too are on the whole beautifully drawn, although their proportions are sometimes defective. But if one remembers that such vases were everyday utensils so far as the ancient Romans were concerned, then the taste and the artistry which have gone into the forming and painting of every such utensil merit the greatest admiration. The Hamilton collection is fairly large and in addition to a number of Roman vessels also includes some Egyptian items — mummies, figures of gods, etc. — which are all very fine. Next we saw a collection of Indian clothes, weapons, deities, vessels, etc. And a natural history collection which was very well preserved, but not as good as the one in the Ceverian [*sic*] Museum. We strolled through the enormous Library [Reading Room], of which we naturally saw little more than its appearance. Mr Parker, the Superintendent of the museum,[70] a very learned gentleman, who showed us round and pointed out and explained everything in the most courteous way, allowed us to see a remarkable collection of old autograph letters written by the most important men in all periods of English history. He showed us the letter which William the Conqueror wrote on arrival in England, another from Oliver Cromwell to his wife, various letters written by Mary Queen of Scots in the early years of her imprisonment, several by Queen Elizabeth (though only the signature of these is in her own hand), and many others written by almost every king of England. This museum certainly has a priceless collection of manuscripts.

Wednesday 19 October. Today we drove to Roehampton to see the country house of the Jew Goldsmith,[71] which has become so famous that even the King has been there. The garden is very pretty and has a very fine view. The house is not large and from the outside not even particularly impressive, but the furniture and the decoration of the rooms are really magnificent.

From there we drove through Richmond Park to Richmond, where we dined.

Thursday 20 October. We dined with Herr Paleske.

Saturday 22 October. We dined with Mr Hennings.[72]

Sunday 23 October. We spent this day at Mr Percival's house in Sydenham.

Tuesday 25 October. We went to see Weak's Museum today.[73] It has a collection of mechanical gadgets which are so unusual, so perfect, ingenious, incredible and valuable that I do not think I have ever seen anything which has amazed me more. Walking through Weak's palace of art one could easily imagine oneself to be in the magic palaces of the *Arabian Nights*!

Wednesday 26 October. This evening we went to Drury Lane with Huttwalker junior[74] and Herr Schwalbe. Not having seen the theatre for some time, I was again surprised by its size and elegance. Only the actors are markedly inferior to those at Covent Garden. They were performing *Marriage Promises* and *Fortune's Frolick*, two very mediocre pieces. But Bannister, a comic actor, was very good.

Thursday 27 October. This morning we went to see St Paul's Church.[75] Although the exterior is probably the best part of it, there is something inexpressibly sublime and awe-inspiring about the interior: the sight of it evoked the same ideas as the Town Hall in Amsterdam. One feels dizzy at the sight of the enormous vaulted dome, and it is strange how very little and insignificant human beings appear in this immense building. It seems as though it was not built for such a puny race. A few very beautiful statues were recently placed in the church as funeral monuments. Two striking groups of statues stand on the tombs of two English naval heroes; and on the tomb of Howard, who inspected and reformed prisons throughout most of the world, there stands a very beautiful statue of himself. We were shown the principal sights of the church. We saw the library, which is insignificant, and the builder's model for the church, which is executed in wood to an even more sublime design than was put into execution when the church was built. Then we were shown the geometrical stairway; it is very ingenious, being made in such a way that each step rests on the next one, with the bottom step supporting the whole staircase. From there we went on to the outside gallery which runs around the dome and from which one has a very extensive view; and I climbed up to the top gallery, which is only just below the globe at the very top of the cathedral, from where I was able to enjoy the remarkable panoramic view of the whole of London. On the way down we saw the famous Whispering Gallery. It is within the lower part of the dome, and although it is so big that it is very difficult to hear what someone on the other side of the gallery is saying, it is nonetheless possible, by putting one's ear to the wall, to hear what someone facing the wall on the other side of the gallery is whispering. This remarkable phenomenon is unique, inimitable, and only came about by chance.

Friday 28 October. In St James's Park today we saw some of the London Volunteers returning from their parade in Hyde Park, which was a very fine spectacle.[76] There were 16,000 men, who are responsible for providing their own uniforms and weapons and were therefore got up most smartly, even ostentatiously. The cavalry had the finest English horses, all belonging to their riders. There are said to be well-nigh a million Volunteers in London nowadays. These are probably, if not the best trained, certainly the most distinguished-looking regiments to be found anywhere.

Saturday 29 October. We dined at Mr Brown's.

Sunday 30 October. We spent today outside the City at Mr Harris's.

Tuesday 1 November. This evening we went to Covent Garden.[77] They performed a very pretty opera, *The Cabinet*, in which the singing of Braham and Signor Storace was heard by everyone with delight and admiration. The afterpiece, *The Jew and the Doctor*, was decent too.

Wednesday 2 November. Today we saw Northumberland House and Norfolk House, two old-fashioned stately houses[78] in which there is little that is worth seeing apart from one or two good pictures (especially in Northumberland House), and some reindeer running around in the courtyard of Norfolk House.

Saturday 5 November. After the last fourteen days in London, each one of which in turn became the day on which we were to depart, we finally departed today and made for Harwich, where we had bespoken a ship to bring us to Rotterdam. Travelling with us, but in a different coach, were Herr Schwalbe and Herr Gleim from Amsterdam, who proposed to embark with us in our ship. At seven o'clock we reached Witham, where we stayed the night.[79]

Sunday 6 November. This morning we left Witham and, after travelling on a very pleasant road, arrived in Harwich at midday.

Monday 7 November. Today we remained in Harwich, partly because the wind was not favourable, but also in order to see to our passports, permits, customs examination, etc.

In Harwich itself there is nothing worth seeing; the town is small and dirty. The countryside round about is very attractive. Today we went for a walk along the coast. From the highest point of the cliffs one has a very good view of the sea, the town, and a little encampment in front of us along the shore, the cheerful sight and sound of which brought the scene to life.

Tuesday 8 November. After we had spent the morning waiting, bored and impatient, for a favourable wind, the skipper eventually came this afternoon to tell us that the wind had changed, and this evening at seven o'clock we embarked.

Notes

1. He means Shooter's Hill, the view from which was famous. 'The delightful prospect from Shooters hill appeared more beautiful than ever & holds a distinguished rank amongst the great variety I have seen. St. Paul's covered with a cloud of sea coal smoak . . .' (*The Diary of Sylas Neville, 1767–1788*, ed. B. Cozens-Hardy, 1950, 264.) In her diary J.S. elaborated on the view:

> From Shooter's Hill, a hill some 26 miles from London, we first saw the huge capital city stretching along the royal river Thames, which was covered with ships. We saw the wonderful dome of St Paul's rising high into the sky, further away the beautiful Gothic twin towers of Westminster Abbey, and close by the towers of well over 100 other churches. It was a fine, bright day; but the smoke rising from so many chimneys made it seem as though we were seeing things through a veil.

When Dorothy Wordsworth saw a prospect of Hamburg, on the other hand, she 'could not but remark how much the prospect would have suffered by one of our English canopies of coal smoke' (see her Hamburgh Journal of 1798). Approaching London from a different direction, some twenty years earlier, Carl Philipp Moritz's first impression was similar to the Schopenhauers'.

> We first descry'd [London] enveloped in a thick smoke, or fog. St. Paul's arose, like some huge mountain, above the enormous mass of smaller buildings . . . Westminster Abbey, the Tower, a steeple, one church and then another, presented themselves to our view; and we could now plainly distinguish the high round chimneys, on the tops of the houses, which yet seemed to us to form an innumerable number of smaller spires or steeples.

(*Moritz's Travels in England*, ed. P.E. Matheson, 1924, 19.) One wonders whether young A.S.'s impression was similar, for he came to regard the English as church-ridden. Shooter's Hill was not only famous for the view from the top; it was also a favourite lurking place for highwaymen and footpads, which the Schopenhauers presumably did not know. The traveller also had to pass by the gallows at the bottom of the hill and, at the top, the gibbet where the bodies of executed malefactors were hung in chains (cf. Lorenz Meyer's letter to A.S. of 22 July); in 1661 Samuel Pepys wrote, 'I rode under a man that hangs at Shooter's Hill and a filthy sight it was to see how his flesh is shrunk to his bones.'

2. The Schopenhauers entered London over Blackfriars Bridge. Dazed by the noise and the crowds, they made straight for their hotel, the York Hotel in Bridge Street, Blackfriars. The hotel was probably recommended by Sir John William Anderson or his partner, Samuel Drewe, as being convenient for the City, including the offices of Anderson, Drewe and Co. in Old Broad Street. The York Hotel occupied the house, on the corner of Little Bridge Street, which Robert Mylne, the designer and builder of the then new Blackfriars Bridge (opened in 1769), had built for himself; the walls of the rooms were adorned with classical medallions, and on the exterior was the date (1780), with Mylne's crest and initials. Dr Johnson, who became friendly with Mylne, dined with him at this residence on at least one occasion (W. Thornbury and E. Walford, *Old and New London*, I, 1873, 207). The building was demolished in 1863. In 1803 the hotel would have struck the Schopenhauers as typical of the new English architecture. A.S. describes it as 'recht gut' in his diary. In her diary his mother comments on the lack of hotels or inns suitable for foreigners, i.e. in which foreigners might conveniently live for some time, although H.F.S. would readily have found in *The Times* an advertisement for a York House Hotel in Albemarle Street which described itself as catering for the nobility and gentry, both English and foreign. The Schopenhauers stayed at the York Hotel for six weeks. Following their return from Scotland in early September H.F.S. and J.S. took rooms in Norfolk Street, where A.S. joined them on being released from his English school. On first seeing London, A.S. was struck by the width of the streets, and by the fact that they were paved and provided with pavements and were therefore relatively clean and safe for pedestrians. On arriving in Paris shortly after leaving England, he commented in his diary (30 November 1803) on the contrast between London and Paris in this respect.

3. Lady Anderson is the wife (*née* Dorothy Simkins of Devizes) of Sir John William Anderson, Bart (1735–1813), who was born in Danzig (son of William Anderson, Esq., of Danzig, merchant, who d. *c.* 1736), settled in London as a merchant, and became Lord Mayor in 1797 and MP for London in 1793, 1796 and 1800; he is discussed in more detail in connection with a letter from H.F.S. to his son dated 26 July 1803. The Andersons lived in Mill Hill. In her obituary in *GM* (1818/2, 648) Lady Anderson was described as 'a woman of great piety and goodness, of most elegant manners, and high accomplishments. She was a mistress of many foreign languages, and when Lady Mayoress, was ranked amongst the most accomplished and respectable ladies in that high department.' She died at the Adelphi on 30 November 1817.

4. 'Mr. Drewe' is Samuel Drewe, Esq., of Kensington Terrace. He was born on 19 November 1759, eighth son of Francis Drewe of Grange, Devon, by his second wife, Mary, daughter of Thomas Johnson of London. He married a Selina Thackeray and had a son, Frederick William, who went up to Cambridge in 1815, and four daughters (Emma, Augusta, Fanny and Anna). Samuel Drewe was a merchant, 'Assistant of the Russia Company', and, for many years a partner of (Sir) John William Anderson. In 1796 Samuel Drewe was lodged in John William Anderson's residence at 33 Charterhouse Square. Following his marriage he moved to Kensington Terrace, which is where he was living with his young family in 1803. In 1803 Sir John Wm Anderson Drewe and Co., merchants, had their offices at 40 Old Broad Street. Old Broad Street, once one of the most fashionable streets in London, was where the Excise Office had been built in 1768; it was essentially a street of bankers. Anderson Drewe and Co. were trading partners of Floris Schopenhauer, and evidently acted as his English bankers and agents. The Russia Company (or Muscovy Company), of which Samuel Drewe was a member, was an influential City of London institution; founded in 1555, it shared in the eighteenth-century revival of Anglo-Russian trade, which was funnelled through Danzig. Following Sir John William Anderson's death in 1813, Samuel Drewe took a new partner by the name of Ouchterlony. Drewe and Ouchterlony continued to operate from 40 Old Broad Street until the late 1820s, when they moved to 6 New Broad Street. What is particularly interesting is the fact that Samuel Drewe, to whom A.S. had to apply for his pocket money, became a director of the Bank of England (1806–26 and 1830–7), Deputy Governor (1826–8) and, finally, Governor (1828–30). He died in 1837. Further details of his family will be found in *Burke's Landed Gentry*, 4th edn, 1863, 390.

5. Astley's, originally a riding school and circus started by an ex-dragoon named Philip Astley (b. 1742), was by 1803 a national institution; it was situated in Lambeth, on Westminster Bridge Road. The original 'Royal Grove' was burned down in 1794; what the Schopenhauers saw was the 'Amphitheatre of Arts' which replaced it. Extraordinarily enough, this new Astley's was itself destroyed by fire on Friday, 2 July 1803, just six days after they visited it; it is surprising that A.S.'s diary does not record the fact. The establishment which replaced it, the 'Royal Amphitheatre', is the one to which Dickens devoted one of his *Sketches by Boz*; he also referred to it more briefly in *The Old Curiosity Shop* (chapter XXXIX):

Dear, dear, what a place it looked, that Astley's, with all the paint, gilding, and looking-glass; the vague smell of horses, suggestive of coming wonders; the curtain that hid such gorgeous mysteries; the clean white sawdust down in the circus; the company coming in and taking their places; the fiddlers looking carelessly up at them while they tuned their instruments, as if they didn't want the play to begin, and knew it all beforehand! What a glow was that, which burst upon them all, when that long, clear, brilliant row of lights came slowly up . . . Then the play itself! everything was delightful, splendid, and surprising!

The horsemanship, for which a circular ride was provided, was by 1803 only part of a mixed entertainment.

6. Mr Robinson most likely belonged to the well known family of Hamburg merchants of that name (mentioned by Crabb Robinson).

7. The Somerset House (in Somerset Place) which the Schopenhauers visited was the new building dating from 1776, home of the Royal Academy, whose annual summer exhibition was held there from 1780 to 1837. Since the Royal Academy will have been of particular interest to the Schopenhauers, it is worth noting the description of it in *The Picture of London for 1803*:

The room on the ground-floor is appropriated to models of statues, plans, elevations, and drawings.

The coved-ceiling of the library was painted by Reynolds and Cipriani. The centre by Sir Joshua, represents the *theory of the art*, under the form of an elegant and majestic female, seated in the clouds, and looking upwards: she holds in one hand a compass, in the other a lable, on which is written:

Theory is the knowledge of what is truly nature.

The four compartments in the coves of the ceiling, are by Cipriani, and represent Nature, History, Allegory, and Fable. These are well imagined, and sufficiently explain themselves.

The adjoining room being originally appropriated to models and casts from the antique, of which this society have a most valuable and curious collection, is plain and unornamented.

The council room is more richly decorated: the stucco is in a good taste; and in the centre compartment of the ceiling are five pictures painted by Mr. West. The centre picture represents the Graces unveiling Nature; the other four represent the four Elements, (from which the imitative arts collect their objects) under the forms of female figures, attended by Genii, with fire, water, earth, and air, exhibited in different forms and modifications. The four large oval pictures, which adorn the two extremities of the ceiling, are the work of Angelica Kauffman, and represent invention, composition, design, and colouring. Besides these nine large pictures, there are in the angles or ospandrells in the centre, four coloured medallions, representing Apelles, the painter; Phidia, the sculptor, Apollodorus, the architect; and Archimedes, the mathematician; and, round the great circle of the centre, eight smaller medallions held up by lions, on which are represented in chiaro-obscuro Palladio, Bernini, Michael Angelo, Flamingo, Raphael, Dominechino, Titian, and Rubens; all these were painted by Rebecca.

A.S. grew up with paintings and works of art, so that the comment in his diary should be taken seriously; Sylas Neville, visiting the annual exhibition at Somerset House in 1793, commented similarly ('this year remarkably poor. It contains, however, a few very good things', *Diary*, 304). The Schopenhauers were just in time for the Summer Exhibition, which closed on Saturday 11 June.

8. The Drury Lane playhouse (Theatre Royal) was built by Holland in 1794. Charles Kemble, who had been in charge there for the two previous seasons, left in 1803, when he moved to Covent Garden. What the Schopenhauers saw with (the unidentified) Mr Jourdan was the first night of *Much Ado about Nothing*, in which Mrs Jourdan played Beatrice to John Bannister's Benedick. The theatre and this particular performance are described at some length in J.S.'s diary, which confirms that they preferred the after-piece, a pantomime in which Joseph Grimaldi was outstanding. Dorothea Jordan was famous for her tomboy roles.

9. Clearly, young A.S. had been expecting a French-style formal garden, whereas St James's Park, prior to its improvement in 1827–9, was essentially rural.

10. The 'Italian Opera' which the Schopenhauers visited was the Old Opera House at Covent Garden (rebuilt in 1792, it was to be burned to the ground in 1808). Evidently A.S., who was to have singing lessons at Mr Lancaster's, enjoyed opera.

11. It has not been possible to identify the Harris family from the little information given by A.S. It is possible that they are related to James Harris, first Earl of Malmesbury, who was Minister at Berlin from 1772 to 1776 and negotiated a new alliance between Britain and Prussia in 1794; his wife was a granddaughter of John Abraham Korteen, a merchant of Hamburg. H.F.S. had many opportunities to get to know James Harris, although this may have no bearing on our present Harris family. In her diary J.S. gives a fuller account of the boarding school for young ladies, which she places in the unlikely setting of 'Southwark' (then a somewhat insalubrious district comprising the northern part of the present borough). The school may have been in nearby Walworth. Perhaps it was the girls from this school that the Schopenhauers saw on their Sunday jaunts into Surrey and Kent, which would inevitably have taken them along the Borough High Street. Be these facts as they may, J.S.'s account of the school is particularly interesting:

Girls' Boarding School

In the course of our outings in the neighbourhood of London we often met, on Sundays, a crocodile of 30 or 40 young girls walking demurely to church along the footpath at the side of the road. It was a charming spectacle. We would meet them dressed in snowy white and wearing pretty straw hats, walking along two by two, some of them just blossoming into youthful beauty, others still with the fresh complexions and rosy cheeks of childhood. Several teachers accompanied them, watching like hawks over every step they took and every look that crossed their faces, in order that no joyful skip or sign of laughter might be allowed to slip out unobserved on their way to church. Occasionally a similar crocodile of boys would approach from the other direction, also churchward bound, accompanied by their masters. The teachers would greet one another as acquaintances, but the children would only peep at one another out of the corner of their eyes and walk on with unnaturally straight faces. The boys were from one of the many boarding schools, who get driven to church twice a day on Sundays. Villages and towns in these parts abound with such academies, all of which flourish since hardly anyone brings up his children at home, where they would cause too much noise and commotion. As soon as boys and girls emerge from the nursery they are packed off to these establishments, and only return to their parental homes when their education is complete and they themselves nearly grown up.

In such institutions girls learn a little of everything, but hardly anything in any depth. They are taught history and geography, and yet an Englishwoman rarely knows what things are like outside her own country and what happened there in history. They also receive instruction in French and Italian, but the foreigner who is unable to speak English profits little by this, being unlikely to find, in society, any woman able to answer him in a foreign language. Music and drawing are practised very superficially, and generally only to be forgotten again as quickly as possible. The girls learn to embroider and to make paper flowers; they make pretty articles of pasteboard, little boxes of gold paper, vases of eggshell, a thousand dainty little things; but the things that they will actually need to know when they have their own establishments, normally remain an unopened book to them. The main aim in life of the majority of headmistresses of such establishments is for themselves and their pupils to shine once a year when the parents and relations assemble for the annual speech-day. Months before this day serious instruction stops and all energies are devoted to training the children to perform on the great day. They are taught pieces of music which they will perform mechanically before the delighted audience; drawings are made with the help of the drawing-master, and so forth, but the main thing is to drill them for the ball which will be held in the evening, and the dancing-master is accordingly hardly off the premises for weeks on end.

A lady of our acquaintance [Mrs Harris], whose daughters attended a boarding school at Southwark, near London, took us to just such a speech-day. The proprietress of the extensive premises received us most politely. We were led into a large room at one end of which the rapturous mothers and other relatives of the young girls were sitting; the pupils themselves were as it were displayed at the end of the hall on benches rising one behind the other as in an amphitheatre. And a very charming spectacle they made. Imagine fifty young girls from eight to sixteen, pretty, blooming with health, simply but tastefully dressed in their uniforms with snow-white short dresses and blue shoes. A silver net over their hair and a silver sash around their waists were their only finery. There they were, aglow with youthful expectation and joy.

Under the direction of the dancing-master the ball finally began. The girls danced various demure dances among themselves; no waltzes, no shawl-dances, no capers, just a kind of minuet for six or eight couples, which the dancing-master had composed specially for them, and which is probably danced nowhere else in the world than in boarding-schools like this. The girls, who danced very well, had little solos to perform as well, in order to show their paces. When the dance was over they were praised and embraced by their mothers and relatives. Just two little Dutch girls were left standing, sad and unnoticed, in a corner; no one bothered about the foreign girls who had been sent here to be educated. We, foreigners too, felt for them, called them over to us, told them that we had not long ago passed through their country, and were soon repaid by seeing happiness shining out of their clear childs' eyes too. When the — rather boring — set-piece dances were eventually over, it was the turn of some English and Scottish dances. Glad to be freed from constraint, the dear children started dancing more spiritedly, and some young cousins and brothers who were present received permission to join in.

We watched their carefree joy with lumps in our throats. As they danced the charming creatures were preparing themselves for life, the full earnestness of which will — as these words are being written — long since have caught up with them. Then so many bright eyes were looking forward to the future as though it too were a dance of joy; now those same eyes are probably filling with tears as they think back with nostalgia to those days that are gone for ever. Thinking with foreboding of the future that awaited them, we left them, joyful as ever, with unvoiced hopes for their future happiness.
(J.S., *SS*, XVI, 251-6.)

12. The Percivals, who lived in upper Sydenham, were probably Samuel and Mary Percival, whose son George was born on 12 April 1789. Young Percival is the only English boy with whom A.S. was friendly. His father was most likely a partner in the banking firm of Willis Wood Percival and Co. of 76 Lombard Street; in August 1792, when John William Anderson was appointed a trustee of the Subscription towards the Succour of the People of Poland (and himself subscribed £100), this was one of the firms of bankers by whom subscriptions were received.

13. Sir James Durno of Atrochie (1751-1807) came from Aberdeenshire; knighted in 1799, he was a retired diplomat and an old friend of H.F.S. and J.S. As British Consul in Prussia (*c.* 1781) and HM Consul-General at Memel he knew the Schopenhauers in their Danzig days and was now glad to repay their hospitality. He was presumably a cousin of the artist James Durno (1750?-95), son of the proprietor of a brewery at Kensington Gravel Pits, who was a native of North Britain; cousin or not, the artist lived in Rome from 1774.

14. The 'panorama' depicting the battle of Lodi was Mr Porter's 'Grand National Painting' of the battle of Lodi, one of the miscellaneous entertainments for which the Lyceum (next door to the Exeter 'Change in

Wellington Street) was used following rebuilding in 1794; 'battle pictures' were one of the main attractions. A.S. went back to the Lyceum on 15 October, when he saw Mr Porter's 'Siege of Seringapatam'. It was there that Mme Tussaud's waxwork figures were first shown in 1802; but in 1789 James Woodforde had already paid 2s to see 'some very curious Wax Work' there.

15. By 'Haymarket' A.S. means the Theatre Royal, Haymarket, late Mr Foote's, managed by George Colman the Younger, author of *The Mountaineers*, a hardy perennial inspired by Cervantes' *Don Quixote*, which was first performed in 1793; James Woodforde saw it at the same theatre in 1794. R.W. Elliston and C.J. Matthews were both famous actors.

16. The Royal Circus, situated near the turnpike in Blackfriar's Road, St George's Fields, was a rival of Astley's; in those days the borderline between spectacle, theatre, burletta and circus was by no means clear-cut. When Sophie von La Roche visited the Royal Circus in 1786 trick riders, tumblers and plays were to be seen; the performance she saw also included an operetta. *The Picture of London for 1803* praises the Royal Circus as an 'exhibition of ballets, pantomimes, and horsemanship'.

17. The kind of execution to which A.S. is referring is described by Crabb Robinson in a letter to his brother Thomas dated 22 October 1804:

> The next day Saturday the 15th [October 1804] . . . The morning was passed in attending an Execution which raised my curiosity but did not gratify it, and which left permanent impressions of disgust which for a long while afterwards haunted my imagination. It was a Beheading, but in a way quite different from ours. I was placed near enough to see the operation but not to see the catholic ceremonies which might have been psychologically interesting. The wretch was drawn in a cart & being a mere vulgar murderer, expressed nothing on his countenance but that stupid despair which does not suffer the spectator to sympathise with the individual, he can only mourn over the degradation of human nature. Near the gallows in Germany there is generally built a sort of circular elevation in the shape of a tub some twenty feet in diameter. After the Victim had at the Entrance performed all the religious ceremonies, With great rapidity he was led by two Men & blindfolded & put into a chair. The Executioner came behind him with a broad Sword which he held under his cloak & in an instant with a back handed blow the head was struck off. And instead of it three spouts of blood were seen which played for some considerable time while the headless trunk sat upright in the chair as if nothing had happened. At the instant the blow was struck a Priest approached the Edge of the circular elevation And addressed the mob with coarse emphasis & a sort of eloquence which I acknowledged to be not unfit for the audience tho' disgusting to me. The first sentence was an exclamation 'See my friends the consequences of not going to confession! . . .'

18. The hanging will have taken place outside Newgate Prison, executions at Tyburn having been discontinued in 1784. A.S. was following the 'ridiculous rage of going to Newgate' condemned by Horace Walpole; presumably he hired a window at the Magpie and Stump, opposite the prison, a custom on which the landlord must have grown tolerably rich.

19. The newspaper in which Fitz-James's performance was advertised was not *The Times*. The combination of swashbuckling stage name (cf. James Fitzjames, Duke of Berwick, 1670-1734, marshal of France) and the preposterous price of the tickets suggests that Fitz-James may have been a self-assured charlatan. It is nonetheless good to see A.S. enjoying himself in 15-year-old style.

20. Cf. diary entries for 16 and 22 June. The Solly family had been involved in the Baltic timber trade since the time of Richard Solly (1694-1729). H.F.S. first knew Isaac Solly [I] (1725-1802), who lived in Jeffrey Square, St Mary Axe, and in the country house in Hoe Street, Walthamstow, purchased by his father. He and H.F.S. no doubt attended the Baltic Exchange together, which was also in St Mary Axe. In 1803 Isaac Solly [I] had recently died; his obituary speaks of his 'long residence abroad', so H.F.S. no doubt first met him in Danzig; he will have seen him again in London in 1787 and 1796. The 'Mr Solly' with whom the Schopenhauers now dined was his son, Isaac Solly [II] (1769-1853), who succeeded his father as Baltic merchant and head of Isaac Solly and Sons, merchants, of 15 St Mary Axe. The scale of his business can be judged from the fact that during the earlier part of the Napoleonic Wars he is reported to have instructed his agent in Danzig to buy up all the oak planks in Prussia and Poland; he had contracts to supply British naval dockyards with Polish oak and Russian hemp. In 1803 he lived at Clapton. The fact that the Schopenhauers were invited to dine with two other members of the family shows that H.F.S. was an old friend. In 1804 Isaac Solly [II] moved into Leyton House, Church Road, Walthamstow, which had been built by David Gansel senior in 1706. There is an undated early engraving of the house in Vestry House Museum, Walthamstow. In later years Isaac Solly [II] had a distinguished public career. He was chairman of the London Dock Company for twenty years, and was offered (but declined) the chairmanship of the company to build Marc Brunel's Thames Tunnel, an enterprise in which another friend of H.F.S., Sir Claude Scott, was involved. For many years a director of Royal Exchange Assurance, he was instrumental in setting up the London Fire Brigade and helped to establish London University. He became chairman of the British and American Steam Navigation Company (the precursor of the Cunard Line) and first chairman of the London and Birmingham Railway. He was a keen supporter of political reform and of charitable work. His bankruptcy in 1837, apparently the result of losing sight of his own affairs, is no excuse for his omission from *DNB*. His obituary said that 'Seldom has a private gentleman left so many behind him to remember him with gratitude.' For these details of his life I am indebted to E.F. Clark's *George Parker Bidder, the Calculating Boy* (1983), and to Lyn Arlotte of the Local Studies Section, Vestry House Museum, Walthamstow. E.F. Clark's book includes a portrait of Isaac Solly II. By a coincidence typical of this story, when Fanny Burney, in 1826, was trying to obtain a pension for Thomas Lancaster's indigent, widowed sister-in-law, one of the friends she approached was a sister of Isaac Solly II, Dame Maria Domville (*c.* 1780-1863; wife of Sir William Domville, 1774-1860, of Southfield Lodge, Eastbourne).

21. From about 1780 to 1828 Exeter 'Change (in Wellington Street, Strand, hard by the Lyceum) housed 'Pidcock's Exhibition of Wild Beasts'

(later the 'Royal Menagerie'). James Woodforde saw 'some very curious wild Beasts' there in 1789, which cost him 1s; what he did not say was that the beasts in question (lions, tigers, monkeys, etc.) were kept in cages and dens *upstairs* in the building. The menagerie was a favourite tourist spectacle.

22. The Covent Garden theatre which the Schopenhauers visited was the 'old' theatre (rebuilt in 1792; burned down in 1808). *The Stranger* was a translation of Kotzebue's *Menschenhass und Reue* by Benjamin Thompson; it appeared (together with other plays, mostly by Kotzebue) in his *The German Theatre* (6 vols, 1800). The second play was Thomas Holcroft's *A Tale of Mystery*, which had been on since the previous November. A fuller account both of the Covent Garden theatre and of these performances is contained in J.S.'s diary.

23. Presumably the Friends' Meeting House in St Martin's Lane, Westminster; unfortunately they did not sign the book.

24. There is an obvious mistranscription: it was, of course, the Leverian Museum, so named after its founder, Sir Ashton Lever (1729–88), who was a passionate collector of natural objects. When his collection was offered to the British Museum in 1783 the Trustees turned it down. In 1788 Lever disposed of his collection, which had cost over a million pounds to assemble, by public lottery; the lottery raised only some 7,000 guineas. The winner, a Mr J. Parkinson, exhibited the collection in a building called the Rotunda specially erected on the Surrey side of Blackfriars Bridge. The museum was disposed of (by auction) in 1806. James Woodforde described the Leverian Museum as 'one of the first Sights in London', which is also how it was described in *The Picture of London for 1803*:

> This is the completest and most interesting collection of *natural curiosities* in the metropolis . . . To describe the contents, would be to re-write Buffon's, or any other voluminous Natural History; the birds in particular, exceed 5000 in number, and contain 1600 several species. Besides quadrupeds, birds, fishes, insects, fossils, shells, and corals, there are a great variety of antiquities and curious relics.

These are the bare bones. It was left to Fanny Burney's sister Susan to provide posterity with an enthusiastic and more informative description of the collection, which she did in a letter to Fanny dated 19 July 1778:

> Saturday Morning we spent extremely well at Mr. L — Sir Ashton Lever's Museum I mean. — Mr. Anson call'd here with Miss Clayton and carried my mother, Charlotte, and myself there. I wish I was a good Natural Historian that I might give you some idea of our entertainment in seeing birds, beasts, shells, fossils, etc — but I can scarce remember a dozen names of the thousand I heard that were new to me. — The birds of paradise, and the humming birds, were I think among the most beautiful — There are several pelicans — flamingos — peacocks (one quite white) — a penguin. Among the beasts a hippopotamus (sea-horse) of an immense size, an elephant, a tyger from the Tower — a Greenland bear and its cub — a wolf — two or three leopards — an Otaheite dog, a very coarse

ugly looking creature — a camelion — a young crocodile — a room full of monkeys — one of which presents the company with an *Italian Song* — another is reading a book — another, the most horrid of all, is put in the attitude of *Venus de Medicis*, and is scarce fit to be look'd at. Lizards, bats, toads, frogs, *scorpions* and other filthy creatures in abundance. There were a great many things from Otaheite — the compleat dress of a Chinese Mandarine, made of blue and brown sattin — of an African Prince — A suit of armour that they say belonged to Oliver Cromwel — the Dress worn in Charles 1st's time — etc — etc — etc — In one of the back rooms we found ourselves within hearing of a delightful Concert — but I dared not stop to listen to it — the ciceroni (Sir Ashton was not in town) told us it was at *Giardini's* house — which overlooks the gardens of Leicester House — He and others were playing quartettos charmingly . . .

(Quoted from *The Early Diary of Fanny Burney*, Bohm edn, II, 1913, 248.) A fuller and no less enthusiastic description of the collection and its founder will be found in *Sophie in London, 1786* (ed. C. Williams, 1933), and it may well have been Sophie von La Roche's description that prompted the Schopenhauers to visit it.

25. Mistranscription: the museum was Merlin's Mechanical Museum at 11 Princes Street, Hanover Square, a celebrated collection of ingenious mechanical devices or 'scientific toys' (as Horace Walpole described them), invented and assembled by John Joseph Merlin (1735–1803; one-time assistant to James Cox of Cox's Museum in Spring Gardens), and established in Princes Street, Hanover Square, in the late 1770s. Merlin was a Frenchman, born at Huys, who came to England in the suite of the Spanish ambassador in 1760, at the age of 25. He was a clever but absurd man, a mechanician always trying new inventions. Fanny Burney writes of him as 'That absurd creature Merlin' and makes fun of his mispronounced English. He was a maker of mathematical instruments, of watches, 'rose-engines' (lathes), etc.; he contrived all kinds of mechanical novelties, from barrel organ-harpsichords to gambling machines. Dr Burney, at whose house Merlin was an ever welcome guest, gives him credit for turning the octave stop on the old double harpischord into a third unison. He improved, as well as tuned, pianofortes, and devised carriages, swings, tables and hairs, all called after himself. The 'Merlin-chair' for invalids was once well known. 'Merlin has been here to tune the fortepianos,' Mrs Thrale wrote to Miss Burney on 4 January 1781, 'He told Mrs Davenport and me that he had thoughts of inventing a particular mill to grind old ladies young, as he was so prodigiously fond of their company. I suppose he thought we should bring *grist*. Was that the way to put people in *tune*, I asked him'. His museum closed in 1808, following his death in 1803. A.S. clearly preferred Weeks's Mechanical Museum, which he visited on 25 October. His reaction to Merlin's Museum is similar to that of the seventeen-year-old Evelina to Cox's Museum: 'It is very fine, and very ingenious . . . but I seem to miss something' (Fanny Burney, *Evelina*, 1778, letter XIX). A full and much more enthusiastic account of Merlin's Museum is to be found in *Sophie in London*.

26. In her diary J.S. has a rather fuller description of Westminster Abbey, but A.S. was more moved by it. Like C.P. Moritz before him, he seems to have been most impressed by Poet's Corner, where he too found what Heine was to call 'my friends in Westminster Abbey'.

27. This remained one of A.S.'s favourite and most characteristic quotations.

28. The Richmond stage left from the White Hart inn, not far from the New Church in the Strand; in 1782 the journey cost 2s. Richmond, and especially the view from Richmond Hill, featured on most travellers' itineraries. The inn from which A.S. got such a prodigious fine view was the Star and Garter, which J.S., in her fuller account of the beauties of Richmond, calls 'one of the finest inns in England', a verdict which most contemporary travellers would have echoed. Sylas Neville wrote that 'the view of the Thames from Richmond Hill is delightful'; he dined at the Star and Garter 'in a room which commands a delightful view of the river' (*Diary*, 8, 21). Richmond did not impress A.S. as deeply as it did his 'sentimental' predecessor, Moritz, who wrote:

> Sweet Richmond! never, no never shall I forget that lovely evening, when from thy fairy hills thou didst so hospitably smile on me, a poor lonely, insignificant traveller! As I traversed to and fro thy meads, thy little swelling hills, and flowery dells, and above all, that queen of all rivers, thy own majestic Thames, I forgot all sublunary cares, and thought only of heaven and heavenly things. Happy, thrice happy am I, I again and again exclaimed, that I am . . . here in *Elysium*, in Richmond!

(*Moritz's Travels in England*, 106.) Contemporary engravings by August[ine] Heckel, a native of Augsburg who lived in Richmond until 1770, both enable us to admire the famous view and show us the old Star and Garter inn. These engravings, reproduced in Hugh Phillips's *The Thames about 1750* (1951), include 'A View from Richmond Hill up the River' and 'West View of Richmond etc. in Surrey from the Star and Garter on the Hill'. The latter is particularly interesting because it shows the famous old Star and Garter inn with its common wooden 'penthouse' for the entrance doorway and a signpost with a large sign standing in front of the inn. This is the inn the Schopenhauers knew; in the latter part of the nineteenth century it was replaced by the Star and Garter Hotel, which became famous for its Bohemian dinner parties. The fact that there was at Hamburg (or, more precisely, at Altona) a hill overlooking a long course of the Elbe, the view from which was compared, by the natives, to the view from Richmond Hill, shows how well England was known in Hamburg at this time.

29. The Royal Botanical Gardens (founded in 1759) also features in J.S.'s diary.

30. Pope's 'villakin' (as he called it) was at Twickenham; an engraving of the villa as it was in 1749 will be found in Hugh Phillips's *The Thames about 1750*. A.S. admired Pope; he later possessed the first five volumes of *The Works in nine volumes* of 1697, which he annotated heavily in the 1850s.

31. It is strange that a 15-year-old schoolboy did not mention the famous maze, just as it is strange — given his interest in animals — that he did

not go to see the mammoth skeleton exhibited at the little Royal Academy (see *The Farington Diary*, 7 June 1803).

32. Although Isaac Solly II had five brothers — Richard (1771-1803), Samuel (1774-1847), Edward (1776-1844), Hollis (1777-1851) and Thomas (1780-1832) — the reference is to Edward Solly (b. Walthamstow, 25 April 1776), who was both 'one of the most remarkable [art] collectors that ever lived' (*The Times*, 22 November 1905) and a successful speculator in the corn trade between Danzig and London. From *c.* 1800 to 1820 he lived in Germany, where he ran the main part of the family business (Solly und Gibsone of Danzig), this consisting chiefly in buying timber in Germany and the Baltic countries and exporting it to England; he also dealt, on his own account, in wheat, tallow and flax. He was twice married, both his wives (Lavinia Pohl and Augusta Crüger) being German. He wrote and spoke fluent German, and lived latterly in a palatial house (No. 67) in the Wilhelmstrasse in Berlin in which at least seven large rooms had walls lined with Italian paintings. He was on friendly terms with many people at court and with government-men like Hardenberg, Altenstein, Scharnhorst and Stein, their esteem and trust underlying the fact that his personal fleet of merchantmen was recognised as part of the Prussian naval reserve. During the Napoleonic wars, when the Solly family business was at its most flourishing, Edward Solly made a vast fortune — not only by buying up all the surplus oak available in Germany and at Danzig in order to sell it to the Admiralty, but also by speculating in corn. Most of his profits were spent on his art collection, which included many of the greatest masterpieces of Western art. Although his collection was also strong in paintings of the Dutch, Flemish and early German schools, Edward Solly's passion was the Italian school, and more particularly the 'different schools of the period of Raphael', which he considered 'the period of perfection'. He was the first English collector to concern himself with the Trecento, and the first to explore the Quattrocento in depth. The main feature of the Solly collection was its 'prodigious, unmatched and unmatchable strength in the Italian Schools' (Frank Herrmann, in the series of articles to which I owe much of this information about Edward Solly: 'Who was [Edward] Solly?', *Connoisseur* Vol. 164, 1967, 229-34; Vol. 165, 1967, 13-18, 153-61; Vol. 166, 1967, 10-18). In fact he assembled two collections, the first and principal one being sold to the Prussian State in 1821; the second was disposed of at Christie's in 1847. The sale of his main collection became necessary when twenty vessels belonging to the Solly fleet of merchantmen, which were plying a contraband trade with England on Prussia's behalf, were captured and confiscated by the Danes in 1809-10. It was to restore his solvency following this loss of ships and cargo that Edward Solly finally sold 3,000 of his paintings to the Prussian State in 1821. The collection had cost him some £750,000 to assemble, an immense sum when translated into today's terms. Both Hardenberg and King Frederick William were involved in the negotiations preceding the sale. The collection went on public view in 1830, in a building specifically designed for the purpose; it formed the nucleus of the collection of the National Gallery of Germany. Charles Eastlake enjoyed a private preview of the collection in 1828, at which time he was Arthur Schopenhauer's dinner companion. In 1803 the Schopenhauers, who were all interested in art, no doubt visited two art

galleries that same morning in preparation for dining with Edward Solly. Following the sale of his principal collection, Edward Solly moved back to England, where he forsook the timber trade and took to dealing in paintings instead. He was not only one of the greatest English collectors; he was also a figure of great importance in the history of Anglo-Prussian relations, a subject on which he wrote in his *Versuch einer Berichtigung deutscher Urteile über Englands äussere und innere Verhältnisse* (1816).

33. No 'Roman Gallery' is listed in contemporary guidebooks or in histories of London; it may be misnamed. The best-known collection of paintings of the Italian school (apart from Northumberland House, which the Schopenhauers later visited) were Lord Radstock's collection and Mr Knight's collection, at their houses in Portland Place.

34. The Shakespeare Gallery, at 52 Pall Mall, was the creation of a rich printer, John Boydell (1719-1804). Boydell, London's most famous print dealer, had a shop in the Strand packed with prints and drawings; Sophie von La Roche left a description of the shop. The Shakespeare Gallery opened in 1789, the year before Boydell became Lord Mayor. His aim had been to 'form an English School of Historical Paintings' depicting 'scenes of the immortal Shakespeare'. He commissioned paintings from many artists, including Reynolds, Romney, West, Fuseli, Opie and Kauffmann. Two of the paintings were by Sir James Durno's namesake (and cousin?), James Durno (1752-95). Owing to financial embarrassments caused by the war Boydell was obliged to dispose of his collection of 170 paintings by lottery in 1804; he died shortly afterwards. James Woodforde, who visited it in 1793, described the Shakespeare Gallery as being 'filled with beautiful Paintings'.

35. What follows is a typical schoolboys' reaction; the emphasis is on the armory, the Crown Jewels and the Tower menagerie. J.S. also wrote about the Tower in her diary, and A.S.'s friend Charles Godeffroy wrote about it in a letter to A.S. in August 1804.

36. Greenwich Hospital is also described by J.S., who no doubt told Sir James Durno about her meeting with Lord Nelson, and by Sophie von La Roche, whose words 'the six buildings of this hospital . . . [create] the impression of summer palaces' (*Sophie in London*, 250) may have been in A.S.'s mind.

37. He was probably writing to his sister and to Charles Godeffroy and Lorenz Meyer, although this is only speculation; none of the letters has survived. The habit of writing letters on Monday persisted throughout his time at Mr Lancaster's.

38. Old Mrs Solly: Mrs Elizabeth Neal Solly, widow of Isaac Solly [I] (1752-1802); she lived in Hoe Street, Walthamstow. In his memoirs one of her grandsons wrote, 'I . . . recollect old Mrs Solly as a stately and rather severe old lady' (Henry Solly, *These Eighty Years*, I, 1893, 3).

39. *John Bull, or, The Englishman's Fireside*, a comedy by George Colman the Younger, had been running at Covent Garden since early March. The farce *The Lying Valet* is by David Garrick; it dates back to 1741, when it was first put on at the theatre in Goodman's Fields.

40. The furniture warehouse was most likely the well known premises of George Seddon at 150 Aldersgate Street, which Sophie von La Roche, who visited it in 1786, described as a large building with six wings

employing 400 men. The Schopenhauers may have been prompted to visit Seddon's by Sophie von La Roche's *Tagebuch einer Reise durch Holland und England* (1788; *Sophie in London*, 1933), for German visitors to England tended to follow in one another's footsteps. In her diary J.S. writes of her 'so vielen, zum Teil trefflichen Vorgängern', which must be taken as implying that she knew the work of Moritz, La Roche, Wendeborn and Archenholz, to say nothing of some other less excellent diarists.

41. If the Schopenhauers had been going back from Aldersgate Street to Old Broad Street, where Anderson Drewe and Co. had their offices, they would have passed 'Bedlam', which was situated in Moorfields; that this is what they did is further suggested by the fact that Herr Paleske, who was apparently associated with Anderson Drewe and Co., was one of those who went to Vauxhall with them that evening. Over the gateway of Bethlehem Hospital, or 'Bedlam', at this time were the statues of 'Melancholy' and 'Raving Madness' '(popularly known as the 'Brainless Brothers') by the elder Cibber.

42. Heilige Geistgasse 117.

43. It seems reasonable to suppose that Captain Barnby may have been employed by Gebrüder Schopenhauer, who ten years previously had owned four ships (none of them at that time skippered by Captain Barnby).

44. Vauxhall Gardens — 'that paradise of enchantment, with its houris in the illuminated walks, and the lamps and the fireworks, and the waterworks, and the hermit in his cave, and the Rotunda, and Madame Saqui on the tightrope, and fowl and ham and rack punch in the boxes, and poke bonnets, and scanty skirts, and roll collars and swallow-tailed coats' (Thornbury and Walford, *Old and New London*, VI, 447) — was a feature of Vauxhall Bridge Road and the old village of Vauxhall from about 1615 until 1859. *The Picture of London for 1803* speaks of 'This fashionable, and much frequented, place of summer's amusement' as being situated 'about a mile and a half from London'; part of its attraction was its 'rural beauty and easy access'. Vauxhall features in Goldsmith's *Citizen of the World* and Dicken's *Sketches by Boz*, both of which A.S. later possessed, in Smollett's *The Expedition of Humphry Clinker*, Fielding's *Amelia*, Thackeray's *Vanity Fair*, etc. Of these it is *Humphry Clinker* that is most to the point, for if A.S. and his mother saw Vauxhall with something at least of the enthusiasm of Lydia Melford —

> Image to yourself, my dear Letty, a spacious garden, part laid out in delightful walks, bounded with high hedges and trees, and paved with gravel; part exhibiting a wonderful assemblage of the most picturesque and striking objects, pavilions, lodges, groves, grottoes, lawns, temples, and cascades; porticoes, colonnades, and rotundoes; adorned with pillars, statues, and paintings; the whole illuminated with an infinite number of lamps, disposed in different figures of suns, stars, and constellations; the place crowded with the gayest company, ranging through those blissful shades, or supping in different lodges on cold collations, enlivened with mirth, freedom, and good-humour, and animated by an excellent band of music. Among the vocal performers, I had the happiness to hear the celebrated Mrs—— , whose voice was so loud and so shrill, that

it made my head ache through excess of pleasure.

In about half an hour after we arrived we were joined by my uncle, who did not seem to relish the place.

— one can imagine that H.F.S. may have seen things, rather, through the eyes of Matt Bramble:

> Vauxhall is a composition of baubles, overcharged with paltry ornaments, ill conceived, and poorly executed, without any unity of design or propriety of disposition. It is an unnatural assemblage of objects, fantastically illuminated in broken masses; seemingly contrived to dazzle the eyes and divert the imagination of the vulgar. Here a wooden lion, there a stone statue: in one place a range of things like coffee-house boxes, covered a-top; in another, a parcel of alehouse benches; in a third, a puppet-show representation of a tin cascade; in a fourth, a gloomy cave of a circular form, like a sepulchral vault half lighted; in a fifth, a scanty slip of grass-plat, that would not afford pasture sufficient for an ass's colt. The walks, which nature seems to have intended for solitude, shade, and silence, are filled with crowds of noisy people, sucking up the nocturnal rheums of an aguish climate; and through these gay scenes a few lamps glimmer like so many farthing candles.
>
> When I see a number of well-dressed people, of both sexes, sitting on the covered benches, exposed to the eyes of the mob, and, which is worse, to the cold, raw, night air, devouring sliced beef, and swilling port, and punch, and cider, I can't help compassionating their temerity, while I despise their want of taste and decorum: but when they course along those damp and gloomy walks, or crowd together upon the wet gravel, without any other cover than the cope of heaven, listening to a song, which one half of them cannot possibly hear, how can I help supposing they are actually possessed by a spirit more absurd and pernicious than anything we meet with in the precincts of Bedlam? In all probability, the proprietors of this, and other public gardens of inferior note, in the skirts of the metropolis, are, in some shape, connected with the faculty of physic, and the company of undertakers; for, considering that eagerness in the pursuit of what is called pleasure, which now predominates through every rank and denomination of life, I am persuaded that more gouts, rheumatisms, catarrhs, and consumptions, are caught in these nocturnal pastimes, *sub dio*, than from all the risks and accidents to which a life of toil and danger is exposed.

45. Moritz, who — unlike the Schopenhauers — could not afford to stay at the Castle Inn, said of Salthill that it 'can hardly be called even a village' (*Moritz's Travels in England*, 125.)

46. Rather surprisingly, A.S. does not seem to have been interested in Sir William Herschel's world-famous giant telescope, which is described at greater length by J.S.; more interesting accounts of Herschel are to be found in *The Diary and Letters of Mme. D'Arblay* (7 vols, 1842-6). Herschel, who came from Hamburg, lived in Slough.

47. In her diary J.S. writes about what is clearly the same occasion, though without the bluntness which she was to criticise in her son and which may betray his knowledge of the satirist 'Peter Pindar' (John Wolcot, 1738-1819). A.S. evidently admired Pindar's use of the telling epithet; he possessed Pindar's *Works* (4 vols, 1794-6), which he probably got to know — and may even have bought — at this time. In view of Mr Lancaster's strongly Hanoverian sentiments, it is not too difficult to imagine his reaction to the discovery of Pindar's works beneath his own roof!

48. The Palace of Oatlands first features in German travellers' accounts of England in 1584, when Lupold von Wedel called there — the court being in residence at the time — to request a passport to enable him to travel to Scotland, which he was granted by Secretary of State Francis Walsingham in person. While A.S. liked the gardens, his mother was more interested in the lonely life lived there by the Duchess of York (formerly Princess Friederike of Prussia).

49. The Rev. Thomas Lancaster's academy, at which A.S. was to spend three months as parlour boarder, was situated in what was (and is) an elegant Jacobean mansion in Wimbledon High Street, facing the Common.

50. Why the Percivals were there is not clear.

51. A.S.'s diary breaks off here until 20 September, when he was allowed to rejoin his parents in London. It may be that he kept a (pretty vitriolic) diary which has been lost or was destroyed by his mother; but it is at least as likely that he was too bored to keep a diary.

52. No doubt all three were merchant friends of H.F.S. Messrs von Hess and Mathiessen were Hamburg deputies; the latter will have been not Johann Konrad Mathiessen (formerly part-owner of the Neumühlen estate of G.H. Sieveking) but his son Erhard Adolf Matthiessen (1763-1831), who, from 1797, was head of a large firm of merchants.

53. Charles Kemble had only just moved to Covent Garden (from Drury Lane); Hamlet was one of his famous parts.

54. *The Rival Soldiers*, an operatic farce first performed at Covent Garden in 1798, was an adaptation by John O'Keefe of his own comic opera *Sprigs of Laurel* (1793).

55. If Lorenz Meyer had included such a story in one of his letters A.S. might well have been critical, but in fact the story is precisely the sort of thing that makes his diary rather livelier than his mother's.

56. Claude Scott (1742-1830) of Sundridge Park, Bromley, MP for Malmesbury. Born in Walthamstow, he married Martha Eyre of Stepney in 1767. When H.F.S. and J.S. were in England in 1787, Claude Scott was a moderately well-off corn factor working in a small counting house in the City, presumably in Great Alie Street, Goodman Fields (where he is found in a 1793 directory). By the time H.F.S. was back in England in 1797, Claude Scott was living at 7 Upper Gower Street; the year before he had purchased the Sundridge Park estate at Bromley. Now, in 1803, the Schopenhauers found him transformed into the affluent owner of a large estate and proud possessor of a brand-new house. When he bought the estate, Claude Scott demolished the ancient manor house and built a large mansion in typical Regency Graeco-Italian style. The mansion, with its three giant porticos and classical facade based on the temple of Ceres outside Rome, was the centrepiece of beautiful parklands. The layout of these

parklands and the building of the house were the combined work of Humphry Repton, John Nash and Samuel Wyatt. In 1803 Claude Scott was MP for Malmesbury Borough, a seat which he held until 1806; from 1809 to 1812 he was MP for Dungannon. Someone who dined with Claude Scott at Sundridge Park in 1803 is reported (in the *Farington Diary*) as saying that he lived 'splendidly'; Mr Scott is described (ibid.) as 'a man of very strong clear sense [who] never pretends to knowledge that he has not'. A.S. will no doubt have been interested in Mr Scott's collection of paintings.

57. The Duke of Dorset's residence at Knole Park is described in more detail by J.S. and by Fanny Burney. Unlike the young A.S., Fanny Burney found 'Knowle' 'monastic and gloomy', but she spoke of the house's pictures as 'a delicious collection' (Diary, 1779). Notwithstanding A.S.'s remark about modern furnishings, Knole is known, above all, for its pre-1590 upholstered furniture.

58. 'Tunbridge Wells . . . has . . . become the general rendezvous of gaiety and politeness during the summer' (J. Sprange, *The Tunbridge Wells Guide* [1797], 115). The Schopenhauers arrived too late. For a description of the delights of Tunbridge Wells at this time, see Fanny Burney's *Camilla* (1796), Book VI, and her Diary for 1779.

59. *Isabella* is Garrick's adaptation (1757) of Southerne's *The Fatal Marriage* (1694). *The Irishman in London* (1793) is a farce by W. Macready.

60. Mr Court, evidently a business associate of H.F.S., lived at Maryland Point, Stratford, a hamlet in West Ham. The 1821 survey of West Ham showed land (a house and garden, together with a meadow) held by Mr Court; this suggests that he was not as well-off as some of H.F.S.'s other business associates. Nothing else is known about him, but he may well be the Mr David Court who in 1802 had premises in New Road, St George's East.

61. Again one sees A.S.'s preference for non-English friends. Young Suirmand, who was apprenticed to Mr Court of Maryland Point, came from Rotterdam. Gebrüder Schopenhauer had business connections with Holland.

62. The reference is to William Mellish, who was elected MP for Middlesex in 1806; he owned an estate at Bush Hill Park in north Edmonton which was sold by his executors following his death in 1839. During the election of 1818 Mellish was spoken of by *The Times* as 'a thick and thin man for the government and a jolly, comely, hereditary Protestant' (*VCH Middlesex*, II, 58). In admiring Bush Hill Park A.S. is in company with Lysons ('The park exhibits some very pleasing scenery. It is said to have been originally laid out by Le Nautre').

63. A.S. evidently knew his Shakespeare already. A generation previously Sylas Neville had enthused about Garrick's performance as Richard III ('Garrick is inimitably great in Richard and very different from the other Richards I have seen; his expression of the dying agony of that wretch is beyond description', *Diary*, 29 September 1768).

64. Perhaps the Schopenhauers read about 'The Invisible Girl' in *The Picture of London for 1803*:

The Invisible Girl; Leicester-square.
The philosopher will here experience an uncommon result of the union of catoptric and acoustic principles. A globe of glass is

suspended by a ribbon, under which four tubes are adapted, but they do not communicate therewith, *and are likewise insulated*; by these conversation is carried on with an invisible lady, who answers every question, breathes on you, and tells every visitor whatever they hold in their hands, in an instant. This exhibition is open from ten o'clock until six. Price of admittance *two shillings and sixpence*.

There is a more detailed description of this extraordinary trick in *The Farington Diary* (II, 1923, 116):

June 28. — Lady Thomond spoke so warmly of the extraordinary contrivance called 'The Invisible Girl', at an apartment in Leicester Square, I went to see it. Four mouths of Trumpet shapes to any of which persons place their ears & hear *as from within* a voice like that of a girl, which answers any question, — describes your person & dress, sings plays on a pianoforte tells you what a Clock it is &c. &c

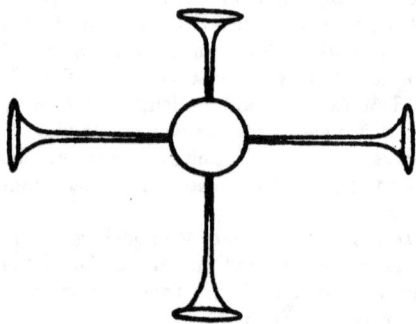

From drawing by Farington.

The Ball is suspended from the Ceiling, and with the Trumpets inclosed within a standing frame. The effect of the voice & the music was surprising, and no conjecture that was made by persons present of the nature of the contrivance seemed satisfactory. — One thought that the sound passed from *below* through Tubes into the mouths of the Trumpets & seemed to the hearer to proceed from the inside of the Ball. — The voice spoke English, — French & German. — The admittance to hear it is 2s. 6d.

So impressed was A.S. by this act that he referred to it in *WWI* (I, 358): 'we find ourselves like the hollow glass globe, from out of which a voice speaks whose cause is not to be found in it; and whereas we desired to comprehend ourselves, we find, with a shudder, nothing but a vanishing spectre'.

65. *The Provok'd Husband, or, A Journey to London* is a comedy written by

Vanbrugh and finished by Cibber; it was first performed in 1728. The afterpiece or 'entertainment' was on a similar theme. Isaac Bickerstaffe's *The Padlock*, first produced in 1768, is based on Cervantes' tale of the *Curioso Impertinente* or jealous husband.

66. The storming of his own capital, Seringapatam, by Tippoo Sahib in 1798.

67. Sheridan's patriotic melodrama *Pizarro* (1799) was an adaptation of Kotzebue's *Die Spanier in Peru* (1796); immensely successful, it serves, indirectly, to remind us that at this time Kotzebue was the most popular German dramatist in England. Sheridan's play takes its title from Francisco Pizarro (1478-1541), Spanish conqueror of Peru, who was known for the excessive cruelty which eventually caused him to be killed by his own soldiers. Spain, which had declared war on Britain in 1796, was unpopular at this time. When *Pizarro* was produced in summer 1799 Sheridan told his friends that the play was 'the finest ever known, though the plan was German'. As D.M. Stuart has written (in his *Dearest Bess: The Life and Times of Lady Elizabeth Foster*, 1955, 84 f.), the King and the Royal Family were present at Drury Lane on 5 June:

> It had been reported that His Majesty's not having gone there for so long was 'owing to Sheridan's not having "lighted him" as was the custom' — by escorting him to and from the royal box with a candle in either hand: but on this occasion the playwright 'went through all the proper ceremony'. King George
>
>> applauded very much, with taste and judgment. The Duchess of York congratulated S. for the honour he had done her country, adding that she had read Kotzebue and knew how much better *Pizarro* was, and the huge audience huzzaed at every speech or allusion to which a loyal or patriotic colour might be given.
>
> The extreme Whigs naturally fell foul of Sheridan for the 'excessive loyalty' evinced in *Pizarro*. Always sensitive as to the feelings of the inveterate enemies of their country, they were particularly affronted by the 'vulture' passage, with its ringing declaration:
>
>> The throne we honour is the people's choice; the laws we reverence are our brave fathers' legacy — tell your invaders this, and tell them, too, we seek no change, and least of all such change as they would bring us.
>
> Sheridan dined at Devonshire House on his return from a visit to the Duke of Bedford at Woburn, where the company had been 'adversely criticizing *Pizarro*':
>
>> To Lady Melbourne, who was also critical, he said, 'You are an admirable *prose* woman, but God denied you a poetic mind. You are fit only to pick out the eyes of potatoes by the dozen:

and as for Fox, he has a certain talent for speaking, and Hare
has a namby-pamby wit with a dextrous arrangement of words,
and FitzPatrick a pompous kind of decorum and propriety of
speech; but as to judgment of the theatre I had as lief talk to
my shoemaker.' Then he turned to me. 'Was not the dedication well done? You could not misunderstand it.' Then he
added in a whisper, 'Tell me anything *you* wish altered in it,
and it shall be done. Oh, that you would come, O, *Peruvienne*,
with me!' He then renewed his protestations, and was very
tender but very entertaining.

Perhaps one should add that Sheridan had been anticipated by Sylas Neville, who back in 1769 christened his horse 'Pizarro'!

68. G.F. Cooke was famous for what Alardyce Nicoll calls 'the constant backslidings of the drunken Cooke', which were, however, readily forgiven by the audience. A.S.'s account is a nice one.

69. For further accounts of the British Museum at this time see J.S.'s diary and Moritz's *Travels*.

70. Presumably 'Mr Parker' was Joseph Planta (1744–1827), FRS, Principal Librarian and Director of the British Museum (from 1799 to 1827). Planta, we are told, was qualified 'both by his knowledge of foreign languages and by his eminent courtesy of manners, for that salient part of the duties of librarianship which consists in the adequate reception of strangers' (E. Edwards, *Lives of the Founders of the British Museum*, 1870, 516). In 1801 it had been laid down that 'Foreigners and others of Rank and Men of Eminence in Science' were to be attended by the Librarians or their Assistants (*British Museum Original Papers, 1785–1809*, 18 May 1801, 745); there was no librarian by the name of Parker at this time. The Rev. Dr C.G. Woide, who showed C.P. Moritz and Sophie von La Roche round the British Museum in 1782 and 1786 respectively (and may well have shown the Schopenhauers round it in 1787), died in 1790. This excellent man and famous orientalist lived at Lisson Street, not far from Paddington (which Moritz described as 'a very village-looking little town'); he was a friend of John William Anderson, who left bequests to Dr Woide's daughters. It is amusing to read in *The Picture of London for 1803* (185 ff.) that

> Persons who are desirous of seeing the Museum, must enter their
> names and address, and the time at which they wish to see it, in
> a book kept by the porter, and upon calling again on a future day,
> they will be supplied with printed tickets, free of expence, as all fees
> are positively prohibited. The tickets only serve for the particular
> day and hour specified; and if not called for the day before, are
> forfeited . . .
>
> The spectators are allowed three hours for viewing the whole;
> that is, an hour for each of the three departments. One hour for the
> manuscripts and medals; one for the natural and artificial produc-
> tions; and one for the printed books.

71. A.S. is referring to Benjamin Goldsmid of 'The Grove', Roehampton, a bullion broker with offices in Fenchurch Street; one of four brothers,

sons of a Dutch banker who had settled in England in 1742, Benjamin Goldsmid built his mansion at Roehampton before the district became what Thackeray called 'a banking colony'; he used to give lavish parties that were reported in the social columns of the press — of a fête which he gave after the victory of the Nile (before Nelson had moved to Merton) it was said that nothing like it had been seen in England. A young visitor to Merton, George Matcham junior, thought the house fine but the decor gaudy and tasteless; he did not relish the 'Jewish food'.

72. Presumably Hennings is from Hamburg and the father of the Mlle Hennings with whom Lorenz Meyer danced at a ball at the Godeffroys' house on 14 March 1804.

73. 'Weak's Museum': Weeks's Mechanical Museum, 3 Tichborn Street, Haymarket, opened in 1803 as successor to Cox's Museum, some of whose mechanical exhibits were displayed there. In summer 1803 Weeks's Museum was a novelty; previous to its opening, two temples were exhibited, nearly 7 ft high, supported by 16 elephants, embellished with 1,700 pieces of jewellery (*The Picture of London for 1803*, 189). It became a popular place of entertainment. The exhibition room, 107 ft long and 30 ft high, and covered entirely with blue satin, was designed by James Wyatt. It contained a variety of mechanical figures and devices, including mechanical mice, birds (notably the bird of paradise) and other animals such as a steel tarantula whose 115 pieces demonstrated the spider's movements, 'much to the alarm of lady visitors'. A.S. was much more interested by it than he had been by Merlin's Mechanical Museum, which he visited on 13 June.

74. Huttwalker junior, evidently a young Hamburg acquaintance of A.S., may be Martin Hieronymus Hudtwalker, later author of a romantic novel, *Bruchstücke aus Karl Bertholds Tagebuch* (1826). *The Marriage Promise*, a comedy by John Till Allingham, was first performed at Drury Lane on 16 April 1803. The after-piece, *Fortune's Frolic*, is also by Allingham.

75. St Paul's and the Whispering Gallery are also described by J.S. in her diary.

76. With A.S.'s enthusiastic reaction to the spectacle of so many Volunteers, contrast his friend Charles Godeffroy's comment that 'The English have an immensely high opinion of their Volunteers, but those that I have seen on parade are less impressive than our Hamburgh soldiers.' Dorothy Wordsworth, for her part, merely remarked that the soldiers in Hamburg wore 'dull-looking red coats, and immense cocked hats'. A.S.'s English schoolmaster was a Volunteer.

77. T.J. Dibdin's comic opera *The Cabinet* was first performed at Covent Garden in February 1802. *The Jew and the Doctor*, also by T.J. Dibdin, was a farce dating from 1798; A.S. was probably amused by it because he associated 'Jews' with the business world which he did not wish to enter.

78. Northumberland House in Northumberland Street was the town house of the Percy family for 300 years. A grand but dull and gloomy mansion, its main feature was the ballroom or grand gallery containing large and very fine copies of celebrated classical paintings. Norfolk House, in St James's Square, was the residence of the Dukes of Norfolk.

79. Both the bespeaking of a ship and the departure from Witham were usual at the time.

IV
Arthur Schopenhauer's English Headmaster

Background

On 27 June 1803 the Schopenhauers drove out to Wimbledon, where they and their friends the Percivals dined with the Rev. Mr Lancaster, the Anglican clergyman who was to be young Arthur's headmaster for the next three months. Mr Lancaster's surname has long been known, but he has never been identified. Biographical exhumation can now reveal that when Johanna Trosiener's future childhood mentor arrived in Dumfries in 1753, her son's future headmaster was living, aged three, in the wilds of the English border country just 60 miles away, at Alston, for the headmaster and founder of what in 1803 was popularly known as 'the Rev. Mr Lancaster's Academy' was the Rev. Thomas Lancaster (1750–1823), eldest son of Thomas Lancaster senior of Alston.

Thomas Lancaster came of an old Westmorland family, the Lancasters of Barton, a cadet branch of the Lancasters of Sockbridge, who traced their ancestry back to the Norman Conquest. His father, who was curate of Culgaith at the time of his eldest son's birth, was one of the younger sons of John (1681–1746) and Agnes (1686–1750) Lancaster of Pooley and Moor End, Barton, Westmorland. In all, John and Agnes Lancaster had ten children (six sons and four daughters), born between 1711 and 1727; their fifth child, Thomas (the father of our headmaster), was, like Sterne's Yorick, born in the year 18. When the time came, he attended the local free grammar school, Barton School, whose most famous headmaster, the Rev. Joseph Wilson, had been appointed on 31 May 1723. As a feoffee of the school John Lancaster would have had a hand in the appointment. His son was one of the first boys to pass through the school in its heyday, as described in James Clarke's *Survey of the Lakes* (1787):

> During the time that Mr. Wilson was master, 1723–1759, scholars were sent to him from the remotest parts of the British Empire. Since his death, in 1759, the School has been much upon the decline.
>
> It is customary for the master to give the scholars a prize to fight cocks for; the master for this gets what is called the 'cock penny', being a present according to the ability of the scholar, and the cock-fighting is held either at Shrove-tide or Easter. This custom seems to have originated in that care which was taken here to instil in youth a martial and enterprising spirit . . .
>
> Opposite to Barton School is a field called Dodgey-Rays, whither Mr. Wilson used always to send any of his boys who were imperfect in their tasks in order to get them better; so common and well-known was this punishment that to send a person to Dodgey-Rays is become a proverbial expression in this country.[1]

After leaving Barton School, Thomas Lancaster senior either worked on the family farm for a few years or was employed as an usher, or tutor. In due course he matriculated at Glasgow in 1739, thus breaking the family tradition by which the Lancasters had been sending their sons to Oxford since 1350, and to Queen's College since 1467. He arrived in Glasgow at more or less exactly the same time that Tobias Smollett was leaving the city which he described as one of the prettiest towns in Europe. Smollett studied at Glasgow in the early 1730s and served his surgical apprenticeship there from 1735 to 1739. No doubt Thomas Lancaster also found the 'college' a 'respectable pile of buildings' and enjoyed an education which Smollett described as in some respects preferable to the English. Thomas Lancaster took his MA in 1742 and therefore left Glasgow a matter of weeks before Alexander Carlyle arrived there; though separated by only a few weeks, they studied under different professors of divinity (Lancaster studied under old Professor Polter, Carlyle under his successor, Professor William Leechman); but they both also studied under Professor Hutcheson (Professor of Moral Philosophy), who performed in Glasgow the same kind of civilising role that John Stevenson performed with such notable success in Edinburgh.

Thomas Lancaster was ordained deacon on appointment as

curate of Culgaith in 1745. Culgaith, about four miles east of Penrith in the northernmost Pennines, is a long, straggling village, beautifully situated on the top of an eminence above the river Eden and commanding an extensive prospect on every side. Thomas Lancaster presumably acted as schoolmaster as well as curate of the ancient chapel, which had long since fallen into decay (it was to be rebuilt in 1758 by his successor). The cure of Culgaith was in the patronage of the vicar of nearby Kirkland (Cumberland), and it was at Kirkland Church, on 29 April 1749, that Thomas Lancaster married Ruth Williamson. Following their marriage they settled at Alston. No doubt Swift's description of the country parson of a generation earlier is still applicable to the life led by Thomas and Ruth Lancaster in those reaches of the north where change happens very slowly:

> He liveth like an honest plain farmer, as his wife is dressed but little better than a Goody. He is sometimes graciously invited by the squire, where he sits at an humble distance. If he gets the love of his people, they often make him little useful presents. He is happy by being born to no higher expectation, for he is usually the son of some ordinary tradesman or middling farmer. His learning is much of a size with his birth and education, no more of either than a poor hungry servitor can be expected to bring with him from college.[2]

The life initially led by his son, Schopenhauer's future headmaster, was much the same.

Thomas and Ruth Lancaster had six children. Thomas, our headmaster, was their eldest; he was born on 8 August 1750 and baptised on 5 September 1750.[3] Shortly afterwards, on Sunday 28 October 1750, Thomas Lancaster senior was ordained priest at a private ordination in Durham Castle chapel held by Martin [Benson], Bishop of Gloucester; he was licensed to the cure of 'Aldstone' (Alston) with Garrigill, then worth £20 per annum, on 18 July 1754, and was instituted vicar of Alston on 11 September 1756; there is a record of his subscription to the 39 Articles on that occasion. He was therefore vicar when Alston Church was rebuilt in 1769. In 1773 he appointed his son, Thomas, to the curacy of Alston. He lived until his son had bought the mansion in Wimbledon which was to house his academy in its heyday. He died on 9 December 1789, aged 73; his arms can be seen in Alston Church. His wife died on 6 March 1807, aged 84.

Thomas Lancaster junior passed both his childhood and his early manhood in the Alston Moor area, a wild, remote and therefore backward district, but one which was just beginning to change. Change, and indeed revolution, is a key factor in the background to our headmaster's life; no doubt it helps to explain his innate conservatism. With his life extending from 1750 to 1823, Thomas Lancaster was a contemporary of men like Goethe, William Blake, Thomas Bewick and R.B. Sheridan. That said, he puts one in mind more of the men of the previous generation. His lifetime included the industrial revolution, the agricultural revolution, the Enclosure Acts (1750–1810), a revolution in transport, the French Revolution, the Napoleonic Wars, and so on. The population of Britain doubled during his lifetime.

The first changes of which he became aware were those connected with the rapid expansion of lead and silver mining in the Alston Moor area from 1750, although his father would also have told him about the fighting in the Penrith area in 1745 and the barbaric executions at Carlisle and Brampton the following year, when those brought to the bar for sentence were told by Chief Baron Parker:

> You, every one of you, prisoners at the bar, return to the prison from whence you came, and from thence you must be drawn to the place of execution; when you come there you must be hanged by the neck, but not till you are dead, for you must be cut down alive; then your bowels must be taken out, and burnt before your faces; then your heads must be severed from your bodies and your bodies divided into four quarters, and these must be at the King's disposal; and God have mercy on your souls.[4]

Such was the fate meted out to a total of 31 prisoners at Carlisle, Brampton and Penrith in October-November 1746. It is the fate to which Richard Jameson would have been exposed if he were out in '45. Whether the newly appointed curate saw them or not, the Highlanders passed through Culgaith on 15 December 1745.

It was, however, the Jacobite rebellion of 1715 that led, indirectly, to the expansion of mining that was to change the face of Alston Moor. When the Earl of Derwentwater was executed for his share in the rebellion, his property, which included the manor of Alston Moor and many adjoining estates, was confiscated. After some delay the estates, with their mineral rights, were granted to Greenwich Hopsital, which already owned some scattered mines in the area. This is not the place to relate the story of the expansion that followed; it is sufficient to say that it was by far the most visible event of Thomas Lancaster's childhood. Thus a new, model village, Nent Head, was built a few miles away from Alston in 1753.

Alston Moor is an area of rough moorland, much of it over 2,000 ft above sea level, with deep valleys and steep fellsides. It is 'a land of steep slopes with rocky crags, and wild moorland bogs, with isolated farms and hamlets at heights that are very unusual in this country'.[5] The principal habitation was Alston, which in 1750 was a market village. It would be difficult to overemphasise the barren wildness of the landscape and the savagery of the climate in winter. When Thomas Lancaster was ten years old Bishop Pococke visited Alston and the surrounding district, presumably calling on his father, the vicar; he left interesting descriptions of the area and, especially, of its inhabitants:

> Alston was on the road from Penrith to Hex[h]am and Newcastle; but since this turnpike road has been made by Burgh they all go that way, so that Alston not being frequented there is a very agreeable, honest simplicity among the people. Most of the miners come home before Sunday, and on Monday carry their provision for the week to the mines; the women wear the large bonnets which were in fashion in the south the latter end of the last century.[6]

Thus Parson Lancaster's own wife may well have appeared the 'goody' described by Swift.

In due course the young Thomas Lancaster was sent to Appleby Grammar School, the nearest such school to Alston. He was there from 1756 to 1768. John Wesley, when he first visited it in 1766, called Appleby 'a country town worthy of Ireland, containing at least five and twenty houses'.[7] A few years later Thomas Pennant described it as a small town consisting of a single street irregularly built on the steep slope of a hill, with the castle on the summit. Nicholson and Burn, writing in 1777, added that the shambles and town hall in the middle of this street greatly incommoded it; if these were taken away, they argued, the street would be very grand and elegant.[8] As it was, any intimations of *grandezza* were countered by the ubiquitous dunghills in the streets which were a frequent cause of concern to the corporation. In the mid-eighteenth century bullbaiting was a common spectacle in the market place, while for the recalcitrant human inhabitants there were the stocks and pillory at the end of the open hall facing the Low Cross, to say nothing of a whipping post and place for branding criminals (with M for malefactor) on the hand. These must have been common sights in young Thomas Lancaster's schooldays.

He attended Appleby Grammar School during the long and distinguished headmastership of Richard Yates, which lasted from 1723 to 1781.[9] It was in 1747 that the chancellor of the diocese of Carlyle, John Waugh, noted that 'Mr. Richard Yates, A.M., of Queen's College, in Oxford, is the present Master and has the school in as good repute as ever has been before his time.' A few years after Thomas Lancaster left the school, Nicolson and Burn commented that:

> He hath executed that office for the space of fifty years, with honour, ability, assiduity, and learning, [and] hath instructed two generations of gentlemen and others, not only in the town and neighbourhood, but from many other parts of the Kingdom, and furnished during that time nearly half the foundation of Queen's College . . . who together with classical precepts, hath been always solicitous, by his example and every method of instruction, to recommend the practice of virtue and religion.[10]

Yates was the outstanding, progressive headmaster of a classical seminary in which Latin grammar and literature loomed large. Textbooks used in Thomas Lancaster's day included Clarke's Suetonius, Cook's Horace, and the Delphin edition of Cicero's *Orations*; Yates took passages for translation into Latin from the *Spectator*. The ushers in young Thomas Lancaster's time were John Farrer (*c*. 1755-6), Thomas Robertson (1756-8), Septimus Collinson (1758-9), Matthew Powley (1759-60) and William Kendal (1760-8). Thomas Lancaster probably also took lessons from the writing-master, Mr Parkinson (1734-?). It is particularly interesting to find him being taught by Septimus Collinson (1740-1827) during the latter's year as usher. Collinson went on to become Provost of Queen's and Lady Margaret Professor of Divinity; he had a reputation for preaching good sermons in a Cumberland accent so strong as to be scarcely comprehensible, and is said to have 'belonged in spirit to the eighteenth century',[11] as did his young pupil after him.

Thomas Lancaster left school in September 1768 and, says the list of benefactors to the school, 'got the school of . . . soon after'.[12] In 1770 he gave the customary half-guinea to the school Library

Fund inaugurated by Yates; ten years later, in 1780, he gave two books to the Bainbrigg Library. As to why he did not go up to Queen's as batteler, as his cousin was to do in 1781, it seems likely that he was not bright enough to win the Thanet Exhibition. Instead, he got the mastership of Maughanby Grammar School soon after leaving school.

Village Schoolmaster

Maughanby is, or was, a hamlet near the village of Glassonby (two or three miles south-east of Kirkoswald) in the parish of Addingham, Cumberland; it was accordingly about ten or twelve miles from Thomas Lancaster's parents' and grandparents' homes at Alston and Barton respectively. Now Maughanby is little more than the name of a farm which the old Free Grammar School buildings have become.

Maughanby School was founded, and endowed with some 70 acres of land, by the Rev. Edward Mayplet, vicar of Addingham and prebendary of Carlisle, some time before his death in 1624. In Bishop Nicolson's notes on his visitation of the diocese in 1703-4 the school buildings are listed as 'A large school house, a mansion house; a barn and a beast house'.[13] This description is, however, misleading (especially as regards the 'mansion house'), for Chancellor Waugh recorded in his copy of Bishop Nicolson's *Miscellany* under 14 May 1748:

> I called at Maughanby School and found the School, House, (now turned into a bier [*sic*], so that no place for the master to live in, or indeed a Farmer) and out Houses very bad — all the Houses and Glebe are neglected and suffered to run to ruin.[14]

In view of this it is most unlikely that Thomas Lancaster lived in the old schoolhouse;[15] he is more likely to have lodged locally, possibly at Kirkoswald with his future wife's family. Be that as it may (in 1769 he was not yet engaged) by 1819 a report was published which stated, 'There is no dwelling house upon the estate.'[16]

The old schoolroom and the old schoolhouse still stand — the latter in the form of a byre — in the farmyard at Maughanby. In Thomas Lancaster's time the master of Maughanby School had either to farm the 70 acres himself or find a tenant to do so. The land provided his main income; it was impossible to live on the master's pittance. One is, inevitably, reminded of the third chapter of Macaulay's *History of England* (1848), with its brilliantly hostile description of the country clergy in the early eighteenth century. The country clergyman, he argues, was not regarded as, and indeed was not, a gentleman, for 'often it was only by toiling on his glebe, by feeding swine, and by loading dungcarts, that he could obtain daily bread'; he was ill-informed, grossly prejudiced, and a passionate supporter of the Tories.[17] It has to be said that this sounds very like the Anglican clergyman as seen by Schopenhauer — in other words, very like Thomas Lancaster as he appeared to his German pupil's eyes. There is no evidence either that Thomas Lancaster worked the school farm himself, or that he did not. While it may be wrong to think of him at this time as a kind of Parson Trulliber, the boorish, semi-illiterate parson who was more farmer than priest *is* an historical fact, for the later eighteenth century was the time of what Gibbon called 'the fat slumbers of the Church'.[18]

Maughanby School was founded as a free grammar school for the teaching of Greek and Latin which would give those of the local children who wanted it (in a hamlet of some 180 souls) the benefit of a free education founded upon the principles of the Church of England. In practice the emphasis was on the three Rs, with a fourth R in the form of religion. The school was open to boys and girls of the parish as soon as they had learned the alphabet.[19] By a bond dating from 1676 the schoolmaster was required to attend church regularly with his pupils, and to instruct them in the principles of religion, particularly the catechism. The 1819 report noted that the children were instructed in reading, writing and arithmetic and in the classics when required; at that time three or four of the 40-60 children in the school were learning the classics.[20] In effect, however, the school had always been a village school in which local children could receive the rudiments of a church-based education; children whose parents wished them to concentrate on the classics were sent to Appleby or to one of the other established grammar schools. Maughanby School never achieved much distinction, partly no doubt because of its obscure location, but partly also because of the punitive endowment which obliged the school to pay £200 upon the death of the lord of the manor (of Melmerby) and upon a change of tenant to farm the school lands. Bishop Nicolson made the obvious comment, way back in 1704: 'What shall subsist the Schoolmaster and his Family, whilst this money is raising, is hard to determine.'²¹ No doubt this continued drain on the school's resources explains the way in which first the old schoolmaster's house, and then the schoolroom — described as a 'hovel' in 1864–5 — fell into ruin.

The Bishops of Carlisle appointed the schoolmasters in accordance with the 77th canon of the *Book of Common Prayer* (1604), which laid down that:

> No man shall teach either in publick school or private house, but such as shall be allowed by the Bishop of the diocese, or Ordinary of the place, under his hand and seal, being found meet as well for his learning and dexterity in teaching or for sober and honest conversation, and also for right understanding of God's true religion.

In practice an ability to read and to subscribe to the 39 Articles was all that was required of would-be schoolmasters. Thomas Lancaster's licence to teach at Maughanby is dated 10 August 1769 and reads as follows:

> Thos. Lancaster to Maughonby School —
> Augst. 10th. 1769. Thomas Lancaster a literate person was admitted and Licenced to be Schoolmaster of the Free Grammar School of Maughonby within the parish of Addingham in the County of Cumberland and Diocese of Carlisle. Upon the Nomination of the Lord Bishop of Carlisle aforesaid. He the said Thomas Lancasteer having first taken all and every the Oaths and made and subscribed all and singular the Matters and Things by Law in this behalf required before the Lord Bishop of Carlisle aforesaid. In the presence of me Isaac Denton Notary Public.²²

He remained at Maughanby until 9 July 1776.

By the time he resigned as master of Maughanby School the Rev. Thomas Lancaster was engaged to be married. It is impossible to imagine an accomplished and spirited young lady with a genteel fortune being keen to start married life in a ruinous schoolhouse in the middle of nowhere. At all events, his fiancée, Ann Burney, was evidently determined not to play Goody to her husband's Parson Trulliber.

In the meantime young Thomas Lancaster had determined, apparently in June 1773 — while Floris Schopenhauer was in

London — to offer himself as a candidate for ordination. In doing so he was not only following the example of his father and many paternal ancestors; he was also taking the best opportunity open to him to escape from a life of certain drudgery and penury. His father, for his part, was pleased to be able to provide his eldest son with his ordination title in the form of the curacy of Garrigill.

Thomas Lancaster's ordination as deacon (1773) and priest (1774) is fully documented in a series of extant papers[23] which include a letter testimonial of Thomas Lancaster's life and behaviour, addressed to the Bishop of Durham by Joseph Railton (rector of Knarsdale), John Farrer (curate of Haltwhistle and former usher at Appleby Grammar School), and John Ellison (curate of St Nicholas, Newcastle). Joseph Railton[24] and John Ellison[25] were friends of Thomas Lancaster senior. John Farrer was a lifelong friend of his son and is an interesting background figure at this stage of our story. Second son of John Farrer of Bousfield, Orton (Westmorland), and his wife, Isabel, he was born in 1735. He received his elementary education at home, and was then placed at grammar school under the care of Richard Yates. At this time the school was a seminary for schoolmasters and parish priests — professions which often went together at this time, when 'all the best schoolmasters are of the clergy', for 'a clergyman is a gentleman by profession and education; and . . . has the knowledge that will ground a boy, and prepare him for entering on any career with credit'.[26] For many poor boys, particularly from the north, to become a cleric was to take the only certain way of becoming something like a gentleman; but these clerical schoolmasters were down-to-earth and by no means 'too high-learnt to bring up a lad to be a man of business',[27] for this is what both John Farrer and Thomas Lancaster in their very different spheres mostly did. One of John Farrer's friends at Appleby was the poet John Langhorne (1735-79), who left the school about 1753, a couple of years before Thomas Lancaster entered it; John Farrer is featured in Langhorne's poems as 'Farrer, whose friendship warms the heart'.[28] On leaving school Farrer became schoolmaster in the village of Aycliffe in County Durham (c. 1753). Soon, however, Richard Yates recalled him to Appleby as usher (c. 1755-60) at a salary of £8 per annum. After a few years as master of Bishop Auckland School (c. 1760-6), he became master of the school at Witton-le-Wear, County Durham, where he remained from 1766 to 1794. He was ordained deacon in 1759, held a variety of cures, notably Witton-le-Wear (1765-1808) and Hamsterley (1770-1808).

John Farrer taught young Thomas Lancaster during his first year or so at Appleby and clearly made a friend of his pupil, as he did of his headmaster. Given that Thomas Lancaster was, as it were, following in John Farrer's footsteps in becoming a village schoolmaster, what more natural than that he should also have followed the example of John Farrer, whose teaching methods were described by a relative and namesake in 1844:

> In the management of his school he kept a respectful eye on the pattern set before him in his own preceptor Mr. Yates; though not without some variation, where he judged he might vary to good effect. It has been observed by one, who had been under the tuition of both, that in the conduct of a lesson Mr. Yates was more of a speaker than a hearer, Mr. Farrer was a hearer and a speaker in turn; Mr. Yates discoursed, and Mr. Farrer catechised. To adapt his teaching to the several exigencies of boys, whose future destinations were much more diversified than those of his associates at Appleby, he took a wider range in the field of education. With grammatical and classical instruction he attended to their proficiency in penmanship, arithmetic, geography, and the elementary branches of general knowledge. And he provided assistants either continued or occasional, to instruct them in French, mathematics, etc. But, in common with his own preceptor, he carefully attended to the morals of his scholars, and never failed to inculcate a serious sense of religion. This was the more special concern on Sundays, when, beside the public service, he kept them engaged in scriptural readings and religious exercises.[29]

Once, when John Farrer was conducting prayers in the old thatched cottage which was the schoolroom at Witton-le-Wear, the whole roof collapsed, to the obvious delight of his pupils, who could recognise a holiday when they saw it. If this is reiminiscent of the near-derelict schoolroom in which his young friend Thomas Lancaster was teaching at Maughanby, so is the Rev. Farrer's method, for his ex-pupil was also a catechiser. Thomas Lancaster appears to have taught in a similar way, although there is no evidence that he won his pupils' respect and affection to the same degree; he even used, as one of his texts, John Farrer's abridgement of Cordery's *Colloquies*. John Farrer was a founder-member of 'The Association of Protestant Schoolmasters of the Counties of

Durham, Northumberland, Cumberland and Westmorland and the Towns of Newcastle-upon-Tyne and Berwick-upon-Tweed'.[30] The association, formed at Newcastle-upon-Tyne in 1774, was open to schoolmasters of 35 or less resident in the area; the lowest-paid subscribed £1 per annum. Thomas Lancaster was probably a member too.

In September 1773, then, the Rev. Thomas Lancaster became an assistant curate in his father's parish of Alston with Garrigill. He retained his schoolmastership, only giving it up after he had added the curacy of Kirkby Thore (Westmorland) to his other duties about 1775; he was replaced as schoolmaster in 1776. The years at Maughanby set the pattern for his whole life, as well as his career, in that while there he not only got ordained but met his future wife, Ann Burney. He clearly enjoyed schoolmastering well enough to make a career of it; but he resolved not to live and teach in a byre. In 1777, shortly before he moved to Sunderland, one of the most distinguished works on education ever, Rousseau's *Emile, ou De l'éducation*, was published just across the North Sea, at Amsterdam. We may be sure that news of it did not reach Thomas Lancaster's ears, and that Rousseau's 'Profession de foi du vicaire savoyard' would in any case have been anathema to him, for the Rev. Thomas Lancaster was a government man in religion, as in all else.

Ann Burney was the daughter of William Burney and his wife Elizabeth (*née* Yates). William was the eighth of the nine children of William Burney (*c.* 1670–1740), a tailor, of Hexham, and his wife Jane (*née* Graham). At the time of his marriage Thomas Lancaster's future father-in-law was an illiterate farmer living at Lanercost, best known for its ruined priory, among whose 'fractured columns . . . ruined arches, choaked up vaults and unroofed walls . . . long secularized' William Gilpin enjoyed a blissful picnic.[31] He married Elizabeth Yates at Kirkoswald on 12 November 1746. They settled at Brampton, a 'very good little village, prettily situated',[32] just a fortnight after the executions to which I have already referred, and which took place on 31 October. It was at Brampton that Ann and her twin brother John were born on 22 August 1747. The Burneys presently had another daughter, Sarah (b. 29 July 1750; she was to marry a surgeon, John Lattimer, in 1781), and a son, Timothy (b. 23 July 1752). Ann Burney grew up at Hemble's Gate, on the outskirts of Brampton, the red sandstone farmhouse now known as Hemblegate Farm, of which her father was tenant. It seems that her mother died early, perhaps in

1761, and that the young family then moved to Kirkoswald, perhaps because William Burney had been offered another tenancy by his wife's affluent relatives. Thomas Lancaster probably lodged with the Yateses and found himself enamoured of their niece and her genteel fortune.

Parson

By summer 1778 our future headmaster had moved to Sunderland, where he became sub-curate and lecturer at the newly built New Chapel (St John's Chapel) attached to the parish church of Holy Trinity. The move to Sunderland was made in preparation for his marriage. At the time of his marriage he was 28 and his bride 31.

Their wedding took place at Kirkoswald on 10 September 1778. The Kirkoswald parish register records it:

> 1778, Sept. 10th, Thomas Lancaster of the parish of Sunderland and County and Diocese of Durham, Clerk, batchelor, and Ann Burney, of this Parish, singlewoman, married.

The marriage, by licence, was witnessed by the bride's sister, Sarah, Thomas Lancaster's eldest sister, Hannah, and the bride's friend Ann Hobson. William Burney, who was iliterate, did not put his mark, although he did so when Ann's younger sister Sarah married John Lattimer (a surgeon) on 22 May 1781. Whether Ann Burney's twin brother, John, was present is not recorded; it may be that he had already gone south, or that he was not invited, for there is some evidence that he was the black sheep of the family. The marriage was reported (inaccurately) in the *Newcastle Courant* on 17 October 1778,: 'Married, last week at Kirkoswald, by the Rev. Mr. Fisher, the Rev. Mr. Lancaster of Sunderland, to Miss Burney, with a genteel Fortune.' Earlier Ann was described, more fully if no less inaccurately, as being of Alston, 'niece to Timothy Yates Esq., a most accomplished lady with an independent fortune of 3,000£'.[33]

It seems likely that Thomas and Ann Lancaster had agreed, before their marriage, that they would move away from the wilderness of Alston Moor to the relative gentility of Sunderland, and that they would use her fortune to enhance their lives and further his career. This only really happened when Ann Lancaster's fortune was invested in Robert Bell's house in Wimbeldon in 1789; unfortunately she did not live to reap the social benefits of the investment.

Sunderland, in 1778, consisted chiefly of 'one good street of great length, another of less consideration in a parallel direction, and several lateral ones diverging from the principal one at right angles'.[34] The population was estimated by Thomas Lancaster himself, in 1784, at about 30,000 inhabitants; this was almost certainly an overestimate, although the town was growing fast. To Spencer Cowper, Dean of Durham from 1746 to 1774, it was 'a large filthy town inhabited by more filthy people',[35] but to the Lancasters, used not to Durham but to the wilds of the northern Pennines, it must have seemed more inviting. Little is known of the Lancasters' life there, although we may safely assume that one of those on whom they called was the Rev. Henry Egerton (rector of Bishopwearmouth from 1776 to 1795), brother of the then Bishop of Durham. Henry Egerton lived in the rectory described by Dean Cowper as 'on the same model with Dr. Sharp's in the College [Durham Cathedral close], so more magnificent than most of his Brethren's'.[36] Being possessed of a large private fortune, Henry Egerton lived in a style splendidly at odds with his position, and had his 'public' days when his house was open to all the gentry of the neighbourhood without invitation. No doubt Thomas Lancaster, who lived in Bishopwearmouth, took advantage of this engaging practice of his clerical neighbour, for he appears to have been something of a toady and something of a snob. Besides, in an age when preferments and opportunities depended so heavily on patronage, an ambitious young cleric had to look for helping hands.

On a less socially exalted plane, Thomas Lancaster naturally knew the curate of St John's, the Rev. Thomas Hall,[37] and various members of the congregation.[38] He knew the litigatious attorney Benjamin Hodgkin, and John Coxon, the rector of Sunderland, who baptised the Lancasters' first four children.[39] More significantly, he presumably also knew Dr Jeffery Ekins,[40] who at this time was a peripatetic public preacher, as well as being rector of Sedgefield (next to Trimdon, where Lancaster was appointed curate in 1780). That Thomas Lancaster met Dr Ekins is as good as certain, for Dr Ekins ended his days at Parson's Green, to which Thomas Lancaster presently moved.

By the terms of the endowment of St John's in 1769, the right of presentation for 21 years was reserved to John Thornhill, subject to the approval of the Bishop of Durham. In April 1769 the Rev. Thomas Hall was presented to the benefice of St John's, with the approbation of the bishop. When Thomas Lancaster was appointed sub-curate no such approval was deemed necessary. How and why he came to be appointed is not known, but it seems likely that the establishment of the Donnison School (a charity school for girls) in 1778 meant that a new, teaching appointment was necessary, for the girls were required to attend religious instruction on Wednesdays and Fridays as well as Sundays. There was also a charity school for boys attached to the chapel; a vestry minute dating from this time (21 July 1781) laid it down that 'each Boy who shall distinguish himself by his quick Improvement in Learning shall be indulged with an additional pair of Shoes at Midsummer every year', and that:

> instead of the Caps usually given to Charity Boys, these boys shall have each a round narrow-brimmed Hat, bound about with a narrow worsted Binding the colour of their Coats, which Binding is to be preserved and kept on under Pain of being discharged.[41]

Is it fanciful to suppose Thomas Lancaster's wife to be behind this attempt to give a touch of tone to the charity school? I think not. Although Thomas Lancaster was not schoolmaster, he was responsible for the religious instruction that will have loomed large in the boys' education.

St John's Chapel was 'a neat edifice built of brick, and ornamented with hewn stone':[42] a plain, solid Georgian building, with a typical interior — two galleries on the north side, one over the other, in theatrical style (the upper gallery being generally appropriated to the use of the soldiers from the neighbouring barracks), double-decker pulpit, and so on.[43] In all, the chapel originally accommodated 1,822 (including 610 children). When he arrived at St John's as lecturer and sub-curate Thomas Lancaster found that a row was brewing between Sunderland Vestry and the proprietors of the chapel. At issue was the question of whether the churchwardens of Holy Trinity were to continue to pay for the maintenance and repair of St John's. In 1780 the proprietors of St John's instituted proceedings in the Durham Consistory Court against the churchwardens of Sunderland in an attempt to compel them to maintain the chapel, to wit: its gates and fence. Two relevant documents exist;[44] dated 15 February 1780, they are signed by George Thompson and witnessed by Thomas Lancaster. A decision of the Consistory Court dated 2 June 1780 made it clear that the churchwardens were not responsible for the upkeep of a private chapel of rest. Thereupon the proprietors, on 15 June 1780, drew up a declaration of independence.

Whether there is any connection I do not know, but in August 1780 Thomas Lancaster was appointed curate of the chapel of Trimdon (near Sunderland). It may well be that he wished to make sure that his position was not adversely affected by the decision of the Consistory Court; he cannot have been thinking of any financial advantage, for he immediately proceeded to appoint a substitute. A letter is extant, dated August 1780, from the Patrons of the Curacy of the Chapel of Trimdon, asking for Thomas Lancaster, Clerk to the Curacy, to be licensed as curate.[45] The request was granted; the Bishop of Durham's spiritual act book shows that Thomas Lancaster was licensed to the curacy of the chapel of Trimdon on 12 August 1780. Thomas Lancaster wrote the following letter to the Bishop of Durham:

> To the Right Revd. Father in God John by Divine
> Providence Lord Bishop of Durham   Greeting
>
> These are to certify your Lordship that I Thos Lancaster Curate of the Perpetual Curacy of Trimdon in the County of your Lordship's Diocese of Durham do hereby nominate & appoint Gilfrid Gates to perform the Office of a Curate in my Chapel of Trimdon aforesaid & do promise to allow him the yearly Sum of Thirty Pounds a Year with the Surplice Fees for his Maintenance in the same & to continue him to officiate in my Church until he shall be otherwise provided of some Ecclesiastical Preferment unless by any Fault by him committed he shall be lawfully removed from the same. And I do hereby solemnly declare that I do not fraudulently give this Certificate to entitle the said Gilfrid Gates to receive Holy Orders, but with a real Intention to employ him in my said Chapel according to what is before expressed.
>   Witness my Hand this)
>   14th Day of Septr. 1780) Thomas Lancaster
>   Curate of Trimdon[46]

Although interesting as one of only three by Thomas Lancaster to have survived, the letter is a formal one, following a prescribed pattern, and written by a scribe.

For the most part the Lancasters' time will have passed fairly quietly, with the occasional minor excitement, which, in Sunderland, had to do mostly with the sea or the weather, although political events will have been very much under discussion too. The Lancasters moved to Sunderland a few months after the death of Chatham, and the War of American Independence was the background to most of their time there, although it will not have dominated their lives to the extent to which the Napoleonic Wars dominated Thomas Lancaster's later life. We shall see presently that he reacted strongly to the French Revolution and to Napoleon, and should remember both that his schooldays coincided with the Seven Years' War, and that England was again at war with France while he was in Sunderland. France to men of his generation was the traditional enemy. In September 1779, when France and Spain were leagued with America against Britain, Thomas and Ann Lancaster may have been among the many who flocked to Town Moor to see Paul Jones's squadron sail past on its way to a memorable victory off Flamborough Head. There was too large a crowd of spectators for it to be safe for Jones to fire his usual insouciant salute, or perhaps the local story is true, that he mistook for soldiers the crowds of women dressed in the then fashionable cloaks of scarlet duffle, this preventing him from attempting the landing which was widely feared.[47]

1781 was the year in which young William Pitt entered Parliament as member for the Lonsdale pocket borough of Appleby. In January 1782, when Ann Lancaster was nursing her infant eldest son, a ship blew up spectacularly in the harbour, and in February 1783 the North York Militia had to be called out to quell a riot caused by press-ganging. Then there were the storms, ever a feature of life in the north-east, particularly in winter. In a sermon published in Sunderland in December 1784 Thomas Lancaster refers to 'our . . . affliction, last winter' and proceeds to describe the 'uncommon visitation, by which our coasts have been, but a few days ago, bestrewed with death and destruction':

> A most destructive storm at sea, such as hath not been equalled in the memory of the oldest man living, began in the night of December [5th], and continued, without intermission, the two succeeding days and nights; by which the greatest part of a fleet of more than 200 sail of light ships, that sailed out of Yarmouth roads, not many hours before it began, were stranded, wrecked, and foundered at sea. — The Author has been informed,

that no fewer than *one hundred and four* corpses of men, washed on shore from ships lost on the coast of Northumberland, were, in one day, interred in a churchyard in that county![48]

Ann Lancaster, particularly if she possessed the *niceness* on which modern dames preened themselves, must have found such storms altogether too much. But more important than any such events, however dramatic, were the official duties to which the Rev. Lancaster had to attend, to say nothing of the young family which soon needed to be cared for. A noteworthy occurrence that closely affected Thomas Lancaster was the burning down, in November 1783, of the recently built Masonic Hall, home of King George's Lodge.[49] The hall had been dedicated shortly before his marriage, on 17 July 1778. The earliest extant minute in the oldest minute book of the lodge shows that 'Rev. Thos Lancaster, Chaplain' was one of those present, on 5 August 1778, at the first meeting of the lodge following the dedication of the hall. The minute not only shows that Thomas Lancaster was a Mason; it is also the earliest reference to his time in Sunderland.

It was during their eight years in Sunderland that the Lancasters' first four children were born: Elizabeth (known as Eliza; b. 23 February 1780, baptised 18 March 1780), Timothy Yeats (baptised 1 December 1781), Ruth (baptised 30 May 1784) and Ann (baptised 1 December 1785). The names chosen for the children are all family ones: Elizabeth was the name of Ann Lancaster's mother; Timothy Yeats was the name of her favourite uncle; Ruth was the name of Thomas Lancaster's mother; and Ann was not only Ann Lancaster's name but a traditional Lancaster family name. All four were baptised in the parish church of Holy Trinity by the rector, John Coxon. We shall return to the Lancasters' children shortly; for now let it simply be remarked that Eliza is the Miss Lancaster to whom Arthur Schopenhauer was advised to apply for a safety pin to tide him over an emergency.

While in Sunderland Thomas Lancaster published *A Sermon Preached in St. John's Chapel, Sunderland, On Sunday December 12, 1784, and Published (By Desire) for The Relief of the distressed Inhabitants of Shetland, now Groaning under the Miseries of Famine.* (By the Rev. T. Lancaster, lecturer. Printed by James Graham, Bookseller, High-Street, Sunderland, 1784 [21 pp.].) I give the whole title as the briefest indication of the contents. This rare item, not in the British library or the Bodleian, is one of the three extant sermons by Thomas Lancaster. While this one — unlike the others — does not exemplify the sort of thing to which Schopenhauer objected so strongly, it is of considerable intrinsic interest, being based on a petition presented to the House of Commons on 3 July 1784 by 'the unhappy people of Shetland', whose crops had failed two years running and who had been brought to their knees by the length and severity of the winter of 1783/4 and its many attendant disasters, and on accounts of this which appeared in the press in October 1784. One of a series of charity sermons, it is a straightforward plea for charitable generosity to those visited by disasters of such magnitude. It is preceded by an 'Advertisement' which speaks for itself:

> The Author, being requested to publish this Sermon, readily embraces the opportunity of eventually benefitting the Charity, for which it was originaly written, by giving up the profits, arising from its sale, for that purpose. He by no means presumes to offer this discourse to the public as a faultless composition; it being only the work of a few mornings, in the ordinary course of his duty. It has been suggested, that the publication of it may do good: if it does, his end is answered: he courts neither fame nor profit.

The Rev. Lancaster's style, it must be allowed, tends towards the pompous; there are too many disclaimers. How much was raised by the sale of the sermon at 2d each (or 1s 9d per dozen) is not recorded. What is known is that the sermon produced a collection of £13 13s 6d[50] This sum was about average for such occasions; it compares well with the £14 2s 8d raised by the annual charity sermon for the same year (1784) given by the fashionable Rev. William Romaine, lecturer at St Dunstan's in the West and vicar of St Anne's, Blackfriars, who was originally from Hartlepool and was noted for his orthodoxy and rigid interpretation of the 39 Articles.

It may be that Thomas Lancaster was prompted by the example of William Romaine to go south and seek to establish himself as a fashionable cleric. Go south he did. The Rev. Romaine may have advised him to make such a move; the idea of heading for Fulham probably came from the Rev. Thomas Hall, who was a Middlesex man. Be that as it may, the Lancasters left Sunderland either in late December 1785, after their infant daughter had been baptised, or early in 1786; the Fulham rate books show that Thomas was paying rates on a house at Parson's Green in winter 1785-6.[51]

Parson's Green

With a house suitable for a boys' academy to be found in the environs of London, a new child expected (a daughter, Ann, born in November), and a long-distance move to be made, 1785 was an exceptionally busy year. In winter 1785/6 the Lancasters moved south with their four eldest children. Eliza was six, Timothy four, Ruth 18 months and Ann just a few weeks old. They were moving because Parson Lancaster, encouraged by William Romaine, or at least by his example, had resolved to invest his wife's fortune in a house suitable for the establishment of a polite academy; no doubt he also had at the back of his mind a pipe-dream of success as a popular preacher à la Romaine. He knew that a distant ancestor of his, William Lancaster (1650–1717), had been rector of the most influential living in London, St Martin's in the Fields, and Archdeacon of Middlesex (1705–17). Thackeray's description of Thomas Newcome's move to London applies almost exactly to Thomas Lancaster:

> When pig-tails still grew on the backs of the British gentry, and their wives wore cushions on their heads, over which they tied their own hair, and disguised it with powder and pomatum: when ministers went in their stars and orders to the House of Commons, and the orators of the Opposition attacked nightly the noble lord in the blue ribbon: when Mr. Washington was heading the American rebels with a courage, it must be confessed, worthy of a better cause: there came up to London out of a Northern county, Mr. Thomas . . . [52]

One wonders whether Thomas Lancaster was wearing, or the luggage wagon was carrying, a clerical scarf to enhance the dignified figure he hoped to cut in the metropolis. At this time a churchman who had not been at Oxford or Cambridge wore a 'pudding sleeve gown'; all clerical dignitaries wore a scarf, and many a country parson brought one to London so that he might be mistaken for a doctor of divinity.[53] Whether Thomas Lancaster did this or not is not known (unfortunately no portrait appears to exist) but he would undoubtedly have been capable of doing so, for it seems that he inherited the archdeacon's vanity.

Parson Lancaster had resigned his Sunderland posts at Easter 1785 in order to be able to devote part of the summer to finding a suitable house, and he found one at Parson's Green. The house was on the east side of the Green, opposite the house to which Samuel Richardson had moved thirty years previously. On 30 October 1754 Mrs Delany noted, 'Richardson is very busy, removing this very day to Parson's Green.'[54] In letters Richardson wrote, 'The Speaker was so good as to call upon me at Parson's Green. He liked the house and situation' (26 November 1754) and 'My wife . . . bids me . . . tell you that she . . . likes her removal to Parson's Green, every day more and more.'[55] Doubtless Ann Lancaster, in spring 1786, liked it no less.

A century earlier Samuel Pepys had described Parson's Green as being 'in the country',[56] which it still was. It was also the most elegant quarter of Fulham, inhabited mostly by gentry and persons of quality. It owed its name to the Parsonage that stood midway on the western side of the Green, which back in 1705 was used by the rector as a bowling green 'for his own and his domesticks' Diversion'.[57] In 1785 it was probably just a patch of grass surrounded by posts and chains, with a muddy footpath crossing it from Rectory Place to Elm House. Elm House was the house which Thomas Lancaster had found to be suitable for his purposes. Back in 1729 it had been advertised for letting in terms which give point to his choice:

> On Parson's-Green, near Fulham, Middlesex, To be Lett a large convenient House, with an Orchard, well-planted Gardens, Stables, Coach-Houses, and Out-Houses, a Row of large Elms before the Gates, pleasantly situated on a very healthy Ground. The House is fit for either Courtier, Merchant, or large Boarding-School.[58]

No doubt it was advertised in very similar terms in 1785. Feret, in *Fulham Old and New*, gives a photograph of Elm House as it was 110 years later, as well as a somewhat confusing history of the property originally known as 'Hore's tenement'.

It was, then, at Elm House, Parson's Green, that Thomas Lancaster established his first academy. Evidence of the academy as such is provided by a sermon published in 1789, in which he described himself as 'master of an Academy at Parson's Green, Middlesex', and by an advertisement in *The Times* in 1789, in which he announced that he had moved his academy from Parson's Green to Wimbledon. We may be sure that it was run, slightly more hesitantly, on the same lines as his school in Wimbledon, of which we have both his own and Johanna Schopenhauer's accounts.

Thomas Lancaster was not licensed to teach at Parson's Green. Having come from dioceses in which schoolmasters were expected to be licensed, he presumably applied to the Bishop of London's secretary for a licence, only to be met with a blank stare, as William Barrow was:

> When I first engaged in the academy in Soho-square, I applied for the licence, which I supposed necessary to every man before he could legally undertake the profession of a schoolmaster; and the secretary's answer surprized me, as much as my application appeared to have surprized him. 'I have been six years in my office,' said he, 'and never heard of such a thing before.' It was then agreed that he should make enquiry on the subject, and inform me of the result. I left my address, and never heard more of the licence.[59]

William Barrow (1754–1836) took his degree at Oxford in 1778 and must have 'engaged in the academy' in the 1780s; his experience with the Bishop of London's secretary therefore explains why there is no record of Thomas Lancaster having been licensed to teach at Parson's Green.

Most of Lancaster's time and energy at this time was devoted to the establishment of his academy, which meant, apart from much else, establishing the 'plan of education' which he was to publish in 1794. His wife probably acted as matron for much of the time, with a nursemaid looking after the children. In what time was left for their social life the Lancasters will have found that society in Fulham was on the whole politer than it had been in Sunderland, although the rector's establishment is unlikely to have rivalled Henry Egerton's at Bishopwearmouth. On the other hand the rector, the Rev. Graham Jepson (1736–1811), was a former assistant master at Eton, and would therefore have been able to advise Parson Lancaster on how to adapt to dealing with a very different class of child and — no less important — a very different class of parent. When Thomas Lancaster's distant ancestor William Lancaster (1650–1717) became Provost of Queen's College, he was known to at least one of his colleagues as the 'Northern Bear' and as 'Old Smoothboots'. If smoothness is a quality which our headmaster had to cultivate at this stage of his life, he will have been helped in this by the new acquaintances he now made, including his next-door neighbour, Lady Ann Simpson of Belfield House, although she moved away in 1787, and very likely including Charles Burney

(1757–1817), son of Dr Burney and brother of Fanny.

After graduating from Aberdeen, Charles Burney was appointed assistant master at Highgate Grammar School, but shortly afterwards moved to Chiswick Academy. In 1786 he moved the school, of which he was by then headmaster, to Hammersmith, where he remained until 1793. Charles Burney and Thomas Lancaster therefore arrived in neighbouring parishes at the same time to set up schools, which makes it very likely that they met. That they were acquainted we know from their (later) common membership of the Society of Schoolmasters. Indeed, it was probably the fact that they were acquainted that later gave Thomas Lancaster's sister-in-law, the mendicant (and indeed mendacious) Mrs Sarah Burney, the idea of claiming to be related to Fanny Burney. The fact that she claimed to have dined with Dr Burney at Greenwich could, if true, be regarded as confirmation that Thomas and Ann Lancaster knew Charles Burney and his wife Fanny, for John and Sarah Burney would be most unlikely to have met Dr Burney except at the Lancasters'. The story may, however, be untrue. We shall meet Mrs Sarah Burney presently in connection with the positively Dickensian Chancery case in which her husband was involved at the time of his death.

At this time the politeness of life at Parson's Green was annually interrupted by the rudeness of the fair which took place on 17, 18 and 19 August, beneath the trees on the east side of the Green — in other words, right outside the Lancasters' house. All the usual concomitants of an old country fair were there: the greasy pole climbing, treacle bobbing, ale broaching, competitive hot tea drinking, and the like; there were oysters, gingerbread and cock-shying ('Poor live cocks used to be tied up by their legs and people threw sticks at them'). Shortly after the Lancasters' time a clown by the name of Billy Burton used to ride a horse which, after completing its performance, would make off at top speed for the White Horse inn at the corner of the Green; many of the fairgoers must have done likewise. Presumably the genteel inhabitants arranged to be away in August.

For the Lancasters, in August 1786, there was no question of jollification, for the family was in mourning. At the beginning of June their eldest son, Timothy Yeats, had died; he was buried at Fulham All Saints on 5 June 1786. Whether he was carried off by smallpox or putrid fever is not known; I have found no record of any epidemic in Fulham in 1786. It may be that his death was the result of an accident; towards the corner of the Green on the

Lancasters' side there was a large pond, one end of which was very deep and therefore represented a real danger to a four-and-half-year-old boy. And, as if this was not enough, Thomas Lancaster's young cousin and namesake, who was staying with them, probably as a newly appointed or potential usher, also died there in September, aged 27; he was buried at Fulham All Saints on 18 September 1786 and is commemorated by a plaque in Barton Church. This double tragedy must have been a terrible blow to Thomas and Ann Lancaster, whose decision to leave Parson's Green three years later may have been in part a desire to start again free of tragedy.

Young Thomas Lancaster, younger son of Samuel and Eleanor Lancaster of New House, Barton, Westmorland, was born in 1759; his father was a younger brother of our Thomas Lancaster's father. Given the same name and similar dates and background, it is not surprising that these two Thomas Lancasters have been confused.[60] Like his uncle, young Thomas Lancaster attended Appleby Grammar School under Richard Yates. Unlike his uncle, he went on to Queen's College, which he entered as a batteler on 30 March 1781. He took his BA in 1784 and was ordained deacon, at Oxford, on Trinity Sunday 1784.[61] His ordination title was a letter from Thomas Kirkby, rector of Kirkhaugh, Northumberland (near Alston), nominating him to be his curate. He is not recorded as having taken his MA, and there is no record of his ordination as priest. He remained in residence at Queen's until towards the end of long vacation 1786. No doubt he heard William Agutter's sermon 'On the Difference between the Deaths of the Righteous and the Wicked, Illustrated in the Instance of Dr. Samuel Johnson and David Hume, Esq.', preached before the University of Oxford on 3 July 1786 (published in 1800), and told his uncle about it, who proceeded to adopt Dr Johnson as emblematical of righteousness. My reason for this supposition is Arthur Schopenhauer's violent objection to Samuel Johnson, which is explained if he had Dr Johnson held up to him as a paragon of all the virtues while he was at Mr Lancaster's. Presumably young Thomas Lancaster carried out no duties at Kirkhaugh. Most likely his uncle had offered him the post of usher. Be that as it may, Elm House was never the same again after this double death in summer 1786.

In going up to Queen's, Cousin Lancaster had been following a family tradition, for the Lancasters had been sending their sons to Queen's since 1467. The member of the family who most made his mark there was William Lancaster, who took his BA in 1674, when he was sent to Paris by Sir Joseph William to study modern languages. In 1704, in a disputed election, he was elected Provost of Queen's, a post which he combined with that of Archdeacon of Middlesex. As R.H. Hodgkin has said of the disputed election;

> It was not surprising that a High Churchman like Lancaster who shed his views about Passive Obedience when it came to a crisis, should have bitter enemies. None was more bitter than Hearne, the Jacobite diarist, whose hatred was fed by Lancaster's refusal to subscribe to his books. So in Hearne's diary Lancaster appears as 'Old Smoothboots' or the 'Northern Bear'; and is branded as vain, ignorant, idle and sottish.[62]

Lancaster went on to become Vice-Chancellor of Oxford (1706-9), and was said — by Thomas Hearne — to have been 'the worst Vice-Chancellor that ever was in Oxon' and an 'old hypocritical ambitious drunken sot' suffering from gout in the stomach.[63] Dr Lancaster is remembered, however, for quite a different reason: because he began the rebuilding of Queen's in 1709. The ramshackle old medieval buildings began to come down, to be replaced by elegant buildings partly designed by Lancaster himself; the rebuilding was completed by his successor.

If it is true that 'as the new buildings of the college went up, its old standards came down',[64] with the result that by the time Thomas Lancaster matriculated in 1781 the college was in decline, it is ironical that one of the last of the old-style fellows was another Lancaster, the Rev. Thomas William Lancaster, born in Fulham in 1787, second (and eldest surviving) son of our headmaster. Thomas William was born at Elm House on 24 August 1787 and was baptised at Fulham All Saints on 27 December 1787. No doubt he was named after Archdeacon Lancaster. He was very much his father's son and a great consolation to his parents, who were to have only one more child, another son, Henry, who was born in Wimbledon.

Before we turn to Wimbledon, where the Lancasters moved in 1789, there remain the other events of that year. The first of these concerns the restoration of the King's sanity in February. A 'Prayer of Thanksgiving' was appointed to be read in all the churches throughout the metropolis on Sunday 1 March, and in all other churches on the following Sunday. Thursday 23 April 1789 was appointed a day of public thanksgiving. Thomas Lancaster seized this oppportunity to compose another occasional sermon; *The Christian Duty of Thanksgiving. A Sermon preached at Hanworth in the County of Middlesex, on Thursday, April 23, 1789, being the day appointed for A Solemn Thanksgiving to Almighty God, for His Majesty's Happy Recovery. By Thomas Lancaster, Curate of Feltham, and Master of an Academy at Parson's Green, Middlesex.* At the time of preaching the sermon Mr Lancaster was not curate of Feltham, but on 9 July 1789 he was licensed to the cure on the nomination of the vicar, the Rev. John Hewit (1734-98), at a stipend of £30 per annum.[65] There is no record of his resignation as curate of Feltham, but Charles McCarthy, AB, was appointed to the cure on 22 April 1792.[66] Parson Lancaster thus became curate of Feltham a few days before the fall of the Bastille. His very characteristic and revealing views on the French Revolution will be discussed later. He can hardly have obtained the curacy on the strength of this sermon which, it has to be said, is unctuous and peculiarly tedious; by far the weakest of his three surviving sermons, it does much to explain Arthur Schopenhauer's horrified reaction to such things. Parson Woodforde, who bought a copy on 12 September 1789 ('To a Sermon on the Recovery of the King by Lancaster pd. 0. 1.0.') refrains from comment. Maybe Lancaster was flying the flag for the new, bigger and higher-profile academy he was planning to open in Wimbledon, seeking to impress the parents of potential pupils and establish himself as a sound (i.e. conservative) man.

No doubt several reasons came together in Thomas Lancaster's mind to produce the decision to move from Parson's Green. The deaths in quick succession of Timothy Yeats and Cousin Thomas had put a blight on Elm house which even the subsequent birth of Thomas William did not entirely remove, but in retrospect it also became clear that Parson's Green had not been the ideal location for the establishment of an academy, partly because there was too much competition. The Lancasters' next-door neighbour, the Rev. Mr (John A.?) Waring of Albion House conducted an academy at which the future Prime Minister, Robert Jenkinson (1770-1828; Prime Minister as Lord Liverpool, 1812-27), studied from about 1776 to 1783. It may be that Lancaster prevailed upon the Albion House dancing-master, M. Du Rosel of Chelsea, to give lessons at his establishment too. On the other side of the Green, the Rev. Thomas Bowen (chaplain of the Bridewell Hospital and minister of Bridewell Precinct) had, only in 1784, established an academy in High Elms which rapidly became successful. To some extent Bowen may have spiked Lancaster's guns; he was, after all, known locally, which Lancaster was not.

Whatever the competition, Thomas Lancaster very likely failed to establish himself fully at Parson's Green because Fulham was by then a smart and relatively populous district in which an obscure north-country clergyman would not have cut much of a figure. In Wimbledon, on the other hand, he was to be the owner of one of the outstanding properties in the parish and therefore a person of some consequence, one of a much smaller number of gentry, and headmaster of a school which quickly flourished because the conditions were right. The move to Wimbledon was, therefore, the decisive step of his career. It took place in summer 1789.

Notes

1. Quoted from E. Hudson, *Barton Records* (1951), 52.
2. *Swift's Writings on Religion and the Church*, ed. T. Scott, I (1898), 267.
3. Their other children were Hannah (b. 24 December 1752; m. Thomas Vipond, 12 December 1784), John (bapt. 17 April 1755, d. 21 September 1757), Agnes (bapt. 27 October 1757; m. Nicholas Rowell, 6 October 1782), Ruth (bapt. 13 November 1760; m. Thomas Atkinson, 7 October 1780) and Samuel (b. 5 November 1763; he moved south to Lavender Hill, where his son Thomas Peirce was baptised by his eldest brother on 27 March 1797).
4. Quoted from Ewanian, *History of Penrith* (1894), 171.
5. A. Raistrick, *Two Centuries of Industrial Welfare: the London (Quaker) Lead Company* (1938), 18.
6. 'Northern Journeys of Bishop Richard Pococke,' in *North Country Diaries (Second Series)*, Publications of the Surtees Society, CXXIV (1914), 212.
7. This and the following details are taken from M. Holdgate, *A History of Appleby*, (Appleby, 1970), 63, etc.
8. J. Nicolson and R. Burn, *The History and Antiquities of the Counties of Westmorland and Cumberland*, I (1777, repr. 1976), 310.
9. See E. Hinchcliffe, *Appleby Grammar School* (Appleby, 1974), 45-53.
10. Nicolson and Burn, *Westmorland and Cumberland*, I, 332.
11. R.H. Hodgkin, *Six Centuries of an Oxford College* (1949), 166.
12. *CWAAS*, XIII, 1893, 33.
13. F.B. Swift, 'Maughanby School', *CWAAS*, LIV (1954), 237.
14. Ibid., 243.
15. Although his married predecessor, the Rev. Joseph Smith, seems to have lived there (ibid., 246).
16. Ibid., 238.
17. The summary of Macaulay is taken from J. Beresford's introduction to James Woodforde's *The Diary of a Country Parson, 1758-1802*, I (1924), 3.
18. Quoted from R. Bayne-Powell, *Eighteenth-Century London Life* (1937), 290.

19. Swift, 'Maughanby School', 238.
20. Ibid., 238 f.
21. Ibid., 237.
22. Preserved in Cumbria RO, Carlisle.
23. Held in the Department of Palaeography, University of Durham.
24. Joseph Railton, son of Joseph Railton of Unthank and his wife Sarah (*née* Rowland), was baptised at Dalston (Cumberland) on 17 May 1713; he was usher at Carlisle Grammar School from 1732 to 1737 and master of Hexham Grammar School from 1737 to 1742. He was ordained deacon at Durham on 30 August 1741 and was rector of Knaresdale from then until his death in 1796. He married three times. By an extraordinary coincidence the school which Thomas Lancaster was to open in Wimbledon was eventually taken over by a school founded in Hammersmith by another Cumbrian by the name of Joseph Railton, presumably a relation.
25. John Ellison, eldest son of the Rev. Dr Nathaniel Ellison, was born on 27 December 1694. He matriculated at University College, Oxford, on 22 March 1710/11 and took his BA in 1715. He was ordained at Carlisle in 1717. He was vicar of Bedlington (1719-73), lecturer at St Andrews, Newcastle (1724/25-66) and curate of St Nicholas, Newcastle. He died on 27 December 1773, just three months after Thomas Lancaster's ordination.
26. Mr. Riley, in George Eliot's *The Mill on the Floss*, Chapter 3.
27. Mr Tulliver, ibid.
28. *Memoir of the late Rev. John Farrer* (Newcastle, 1844), 9.
29. Ibid., 12.
30. See F.J.G. Robinson and P.J. Wallis, 'The Association of Protestant Schoolmasters in the North of England', *Transactions of the Architectural and Archaeological Society of Durham and Northumberland*, III (1974), 87-99. Thomas Lancaster is not among the known members, but the records are incomplete; he was given to joining societies.
31. See *My dearest Betsy: a self-portrait of William Gilpin, 1757-1848*, ed. P. Benson (1981), 189 f.
32. Boswell, 'Journal of My Jaunt.
33. *Newcastle Courant*, 19 September 1778.
34. R. Warner, *A Tour through the Northern Counties of England*, I (Bath, 1802), 306.
35. *Letters of Spencer Cowper*, ed. E. Hughes (1956), 142.
36. Ibid.
37. Son of Benjamin Hall and his wife Sarah, Thomas Hall was born on 1 August 1736 in Clerkenwell, studied at Jesus College, Cambridge, taking his BA in 1760, and was ordained deacon at Norwich — for Durham — in December 1762. He was curate of Sunderland from 1762 to 1769, when he was appointed curate of St John's, a position he resigned in 1787 on moving to the cure of Swillington. He was to die at Sandal Magna on 12 October 1790.
38. Including John Thornhill (the rich coal fitter and proprietor of the chapel), Captain George Thompson, Thomas Simpson (master, from 1783, of the charity school attached to St John's), and William Russell, a particularly interesting figure. Partner in the Sunderland bank of Russell, Allan and Maling, he was born in 1734, second son of the squire of

Rowenlands. He acquired his interest in the bank from his uncle, Matthew Russell, and subsequently became proprietor of Wallsend Colliery, the coals from which, 'Russell's Wallsends', were once famous. He was thought to be one of the wealthiest commoners in England; in 1795 he raised, at his own expense, a large body of infantry Volunteers. He lived for some time at Newbottle, and later purchased Brancepeth Castle, outside Durham; he died on 8 June 1817, aged 83.

39. John Coxon was born in Closehead, Cumberland, in 1708, studied at Queen's College, Oxford, taking his BA in 1729, and was ordained deacon, at Carlisle, in 1731. He was curate first of Brampton and then of Morpeth, before becoming rector of Sunderland in 1762. He died in November 1787, and in 1793 Thomas Lancaster's old friend John Farrer became rector.

40. Dr Ekins did not reside at Sedgefield, but his death at Parson's Green speaks for itself.

41. *Antiquities of Sunderland*, IX (1908), 142.

42. G. Garbutt, *A Historical and Descriptive View of . . . Sunderland* (Sunderland, 1819), 206.

43. There is an attractive engraving of St John's in Garbutt, *Sunderland*.

44. In the Department of Palaeography, University of Durham.

45. Ibid., Church Commission Box 218.

46. Ibid.

47. See J.W. Summers, *The History and Antiquities of Sunderland* (Sunderland, 1858), 81 f; and Mrs Gaskell, *Sylvia's Lovers*, Chapter III ('Buying a New Cloak'). Details of other contemporary events from M.A. Richardson, *The Local Historian's Table Book*, Historical Division, II (Newcastle upon Tyne 1843); and J. Sykes, *Local Records*, I (Newcastle-upon-Tyne, 1833).

48. Thomas Lancaster, *A Sermon preached in St. John's Chapel, Sunderland* (Sunderland, 1784), 13.

49. See Garbutt, *Sunderland*, 287-96; T.O. Todd, *The History of the Phoenix Lodge, No. 94, Sunderland* (Sunderland, 1906).

50. *Antiquities of Sunderland*, IX (1908), 145.

51. *The Auckland Castle Episcopal Records: Clergy Visitation Returns, 1791-92* (preserved in the Department of Palaeography, University of Durham) reveal that Thomas Lancaster's successor as curate of Trimdon was inducted on 6 April 1785.

52. Thackeray, *The Newcomes*, Chapter 2.

53. Bayne-powell, *London Life*, 290.

54. S. Richardson, *Correspondence*, ed. A.L. Barbauld, III (1804), 296.

55. Ibid., III, 99.

56. *Diary*, 24 August 1667.

57. C.J. Feret, *Fulham Old and New*, II (1900) 87.

58. *Country Journal*, 5 July 1729 (quoted from Feret, *Fulham*, II, 102).

59. W. Barrow, *An Essay in Education*, I (1802) 196 f.

60. Notably by J. Foster in his *Alumni Oxonienses* (1887-91).

61. By letters dimissory from Durham. His ordination papers are preserved in the Department of Palaeography. University of Durham.

62. Hodgkin, *Six Centuries*, 133. Two generations later James Scott (1733-1814) used 'Old Slyboots' as a *nom de plume*; presumably this goes

back to Thomas Hearne (the 'Wormius' of the *Dunciad*).
 63. J.R. Magrath, *The Queen's College*, II (1921) 78 f.
 64. Hodgkin, *Six Centuries*, 160.
 65. Bishop of London's Act Books, preserved in the Guildhall Library (MS 9549, fol. 194).
 66. Ibid. fol. 230.

V

Parson Lancaster at Wimbledon

The Eligibility of Wimbledon

In 1789 Thomas Lancaster used his wife's 'genteel fortune' to buy, for £2,300, a Jacobean mansion in Wimbledon High Street which had come on the market following William Grenville's election as Speaker on 5 January 1789. He immediately proceeded to sell off, for building, most of the 17 acres that went with the property, thus very considerably reducing the price he had paid for the house. As a result he and his wife were left in possession of a modest private income.

Mr Lancaster's new house (known from 1789 to 1805 as 'Mr Lancaster's') was — and is — a most imposing one.[1] Described in a survey made in 1617 — at which time there were just 46 houses in Wimbledon as opposed to 248 in 1806) — as a 'fayre new house', it was built c. 1613 by Robert Bell (1565-c. 1640), a member of the Girdlers' Company of London and an original member of the East India Company.[2] Following Bell's death, the house was bought in 1647 by Richard Betenson of Layer de la Hay in Essex, who settled the house and land on his son Richard in 1658, on the occasion of his marriage with Albinia, granddaughter of Sir Edward Cecil, Lord Wimbledon. The Betensons sold the property in 1700 to Richard Ivatt, alderman of London, in whose family it remained until 1766. From 1766 to 1789 the house, with its land and the Rose and Crown tavern (later the turning point on Swinburne's daily walk from Putney Hill), was let for £116 8s per annum to Viscount Duncannon, to a Marquess of Bath, to Sir William Draper and, finally, from 1787 to 1789, to the most interesting of its occupants, the Rt Hon. William Grenville (1759-1834). Grenville was a relative and colleague of Pitt, who often stayed in the house during

Grenville's tenancy, so that tradition came to give the name of 'Pitt's room' to one of the main bedrooms, the one with a fine plaster ceiling on the right of the library, overlooking the garden, on the mezzanine floor. Grenville was the last private resident of the house for a century, for it served as a school from 1789 to 1887.

While Thomas Lancaster will have not failed to rehearse to parents of prospective pupils the names of the previous occupants of his house (particularly William Grenville, whose career was then at its height), the house itself was even more important to him. It was well described by a later owner as 'perhaps unique as a survival of the smaller rural or semi-rural homes of the prosperous London merchant in the seventeenth century',[3] although to speak of it as an exemplary 'Jacobean mansion of the smaller kind'[4] is somewhat misleading, for it is a very large house by modern standards. It is a house of ten gables, built of red brick with stone quoins and, in the lower storey, stone-mullioned windows. Like Hardwick Hall, the house originally had 'More window than wall'; by Lancaster's time some of the windows had been blocked up. The house is massively built, with very high ceilings, the plasterwork of which is one of its most remarkable features. In 1789 the principal rooms were probably still wainscoted, as they had been in 1763, when it was expressly stated that the lessee 'shall not . . . do any injury to the wainscot of the parlour'. One can imagine Thomas Lancaster warning his charges not to carve their initials on the panelling! That they had penknives in those days is shown by the fact that Schopenhauer's was stolen. In the eighteenth century many of the rooms retained their ceiling-high carved Jacobean mantelpieces. The ornate plasterwork of the ceilings survives to this day, and one can only agree with T.G. Jackson, who wrote a century ago:

> Considering that all the best rooms upstairs had been boys' dormitories, it [was] a constant surprise to me that the plaster enrichments of the ceiling had esaped the destructive propensities natural to British youth, who generally regard anything unusual as a proper object for a catapult or a 'cock-shy'; but I ceased to wonder, when a friend who was here one day said: 'I was at school in this house, and I slept in this room, but I am quite sure I never saw this ceiling till today.'[5]

If the house was calculated both to impress parents and to make an interestingly rambling place for the boarders to live, the grounds were also impressive. In front was a large playground, while at the side and rear of the house were extensive gardens, orchards, vegetable gardens, stables, and the like. T.G. Jackson wrote that:

> Behind the house is the old garden with a raised terrace at the far end — the 'mound' which was a usual feature of a Jacobean pleasaunce — thrown up no doubt with the earth from the foundations. A modern lawn has replaced the old formal garden, but in a dry season the eye still seems to trace the lines of the curious knots and parterres where Mrs. Bell grew her roses and gilly flowers.[6]

Whether the formal garden remained — as the headmaster's garden — in 1789, I do not know. The boys would in any case, judging by contemporary novels, have been far more interested in the orchard. In 1789 the eagle which now surmounts the middle front gable of the house, and which gave the house its modern name, Eagle House, was not there. From 1789 to 1805 the school was known as 'The Rev. Mr Lancaster's Academy' or, more properly, as Wimbledon School.

Eagle House came perilously close to being demolished in the 1880s. Thomas Lancaster is commemorated in the names of Lancaster Road, Lancaster Place and Lancaster Cottages, all of which were built on the land he sold off after buying the house. They all exist still, as does the Common, on which the boys were taken for compulsory walks. Naturally the Eagle House that can be seen today is not identical with the house in which Arthur Schopenhauer spent some of the most miserable days — and all the most wretched Sundays — of his life; but a comparison of the house with a pen-and-ink drawing by R.B. Schnebbelie (c. 1780–c. 1849) of 'The Rev. Mr. Lancaster's Academy , 1810'[7] shows that it is still substantially the same. Today's Eagle House is close in appearance to the house as it was in 1789 — or 1803 — because in 1887 T.G. Jackson, having bought it, restored the building, removing most of the accretions it had acquired during its century as a school. Thomas Graham Jackson was the architect who was to leave more of a mark on Oxford than any other architect since Wren, both by the sheer volume of his work between 1877 and 1914 (Examination Schools, Radcliffe Science library, new buildings for Lincoln, Brasenose, Trinity, Corpus Christi and Hertford Colleges, etc.) and — more especially — by the 'Anglo-Jackson' style which he evolved, a personal brand of the Jacobean style exemplified by his own house at that time. Hence Lancaster's house may be said to have left its mark on Oxford.

Although, as we shall see, he was bored and made miserable by the typical English boarding-school regime carried on there, Arthur Schopenhauer cannot have failed to be impressed by the elegance of the house, with its magnificent Jacobean staircases, oak wainscoting, elaborately carved chimneypieces, artistically fretted plaster ceilings, partly original furniture, and terraced, Elizabethan-style garden, for his travel diary, which includes an account of a visit to a London furniture-maker, makes it clear that he noticed such things, which reminded him of home.

By August 1789 Thomas Lancaster and his family had moved to Wimbledon, where his school opened again, under the name of Wimbledon School, on 18 January 1790. This is revealed by a notice which appeared in *The Times* on 6 January 1790:

WIMBLEDON SCHOOL,
FOR YOUNG NOBLEMEN AND GENTLEMEN.

THE REV. THOMAS LANCASTER respectfully informs the Nobility and Gentry, that he has removed his Academy from Parson's Green, to a large and commodious House at Wimbledon, Surrey, which he has lately purchased, and fitted up in a style suitable to the Title of this Advertisement. His School-room is at once large and comfortable, Playground and Gardens extensive, Apartments spacious and lofty; and situation most healthful, with the additional advantage of an excellent Cold bath.

It will be his ambition to establish a preference to his Seminary, on the solid foundation of the general improvement and comfort of his pupils; and a Sketch of his Plan and Terms will be delivered or sent to any Nobleman or Gentleman applying for it, at No. 2, St. Mary's Hill, Eastcheap; No. 19, Thavies Inn, Holborn; No. 10, Henrietta-street, Covent Garden; No. 11, Lisle-street, Leicester-square; Mr. Hodgson's, No. 50, Strand; or to himself, at Wimbledon, Surrey; where a visit will be esteemed a favour, and will enable those who do him that honour to satisfy themselves of the truth of what is here advanced.

N.B. His School opens again on the 18th instant.

*** Wanted a Latin Assistant, whose character and qualifications will bear the strictest scrutiny. An Oxonian will be preferred. Address as above.

✝✝✝ Mr. Lancaster's Thanksgiving Sermon, on the happy Recovery of his Majesty, may be had of Mr. Beetham, No. 27, Fleet-street, or any of the Booksellers.

Mr. Lancaster's preparations for the reopening of his school were interrupted by the news of his father's death on 9 December 1789.

When he came to compose his *Plan of Education* (1794), our headmaster spoke of his school as being 'established in a *most eligible* situation, at an easy *Distance* from Town', enjoying 'A just Elevation, on a light Soil' and therefore free of the 'Damps and stagnant Vapours' to which Low Situations are subject. In 1769/70 nearby Merton, of which Thomas Lancaster was eventually to become perpetual curate, was described by Alexander Carlyle (whose youngest sister, Janet, was living there with her husband, Thomas Bell) as 'a very agreeable place'.[8] Johanna Schopenhauer, for her part, wrote enthusiastically of Wimbledon Park and the countryside around Wimbledon and Roehampton:

> A mile and a half further on one comes to the beautiful park at Wimbledon, which belongs to Lord Spencer. So many beautiful and charming things are thus concentrated in this happy area, which is only a few miles across, and which by itself is well worth the journey from London.[9]

It is hardly surprising that her son, in the diary entry referring to his first visit to the Wimbledon area, does not mention its charms. Lord Jeffrey, on the other hand, who moved to Wimbledon in 1831, gave a fuller and more poetic account of its attractions:

> I am delighted with this place. It is much colder than London, but dry and bright. Fine old trees, skirting a bright green common, in tufts and masses; some shining ponds glistening in the turf; a boundless horizon, with the Richmond woods on one side, and the Surrey hills on the other; a gay but quiet village, sinking into the wood, and a garland of large shady villas sweeping in a full crescent round a broad bay of the common.[10]

Three years earlier Prince Pückler-Muskau had found that 'Wimbledon Park, stretching over several hills and full of beautiful groups of trees, presents fine views, but the effect of the whole is spoiled by some degree of monotony.'[11]

By this time, thanks to the preference for Wimbledon shown by so many statesmen and noblemen of Thomas Lancaster's generation, Tory and Whig alike, a 'country house at Wimbledon' had become (according to Thackeray's *Vanity Fair*) part and parcel of the expectations of the worldly young woman.[12] The life led by Ann Lancaster and, following her death, by Miss Lancaster must have been closer in some ways to that led by poor Jemima at Miss Pinkerton's academy for young ladies. ('Honest Jemima had all the bills, and the washing, and the mending, and the puddings, and the plate and crockery, and the servants to superintend'.)[13] If Ann Lancaster had the supervision of the school servants George Higgins and Thomas Hammon at the time of their subscription to the militia, it was her daughter Eliza who made out the bill which impressed Floris Schopenhauer by its size, to say nothing of providing safety pins for his son or of being called upon for help when he tore his inexpressibles (trousers)![14]

Although no copy of Mr Lancaster's 'Sketch of his Plan and Terms' has been found, the sketch was, in the course of the next four years, amplified into a full-blown *Plan of Education* (1794, 2nd edn 1797), which is discussed presently, while we know something of terms from Heinrich Floris Schopenhauer's grudging reaction to his bill ('they certainly know how to charge'). It is certain that an Oxonian usher was duly appointed, although his identity is not known.

In the history of England the years 1789-92 were somewhat unreal, as Pitt ignored the French Revolution for as long as possible. But beneath the flat, prosperous surface there were seethings of sedition, particularly in the north. For Thomas Lancaster, with a new and larger school to establish, to say nothing of a new and more exposed social position, these were busy, crucial years. The two-year-old Thomas William was making increasing demands on his mother, sisters and — presumably — nursemaid, and Parson Lancaster still had the duties of his curacy at Feltham to attend to. He remained curate of Feltham until 1792, when we find him signing the marriage register at St Mary's, Merton, as assistant to the perpetual curate, the Rev. Charles Frederick Bond, who was also curate of Calbourne. Charles Frederick Bond, who was a Surrey man and presumably related to the last owner of Thomas Lancaster's house, was born in 1765, took his BA at Cambridge (St John's) in 1788 and was ordained deacon at Salisbury the same year. He remained perpetual curate of Merton until 1814, although he did not reside. Prior to 1801 Thomas Lancaster occasionally deputised for the Rev. Bond. From 1801 to 1811 he was nominally non-stipendiary assistant curate, but in all but name he was the incumbent. He became perpetual curate only in 1814 (from 1811 to 1814 he was stipendiary assistant curate); he held the position until his death in 1823[15] and resided in the parsonage following his retirement as schoolmaster in 1811.

In addition to everything else, the Lancasters soon had another son to look after, Henry, born in Wimbledon and baptised there on 30 June 1791. Presumably both Thomas William and Henry were educated at their father's school and therefore met Arthur Schopenhauer. Thomas William was almost exactly the same age as young Schopenhauer, and in 1803 Henry was twelve. I cannot imagine Schopenhauer relishing the company of Thomas William Lancaster, who was very much a chip off the old block. The more dashing Henry would have appealed to him more, had he not been too young to be worthy of notice. It was no doubt also in summer 1791 that Thomas Lancaster was visited by Daniel Lysons, who was preparing his *The Environs of London*, in which he refers to 'the ancient house where the Reverend Mr. Lancaster now keeps an academy'.[16] At the time there were 230 houses in Wimbledon, and baptisms and burials ran at about 35 a year; Merton was smaller — 116 houses and 20 births and deaths a year. It was in 1792 that Horne Tooke moved to Wimbledon, where (even before his trial for high treason in 1794) he became one of the most colourful residents. In summer 1793 the Prime Minister, William Pitt, spent ten days at Henry Dundas's Wimbledon villa, and in September that same year Pitt, Burke and Henry Mackenzie ('the man of feeling') were among Dundas's guests at a party. Parson Lancaster is unlikely to have been present, but will inevitably have met government men at Wimbledon from time to time. Among those who lived or had recently lived there were Earl Spencer, Dundas, Rockingham, Fox, Grenville and Wilberforce. In 1796 another colourful character took up residence: Sir Francis Burdett. Among the most frequent of the many famous visitors and dinner guests were Pitt and Porson. Lord North, Henry Dundas's friend and former chief, was among them too, and Thomas Lancaster probably met him, for his son (Thomas William) later became domestic chaplain to North's daughter-on-law, the Dowager Countess of Guildford.

The Symposiacks of Wimbledon

On 30 January 1793 Bishop Samuel Horsley, in a notable sermon preached before the House of Lords, spoke on a subject close to Thomas Lancaster's heart: the dangers of the revolutionary spirit. Member of Johnson's Club at the Essex Head (1783), friend of William Windham, and Bishop of Rochester since 1793, Samuel Horsley was known for his strength, acuteness and occasional coarseness of manner. In 1795 or thereabouts, in a waggish satire in the form of a poster, he appears as 'Cardinal Horsly'. The exuberantly droll poster, a copy of which has survived,[17] purports to advertise a 'Grand Exhibition at Wimbledon', to take place on Wednesday 25 February [1795] at — readers of the poster would conclude — the West Side residence of the Rt Hon. Henry Dundas, the Secretary of War.

The late eighteenth century was celebrated both for high jinks and boisterous parties, and for its political satires, squibs and spoofs. It would be nice to see the poster as advertising a real party, perhaps attended by Parson Lancaster, but there is no reason to think it anything but a satire. This Wimbledon entertainment, which purports to show a number of government men making an exhibition of themselves, is very much in line with the political skits and burlesques of the 1780s and 1790s (*The Rolliad*, the *Political Eclogues* and *Probationary Odes*, the work of Peter Pindar, the *Anti-Jacobin*, and so on) which derive from the forceful satires of Charles Churchill in the early 1760s. More especially, the 'entertainment' announced by Sieur Henrico Dundassio, and featuring a Bottle Oration by the Sublime Pittachio, belongs together with a 'Political Eclogue' dating from the same year, Mr. M-s-y, *Pitt-Clout and Dun-Cuddy* (1795), to say nothing of the later *Political Creed* (A Satire on Wm Pitt and H. Dundas, parodying the Apostles' Creed, 1797?) and I-Spy-I's *The Melviad, or, The Birth, parentage, education and achievements of a grete Mon (Harry D)* (3rd edn, 1805). In the *Political Eclogues* Pitt and his friends appeared as Virgilian Shepherds; presently they appeared in less flattering guises in the work of Peter Pindar and elsewhere.

About 1803 Peter Pindar (pseudonym of John Wolcot), the satirical poet whose work Arthur Schopenhauer evidently relished, was to be a *habitué* of Lady Hamilton's arty gatherings at Merton Place, where Thomas Lancaster may well have met him. What concerns us now, however, are the political gatherings at Wimbledon, which were well known, for the pro-government satirist Thomas Mathias (1754?-1835, librarian at Buckingham House) wrote of

Grand Exhibition at Wimbledon!!!

On WEDNESDAY, the 25th of FEBRUARY, the Famous

SIEUR
Henrico Dundassio

Will entertain a Select Party with Amusements and Devotions suited to the Day.

FIRST,

A Grand Eating Match,

By Messrs. HAWKESBURY and SPENCER.

Which will prove (beyond all Doubt) the Probability of a FAMINE!

SECONDLY,

A BOTTLE ORATION, By the Sublime PITTACHIO,

In which he will blend, with the most familiar Ease, Wine and Politics, Private Interest, and Public Welfare, &c. &c. To conclude with a Denunciation of the Jacobins, and a Plan for Marching to Paris!

Thirdly,—An Essay on the Beneficial Effects resulting from

PLACES AND PENSIONS!! by Master JENKINSON.

To which will be added, a succinct Account of the

BLESSINGS OF APOSTACY,
By the WARLIKE SECRETARY.

Who will favour the Company with a Song, entitled

"WAR BEFORE COMMERCE,"

Fourthly,—A Serio-Comic Entertainment, call'd

All Under the Table:
Or, WINE FLIES UPWARDS!

In which, "A FORM OF PRAYER" will be read to the PROSTRATE COMPANY,
BY CARDINAL HORSLY,

Who has been engaged at a considerable Expence, and undertakes to prove the Infallibility of the Romish Religion.

The Whole to conclude with a Solemn and Moral DIALOGUE, (after the Manner of *Peach'em* and *Lockit*) entitled,

WATT's GHOST!
Or, DEAD MEN TELL NO TALES.

The Company are requested to pay particular Attention to this Piece, as it developes the real Management of

The SPY SYSTEM.

N. B.—If Time and Circumstances will permit, Mr. HAWKESBURY will recite a HUMOROUS STORY, of his own Composition, call'd

KING's FRIENDS;
OR, THE DUPE.

Which in due Time will be published to the Astonishment of the Public.

⁂ Sieur HENRICO DUNDASSIO returns his grateful Thanks to his Friends and the Public for their hitherto unmerited Confidence and Encouragement—and begs Leave to inform them, that, as he entertains some Apprehensions of being deprived of his Licence by the Swinish Multitude, and as this is in all Probability, the very *last Time* that he shall be *permitted* to perform, nothing shall be wanting on his Part to render the Entertainment complete, and agreeable to that Description of Persons who will alone be permitted to partake of it.

Vivant Rex et Regina.

'the symposiacks at Wimbledon'.[18] Naturally Peter Pindar, the anti-government satirist, has a good deal to say about the goings-on at Wimbledon. He makes repeated reference to Wimbledon and the doings of 'Messieurs Pitt and Dundas'. Indeed, Pindar's favourite butts are the King, Pitt, Dundas and 'Jenky' (Charles Jenkinson, Baron Hawkesbury). In the fourth volume of his works, which Schopenhauer possessed, Pindar wrote:

> O say, where first was planned thy Powder scheme?
> At *Wimbledon* arose the golden dream;
> Where thou [Pitt], and honest Rumbold-hunting Harry [Dundas],
> Project, and *re*-project, and oft miscarry.[19]

In a long poem entitled 'Mr. Pitt's Flight to Wimbledon' Pindar portrays Pitt as fleeing to Wimbledon, to 'Dundas's hay-loft', to escape the angry Mob. He writes of 'Lord Hawk'sb'ry, turned, by Royal Love, / From Jenkinson, a clod of meanest mould' and describes 'Messieurs Pitt and Dundas' as 'pot-valiant'. These references to some of Parson Lancaster's political heroes Schopenhauer will have known. In the fifth (1801) volume of Pindar's works, which he did not possess, such references occur even more frequently: 'Messieurs Pitt, Dundas, Jenkinson & Co', 'Dundas, Pitt and Jenky', 'Pitt, Dundas and Jenkinson . . . / That spotless Trinity of Courtly Pow'r'. Pindar writes of Wimbledon:

> I'll pierce of Wimbledon the midnight scene,
> Where Taxes spring, and Riot's orgies reign
>
> Who says of Wimbledon a slighting word,
> Where Pitt, the Punch of Showman Harry, steals
> To learn State tricks.

And also refers to the heavy drinking in which Dundas and Pitt reputedly indulged. He writes of 'the dozing fountain of Dundas's port', and 'Ode X. To Henry Dundas, Esq.' includes an imaginary advertisement by Henry Dundas for a new job as butler and ends, 'Please to direct to Mister H. Dundas, / At the *Old Sign* — the Bottle and the Glass.'[20]

These references are so close to our satirical poster that one might well wonder whether Peter Pindar was responsible for it. Whether he was or not, there can be no doubt that the 'Grand Exhibition at Wimbledon' was not a real event but the product of some wag's imagination; it may even be that John Horne Tooke and James Perry had a hand in it. The poster is a satire against the hard-drinking Dundas-Pitt coterie by someone familiar with their ways. The identities of those taking part are self-evident. Sieur Henrico Dundassio is Henry Dundas, whose 'villa at Wimbledon was a most popular rendezvous for all his friends. His social qualities, his generous hospitality, and the excellence of his wine cellar, made him a splendid host, and his parties were frequent and large.'[21] Henry Dundas, Secretary for War and a Tory — he studied at Edinburgh a few years after Richard Jameson — was a friend and supporter of Prime Minister Pitt. Those taking part in the Grand Eating Match are presumably Baron Hawkesbury (1727-1808), then President of the Board of Trade, and Earl Spencer (1758-1834), First Lord of the Admiralty, a leading moderate and a friend of Dundas; if our poster dated from 1796 or later, 'Hawkesbury and Spencer' would be Robert Jenkinson (Lord Hawkesbury, 1796) and his Oxford friend, Lord Henry Spencer, but it apparently dates from 1795, the year of Robert Jenkinson's marriage at Wimbledon, so he is probably 'Master Jenkinson'.

The Sublime Pittachio is, of course, Pitt, a frequent visitor to Wimbledon. A room — Mr Pitt's room — was set aside for his use in Dundas's villa, and 'very often the Premier . . . accompanied Dundas out to Wimbledon',[22] which is why Peter Pindar portrays Pitt as fleeing to Henry Dundas's hay-loft. The name Pittachio not only links with Pindar's 'Pitt, the Punch of Showman Harry', but also casts some doubt on the Prime Minister's sobriety. Master Jenkinson of 'Places and Pensions' could be identical with Pindar's 'Jenky', a reference to the most famous of 'Court Crawlers' or 'state-sycophants' (Peter Pindar), Charles Jenkinson, Baron Hawkesbury. But the reference is more likely to be to 'young Jenkinson', Robert Banks Jenkinson (1770-1828), the second Earl of Liverpool and future Prime Minister. Educated at Charterhouse and Christ Church, he had witnessed the capture of the Bastille in 1789, and a few years later 'Lord Hawkesbury's March on Paris' became a stock jest. Thomas Lancaster probably knew the future Prime Minister from this time, hence the dedication of his 1814 sermon. Young Jenkinson not only married at Wimbledon in 1795, he was also at the time MP for Thomas Lancaster's school town of Appleby. Even if Thomas Lancaster did not meet him in 1795, he will have met him soon afterwards, for young Jenkinson and his wife (by then Lord and Lady Hawkesbury) bought Coombe House (or Coombe Wood, as it was also called) in 1801, and therefore joined the symposiacks of Wimbledon. Coombe Wood was where the notorious highwayman Abershawe was said to have lived. The 'Master Jenkinson' of our poster cannot be Charles Cecil Cope Jenkinson (1784-1851), the future third Earl, for he went to sea before the age of ten.

The 'Warlike Secretary' is again Henry Dundas, noted for his pro-Catholic attitude (hence the 'Blessings of Apostacy'). His song, 'War before Commerce', is directed at Pitt, who put commerce before war and was the prime example of the sophisters, economists and calculators at whom Burke raged. 'Cardinal' Horsly is none other than Bishop Horsley, anti-Jacobin and anti-Catholic, notorious for his aspersions on Catholics in 1789/90, who was connected with the Dundas circle through their mutual friend William Windham.

The concluding item, 'Watt's Ghost! Or, Dead Men Tell No Tales', involves only a passing reference to Peachum the informer and Lockit the warder of Newgate in Gay's *Beggar's Opera* (1728). Assuming the apostrophe to be in the right place, the reference is probably — via James Watt's contemporary work on steam as a motivating force — to the huge bowl of steaming hot whisky punch with which Dundas's jollities were wont to climax. Those to whom the poster is addressed would also have known that Watt's son, James (1769-1848), took part in the French Revolution, being at first in high favour with the leaders of the movement. When he showed a distaste for their later excesses he was denounced by Robespierre before the Jacobin Club and forced to flee to Italy, whence he returned to England in 1794. There is, however — particularly in view of the laxity with which apostrophes are treated at this time — a further point, for 'Watt's Ghost' could also refer to Charles Jenkinson's or 'Hawkesbury's' marriage to the part-Indian Amelia Watts. Be that as it may, Hawkesbury, a colleague of Pitt and Dundas and a leading King's Friend, was no doubt in Peter Pindar's mind when he wrote, 'some there are . . . / That flutter in the sunshine of a Court; / Who . . . / Loose the gaunt dogs of Stage, and bawl "Sedition!" '[23] A dupe to members of the Fox Club, Hawkesbury was a man of whom Thomas Lancaster evidently approved; both would have used in all seriousness the phrase which Pindar uses ironically: 'Low Democracy, the Brute'.[24] It was not for nothing that Lancaster dedicated his last published sermon to 'Jenky's' son, the second Earl of Liverpool.

This waggish satire is most likely the work of John Wolcot (Peter Pindar), or of members of the Fox Club, or even of the maliciously waggish George Canning, who was given to versifying and indeed to publishing spoof posters. I am thinking of Canning's anti-Jenkinson 'recruiting sergeant' poster, issued at much the same time as our poster, in which Canning produced a malicious parody of one of Jenkinson's own posters. Canning's poster contained some 50 lines of satirical verse, beginning:

> Tight lads, who would wish for a fair opportunity,
> Of defying the Frenchman, with perfect impunity . . .
> 'Tis the bold Colonel Jenkinson calls you to arm,
> And solemnly swears you shall come to no harm.

At a dinner party given by a friend, Canning caused a packet of these posters to be delivered as from a printer, in fulfilment of an imaginary order; it was implied that copies had already been posted in the streets of London. The somewhat sensitive 'Jenky' (as he was known in Canning's circle) was upset. Here, then, is a 'poster' of a similar kind to our present one, which is both an interesting piece of anti-government satire and a useful way of putting Parson Lancaster into his political context and part of his social context. (I say 'part' because his social life was divided between Wimbledon and Merton.)

Wimbledon and Merton society at this time was both brilliant and sharply divided. In addition to the circle of government men revolving around Henry Dundas, there was a circle of 'levellers' (as Parson Lancaster will have called them) centred on the Fox Club, and — from 1801 — a group of whom Thomas Lancaster saw rather more: the Nelson-Hamilton household, and associated relatives (members of the Nelson, Matcham and Bolton families; Emma Hamilton's mother, Mrs Cadogan), to say nothing of 'My Lady's' exotic visitors, who included a number of literary men. Then there were the local landowners, who included Earl Spencer, Abraham Goldsmid, Benjamin Goldsmid, Daniel Henry Rucker, Sir Robert Burnett, Benjamin Paterson (owner of a copper mill), Robert Reid (farmer), and so on. There were the local nobility and gentry, who included, in addition to some of the above, the Countess of Buckinghamshire, Sir William Bush and Sir Stephen Lushington. There was Captain Francis Fowke of the Wimbledon Volunteers (to which Parson Lancaster and Earl Spencer belonged), and other more humdrum neighbours, of whom the Lancasters presumably saw more. These will have included Dr John Parrott and his wife Charlotte, who lived in Upper Mitcham (Dr Parrott was the local physician;

his wife most likely nursed Ann Lancaster in her final illness); the Rev. Herbert Randolph (a fiercely conservative and orthodox cleric and therefore a man after Thomas Lancaster's heart); John Castle (master of the local elementary school in 1795, and subsequently vestry clerk); Mr Newton and Mr Halfhide, both of them calico printers; Allen Chatfield (distiller); John Watney (brewer); and so on. At this time Wimbledon had a high proportion of well-to-do ratepayers. So far as Thomas Lancaster is concerned, prospective parents (like the Schopenhauers) will also have needed to be dined and impressed.

From our point of view the most interesting are the groups of whom most is known: the Fox Club circle and the Nelson household. The story of the Lancaster family's connections with Nelson belongs a little later, for it concerns the years 1801–5. In the meantime let us return to John Horne Tooke and friends.

One of the foremost residents of Merton in Thomas Lancaster's day was James Perry (1756–1821), who lived in Tavistock Square, London, but also rented Wandle Bank House, Wimbledon, adjoining Lord Nelson's Merton Place. Perry bought the *Morning Chronicle* in 1789 and became famous as the editor of what his old friend Thomas Holcroft called 'the only constitutional paper that remains'. Thomas Lancaster would have been more likely to approve of Thomas James Mathias's description of 'Mr. Perry's *little democratick closet* . . . at the Morning Chronicle office'[25] — 'democratick', when used by such men, being tantamount to 'seditious'. Thomas Lancaster could have met James Perry in the 1770s, when Perry (with Thomas Holcroft, and William Shield, the celebrated composer) was a strolling player with Booth's company in the north-east of England. Like Henry Dundas, Perry was a Scot; he gave up the stage on being told that his Scottish accent unfitted him for it, whereupon he took up writing. It was Perry who advised Holcroft to turn his hand to writing. Whether Thomas Lancaster ever saw Perry on the stage or not, that part of Perry's life no doubt came up in conversation when they found themselves dining together in Wimbledon and Merton, as will have happened not infrequently. Both men were friendly with Nelson. How well they got on together is subject for speculation. When Perry died a tablet was erected to his memory by the Fox Club, 'in testimony of the zeal, courage, and ability with which he advocated the principles of civil and religious liberty'. This would have made him a 'leveller' to Thomas Lancaster, whose attitude to Perry may well have been similar to that of Coke Clifton's attitude to Frank

Henley in Thomas Holcroft's *Anna St. Ives* (1792):

> The absurdity of his tenets can only be equalled by the effrontery with which they are maintained. Among the most ridiculous of what he calls first principles is that of the equality of mankind. He is one of your levellers![26]

Thomas Lancaster was well established at Wimbledon when John Horne Tooke took a house there in 1792. The house in question, Chester House (West Side), just down the road from Henry Dundas's, was detached and pleasantly situated. Two fields in front enabled Horne Tooke to keep a couple of cows, while a large garden enabled him to grow the vegetables and fruit that were to grace his table. The Sunday dinner parties which he gave soon became famous; they were said to have been paid for by 'Colonel' (William) Bosville and (from 1796) Sir Francis Burdett alternately. In his *Memoirs of John Horne Tooke*, published in 1813, A. Stephens included a chapter entitled 'From 1803 to 1804. A Description of the Entertainments of Wimbledon — An Account of some of the Company'.[27] Thomas Lancaster is not mentioned by name, but the 'clergyman of acknowledged orthodoxy'[28] must be either the Rev. Lancaster or the Rev. Randolph. Horne Tooke was not only an eccentric; he was also given to mixing his company rather puckishly, so that a banker (e.g. Samuel Castell) would have to find common ground in conversation with a man of letters (e.g. Samuel Rogers), an atheist (e.g. Tom Paine) with a clergyman (e.g. Thomas Lancaster), a professor (e.g. Porson) with a merchant (e.g. Daniel Henrey Rucker).[29] Horne Tooke would have been perfectly capable of seating Thomas Paine and Thomas Lancaster side by side, for he disliked Paine and can hardly have liked Lancaster. Thomas Lancaster, who would not have been so fond of speaking of 'levellers' had he believed in equality, would have had virtually nothing in common with the author of the *Rights of Man* (1790-2) and *The Age of Reason* (1793), although both men were typical of the age.

Other men who constantly enjoyed Horne Tooke's hospitality and whom Parson Lancaster would have met there included Thomas Erskine (the Lord Chief Justice); Sir Francis Burdett; Professor Porson; William Scott (brother of Lady Oxford); 'Colonel' Bosville, Joel Barlow (an American) and Count Zenobio (a Venetian nobleman), all three members of the 'Society for Constitutional Information'; Sir James Mackintosh; the poet Samuel Rogers; and many others. Of these the famous Greek scholar Richard Porson, who married James Perry's sister in 1796 (she died the following year), is the subject of the best stories, including the one first and most reliably told by Horne Tooke's biographer:

> I was told by Mr. Tooke, that he [Porson] one day called on him at Wimbledon, and was detained to dinner. Some expressions of a disagreeable nature are said to have occurred at table, and the professor, at last, actually threatened both to *kick* and to *cuff* his host. On this the philologist, after exhibiting his own brawny chest, sinewy arms, and muscular legs, to the best possible advantage, endeavoured to evince the prudence of deciding the question as to strength, by recurring to a different species of combat. Accordingly, setting aside the port and sherry, then before them, he ordered a couple of quarts of brandy; and, by the time the second bottle was half emptied, the Greek fell vanquished under the table. On this, the victor, at this new species of Olympic game, taking hold of his antagonist's limbs in succession, exclaimed: 'This is the foot that was to have kicked, and the hand that was to have cuffed me!' and then drinking one glass more, to the speedy recovery of his prostrate adversary, ordered, 'that great care should be taken of Mr. professor Porson;' after which he withdrew to the adjacent apartment, in which tea & coffee had been prepared, with the same seeming calmness as if nothing had occurred.
>
> I should not have mentioned this scene, but that it is well known to all Mr. Tooke's friends, and almost to every one, who ever visited at Wimbledon.[30]

Another famous story was told by P.L. Gordon:

> He [Porson] had engaged to make a copy of this [his Greek] Lexicon . . . During the summer months he had taken up his quarters with his friend Mr. Perry at Merton, and when he had laboured for three years on it, his room caught fire, and destroyed all his papers. Mrs. Perry, on condoling with him on the irreparable loss he had sustained, asked him what he meant to do? 'The loss, Madam,' he replied, 'is, I hope, *not irreparable*, I had got to *iota* — I must now *begin* at the *beginning*, and go back to *alpha*!' When he had finished his breakfast, he retired to another room, renewing his labours as if nothing had happened to disturb them.[31]

Parson and Porson almost certainly met socially; maybe Mr Lancaster called to condone with Porson on the loss of his manuscript.

Anti-Jacobin and Volunteer

More important than Wimbledon and Merton society are the political events of the time, in which many of our 'symposiacks' were involved, for Thomas Lancaster's later life was dominated by the French Revolution and the Napoleonic Wars. In an interesting sermon published in 1814 he looks back at the main events and personalities of the period from 1789 to 1814, virtually that of his Wimbledon schoolmastership.

In referring to the events of late 1792, to the Volunteers and to Nelson, he is, as we shall see, referring to his own part in the historic events of the period. Of most fundamental significance is the way in which he refers to the accursed 'atheistical and levelling principles' of the French Revolution, and to the 'torrent of sedition which, in the latter end of 1792, threatened to overthrow every thing' in the country. The gentrified north-countryman can be heard speaking here, for his 'latter end' is a genteel version of the normal 'back end' (meaning: end) of the northerner; but more important than how he is saying it is what he is saying. In speaking of a 'torrent of sedition' Parson Lancaster is no doubt thinking of the riots in several parts of the country in summer 1792 and of the associations for preserving liberty and property against 'republicans and levellers' which were established at meetings of the inhabitants of many parishes in December 1792. One such meeting took place in Wimbledon. At a series of vestry meetings in 1797 it was resolved to *renew* the Association established in 1792 for the Protection of the King and Constitution of the Country and for stopping the Propagation of Sedition. Among those who attended the crucial meeting at the Dog and Fox (landlord: James Steele) was Thomas Lancaster.

In speaking of a 'torrent of sedition' Lancaster was probably also thinking of the activities of the several Jacobinical societies (Corresponding Society, Society for Constitutional Information, Society of the Friends of the People, Revolution Society) and of the no less hotly Jacobinical dissenting clergymen who, in his view, were fomenting sedition. The sermon 'Discourse on the Love of our Country', given on 4 November 1789 by Dr Richard Price, would have been anathema to him. It was because of such activities that the government introduced a series of coercive measures on 21 May 1792. As a result, Thomas Holcroft, who had become a member of the Society for Constitutional Information in November 1792, found himself summoned to appear at the Old Bailey on 1 December 1794 on a ludicrously inept — but sinister — charge of high treason. He was acquitted, but his *A Narrative of Facts relating to a Prosecution for High Treason* (1795) and *A Letter to the Right Hon. W. Windham* (1795) show the other side of the coin. Thomas Lancaster, in speaking of sedition in such a loose way, twenty years after the event, reveals himself as a dyed-in-the-wool government man. Is it even possible that he went so far as to join the society for Tory schoolmasters, one of the anti-revolutionary societies that sprang up following the French Revolution and the 'sedition' to which it led in this country? I am thinking of the following advertisement, which appeared in *The Times* on 1 January 1793:

To SCHOOL-MASTERS

THE MASTER of a BOARDING SCHOOL, in the vicinity of London, submits to the consideration of his Bretheren in the same employment, whether it would not be very proper for them, at this critical time, collectively to express their esteem for, and attachment to our excellent Constitution, and their Resolution, to preserve and promote, Peace and good Order, by all means in their power.

Gentlemen of the Profession who approve of this proposal, are requested to meet at King's-Arms Hall, Change Alley, Cornhill on Tuesday, the 8th Instant, at Twelve at noon.

Schoolmasters of every description and of every religious denomination, are hereby invited.

N.B. The Chair will be taken precisely at One.

The self-important passages in Thomas Lancaster's 1814 sermon, and the fact that he prided himself on 'doing his bit', even make one wonder whether it may have been he who took the initiative and placed the advertisement. The first paragraph is wholly in line with what was evidently his attitude at the time. It is, however, unlikely that such was the case, for there is no reason to think that he was sufficiently open-minded to wish to share his patriotism with dissenters and Catholics. It seems likely that relatively few schoolmasters responded — maybe they were too busy, or were mostly Whiggishly inclined, like Samuel Parr and Charles Burney

— for no follow-up resolution appeared in *The Times*.

So far as the French Revolution was concerned, Thomas Lancaster was clearly on the side of Burke (with whom Pitt had broken, in tears, in 1791) and Bishop Horsley rather than of Fox, the idol of a number of his Wimbledon friends. The lord of the manor of Wimbledon, Earl Spencer (George John Spencer, second Earl Spencer, 1758-1834), a moderate Whig, was one of those who deserted Fox when he persisted in his view that the French Revolution was 'the greatest event that ever happened in the world, and . . . much the best'. Thomas Lancaster, evidently a less moderate man than Lord Spencer, must have been involved in many dinner-table conversations, some of them heated, on the subject of the French Revolution, the political repercussions of which were felt in Wimbledon, where the Fox Club, in the person of men like James Perry and John Horne Tooke, was dedicated to 'the principles of civil and religious liberty' — precisely those 'atheistical and levelling principles' which Lancaster described as 'accursed'. The gregarious Horne Tooke, whose dinner parties were famous, 'gave his unqualified assent to the proceedings of the Parisians. The capture of the Bastille was of course a subject of triumph, and he ordered a fragment of that imposing mass . . . to be deposited in a conspicuous place in his study.'[32] For Parson Lancaster this must have been the proverbial 'Stein des Anstosses'. When Horne Tooke was brought to trial in 1794 on a charge of high treason, the Rev. Lancaster was probably righteously satisfied — the more so, since the then Home Secretary was another Wimbledon man: Henry Dundas. Horne Tooke regarded the views of Tom Paine (a frequent visitor) as extreme, but to Lancaster Horne Tooke's less radical views will already have been plain 'seditious'.

Labels are particularly misleading at a time when 'it was becoming increasingly difficult to say who, from the angle of practical politics, should be considered a Tory and who a Whig'.[33] When Boswell, in 1778, quoted Eld's definition of a Tory as 'a creature generated between a non-juring parson and one's grandmother', Samuel Johnson added that 'the first Whig was the Devil'.[34] Less amusing, but truer, was Horace Walpole's opinion, expressed in 1762, that 'Tories were Whigs when they got places'.[35] By the time of the second Pitt administration, Whig and Tory overlapped and there were, frequently, wider differences between different kinds of Whig than there were between Whig and Tory as such; indeed, the distinction between Jacobin and Tory is more to the point. The governments over which Pitt (a Tory who called himself a Whig) presided from 1783 to 1801 were, after all, coalitions of moderates, with the more extreme Whigs and others in opposition.

Parson Lancaster was essentially what one would expect him to be: an old-fashioned Whig, in other words a conservative, strongly opposed to Jacobinism and democratick notions of whatever kind. He shared George III's own bigotry: his 1789 sermon identified him as a clerical King's Friend, as did the reference to 'our rebellious colonies' in his 1814 sermon, for it was George III who had spoken of the Americans as rebels. This latter sermon being dedicated to the then Prime Minister, the Earl of Liverpool, is both a reflection of the changed political circumstances of the country and an indication that Thomas Lancaster was essentially a *status quo* man, a government man, who in any case could not afford to alienate too many parents, and had probably known Liverpool since the early years in Wimbledon. Leaving contemporary political labels aside, he was as conservative as his son Thomas William turned out to be, and, like him, will have been regarded as old-fashioned by many of his parishioners. He had little in common with the radical Whigs of Wimbledon, although he was well acquainted with James Perry, a genial soul who left his more radical opinions at his office.

In 1797 Parson Lancaster, in common with many others, decided to do his bit to 'oppose and subdue' the invasion almost hourly expected from 'our implacable enemy' by joining the Volunteers. There had, of course, long been a militia or 'constitutional force' upon which the defence of the country and the maintenance of order were supposed to depend, but by the end of the seventeenth century this body, composed largely of poachers and idlers, had become largely useless:

Stout once a month they march, a blustering band . . .
Of seeming arms to make brief assay,
Then hasten to get drunk, the business of the day.[36]

When 1715 and 1745 gave them a chance to prove their metal, they did so by running away. In 1757 the militia was reorganised and morale rose as the news of victories in America and Germany came in:

The militia, arrayed in red coats with white facings, red waistcoats and breeches, white gaiters and cocked hats, armed with musket, bayonet and sword, marched up and down Surrey, Kent and Sussex, quartered in public houses on the march, drew a shilling a day and had no more onerous duty to perform than the guarding of French prisoners.[37]

In 1780, during the Gordon riots, the Surrey militia were marched up to St George's Fields, where official irresolution kept them undeployed while the mob demolished the Surrey prisons and wrecked private property. Eventually, on 8 June, they were deployed and used to clear Blackfriars Bridge.

Following the French Revolution and the subsequent widespread 'sedition' in this country, the militia was embodied on 1 December 1792, before war as such had begun, after the previous tenant of Thomas Lancaster's house, the Foreign Secretary (Grenville) had urged the necessity of popular support for the government in rousing words:

> If the country is to be saved, the work must not be left to the hands of the Government, but every man must put his shoulder to it, according to his rank and situation in life, or it will not be done.[38]

In 1794 Pitt created the Secretariat of State for War and appointed Henry Dundas to be the first Secretary. That same year an Act[39] was passed to encourage the raising of a supplementary militia of volunteer corps, and a subscription was opened in Surrey for providing arms for the public defence. By the end of 1794 six corps of 'Light Horse' or 'Yeomanry Cavalry' had been formed there. No doubt their 'readiness to afford every assistance in the maintenance of order and good government'[40] was gratifying to the conservative property owners of Wimbledon. An Act[41] passed on 11 December 1796 went further than the 1794 Act and required 63,878 volunteers to be raised to supplement the militia in the defence of the kingdom. Each county, and indeed each parish, had its appointed quota which had to be filled either by volunteers, who were generally paid two guineas, or by ballot. The Volunteers were to be called out for 20 days' training in the year, but were otherwise not to be embodied except in an emergency.

In March 1797 Pitt suggested to the Lords Lieutenant of counties the desirability of the inhabitants of parishes forming Armed Associations for their own protection. Henry Dundas, as Secretary of War, was responsible for the War Office document 'Plan of General Association of the Inhabitants of the Parish of . . . to serve without Pay, for the protection thereof, in case of an Emergency, at the Requisition of the Civil Power, to be submitted to the consideration of a Vestry to be called for that Purpose'.[42] To defray such incidental expenses as might be incurred, it was suggested that a subscription should be opened in the parish, to which every householder might be invited to contribute.

At Wimbledon the government plan was considered at a series of vestry meetings in summer 1797, when it was decided to renew the Association established in 1792 for the Protection of the King and Constitution of the Country and for stopping the Propagation of Sedition. Among those who attended the meeting at the Dog and Fox was Parson Lancaster. The 'Rules and Orders of the Association' were agreed at a vestry meeting on 20 June 1797; they make it clear that the Wimbledon Corps of Horse and Corps of Foot were founded for the protection of King and Constitution. It was agreed that the Corps of Horse should be armed with a 'Pistol, Sabre and Cartouch Box'. Volunteers carried only one pistol, the second holster being used for ball and powder, handkerchief and one day's provisions. At another vestry meeting on 26 June 1797 Thomas Lancaster announced his intention of associating in the Corps of Horse;[43] others to do so included Earl Spencer. In announcing his intention of joining the mounted Volunteers he was not only doing his bit for public order and the defence of the realm; he was also fighting the good fight for Christianity, and was making a personal sacrifice, because his wife, Ann, was ill. She was to die a month later, aged 50. Volunteer affairs will then have helped to keep him from brooding on this further family misfortune, which was not to be the last. His family and servants did their bit too. At this time the Misses Lancaster were among those ladies of Wimbledon who subscribed towards furnishing flannel waistcoats to the 'Infantry Wimbledon Volunteers', and the Wimbledon Militia Book, dating from Michaelmas 1797, lists 70 subscribers, most of them servants, including George Higgins and Thomas Hammon, both of whom worked for Lancaster, presumably as school servants.[44]

On being enrolled in the Corps of Horse or Volunteer Cavalry by its commanding officer, Captain Francis Fowke, Parson Lancaster will have taken the oath of allegiance in words similar to those used in 1803:

I, [Thomas Lancaster], do sincerely promise and swear that I will be faithful and bear true Allegiance to His Majesty King George the Third, and that I will faithfully serve His Majesty in Great Britain for the Defence of the same against all His Enemies and Opposers whatsoever. So help me God.[45]

Wimbledon Vestry minutes make it clear that members of the Corps of Horse furnished themselves with 'Clothing Arms and Accoutrements'[46] at their own expense, to say nothing of needing to possess a horse, which cost £50 to buy and £45 per annum to maintain. If Thomas Lancaster — as is likely — served as padre rather than cavalryman, he will not have had to spend so much on accoutrements; but he will certainly have paid — and paid gladly — for the privilege of protecting King and Country.

In 1798 meetings were held throughout the country by the Lords Lieutenant and their deputies to devise special measures for resisting invasion, including the organising of supplies of food, horses, cattle and wagons for transport; owners of horses were asked to state the terms on which they would be prepared to give their services to the government. Not surprisingly, local defence matters continued to dominate vestry meetings in 1798. At a vestry held on 28 February a parish committee was formed to co-ordinate parish activities for the defence of the county. In April 1798 a further Act was passed[47] which was intended, in Dundas's words, 'for the purpose of giving a general direction to the zeal of the country'.[48] On 8 May Wimbledon Vestry formally resolved 'that we do engage to Embody ourselves in a Corps of Cavalry'. The local defence association — presumably including the Corps of Horse — used to muster twice a week, on Tuesdays and Thursdays, on the Common; there were forfeits for non-attendance on muster nights. The fact that Thomas Lancaster's name does not appear in the muster rolls means either that he served (as one would expect) as padre, or that his role was restricted to being on the committee of the 'armed association'. Be that as it may, it was enjoined that 'the uniform, arms and accoutrements of the gentlemen serving in Volunteer corps should ever be kept contiguous to their beds, that they may be alarmed and assembled at the shortest possible notice or alarm'.[49]

It appears that the Wimbledon Volunteers, unlike their brothers-in-arms in many other places, did not muster on Sundays. It was usual at this time for Volunteers to march to their parish church in uniform and be put through their paces on the village green at the conclusion of the service. Attendance at morning service was regarded as part of the Volunteer's duties. The idea of Sunday exercise went back at least as far as Henry VIII's time, but there was opposition to the idea in 1803 when the Military Service Bill was at the committee stage. Pitt could see nothing in the idea of Sunday parades that was antagonistic to the principles of the Church of England, although the Evangelical party, headed by Wilberforce (yet another Wimbledon man) objected. Eventually it was agreed that Volunteers having religious scruples in regard to Sunday training would be allowed to train on another day of the week. This was a purely religious difference, for Whig and Tory served side-by-side in the Volunteers. It is reasonable to suppose that Parson Lancaster was one of those who argued against the Wimbledon Volunteers parading on Sundays, and that this argument won the day.

On 4 July 1799 King George III reviewed the Surrey Volunteers on Wimbledon Common, the force numbering 676 cavalry and 1,958 infantry. Of the cavalry Lord Leslie's Surrey Yeomanry, 253 strong, was the largest corps; there were ten other troops varying in strength from 80 to 25, one of them being the Wimbledon Corps of Horse under Captain Fowke, who numbered just 29. The King is said to have derived much pleasure from the 'regularity order and military appearance' of the Volunteers.[50] Peter Pindar, in a poem which Schopenhauer knew, derived his pleasure from a description of the King:

> Though on Blackheath, and Wimbledon's wide plain,
> George keeps his hat off in a show'r of rain;
> Sees swords and bayonets without a dread,
> Nor at a volley winks, nor ducks his head:
>
> Although at grand reviews he seems so blest,
> And leaves at six o'clock his downy nest,
> Dead to the charms of blanket, wife and bolster,
> Unlike his officers, who, fond of cramming,
> And at reviews afraid of thirst and famine,
> With bread and cheese and brandy fill their holsters.[51]

If it seems surprising to find Parson Lancaster associated in the Corps of Horse, let us remember that 1797 was the year which Lord Rosebery, in his *Pitt*, described as 'the darkest and most desperate that any British minister has ever had to face'.[52] It was in October 1797 that the Directory named 'Citizen-General Bonaparte' commander-in-chief of the 'Army of England' which was to undertake the descent upon England. For months on end, both in

1797/8 and again in 1803, invasion was daily expected, and so confident was Napoleon of success that he had already struck medals to commemorate the success; they were stamped 'Frappée à Londres en 1804'.⁵³ A meeting of bishops had decided that whilst it would not be consonant with the duties of the profession for clergymen to take up arms, in the event of actual invasion or dangerous insurrection it would be the duty of every priest to give such assistance to the civil or military power as the emergency of the moment might require. This decision in fact amounted to an encouragement to patriotic clerics, of whom there were many, for it only meant that they could not actually fight except, perhaps, in an emergency. Whether Parson Lancaster served as padre or cavalryman — that is, whether he was armed with bell, book and chasuble or with pistol, sabre and cartouche — is not recorded. We should, however, remember what Thomas Hardy later wrote, 'The religion of the country had, in fact, changed from love of God to hatred of Napoleon Buonaparte; and, as if to remind the devout of this alteration, the pikes for the pikemen [of the Infantry Volunteers] were kept in the church of each parish.'⁵⁴ In associating in the Corps of Horse Thomas Lancaster was moved not only by patriotism but by his militant faith, which demanded that he do everything in his power to oppose the accursed atheistical and levelling principles of the French Revolution. If there were ever any doubt as to his position as a conservative Georgian clergyman, it would be dispelled by the wording of his 1814 sermon. The fact that he chose the Corps of Horse does not necessarily mean that he was a hunting person, but does reflect the fact that he had, necessarily, grown up on horseback.

The clearest possible confirmation of this near-hysterical hatred of Napoleon as the devil incarnate rings out of the central passage of Thomas Lancaster's thanksgiving sermon of 1814, the most remarkable and revealing thing he ever wrote. It deserves to be quoted in full:

> Let us consider . . . What great things the Lord hath done for us.
> 1. Look back to the French Revolution, the commencement of which many of us can remember. That Government afforded assistance to our rebellious Colonies, and by that means hastened its own downfall. The wits and pretended philosophers of that nation, with execrable industry, diffused atheistical and levelling principles, not only among their own people, but throughout all Europe.

This country was inundated with them.

In most *other* countries these accursed principles took root downwards, and brought forth fruit upwards. — But what was the case in this country? The torrent of sedition, which, in the latter end of 1792, threatened to overthrow every thing, was, in the beginning of 1793, succeeded by an universal burst of loyalty and love of good order. Was this, think ye, the work of man, or of God? Doubtless it was the work of Him, who alone can rule the hearts of men.

2. The short duration of the last peace, may be accounted as one of 'the great things which God hath done for us' of his nation. We know how highly the character of our arch-enemy was estimated by great multitudes of our misguided countrymen, before that period. We have no need to be told, how they applauded all his actions and arrangements, with a degree of zeal and devotion, which would have done honour to their piety, if they could have been found displaying the same animation in praising the Lord their God. But the object of their idolatry was doomed soon to lose the incense of his worshippers. It pleased God, that the short interval of about eighteen months peace, in the midst of twenty years of war, carried on with unequalled fury and devastation, gave the man an opportunity of shewing himself, in such a manner, as put to silence nearly the whole of his admirers in this country. This was a great mercy to us; because it enabled us to enter into the present contest, with increased unanimity, and of course with an increase of strength and resolution.

3. Contemplate the invasion of this country, so long, and so often, threatened by our implacable enemy; and so seriously expected by all, from the highest to the lowest. Recollect their hills, opposite to us, whitened with the tents of hostile armies, eager to riot in the plunder of this devoted country. Call to mind their immense flotillas and rafts, for the transport of those who were to conquer, and deprive us of every comfort.

On the other side; behold our brave countrymen, with one heart and mind, united as one body, presenting themselves, as volunteers, to oppose and subdue the invaders; had their temerity led them to realize their threats. This happy spirit, pervading our whole population, at that important crisis, answered its end; insomuch as it deterred our enemy from undertaking the threatened invasion.

But it seems probable, that the idea of invading this

country would still have been holden out as a bugbear; had it not pleased God to enable the greatest naval Hero, that ever adorned this, or any other country, to annihilate the maritime power of the enemy, in the ever memorable, and ever lamented battle of Trafalgar! Here, the hand of God was evidently, and eminently, with us.

4. Again; shall I remind you, how often this dealer in blood over-ran Germany, Italy, and the neighbouring countries? How he overspread the Peninsula with his armies, under the deceitful pretence of friendship? How he arrogantly dethroned kings, and set up kings, as if he were a god upon earth? How (with an audacity peculiar to himself) he, from time to time, annexed the states and territories he had conquered, to that fine country, of which he had acquired the sovereignty by stealth? Can you hear of this mad-man losing his numerous and powerful army, and almost himself, on the snowy plains of Russia, in a manner little less providential, than the destruction of the blasphemous Sennacherib's might host; and not perceive, 'that the Lord your God is he that hath fought for you?' Have [not] his armies been gradually expelled from the whole Peninsula (except one province) by the brave and persevering efforts of the greatest Commander now living, even in this age, prolific as it is of eminent military characters [?] — And is not your gratitude for the merciful interposition of the Almighty, heightened by the usurper's recent discomfiture at Leipsic; and by the still more recent resolution of a people, attached to us by vicinity and friendly intercourse, to free themselves from the dominion of the tyrant, and reclaim their ancient freedom and independence?

5. Once more; in all these troubles that have agitated and tormented Europe, from one end to the other, *this country has never been the seat of war.* You, my brethren, have sat, 'every man under his vine, and under his fig-tree', as if it were peace.[55]

Thomas Lancaster is here looking back, in 1814, on events recently over. What is most important in the present context is the fact that the summer of 1803, when Arthur Schopenhauer was at Wimbledon — *what* a pity it is that he did not keep a diary! — was precisely the time at which the hatred and hysteria which can still be heard in Lancaster's sermon were heard on all sides, for instance in a broadside issued on 1 August 1803, which Arthur

Schopenhauer must have heard read out in church (or at school) on Sunday 7 August:

> PROCLAMATION
>
> Made to every man in the United Kingdom of *Great Britain and Ireland*, this first day of August, in the Year of our Lord One Thousand Eight Hundred and Three, and in the Forty-Fourth Year of the Reign of our especially dear Son, KING GEORGE THE THIRD.
>
> WHEREAS by the Blessing of God, the Patriotism, Courage, and Industry of Englishmen, the natural Advantages of our Situation, the Excellence of our Constitution, and the Wise Administration of our Government, we are a Glory to ourselves, the Seat of Freedom, the Empire of Happiness and Wealth, and *Mistress of the Seas*. and whereas at the Head of the Corrupt and Despotic Government of the Neighbouring Realm of France, there is an USURPER, a *Corsican* by birth, and called by the Name of Napoleone Buonaparte, who having subjugated to the most abject Slavery the whole of the vast Empire over which he unjustly reigns, and on the Continent of *Europe*, as well as in *Asia, Egypt*, and *Syria*, and divers other places, spread MURDER, RAPINE, SLAVERY, and DEATH in *Cruel and Horrible Wantonness*; and not having the Fear of God before his Eyes, but being thereto moved by the instigation of the Devil, and filled with Envy, Malice, and Hatred to Us for the aforesaid Blessing We enjoy, as well as at our Magnanimous Resolution to resent effectually his Outrages and Insults, both presumptuously threatened, and doth actually intend to attempt an INVASION OF OUR LAND, and for which said diabolical Purpose he hath been, and at present is, collecting a vast Armed Force whose Orders are to *Murder all our Inhabitants bearing Arms in our Defence, violate the Wives and Daughters of our People, and plunder our Cities*; and all this to reduce this Happy and Independent Empire to a mere Province under his Vile Dominion: We have therefore thought fit to address this Proclamation unto you, calling upon you, as you would express your Love to us, and your wish to transmit to Posterity your Country as you received it from the hands of your Forefathers, and to preserve yourselves and yours from the aforesaid Barbarous and Sanguinary Measures, that you, with one heart, immediately give effect to the Wise and Salutary Proceedings of our Government,

thereby exhibiting to those who would destroy You, an ARMED HOST OF BRITISH FREEMEN, READY TO DIE IN OUR DEFENCE. — And altho' in reliance on God we know the Blood and utter discomfiture of the Enemy will be the price of his Temerity, yet it is your Duty so to arouse and prepare yourselves and so vigorously and unanimously to join in the Common Cause, that you may be able not only to inflict an Awful Punishment on the Legion of Murderers who may assail you, but by a Grand and Dreadful Direction of your Vengeance, strike Deadly Terror and Confusion into the hearts of all your Enemies: And as our brave SEAMEN, should they meet them, will save you on Land great part of the trouble, if not the whole, yet as in the nature of things our Fleets may miss them, have no other reliance for your safety than what arises from TRUST IN PROVIDENCE, CONFIDENCE, UNANIMITY, AND VIGOUR AMONG YOURSELVES.

Given at our Metropolis of London.
BRITANNIA![56]

Though we hear nothing of them in Schopenhauer's diary or in his parents' letters to him, broadside after broadside fluttered from the press during his stay in England, in all of which patriotic appeals to the nation were mixed with execrations and curses levelled at the person of Napoleon. One of the more dignified was Sheridan's *Address to the People* beginning 'OUR KING! OUR COUNTRY! AND OUR GOD!'[57]

In summer 1803 the number of Volunteers was increased following the rupture of the Treaty of Amiens, as a result of which England declared war on France again on 18 May, news of this reaching Calais a week later, according to Arthur Schopenhauer. It was now that the parish of Merton offered, and government accepted, a separate company of 60 rank and file; Thomas Lancaster, who served on the committee of the Merton Armed Association, dedicated the colours in November 1803. In summer 1803 there will have been not infrequent reviews on Wimbledon Common. Musters of the Corps of Horse will also have been a common spectacle and one which will, surely, have given some amusement to the boys of Mr Lancaster's academy, and particularly to Arthur Schopenhauer, who will have had a keen eye for anything bordering on the ludicrous in the conduct of his *bête noire*: the parson on horseback, full of patriotism and self-importance.

On Friday 28 October 1803 Arthur Schopenhauer was among those who saw 16,000 men of the London Volunteers returning from a parade in Hyde Park; he was most impressed, describing them as 'a fine spectacle' and 'most distinguished-looking'. No less impressed was King George III, who caused the Duke of York to issue the following General Order the following day:

> His Royal Highness the Commander in Chief has received the King's Commands to convey to the several Volunteers and Associated Corps which were reviewed in Hyde Park on the 26th and 28th inst. His Majesty's highest approbation of their appearance, which has equalled His Majesty's utmost expectation.
>
> His Majesty perceives, with heartfelt satisfaction, that the spirit of loyalty and patriotism, on which the system of the armed Volunteers throughout the Kingdom was originally founded, has risen with the exigencies of the times, and at this moment forms such a bulwark to the constitution and liberties of the country as will enable us, under the protection of providence, to bid defiance to the unprovoked malice of our enemies, and to hurl back with becoming indignation, the threats which they have presumed to vent against our independence, and even our existence as a nation.
>
> His Majesty has observed with peculiar pleasure that, amongst the unprecedented exertions which the present circumstances of the country have called forth, those of the capital of his United Kingdom have been eminently conspicuous; the appearance of its numerous and well-regulated Volunteer Corps, which were reviewed on the 26th and 28th inst., indicates a degree of attention and emulation both in officers and men, which can proceed only from a deep sense of the important objects for which they have enrolled themselves, a just estimation of the blessings we have so long enjoyed, and a firm and manly determination to defend them like Britons, and transmit them unimpaired to our posterity.
>
> The Commander in Chief has the highest satisfaction in discharging his duty, by communicating these, His Majesty's most gracious sentiments, and requests that the Commanding Officers will have recourse to the readiest means of making the same known to their respective Corps.
>
> (Signed) FREDERICK
> *Commander in Chief.*[58]

Arthur Schopenhauer's reference to seeing the London Volunteers returning from a review in Hyde Park in October 1803 is an isolated one; he shows no awareness of the preparations for defence going on everywhere, and no awareness of the universal hatred of Napoleon,[59] although he must have heard enough about such things from his English headmaster. This is an extraordinary state of affairs, only partly explicable in terms of there being no diary of his time at Wimbledon. His father was, after all, in England in autumn 1797, when defence associations were being formed in parishes up and down the country and were very much in the news. It is therefore doubly surprising that young Arthur, on seeing such things for himself, did not refer to them in a letter. One can only conclude that he was too self-absorbed in his misery to take much interest in the 'real' world.

Thomas Lancaster and Lord Nelson

In his sermon of 1814 Thomas Lancaster called Nelson 'the greatest naval Hero, that ever adorned this, or any other country', which was not only a florid tribute to his most distinguished acquaintance but fully justified, for following Trafalgar 'the danger of any invasion of England rolled away like a dream'.[60] But if Nelson and the Royal Navy had thus carried out the task for which the Volunteers were established, Nelson, in 1802, had in turn paid tribute to the Volunteers when he said, 'If ever war was again to take place, I would send every ship and every regular soldier out of the Kingdom, and leave the nation to be protected by the courage of her sons at home.'[61]

Thomas Lancaster's relationship with Nelson is the most interesting and best documented part of his life. In his invaluable Oxford alumni lists Foster not only confused Thomas Lancaster with his cousin and namesake, but was also inclined to think that Thomas Lancaster was chaplain to Nelson. While this was not the case (Nelson's chaplain from 1801 was the Rev. A.J. Scott), it was not far wrong. The fact of the matter is that Nelson went to live in Merton in 1801 and soon came to know Thomas Lancaster well; in a letter to Parson Lancaster he signed himself 'your friend'. Nelson was Lancaster's junior by eight years, but he was also, like him, the son of a country clergyman, and was by no means averse to sincere flattery and admiration. Thomas Lancaster's Christian patriotism and snobbery were both involved in his attitude to the admiral, though his friendship seems to have been as sincere as the admiration for Nelson which he shared with his children. During the eighteen months he spent at Merton in 1801-3 Nelson regularly attended the parish church and was obviously more appreciative of Parson Lancaster's sermons than was Arthur Schopenhauer. On at least one occasion[62] Mr Lancaster administered Holy Communion to Nelson at Merton Place; this is no doubt the origin of Foster's reference to Thomas Lancaster being '? Chaplain to Lord Nelson'. This friendship with Nelson was the high point of Thomas Lancaster's life.

On 13 September 1801 Nelson purchased Merton Place from Mr Greaves for £9,000, most of which he had to borrow. Merton Place was an old house of considerable charm dating from the end of the seventeenth century and lying in some 70 acres of beautiful grounds on either side of Merton High Street, not far from what is now South Wimbledon Underground station; the house and 40 acres lay in the parish of Merton, the rest of the grounds in Wimbledon. Even before he had seen it, Nelson called Merton Place 'the Farm', probably because of Sir William Hamilton's letter of 16 October — Sir William and Lady Hamilton moved in early in October, Nelson following them on 22 October — in which Nelson's old friend and husband of his mistress wrote:

> We have now inhabited your Lordship's premises some days . . . The proximity to the capital and the perfect retirement of this place are . . . beyond estimation . . . It would make you laugh to see Emma and her mother fitting up pig-styes and hen-coops, and already the Canal is enlivened with ducks, and the cock is strutting with his hens about the walks.[63]

Emma Hamilton even had the stream in the garden enlarged to provide a 'street of water' on which she was — at his suggestion — to row Nelson in the rowing boat which she had also procured. 'You are to be,' Nelson had written to her, 'Lady Paramount of all the territories and waters of Merton.'[64] This is precisely what she was to be.

It was a red-letter day for Thomas Lancaster and his parishioners when the victor of the Nile took up residence among them on 23 October 1801. 'Never had Merton experienced such excitement since one of the first Parliaments had *there* told Henry III that the Laws of England could not be changed.'[65] Merton Place was the talk of the village, particularly when an incessant stream of visitors started to appear, most of them celebrated or notorious, some of them exotic, some barely respectable:

> Nelson's father was one of their first visitors. Then came his sisters, with their families — the Boltons with six children, the Matchams with eight, and his clerical brother, still anxious for further preferment, with his Charlotte; and little Horatia [Nelson's daughter by Emma Hamilton]. Emma's relations were also invited, with Italian singers, the theatrical and musical Mrs. Lind, Mrs. Billington, and Mrs. Denis; [the] Duke of Queensbury, 'Old Q' from Richmond, Dr. Fisher from Doctors' Commons, Naval friends and Admiralty bigwigs, disappointed officers and enterprising journalists; foreign bearers of Nelson's decorations, the Abbé Campbell, 'a Mysterious Monk', Prince Castelcicala, the Neapolitan Ambassador and Prince Leopold, Queen Maria Carolina's son. All were indiscriminately welcomed. 'It was a menagerie,' says Walter Sichel.[66]

Most days a dozen guests sat down to dinner. Thomas Lancaster must have met many of them; unfortunately his thoughts on the subject of these exotic guests and the *ménage à trois* which they were visiting are not recorded.

Other residents of Merton at this time included Abraham Goldsmid of Morden Hall (the Schopenhauers visited his brother Benjamin's house at nearby Roehampton); Rear-Admiral Sir Isaac Smith (cousin and fellow voyager of Captain Cook) of the Abbey Gatehouse; James Perry of Wandle Bank House (editor of Nelson's favourite newspaper); Sir Robert Burnett of Vauxhall Distilleries; the Parrotts of Upper Mitcham; the Newtons; the Halfhides, who lived next door to Merton Place; Mr Thoytt (owner of a copper mill); old Mr Axe of Birchin Lane; and so on. Over the parish boundary in Wimbledon there were, as we have seen, many distinguished residents, including members of the government well known to Nelson (Earl Spencer, Henry Dundas). Dundas, who was treasurer of the navy from 1784 to 1800 and Secretary of War from 1794 to 1801, planned and carried out the Egyptian campaign of 1801 against the advice of Pitt and the King, while Earl Spencer, who was First Lord of the Admiralty from 1794 to 1801, singled Nelson out and sent him to win the battle of the Nile (1798).

When Nelson arrived at Merton Place,[67] the house which had until recently gone together with the rectory, one of the first who presented themselves was the Rev. Thomas Lancaster, who had been acting curate of Merton since the previous April. It seems that Nelson and the Hamiltons closely associated themselves with the church, and therefore with its assiduous incumbent. In his letter to Emma Hamilton of 26 September 1801 Nelson had written, 'Have we a nice church at Merton? We will set an example of goodness to the under-parishioners.'[68] If, as Philip Rathbone has said,[69] church-going is an example of goodness, the Rev. Thomas Lancaster had nothing to complain about. He was, of course, far from being predisposed to complain, and Nelson, the 'thorough clergyman's son',

> does not seem to have reflected that the . . . parishioners might not consider his way of life a very striking example of goodness, or that their parson might be difficult about the presence in his church of his great parishioner's curious ménage. His faith was justified: the Reverend Mr. Lancaster was . . . transported with delight to find this aristocratic household among his flock.[70]

Nelson and Lady Hamilton were regular members of the congregation, often accompanied by Nelson's nieces and nephews; in the old church the Nelson party had their own horse-box pew. Nor was Nelson's goodness in any way confined to churchgoing. When Sir Harris Nicolas was preparing his edition of Nelson's letters (1844-6), Thomas Lancaster's daughter, Mrs Ruth Ullock, wrote to him:

> In revered affection for the memory of that dear man, I cannot refrain from informing you of his unlimited charity and goodness during his residence at Merton. His frequently expressed desire was that none in that place should want or suffer affliction that he could alleviate, and this I know he did with a most liberal hand: always desiring that it should not be known from whence it came. His residence at Merton was a continued course of charity and goodness, setting such an example of propriety and regularity that there are few would not be benefitted by following it.[71]

Given that Nelson only spent a little over eighteen months at Merton, this is a remarkable tribute. It also testifies to the deep affection and admiration in which he was held by the Lancasters.

No doubt Ruth Ullock, in paying tribute to him in these terms, was thinking of his habit of visiting the poor of Merton and doing what he could to relieve them; it may well be that Thomas Lancaster sometimes accompanied him on these charitable visits.

As Carola Oman wrote in her admirable biography, 'The relations of Merton Place with the [Rev. Thomas Lancaster] had been cordial from the first.'[72] Mr Lancaster met, both in his congregation on Sundays, and at the dinner parties which were such a feature of life at Merton Place, most members of the Merton Place circle, including the Rev. Edmund Nelson; the Rev. and Mrs William Nelson, their daughter Charlotte and son Horace; Mr and Mrs George Matcham and their son George; Mr and Mrs Thomas Bolton and their sons Tom and George. Following Nelson's arrival in Merton, Thomas Lancaster lost no time in inviting the Merton Place party to dine. In November 1801 Lady Hamilton wrote to Mrs Sarah Nelson (Nelson's sister-in-law), 'Wednesday we return to Merton, dine at Mr. Lancaster's Thursday.'[73] When Mr Lancaster dined at Merton Place, which he did not infrequently, it was allegedly not unknown for him to recite occasional verses in honour of Lord Nelson:

> Mr. Lancaster was a romantic gentleman, given to the composition of poetic effusions which Emma kindly allowed him to recite in her drawing-room. Whatever their quality, he meant them as a sincere tribute to My Lord and My Lady, his parish's chief benefactors.[74]

The evidence does not bear out the idea that Thomas Lancaster was a 'romantic gentleman' except in terms of his hero-worship of Nelson; maybe his slightly embarrassing verses, sincere as they would certainly have been, were prompted by the *vers de société* to which some other members of the circle (Lord William Douglas, Cornelia Knight, even James Harrison) were given. Piquancy is added by the fact that one of those whom Thomas Lancaster probably met at 'My Lady's' *c*. 1803 was the rugged and caustic satirist John Wolcot (Peter Pindar), who had made his name partly through vitriolic anticlerical verses; the anonymous author of the *Memoirs of Emma Lady Hamilton* reported that:

> Among other persons who were entertained at Merton was Dr. Wolcot, generally known by his poetical appellation of Peter Pindar. This eccentric character, having indulged rather

freely one evening in his favourite potation, set fire to his night-cap on going to bed. The cap belonged to Lord Nelson, and the next morning the bard pinned a paper to it with these lines:
> Take your night-cap again, my good Lord, I desire;
> For I wish not to keep it a minute
> What belongs to a Nelson, wher'er there's a fire,
> Is sure to be instantly in it.[75]

If he had known about it, Arthur Schopenhauer would have relished the idea of a meeting between Peter Pindar and Parson Lancaster, who continued to be invited to Merton Place after Nelson's death. On 28 October 1807, on the occasion of 'little Horatia's' birthday, we find him favouring the company with a song which young George Matcham, who was something of a wag, claimed to have mistaken for a funeral oration;[76] but then young Matcham also described a song, given at Merton Place by William (*Vathek*) Beckford, as 'a very horrible noise'.[77]

In her account of Mr Lancaster's academy Johanna Schopenhauer wrote that 'Lord Nelson had two of his nephews educated there.'[78] She appears to attribute this statement to Lancaster himself. Whatever its origin, the story seems to be at best exaggerated. Of the nephews in question only George Matcham junior (1789-1877) may have attended Mr Lancaster's. St John's College, Cambridge, Tutor's Book records only that he received 'private tuition' before going up to Cambridge. If he had attended Mr Lancaster's the chances are that the fact would have been recorded. Thomas Bolton (later Nelson; 1786-1835) was educated 'at the High School, Norwich, and afterwards at Byfleet under the Rev. Mr. Haggett',[79] which seems conclusive, although it is possible that he attended Mr Lancaster's briefly, going on to Mr Haggett's because it was unsatisfactory. In a letter to Mrs Bolton dated 11 June 1802 Nelson sent £100 'towards the education of your children'.[80] Horace Nelson (1788-1808) went to Eton. While it is likely that all three boys visited Mr Lancaster's socially, there is no evidence that there was more to it than that. It is possible that George Matcham and Tom Bolton attended Mr Lancaster's on a temporary basis, although I doubt it. The most likely explanation is that a social visit has been construed into attendance as a result of the snobbery both of Thomas Lancaster and of Johanna Schopenhauer. Johanna Schopenhauer's stories seem to be at their most vulnerable where they concern Nelson.

So far as Thomas Lancaster was concerned, Nelson was the perfect Christian hero doing battle with the powers of darkness. Nelson could therefore do no wrong in his eyes, for he 'either did not see or did not want to see any imperfections in the new members of his flock'.[81] The implication is that a *ménage à trois*, provided it involves a national hero, is deemed concomitant with the rigid orthodoxy practised at Mr Lancaster's academy. Young Schopenhauer, who must have heard not a little of this remarkable household, in which the intimacy between Nelson and Lady Hamilton was obviously not of a purely platonic character (for this we have the evidence of Thomas Saker, the Merton Place factotum), no doubt regarded the Rev. Thomas Lancaster's attitude to it as a prime example of English hypocrisy.

Although the boys at Mr Lancaster's are more likely to have erred on the side of ribaldry than of charity, Lady Spencer seems to have been persuaded — like Thomas Lancaster — of the innocence of Nelson's relationship with Emma Hamilton. In the diary of Frances Lady Shelley there is an account which presumably derives from Lady Hamilton (otherwise it could only come from the Rev. Lancaster, a much less likely story):

> One day, she [Lady Spencer] came to her daughter-in-law, and said: 'Lavinia, I think you will *now* agree that you have been to blame, in your opinion of Lady Hamilton. I have just assisted at a private Sacrament with them both, which Nelson has taken before he embarks. After the service was over, Nelson took Lady Hamilton's hand, and, facing the priest, said, "Emma, I have taken the sacrament with you this day, to prove to the world that our friendship is most pure and innocent, and of this I call God to witness!" '
> What horrible sacrilege! [Lady Shelley's comment.][82]

Thomas Lancaster was either too unworldly, or too worldly, to see the occasion in the same light as Lady Shelley, for he was the priest, and the ceremony took place in Merton parish church on Friday 13 September 1805:

> Some time that day Nelson and Emma went to Merton Church and took Holy Communion together. Before the altar a gold ring was solemnly put on to the wedding finger of her who was a wife in his sight, 'for', said Nelson, 'we both stand before our God with pure hearts and affection.'[83]

A few hours later Nelson and the Rev. Lancaster were both on their way to Portsmouth in separate carriages, Thomas Lancaster carrying a farewell note to Nelson from Lady Hamilton.

Further evidence of the Rev. Lancaster's relationship with Merton Place comes from the Merton parish register. Thus on 26 April 1802 Mr Lancaster baptised Lady Hamilton's maid: 'Hamilton, Fatima Emma Charlotte Nelson, from Egypt, a Negress, about twenty years of age, under the protection of the Right Honourable Lady Hamilton, was baptized April 26th 1802. Thomas Lancaster, Minister.' That 'Right Honourable' shows that Mr Lancaster's attitude to Emma was nothing if not respectful. 'Fatima' is the Coptic girl Quasheebaw whom Nelson had brought back from Egypt as a present for Emma, who adopted her and gave her the names in which she was baptised. She appears in Lord William Douglas's comic saga of the Merton Place circle, written in 1801:

Let not poor Quasheebaw, fair Lady, think,
Because her skin is blacker than this ink,
That, from the Muse, no sable praise is due,
To one so faithful, so attached and true!
Though in her cheek there bloom no blushing rose,
Our Muse nor colour nor distinction knows,
Save of the heart — and Quasheebaw's, I know,
Is pure and spotless, as a one night's snow.[84]

Later poor Quasheebaw's mind gave way and she ended her days in an asylum. The Rev. Lancaster's admiration for Nelson is shown again by a long and quite inappropriate note which he inserted in the Merton register of baptisms on the occasion of the baptism of the son of Nelson's uncle, William Suckling, who had remarried some years earlier:

Nelson, son of William Suckling, Esq., and Wibrew, his wife, born in the morning of the thirty-first day of December, eighteen Hundred and three [A note in the margin reads: 'N.B. Not four but three. — T.L.'] in the Borough of New Windsor, Berkshire, and Christened in the Parish of Merton, Surrey, on the sixth day of September, eighteen hundred and five; which Christening was postponed on account of Lord Viscount Nelson (one of his God-fathers) being out of England on his Majesty's service.

This must have been one of the last occasions Thomas Lancaster saw Nelson in his church.

If, then, Lord Nelson was at Merton in 1803 and was inclined to befriend the Rev. Thomas Lancaster, it would follow that young Schopenhauer might have been presented to him at this time, and indeed might have been one of the boys to recite before him. Richard Milward has written that 'Among [the boys at the Rev. Mr Lancaster's academy who recited before Lord Nelson] might have been the famous German philosopher, Arthur Schopenhauer.'[85] The occasion as such was most fully described by T.G. Jackson:

> Mr. Brackenbury . . . tells me he has talked with an old man who was at school with Mr. Lancaster, and who remembers being brought with some of his schoolfellows into the front room downstairs, which was then the drawing room, and seeing Nelson and Lady Hamilton sitting on the sofa; the boys recited their pieces before these distinguished visitors, and were rewarded with a half-holiday.[86]

It is easy to imagine the scene, with the young philosopher-to-be bowing to the visitors and reciting, perhaps, Milton's 'On Time', which he translated into German at about this time. Gwinner stated categorically that Schopenhauer met Lord Nelson and Lady Hamilton, although he did not name the occasion. Unfortunately it is clear that this scene never took place.

The idea that Schopenhauer might have been present on this occasion has arisen partly because the dates of his attendance at Mr Lancaster's have not been known, and partly because there has been some confusion over exactly when Nelson was at Merton Place. The facts are these. Schopenhauer attended the school from 30 June to 20 September 1803, and appears not to have visited it at all until 27 June 1803. Nelson was at Merton Place from 21 October 1801 to 18 May 1803, and for a few weeks in 1805; he left Merton for the last time on Friday 13 September 1805. It therefore follows that Schopenhauer missed seeing or even meeting Nelson by a matter of weeks, although he will no doubt have heard a good deal about him, for the Rev. Lancaster was not inclined to play down his relationship with the national hero. When Arthur Schopenhauer and his parents dined with Lancaster on Monday 27 June 1803 the conversation no doubt turned to Nelson, with Johanna Schopenhauer as keen to impress the Rev. Lancaster as he was to impress her. Thomas Lancaster will have been genuinely interested to hear about the Grand Gala which the English merchants of Hamburg gave for the Nelson/Hamilton party in October 1800.

The most interesting evidence of the relationship between Schopenhauer's headmaster and Lord Nelson is provided by an exchange of letters between the two men in 1803-4. Thomas Lancaster wrote first, in a letter which has until now remained unpublished. It reads as follows:

My Lord

I beg Leave to offer you my most sincere Congratulations on the Triumph of Justice & Rectitude over an absurd naval Etiquette, in the Decision of Lord Ellenborough, in your Favour, last Monday, in the Court of King's Bench.

And the Committee of the Merton armed Association, to whom I mentioned this Decision, desire your Lordship to accept also their Congratulations on the Occasion, together with their hearty Wishes for your safe & happy Return Home.

The Parish of Merton has offered, and Government has accepted, a Company of 60 Rank & File, exclusive of commissioned & non-commissioned Officers: tomorrow at ten o'clock, I am to deliver the Colours to them at Church previous to their being inspected by Colonel Hardy at twelve.

I hope your Lordship enjoys good Health amidst the Fatigues of your important Command. And that you may soon happily & completely effect its Purposes, & return to cheer the Parish of Merton with your Presence, is the ardent Wish of rich & poor; but of none more than of him who is, with great Truth & Esteem,

My Lord,
Your Lordship's
Wimbledon,   most obliged and
Novr. 18th 1803   obedient Servant,
Thomas Lancaster

P.S. All my Sons & Daughters entreat your Lordship to accept the Tribute of their grateful & affectionate Regard.[87]

Nelson's letter to 'The Rev. Mr. Lancaster, Merton' addressed from HMS *Victory* on 14 February 1804 was a reply to this hitherto unknown letter. It reads as follows:

My Dear Sir,

Many thanks for your kind letter, and for all the good wishes of my friends at Merton, who I shall some happy day hope to thank in person. Nothing shall be wanting on my part to merit the continuance of their esteem by every exertion in my power to bring about an honourable and speedy Peace. — With my respectful compliments and good wishes to all your family, believe me ever, my dear Sir, your much obliged friend,

Nelson and Bronté

You must excuse short letters, for my time will not afford to turn over the leaf.[88]

In the first paragraph of his letter Thomas Lancaster is referring to Nelson's attempt to recover the one-eighth share of prize money to which he considered himself entitled; in a judgement delivered in the Court of King's Bench on Monday 14 November 1803 Lord Ellenborough found in Nelson's favour.[89] The second paragraph of Mr Lancaster's letter not only implies that he was himself a member of the committee of the Merton Armed Association, as we should expect him to be, but confirms that, following the collapse of the Treaty of Amiens, the Surrey Volunteers were re-embodied and expanded. In summer 1803 Schopenhauer's headmaster clearly had the affairs of Merton Armed Association very much on his mind.

Mr Lancaster's wishes were, of course, granted; Nelson returned safely to spend a few weeks at Merton in 1805, by which time Mr Lancaster had probably forgotten his somewhat ructious German pupil. On the first Sunday after Nelson's return, 25 August, his daughter Horatia took her place among the other children of the parish at Thomas Lancaster's afternoon service. Winifred Gérin has made the obvious comment:

> If . . . Mr. Lancaster had any suspicions about the little girl introduced to Merton, Nelson's countless virtues outweighed everything else in his eyes. It must have been hard for him to believe that Nelson could do any wrong; he knew the admiral's unobtrusive charities better than any.[90]

After Nelson's death Mr Lancaster used to help Lady Hamilton to preserve the myth of Horatia's identity by attending her birthday party. On Friday 6 September 1805 he christened the infant son (Nelson) of Colonel and Mrs William Suckling, apparently in the presence of the Duke of Clarence.[91]

It was in early September 1805, when Nelson was at Merton Place for the last time, that the recital (of which we have heard) took place, and indeed that 'Wimbledon School' was renamed 'Nelson House'. Carola Oman writes:

> On an unascertained morning of this week [the first week of September 1805], Lady Hamilton fulfilled a promise. An open chariot breasted Wimbledon Hill, and drew up outside a handsome house in the Dutch-Jacobean style, to be renamed in honour of this day's occasion 'Nelson House'. Here some favoured young gentlemen in blue coats with brass buttons were summoned to the front parlour and ordered by their clerical pedagogue to recite to the Victor of the Nile, an ordeal which ended happily for all with a request from the chief guest for a half-holiday for the school, and with three hearty cheers for Lord Nelson and Lady Hamilton.[92]

Within a week or so Nelson left Merton Place for the last time. There are different accounts of the occasion. What seems to be further interesting light on the Rev. Thomas Lancaster's relationship with him is provided by Kathleen Denbigh, who has written:

> Nelson's last day at Merton was Friday, 13 September . . . On arrival at Portsmouth, Nelson sent a scrawled note to Emma via Mr. Lancaster, the vicar of Merton, who was a friend and admirer and who was there to see him off.[93]

In fact the Rev. Lancaster was present at Portsmouth for a different reason altogether. The true basic facts are given by Carola Oman, who writes that on leaving Merton Place for the last time on 13 September 1805:

> He [Nelson] drank tea, by candlelight, at the 'Anchor', Liphook, and arrived at the familiar 'George', Portsmouth, at 6 on the morning of September 14. Outside its doors he saw the carriage of the Vicar of Merton, who had just parted with a fourteen-year-old son, going as a volunteer, first-class, to the *Victory*, and Mr. Lancaster waited while the Admiral dashed off four lines, opening 'My dearest most beloved of Women, Nelson's Emma!'[94]

With the exception of those opening lines, this account squares with all the facts, including, most importantly, Nelson's own letters. The note to Lady Hamilton, in reply to one from her which Mr Lancaster had carried with him to Portsmouth, read as follows:

> My dearest Emma,
> I arrived here this moment, and Mr. Lancaster takes this. His coach is at the door, and only waits for my line. Victory is at St. Helen's, and, if possible, shall be at sea this day. God protect you and my dear Horatia, prays
>   Yours ever,
>   Nelson and Bronté
>
> 6 o'clock, George Inn,
> Sept., 14th, 1805.[95]

Clearly the Rev. Lancaster did not go to see Lord Nelson off. Nor did he travel in the same coach. He travelled down to Portsmouth, in his own coach, to see his son off, Henry, who was starting his naval career on HMS *Victory*, 'under the especial patronage' of Lord Nelson (as Henry Lancaster later put it). Nelson shows no surprise at Mr Lancaster's presence because he had himself arranged for young Henry to begin his service as a volunteer, first class, on board the *Victory*. Henry Lancaster had thus been more fortunate than Lionel, the eight-year-old son of Benjamin Goldsmid, who had clamoured to be taken on like Henry Lancaster but had been declared by Nelson to be too small.

It is to Henry that Nelson refers in a further letter to Lady Hamilton dated 18 September 1805, when he wrote, 'Tell Mr. Lancaster that I have no doubt that his son will do very well.'[96] In entering the navy Henry Lancaster was following another family tradition, to say nothing of following a general custom of the time, for 'It has been from time immemorial the heathenish custom to sacrifice the greatest fool of the family to the prosperity and naval superiority of the country, and at the age of fourteen, I was selected as the victim.' The words belong to Marryat's Peter Simple,[97] but a generation earlier Henry Lancaster, as the proverbially unfortunate younger son, had been offered up to the same tradition. However, if he was unfortunate in a general sense, he was doubly fortunate to begin his service under Nelson on *Victory*, for, as Southey noted:

> To his midshipmen he [Nelson] ever showed the most winning

kindness encouraging the diffident, tempering the hasty, counselling and befriending both. 'Recollect', he used to say, 'that you must be a seaman to be an officer; and also, that you cannot be a good officer without being a gentleman.'[98]

Indeed, Nelson was in the habit of referring to his midshipmen as his 'children'. He will have been particularly predisposed to be sympathetic towards Henry Lancaster, since he had lost his own mother at the age of nine. Like Nelson's father, the Rev. Thomas Lancaster lost his wife early and was left 'double parent', in his case to a flock of six children ranging from 6 to 17. Born in 1791, Henry Lancaster commenced service in 1805 at the age of 14. (Nelson entered as midshipman at twelve years and three months, a not unusual age!)

Henry Lancaster entered the navy as a volunteer, first class, serving on the *Victory* at Trafalgar. After the death of his patron and his father's friend he served as a midshipman in the *Ocean*, also on the Cadiz station. Vice-Admiral Lord Collingwood, under whom he was serving, may have been a distant relative, for in a letter to J.E. Blackett dated from HMS *Ocean* on 1 May 1806, when Midshipman Henry Lancaster was on board, Collingwood wrote, 'I have a letter from a kinsman of mine . . . who derives our descent from Lancaster (Talebois), who came with William the Conqueror.'[99] This would have made Henry Lancaster a kinsman, although presumably not the 'kinsman' in question. Henry Lancaster saw most of his active service, however, in the Mediterranean; the most interesting part of his service took place when he was serving on the *Apollo* from 1808 to 1813. In O'Byrne's *Dictionary of Naval Biography*, for which Henry Lancaster wrote an account of his career,[100] this period is described:

> we find him employed, chiefly on the Mediterranean station until promoted to the rank of Lieutenant, 20 Oct. 1813. While in the [*Apollo*] Mr. Lancaster served in her boats, with those of a squadron under Lieut. John Tailour, on the night of 31 October 1809, at the capture and destruction, notwithstanding a fearful struggle and a loss to the British of 15 men killed and 55 wounded, of the French storeship Lamproie of 16 guns and 116 men, bombards Victoire and Grondeur, and armed xebec Normande, with a convoy of seven merchant-vessels, defended by numerous strong batteries in the Bay of Rosas [*Gazette*, 1809, p. 1907]. He also assisted in capturing, 13 Feb. 1812, the French frigate-built store-ship Mérinos of 20 guns

and 26 men, under the batteries of Corsica, and, on 20 of the following Sept., the national xebec Ulysse of 6 guns. He was further . . . present at the reduction, in Jan. and Feb. 1813, of the islands of Augusta and Curzola, as well as on shore, as a volunteer, in 1813, at the siege of Trieste . . .

While serving on the Mediterranean station he therefore did very well, as Nelson had told his father he would. He evidently cut quite a dashing and daring figure, volunteering for boat service and raiding parties, to say nothing of twice jumping overboard to save life. He had, while serving in the *Apollo*, a personal friend and no less dashing shipmate in the person of Tom Ullock, the purser. Tom Ullock had entered service (as purser) at the same time as Henry Lancaster, in September 1805. While serving in the *Apollo* his exploits were twice noticed in the *Gentleman's Magazine*.[101] In April 1813 he was wounded when the *Apollo* and *Cerberus* took temporary possession of Devil's Island, near the north entrance to the harbour of Corfu; and in May 1813 (unusually for a purser) he volunteered to join a boat party to spike the guns in one of the enemy batteries on the island of Lagosta. On his next leave he was no doubt fêted not least by Henry Lancaster's family, for he went on to marry Henry's sister Ruth.

For all his dashing Mediterranean adventures, Henry Lancaster's naval career was neither as active as that of his contemporary Edward John Trelawney nor as long and distinguished as that of another contemporary, Frederick Marryat.[102] Like so many naval officers of his generation, he found himself paid off and put on half pay shortly after the outbreak of peace with France. He was eventually retired as a commander on half pay on 28 July 1851, having been promoted commander by an Order in Council of 25 June 1851 by way of reward for long service. But if Henry Lancaster missed the egregious adventures of Trelawney, he did at least get to Trafalgar on time. For the newly joined 15-year-old midshipman Trafalgar must have provided enough terror, excitement and reflected glory to last a lifetime. Trelawney has, in his *Adventures of a Younger Son* (1831), a finely written scene in which the great hulk of the *Victory*, battered by storms and bearing against the tempests the dead body of Nelson (pickled in brandy), looms up through the darkness of an Atlantic storm; but Henry Lancaster was actually on board.[103]

The painting 'Death of Lord Nelson, 1805' by B. West (engraved by J. Heath and published in 1811) included 'Mr. Lancaster

(Midshipman)'. No doubt a copy of the engraving was one of Thomas Lancaster's proudest possessions.

By the time he came to give his Thanksgiving Day sermon in 1814 Parson Lancaster will have heard of the exploits in the Mediterranean of his son, Lieutenant Henry Lancaster, and his friend Tom Ullock. He will have been thinking of his family's relationship with him when he said of Nelson:

> it seems probable, that the idea of invading this country would still have been holden out as a bugbear; had it not pleased God to enable the greatest naval Hero, that ever adorned this, or any other country, to annihilate the maritime power of the enemy, in the ever memorable, and ever lamented battle of Trafalgar! Here, the hand of God was evidently, and eminently with us.[104]

As a naval man Henry Lancaster was not given to such florid language as his father, but he remained extremely proud of having commenced service under 'the illustrious Nelson' and, forty years later, performed the greatest possible posthumous service to Nelson by taking up the pen on behalf of his daughter, Horatia.

Once Horatia Nelson's parentage had been published in 1849, her friends — including her lifelong friend Henry Lancaster — decided to organise a committee to try to secure her a pension.[105] In seeking support the committee went to the top, to Prince Albert and the Prime Minister of the day, Lord Aberdeen. It was Henry Lancaster, in a series of letters, some of which are preserved in the National Maritime Museum, who kept Horatia Nelson-Ward (a reluctant but needy beneficiary) informed of the progress of their efforts on her behalf. The decisive step was taken on 21 July 1853, when a deputation of the committee, including Henry Lancaster, called on the Prime Minister. The eventual outcome was that Queen Victoria offered Mrs Ward a pension of £300 per annum for herself or an annual pension of £100 to each of her three daughters. Mrs Ward accepted the latter. This was the final tribute by a member of the Lancaster family to the memory of Lord Nelson.

Later Life

If the Lancasters' move to Wimbledon coincided with the outbreak of the French Revolution, it was the aftermath of the revolution in the form of the Napoleonic Wars that dominated Thomas Lancaster's life there. From 1797 to 1805 he was preoccupied with the Wimbledon and Merton Armed Associations as well. From 1801 to 1805 and beyond his social life revolved around Merton Place. However, while he was doing his bit for King and Country and the downfall of the seditious, and while he was cultivating the friendship of the great if not of the good, he was also running a school which had begun to flourish, to say nothing of having a family for which he was solely responsible from 1797. When his wife Ann died on 29 July 1797, at the age of 50, Eliza was 17, Ruth 13, Ann 12, Thomas William 10 and Henry 6. This meant that Miss Lancaster, at the tender age of 17, inherited the positions of mother and school matron. In 1794, vestry minutes reveal, the Rev. Mr Lancaster was given two pews in Wimblebon St Mary's for the use of his school. By 1802 the school had expanded to such an extent that further accommodation in the parish church was urgently needed. At a meeting held at the Dog and Fox on 15 October 1802, the vestry 'proposed to Revd. Thos Lancaster that the Singing Gallery in the church should be altered and fitted up for the reception of the Young Gentlemen of his Academy who now occupy certain pews in the Church[,] upon Condition that Mr. Lancaster do retain such pew or pews only as he shall deem necessary for the accommodation of his own private family'. Mr Lancaster having accepted the proposal, alterations were put in hand straight away, which means that the scene of Arthur Schopenhauer's miserable Sundays a few months later was the singing gallery of Wimbledon Church; it was there that he had to sit through the tedious, old-fashioned, intolerant sermons of the Rev. Herbert Randolph. No doubt Thomas Lancaster's *Plan of Education* (1794, new edn 1797) was partly responsible, as it had been intended to be, for the success of his school, although his assiduously cultivated social connections will have helped, as will the 'Nelson factor'.

When he moved to Wimbledon Thomas Lancaster was curate of Feltham. He retained the position until April 1792, when he resigned in order to concentrate on schoolmastering. It was not until January 1801, when he was appointed non-stipendiary assistant curate of Merton, that he again had a preferment, although from 1790 onwards we find him signing the *Wimbledon* marriage register as 'Minister'. Dating from 1801 is a drawing of Merton Parsonage, 'by Henry Lancaster 1801 after Eliza Lancaster', which survives in Merton Vicarage.

By 1801, when Viscount Nelson moved into Merton Place,

Henry Lancaster was 10. His eldest sister, Eliza, was 21. Of the other children Ruth was 17, Ann 16 and Thomas William 14. During the period from 1801 to 1805 and beyond the Lancaster children will have benefited socially from their father's friendship with his important (and child-loving) new parishioner, with whom social visits were exchanged. Frequent visitors to Merton Place were Nelson's nephews and nieces, some of whom were much the same age as the Lancaster children. In 1801 Tom Bolton was 15, his sister Eliza 12 and Ann 10; George Matcham was 12 and his eldest sister Catherine 9; Horace Nelson was 12 and his sister Charlotte 13. The young Lancasters both met their young contemporaries and were fussed over by Nelson himself. He was particularly fond of children and was given to addressing local boys in the street at Merton, so how much more friendly will he, the clergyman's son and brother, have been to the motherless children of 'his' new clergyman. The postscript in Mr Lancaster's letter of 18 November 1803 ('All my Sons and Daughters entreat your Lordship to accept the Tribute of their grateful and affectionate Regard') shows that such was the case.

The Lancasters also had their own visitors, including Maria Lattimer (witness at a wedding in Wimbledon in 1797, she was the daughter of Ann Lancaster's younger sister, Sarah, and her husband John Lattimer; she was born *c.* 1781), Ann Vipond (witness at a wedding in Wimbledon in 1801, she was Thomas Lancaster's niece, daughter of his eldest sister, Hannah, and her husband, Thomas Vipond of Alston). No doubt other nephews and nieces occasionally visited their uncle in his impressive establishment. His own and his wife's brothers and sisters, most of whom continued to live in the Alston district, were probably more reluctant to make the long journey south. At least two of them, however, were living in the London area at this time. On 27 March 1797 Thomas Lancaster baptised Thomas Pierce, son of Samuel Lancaster of Lavender Hill and his wife Sarah. Samuel Lancaster is presumably Thomas Lancaster's youngest brother, although he could conceivably be a cousin born the same year (1763); in any case he and his wife will have been frequent visitors in nearby Wimbledon. Samuel Lancaster married Sarah Pierce on 15 December 1792 at St Martin Outwich; their eldest son, Samuel, had been baptised at St Katherine Colman on 19 October 1795.

Less frequent, and far less welcome, visitors will have been Ann Lancaster's twin brother, John Burney, and his vulgar wife Sarah. Like his future brother-in-law, John Burney went south; but he probably did so before his twin sister's marriage to Thomas Lancaster. Little is known of him except that he worked as steward or land agent to John Cator (1728-1806)[106] and his nephew and heir, John Cator (1781-1858). John Cator (I), Henry Thrale's trusted friend and exact contemporary,[107] was an affluent timber merchant who had his lumber yard near Thrale's brewery in Southwark and also owned a fine country house, Beckenham Place (Kent),[108] which he acquired in 1773, probably shortly before John Burney was appointed steward. From 1772 to 1780 Cator was MP for Wallingford, and when John Burney's widow, Sarah (whose maiden name and origins have proved impossible to trace), told Fanny Burney that her husband had 'worked under government' for forty years, she may well have had in mind that he worked for John Cator when he was an MP, and continued to work for him and his heir for some forty years. That John Burney worked for the Cators was confirmed by John Cator (II) and his wife, who supported his widow's application to the National Benevolent Institution for a pension. Mrs Sarah Burney also told Fanny Burney that her husband 'supported a Chancery suit 30 [years]',[109] which appears to be quite untrue. What is true is that John Burney was involved in a chancery suit from 1804, this being undecided at the time of his death in 1816. The case arose because in 1799 he lent £1,000 on bond to Dame Elizabeth Pryce of Earley Court (Berkshire), whose heavily mortgaged estate had been plundered in a mock sale. Dame Elizabeth's husband, Sir John Powell Price, Bart, had died in 1777, blind and a prisoner in the King's Bench, having been unable to repay John Burney his £1,000. She herself died in 1806, also within the rules of the King's Bench. When John Burney died in 1816, his wife sought to revive the suit. She was successful in this,[110] although she died before claims against the estate were settled in 1849. The case, straight out of the pages of *Bleak House*, would need a novel to do it justice.

What all this means is that John Burney died an aggrieved man. In 1803, when Schopenhauer was at his brother-in-law's school, he was on the point of beginning the suit to recover his £1,000. When John Cator (I) died in 1806 John Burney was kept on by John Cator (II). His wife, who was illiterate as well as untrustworthy, and must have been a considerable embarrassment to her brother- and sister-in-law, approached Charles Parr Burney and Fanny Burney in 1826, claiming — fraudulently — to be their kith and kin. Fanny was annoyed to find that the claim was false — in typical Burney style she speaks of 'cozenage'[111] — although she did settle £5 per annum on the wretched mendicant and, more important, agreed to plead her case to the National Benevolent Institution. By one of those extraordinary coincidences with which this history is littered, she did this via her friend Dame Maria Domville (*c.* 1780-1863, wife of Sir William Domville, 1774-1860), daughter of Isaac Solly I. Thomas William Lancaster comes into the story too, for on 1 December 1827 Fanny wrote to Charles Parr Burney:

> I much rejoice to find that the Revd. Mr. Lancaster, Rector of Banbury, Oxfordshire, and her late Husband's Nephew, by a Miss Burney, his Wife, is now one to sign her Certificate. As well as her own Lawyers, Graham & Co., which authenticates her lamentable case, Mr. Cater of Beckonsfield is her friend; her husband, John Burney Esq., was his Land surveyor or Land Steward.[112]

The Rev. T.W. Lancaster duly signed the certificate, and his name appears on the card which Sarah Burney and her supporters used in an effort to get votes from NBI subscribers, but he seems to have done little else, for on 26 February 1835 Fanny Burney wrote to Mrs Elizabeth Temple:

> The chief supplication of this poor woman is that you would have the kind pity, Madam, of her time of life (84, I think,), her poverty, & her Relationship, to represent her excessive want to her Nephew . . . & prevail with him to join you in affording her some little quarterly relief for the rest of her now certainly very short remaining earthly pilgrimage.[113]

Sarah Burney died in 1840. At the time of her death she was living in Stepney. At one time, she told Fanny Burney, she and her husband had lived in Beaufort Row, Chelsea.

Whether Thomas Lancaster's brother-in-law was also the John Burney, timber merchant and chapman, of Tottenham Court Road, formerly of Bankside, Southwark, whose bankruptcy was announced in the *London Gazette* on 6 December 1785, I do not know; there were various other John Burneys living in London at the time. Henry Thrale's clerk by the name of Lancaster, who absconded with £2,000 in January-February 1781[114] was no relation.

John Burney's Chancery suit began in 1804, but in summer 1803, when Arthur Schopenhauer was living within the rules of

Mr Lancaster's academy, he must have been getting increasingly desperate about his money, and was probably pestering his brother-in-law (among others) for advice. If this was the case, he would have been encouraged to hear that the Chief Justice of the Court of King's Bench, Lord Ellenborough, had decided in Lord Nelson's favour in another case which, like the majority of Chancery cases, involved money.

It was in 1804 that Thomas William Lancaster went up to Oxford. Assuming him to have been taught in his father's school, he will have known Arthur Schopenhauer, for they were much the same age. By 1803 Thomas William may even have been acting as usher at Wimbledon School, although, if that were the case, he is unlikely to have been much involved in the teaching of a foreign parlour boarder. Be that as it may, he went up to Oxford the next year, matriculating not at Queen's but at Oriel, on 26 January 1804. He took his BA in 1807, remaining a member of Oriel until 15 July 1808, when he obtained a fellowship at Queen's, which he held until 1816, when he married. He was first curate and then vicar of Banbury (1815–49), but did not get on with his parishioners and lived mostly in Oxford. From 1840 to 1849 he was an usher at Magdalen College School, and seems to have been a very different kind of schoolmaster from his father, being famous for relying on good and bad marks rather than the cane, which may or may not explain his lack of success. He was the author of a number of theological works, and was best known for his Bampton Lectures of 1831 on *The Popular Evidence of Christianity*. He was an old-fashioned 'high and dry' clergyman, violently opposed to the theological liberalism of the time. There is absolutely no reason to suppose that his father was any different. That Thomas William Lancaster objected to London University being founded 'freed from those exclusions and religious distinctions which abridge the usefulness of Oxford and of Cambridge'[115] speaks for itself. No doubt he was expressing a point of view which had also been his father's. He even seems to have inherited his father's predilection for genteel society; at one stage he was chaplain to the Dowager Countess of Guildford (widow of George Augustus North, third Earl of Guildford, son of Lord North). He died on 12 December 1859.

1804 was also the year in which Thomas Lancaster was one of the more well-to-do Wimbledon residents to subscribe

> towards the support of a Nightly Watch to Patrole the Village Street and Cry the hour through the same from 9 o'clock

every Evening untill 5 o'Clock in the morning in the Winter and from 10 o'Clock every Evening untill 4 o'Clock in the Morning in the Summer.[116]

This serves to remind us that Wimbledon was still at the time a village, albeit one already being used as a dormitory suburb. Back in 1796 Thomas Lancaster had been one of the subscribers to the 'Patrole Guard' on Wimbledon Common, organised, no doubt, to look out for lurking levellers.

The year 1805 was notable for the departure from home of Henry Lancaster, and for the death of Nelson. Presumably the Rev. Lancaster saw Nelson's funeral, which young George Matcham described as 'the most awful sight I ever saw'.[117] For Henry Lancaster, marching in the procession to St Paul's, it will have been the most unforgettable moment of his life. On a brighter note, 1805 was also the year in which one of Thomas Lancaster's oldest friends, the Rev. John Farrer, whom he had known since his Appleby days, visited London for the first time in his life, at the age of 70. For the past forty years he had been teaching at Witton-le-Wear in County Durham. John Farrer stayed in London for three months, during which time some of his old pupils dined him at the London Tavern. I like to think that Thomas Lancaster was of the company. In the course of his three months in the south Farrer also went to Oxford to visit his and Thomas Lancaster's old schoolfriend, Septimus Collinson.

Thomas Lancaster was a confirmed joiner of good causes, good causes in his view being those which had to do with religious orthodoxy, charity, and the protection of King and Country. Even in default of proof, we may be sure that he was a member of the Association of Protestant Schoolmasters [in the North of England]; he was a Freemason and a member of the committee of Wimbledon and Merton Armed Associations; he may have been a member of the Society of Tory Schoolmasters, and was certainly a member of the Society of Schoolmasters, which was instituted to assist their widows and orphans, and to relieve distressed schoolmasters and ushers. He joined the Society of Schoolmasters in 1807, when he subscribed £5 5s. By the time of his death he had donated £21 and thereby become a Benefactor, entitled to act as a member of the committee without election. Other Benefactors included Earl Spencer, who may well have been prevailed upon to subscribe by Thomas Lancaster. Mr Lancaster will therefore have known Samuel Parr, Charles Burney and William Barrow (all vice-presidents), and Charles Parr Burney (a fellow Benefactor). Other members of the Society of Schoolmasters included Richard Brant and the Rev. Joshua Ruddock, both of whom lived in Wimbledon.

The year 1807 also saw the death of Thomas Lancaster's mother, who died on 6 March. At this time he was still being invited by 'My Lady' (Emma Hamilton) to Merton Place, although the gatherings were never the same after Nelson's death. Two years later, in July 1809, he lost his youngest daughter, Ann, at the age of 24. Even given the high mortality rate of those days, he was particularly unfortunate, and it may well be that he became too dispirited to carry on schoolmastering, for he retired two years later. In the meantime there was better news in the form of Thomas William's fellowship at Queen's (1809) and ordination (1810), at which Thomas Lancaster will have met the Provost of Queen's, Septimus Collinson. His thoughts must have turned not only to his days at Appleby and his own ordination but also to the death of his cousin and namesake so soon after his ordination at Oxford.

The other main event of 1810 was Thomas Lancaster's decision to try to put himself in line to succeed Herbert Randolph as vicar of Wimbledon. Among the Althorp papers[118] there is a letter which he wrote to Earl Spencer in 1810:

My Lord,
    That intercourse which sometimes takes place between the superior orders and their inferiors, emboldens me to address you on this occasion.
    The recent appointment of Mr. Randolph by his brother to the valuable Rectory of Hanwell, and the probability which has been stated to me, that he will soon have another more valuable added to it, suggest the idea that he will ere long find it convenient to vacate his Curacy of Wimbledon. After a residence of 20 years in your Lordship's immediate neighbourhood, I will not suppose that you want to be informed how far I may be a fit person to succeed him. Should you think me so, I shall be obliged by the favour of your interest with the Chapter of Worcester for that purpose.
    I shall only add that in the case of my appointment, I will restore the Evening Service during the winter half-year, and shall be happy in all cases to conduct my ministry on such principles as shall best conduce to the edification

of all who are interested in it.
                    I have the honour to be, my Lord,
                            Your Lordship's most obedient servant,
                                    Thomas Lancaster
Nelson House
Jan 27, 1810.

This letter did not lead to his being appointed vicar of Wimbledon, but it may have led indirectly to his appointment as stipendiary curate of Merton.

In 1811 Thomas Lancaster decided to retire at the age of 61; he sold his school as a going concern to Isaac Hellier junior, son of a local calico printer and brewer. In May 1811 the Bishop of Winchester apparently suggested (maybe after being approached by the Bishop of Worcester) that, in view of his impending retirement, Thomas Lancaster should get himself nominated (by Charles Bond, the titular perpetual curate of Merton) as stipendiary curate of Merton. The bishop would have known that Charles Bond would be willing to make the nomination, because he was beginning to think in terms of retirement. Since 1801 Thomas Lancaster had been non-stipendiary assistant curate, although he carried out all the duties of the cure. On 29 May 1811 Charles Bond wrote to him:

Dear Sir,
    I think it highly proper that you comply with the Bishop's request; I have therefore sent you a nomination to the Curacy — May you yet be many years a successful labourer in the vineyard of the Church, & live to see the good Fruits of your endeavours —
    I shall add a check on my banker for your half year's stipend & bounty — & with our united good wishes to you and yours I remain
                            Dr Sir
                                Yours ever & sincerely
                                    Chs. Bond[119]
May 29. 1811

Two days previously Charles Bond had written to Bishop Brownlow nominating Thomas Lancaster to be curate and promising to allow him £40 per annum; he asked for Mr Lancaster to be licensed as curate. The licence was granted on 1 June 1811.

Three years later Thomas Lancaster became perpetual curate

on the resignation of Charles Bond. On 23 May 1814 three of Thomas Lancaster's clerical friends, J.D. Myers (vicar of Mitcham), John Buckland (rector of St George's, Southwark) and George Savage (vicar of Kingston, Surrey), sent the statutory testimonial to Bishop Brownlow in favour of Thomas Lancaster, who had signified that he expected shortly to be nominated curate of Merton. On 4 June 1811 the patron of Merton, Essex Henry Bond, duly nominated him, and he was licensed as perpetual curate on 11 June 1814. It is possible that his 1814 sermon, given in January and published shortly after, was intended to enhance his indubitable claim to the perpetual curacy.

In summer 1811, when he retired as schoolmaster and became stipendiary assistant curate of Merton, Thomas Lancaster presumably moved into Merton Parsonage, there to be looked after by his eldest daughter, Eliza.[120] He died in October 1823, aged 73. The Elizabeth Lancaster who married in London in 1824 may well have been Eliza, having not felt free to marry during her father's lifetime.

We have seen that Thomas Lancaster was, in modern terms, a conservative, violently opposed to the French Revolution and all its liberal works. He was equally clearly an old-fashioned Georgian High Churchman, like his son Thomas William after him, insisting on the old basics, above all 'a regular attendance upon divine service'. His heart was in the right place — his published sermons are concerned with charity to the poor — but he chose to cater for and to mix with the well-to-do. He was not an intellectual and was not, by comparison with his young German pupil, a well educated man; he had not even had the benefit of studying under those whom his pupil was pleased to call the 'orthodox oxen of Oxford'.

Thomas Lancaster was, I am sure, jealous of his position. Belonging to the minor gentry, he improved his lot considerably by a brilliant marriage, and was clearly much flattered by his friendship with Lord Nelson. Like Trollope's Rev. Jeffrey Wortle, DD, the Rev. Thomas Lancaster was, it seems, 'a man much esteemed by others — and by himself'.[121] The 'advertisement' to his sermon published in Sunderland in 1784 says — unnecessarily — that he does not court fame. Five years later he published a wordy, bombastic sermon dedicated to the King on the occasion of his Happy Recovery. The dedication speaks for itself:

> I am desirous, *with all Humility*, to lay at your Majesty's Feet, a Discourse, preached on that most happy Occasion.

The Obscurity of its Author, and its own Imperfections, might have dictated its Suppression. But the Magnitude of the Event . . . and your Majesty's *known Condescension* — have outweighed all other Considerations, and determined me to send it into the World, under the Sanction of your Majesty's *illustrious Name*.

Dedications, Sire, are often rendered nauseous by *fulsome Adulation*: and even *just Praise* is not always acceptable to the best Minds. Therefore, though the *public and private Virtues* which have *deservedly enthroned* your Majesty in the Hearts of your People, afford a copious Theme for the latter, I will not presume to approach with an Offering which is *often counterfeited* — often *most lavished* upon Characters *most opposite* to that of your Majesty.

That your Majesty may long *thus* reign, in *Health, Happiness and Peace*, — blessed with the Society of the *best of Queens*; — and that your Majesty's *Royal Descendants* may wear and adorn the crown of these Realms to the End of Time; is the devout Prayer of

     Your Majesty's
    Most loyal and dutiful Subject,
     And obedient Servant,
      Thomas Lancaster.

The man who wrote that dedication is, it seems to me, not only a pompous toady but a palpable placeseeker and 'King's Friend'. The pious hopes of peace were singularly inept, for the sermon was written at Parson's Green on 20 July 1789, when the fabric of despotism and privilege in France had already begun to crumble and events were set on the course which was to lead to war between England and France lasting for most of the rest of the lives of Thomas Lancaster and his monarch.

If Thomas Lancaster thus nailed his colours to the mast of the political establishment, he did so again in different form when, in 1794, he published *A Plan of Education*, 'By A Clergyman of the Established Church'. In addition to proclaiming his orthodoxy, he goes on to imply himself to be a 'most active and diligent Tutor':

The management of a school is considered difficult: but to a man who can bring himself to delight in the various functions it requires, and will give himself the trouble to gain the affections of his Pupils, without diminishing their respect

for him, habit will render it easy and pleasant.
  This occupation is confessedly of very great importance . . .

There is no false modesty here.

Then there is, finally, the last of Lancaster's published sermons, the one published in 1814 complete with a long, bombastic, and — surely — very old-fashioned dedication to the Prime Minister, the second Earl of Liverpool. Mr Lancaster had, no doubt, met the Earl socially, in Wimbledon, but the fact remains that in this retrospective sermon, his most public and frank performance, he also appears not a little ridiculous, for people simply did not write dedications like that any more. He was evidently something of a snob who preferred moving in genteel circles, and may also have been a somewhat lugubrious character, for young George Matcham, admittedly something of a wag, wrote in his diary on 28 October 1807, 'After supper Mr. Lan—ster with solemn deportment . . . favoured us with a song, which I mistook for a funeral oration.'[122] It would be nice to think that the song to which Mr Lancaster treated the company may have been that popular satire of a few years before:

When lawyers strive to heal a breach,
And parsons practise what they preach;
Then Boney he'll come pouncing down,
And march his men on London town!

Thomas Lancaster is unlucky in being remembered in connection with perhaps the person who had the lowest opinion of him and all his works, but it is probably fortunate for him that his pupil's letters (and diary?) from Wimbledon have not been preserved.

Notes

1. I am most grateful to Mr L. J. Schwarz for allowing me to see the house.
2. On the history of the house, see T.G. Jackson's two articles on 'Eagle House, Wimbledon', *Surrey Archaeological Collections*, X (1890-1), 150-65, and *The Wimbledon and Merton Annual* (1903), 9-25.
3. Jackson, in *Wimbledon and Merton Annual* (1903), 22.
4. Jackson, in *Surrey Archaeological Collections*, X (1890-1), 151.
5. Ibid., 164.
6. *Wimbledon and Merton Annual* (1903), 16.

7. On file in Wimbledon Village Museum is a photograph of this '1810 water-colour': P 163 B, Accession No. 326.
8. Carlyle, *Autobiography*, 499.
9. J.S. *Sämmtliche Schriften*, XVI (1834), 348 f.
10. Quoted from C. Matheson, *The Life of Henry Dundas* (1933), 120.
11. Prince Pückler-Muskau, *Tour in Germany, Holland and England, in 1826, 1827 and 1828*, III (1832), 184.
12. See Thackeray, *Vanity Fair*, Chapter XII.
13. Ibid., Chapter I.
14. See his mother's letter of 13 September.
15. The Rev. Lancaster signed Merton parish register from 11 January 1801 to 7 July 1822.
16. D. Lysons, *The Environs of London* I (1792), 539.
17. In the British Library.
18. In his anonymously published *The Pursuits of Literature: A Satiric Poem* (1794), x.
19. Peter Pindar, *Works*, IV (1796), 46.
20. Starting with 'Mr Pitt's Flight to Wimbledon', the references to Peter Pindar's *Works* are as follows: IV, 97–105; IV, 111; IV, 493; V, 62, V, 71; V, 85; V, 10; V, 73; V, 128; V, 309.
21. Matheson, *Dundas*, 120 f.
22. Ibid.
23. Peter Pindar, *Works*, IV, 51.
24. Ibid., IV, 94.
25. *The Pursuits of Literature*, 336.
26. Holcroft, *Anna St. Ives*, letter XXVIII.
27. A. Stephens, *Memoirs of John Horne Tooke*, II (1813), 291–334.
28. Ibid., 297.
29. Although the particular examples are mine, the dinner-table combinations come from M.W. Patterson's *Sir Francis Burdett and his Times* (1931), 120.
30. Stephens, *John Horne Tooke*, II, 315 f.
31. Gordon, *Personal Memoirs*, I, 267 f.
32. Stephens, *John Horne Tooke*, II, 112.
33. L.B. Namier, *England in the Age of American Revolution* (1930), 206 f.
34. Boswell's *Johnson*, under 1778.
35. Letter of 20 December 1762.
36. Dryden, quoted from *VCH Surrey*.
37. *VCH Surrey*.
38. Dropmore Papers, II, 281; quoted from C. Sebag-Montefiore, *A History of the Volunteer Forces* (1908), 165.
39. 34 Geo. III, cap. 16.
40. Sebag-Montefiore, *Volunteer Forces*, 170.
41. 37 Geo, III, cap. 3.
42. The principal features of the government plan, which was no doubt drawn up by Pitt and Dundas, probably during a weekend at Wimbledon, were these:

(a) A General Association to be formed, composed of the householders of the parish, to which such other inmates as should be approved by the Association may be added. (*b*) The parish to be divided into districts, and the inhabitants of each district enrolled for service to be divided into classes or companies of fifty each; the companies to be severally commanded by captains recommended by a Committee of the Association to the Lord-Lieutenant for his Majesty's Commission. (*c*) The several companies to hold themselves at the requisition of the civil power, and to assemble on an alarm at a rendezvous appointed by the captain. (*d*) A place of general rendezvous for all the companies to be appointed by the Committee of Association. (*e*) All persons enrolling themselves to furnish their own arms, subject to the approval of the Committee. (*f*) A list of the members of each company to be made, and a copy thereof to be lodged with each member of the company; together with a copy of such instructions as may be deemed necessary to facilitate the assembling of the class in the case of alarm. (*g*) Exercise not to be made compulsory, but the captain of each company to be at liberty to muster his men under arms at such times as may be agreed upon. Government to allow to each company a serjeant or corporal to teach the use of arms. (*h*) The companies to carry distinguishing flags, and to adopt some kind of uniform if they should choose it. (*i*) Not to go out of the parish except of their own initiative.

(Quoted from Sebag-Montefiore, *Volunteer Forces*, 184).
 43. Vestry Minutes.
 44. Ibid.
 45. 43 Geo. III, cap. 96, sect. 20.
 46. The uniform worn by the Church Militant in the person of Parson Lancaster involved a red jacket and would have been very similar to the uniform worn by the Light Horse Volunteers in April 1797:

Hair powdered and queued, six inches long close to the head; turban of the helmet and feather cleaned and renewed; black leather stock and turnover; new Hussar jacket; sword well polished; cross-belts well whitened, and pistol-belt over them; white washleather gloves; white leather breeches; regimental boots and spurs; one pistol only, and that in the left holster; the right for a handkerchief or anything else; chain bridoons; horse-collar and coat-case well cleaned and whitened; necessary-bag under the coat-case, and nose-bag between the two.

(Quoted from Sebag-Montefiore, *Volunteer Forces*, 217.)
 47. 38 Geo. III, cap. 27.
 48. Quoted from Sebag-Montefiore, *Volunteer Forces*, 189.
 49. Ibid., 216.
 50. Sebag-Montefiore, *Volunteer Forces*, 222.
 51. Peter Pindar, *Works*, I, (1794) 29.
 52. Lord Rosebery, *Pitt*, 1891, 133.
 53. Quoted from Sebag-Montefiore, *Volunteer Forces*, 308 f.
 54. Thomas Hardy, *The Trumpet-Major*, Chapter XXIII.
 55. Thomas Lancaster, *Sermon* (1814), 12–19.

56. Quoted from Sebag-Montefiore, *Volunteer Forces*, 390 f.
57. Ibid., 246 f. The *Address* reads:

MY BRAVE ASSOCIATES — Partners of my Toil, my Feelings and my Fame! — can Words add Vigour to the VIRTUOUS ENERGIES which inspire your hearts? — No. — You have judged as I have, the *Foulness* of the *crafty Plea* by which these bold INVADERS would delude you. — Your generous Spirit has compared, as mine has, the *Motives* which in a War like this can animate *their* Minds, and OURS. — THEY, by a strange Frenzy driven, fight for Power, for Plunder and extended Rule — WE, for our Country, our Altars and our Homes — THEY follow an ADVENTURER, whom they fear, and obey a Power which they hate — WE serve a *Monarch* whom we love — a GOD whom we adore. — Whene'er they move in anger, *Desolation* tracks their Progress! — Where'er they pause in Amity, *Affliction* mourns their Friendship! — They boast, they come but to improve our State, enlarge our Thoughts, and free us from the Yoke of Error! — Yes — THEY will give enlightened Freedom to *our* Minds, who are themselves the *Slaves* of Passion, Avarice, and Pride. — THEY offer us their Protection — Yes, such Protection as *Vultures* give to Lambs — covering and devouring them! — They call on us to barter all of Good we have inherited and proved, for the desperate Chance of Something better which they *Promise*. — Be our plain Answer this: The one WE honour is the PEOPLE'S CHOICE — the Laws we reverence are our brave Fathers' Legacy — the Faith we follow teaches us to live in Bonds of Charity with all Mankind, and die with Hopes of Bliss beyond the Grave. Tell your Invaders this; and tell them too, we seek no Change; and least of all, such Change as *they* would bring us. R.B. SHERIDAN.

58. Ibid., 292 f.
59. On 28 November 1803 A.S. saw Napoleon at the Théâtre des Français in Paris.
60. J.R. Green, *History of the English People*, IV (1880), 362.
61. Quoted from Sebag-Montefiore, *Volunteer Forces*, iv.
62. See n. 77 below.
63. Morrison MS 638, quoted from the most readily available source: Carola Oman, *Nelson* (1950 ed), 421 f.
64. Ibid., 421.
65. Walter Sichel, *Emma Lady Hamilton* (1905), 380.
66. J.E. Jagger, *Lord Nelson's Home and Life at Merton* (Merton Park, 1926), 6 f.
67. Before he moved into Merton Place, Nelson had written to Emma Hamilton from HMS *Amazon* on 26 September 1801: 'To be sure we shall employ the tradespeople of our village in preference to any others in what we want for common use, and give them every encouragement to be kind and attentive to us.' (In *Nelson's Letters to his Wife*, ed. G.P.B. Naish, 1958, 591.) The tradesmen who supplied Merton Place included Messsrs Greenfield (butcher), Woodman (chandler), Peartree (stable-keeper),

Wyld (cheesemonger), Gadd (baker), Lucas (milkman) and Footit (home brewing supplies). No doubt they later also supplied Merton parsonage, where Thomas Lancaster lived from 1811 to 1823, looked after by his daughter Eliza. Whether the parson's washing, like the admiral's, was taken in by Mrs Cummins is not known; it is only heroes' washerwomen who are remembered. The three cottages on Merton Place estate were presumably occupied by Thomas Cribb (the gardener), James Hudson (his son-in-law and assistant) and Thomas Saker (carpenter and factotum).

68. Quoted from Oman, *Nelson*, 424.
69. Philip Rathbone, *Paradise Merton: The Story of Nelson and the Hamiltons at Merton Place* (1973), 7.
70. Mollie Hardwick, *Emma, Lady Hamilton* (1969), 121.
71. *The Dispatches and Letters of Vice-Admiral Lord Viscount Nelson*, ed. Sir N.H. Nicolas, VII (1846), 228.
72. Oman, *Nelson*, 514.
73. Quoted from Hardwick, *Emma*, 119.
74. Ibid., 121.
75. *Memoirs of Emma Lady Hamilton*, ed. W.H. Long (1891), 276 f.
76. In M. Eyre-Matcham, *The Nelsons of Burnham Thorpe* (1911), 261.
77. Ibid., 231.
78. Her whole account is in the next chapter.
79. Peterhouse Admission Book.
80. See *Nelson's Letters to his Wife*, ed. Naish, 600.
81. Hugh Tours, *The Life and Letters of Emma Hamilton* (1963), 188.
82. *The Diary of Frances Lady Shelley, 1787-1817*, ed. R. Edgcumbe, I (1912), 79.
83. Hardwick, *Emma*, 193.
84. Quoted from ibid., 97.
85. 'How Eagle House got its Name', *Wimbledon News*, 22 December 1972.
86. *Surrey Archaeological Collections*, X (1890-1), 163 f.
87. MS in the Phillipps collection, National Maritime Museum (ref. CRK/8, L/87).
88. *Dispatches and Letters of Nelson*, ed. Nicolas, VII, ccxviii f.
89. See *English [Law] Reports*, Vol. 102 (1910), 821-30, 'Lord Viscount Nelson v. Tucker'.
90. Winifred Gérin, *Horatia Nelson* (1970), 92.
91. Eyre-Matcham, *The Nelsons*, 230.
92. Oman, *Nelson*, 590.
93. Kathleen Denbigh, *History and Heroes of Old Merton* (1975), 92.
94. Oman, *Nelson*, 604.
95. In T.J. Pettigrew, *Memoirs of the Life of Lord Nelson*, II (1849), 496 f.
96. In *Dispatches and Letters of Nelson*, ed. Nicolas, VII, 40; and in *The Letters of Lord Nelson to Lady Hamilton*, II (1814), 98.
97. Marryat, *Peter Simple* (1834), Chapter 1.
98. *Southey's Life of Nelson* (Folio Society ed, 1956), 248. John Whichelo's portrait of Nelson, sketched at Merton in September 1805, a few days before Nelson sailed for Trafalgar, faces p. 224 of this edition.
99. *A Selection from the . . . Correspondence of Vice-Admiral Lord Collingwood*, ed. G.L. Newnham Collingwood (2nd edn, 1828), I, 299.

100. 'Had the Honour of entering the Service under the especial patronage of the illustrious Nelson and was with him in the Victory at the battle of Trafalgar 21 Oct. 1805. Served afterwards in the Ocean, bearing the flag of Vice Admiral Lord Collingwood until 1808, when he joined the Thames 32 Frigate, Capt. B.W. Taylor, and followed him into the Apollo 38 on his appointment to that ship 3 Sept. 1808. Assisted in the Apollo's launch at the burning and cutting out of the French Convoy moored under the Citadel of Rosas on the 1st Nov. 1809, and in much boat service on the coasts of Catalonia, Italy and the Ionian Islands. Assisted at the Capture of the Islands of Augusta and Curzola in the Adriatic. Was nearly drowned in an Italian Brig prize that foundered about an hour after her capture on the 20 January 1812 off the bay of Prajus. He was twice instrumental in saving life by jumping overboard, once in the Adriatic and once in the channel of Malta at night. Received his appointment as Lieut. in Sept. 1813 and served on shore as a Volunteer at the siege of Trieste when he was slightly wounded [crossed out: in the left hand], and on the fall of the place received the thanks of Admiral Sir Thos F. Fremantle and a particular Letter of introduction to Sir Sidney Smith, being appointed to his flag-ship. On joining the fleet at Port Mahon, he found a fresh appointment to the Prince of Wales, Capt. John E. Douglas. He was present at the Capture of Genoa and Savona in March 1814. At the Peace returned to England in July when the ship was paid off. In Sept. he was appointed to the Myrtle 18 Nov. 1815, since which period he has not been employed.' ('Formula requested to be filled up for Mr. O'Byrne's Biographical Dictionary', completed by Henry Lancaster, in the National Maritime Museum.)

101. *GM*, 1813/II, 174, 480.

102. Frederick Marryat, for his part, born in 1792, entered the navy in 1806, was appointed lieutenant in 1812, and attained the rank of post-captain before resigning in 1830. As the second son of Joseph Marryat of Wimbledon House he spent part at least of his childhood at Wimbledon, which he came to dislike; in 1839, when he was staying with his mother there, he wrote, 'it is very dull and *triste*, and one might as well be shut up in a penitentiary' (In Florence Marryat, *Life and Letters of Captain Marryat*, II, 1872, 90; dull and 'trist' is precisely how Emma Hamilton had found Merton after Nelson's death). Little detailed information about Marryat's early life is available, but there is no reason to think that the various private schools which he attended included Mr Lancaster's.

103. Cf. *A History of HMS 'Victory'*, 1891, 14:

The 'Victory' had suffered severely in the fight [Trafalgar]; 57 of her crew were killed and 75 wounded; as regards the ship herself, an eye-witness thus describes her condition on her arrival at Spithead: 'She is very much mauled both in her hull and rigging, has upwards of 80 shot between wind and water, the foremast very badly wounded indeed, and though strongly fished has sunk about 6 inches; the mainmast also is badly wounded and very full of musket shots; she has a jury mizen-mast and fore and main top-masts, and has a great many shot in her bowsprit and bows; one of the figures which support the arms has both the legs shot off.'

104. Thomas Lancaster, *Sermon* (1814), 17.
105. Details in Gérin, *Horatia Nelson*. Additional material in the National Maritime Museum.
106. John Cator (I) was a friend of Samuel Johnson, who paid him a nice tribute when he said that there was 'much good in his character and much usefulness in his knowledge'; he added, 'Cator has a rough, manly, independent understanding, and does not spoil it by complaisance.' (Boswell's *Johnson*, under 1784.)
107. Mrs Thrale, while agreeing that he was 'acute in his Judgement, skilful in Trade, and solid in Property', found him 'Rough in his manners ... a coarse man'. (*Thraliana*, ed. K.C. Balderston, 2nd edn, 1951, I, 418.)
108. Dr Johnson 'found a cordial solace' at Cator's seat at Beckenham, which, Boswell adds, is 'one of the finest places at which I ever was a guest'. (Boswell's *Johnson*, under 1784.)
109. See *The Journals and Letters of Fanny Burney*, ed. Joyce Hemlow, XII (Oxford, 1984), 666-81, 690-5, 706-11, 860-3.
110. See 'Morgan *v.* Barney [*sic*]', *Law Journal*, old series. (1823), I, 228 ff.; also, on Pryce of Earley, *VCH Berkshire*.
111. *The Journals and Letters of Fanny Burney*, ed. Hemlow, XII, 679.
112. Ibid., 694.
113. Ibid., 862.
114. *Thraliana*, ed. Balderston, I, 483.
115. See his *The Alliance of Education and Civil Government, With Strictures on the University of London* (1828).
116. Vestry Minutes.
117. Eyre-Matcham, *The Nelsons*, 247.
118. Althorp papers G. 84. I am grateful to Richard Milward for drawing my attention to this letter.
119. The papers concerning Thomas Lancaster's nomination as stipendiary (assistant) curate in 1811 and as perpetual curate in 1814 are preserved in Hampshire RO (ref. F/9/B).
120. It was at this stage that three of his four remaining children married. The first to do so was Ruth, who married Henry's friend, the dashing Tom Ullock, at Merton, on 6 April 1815. She was 31 at the time and had known Tom Ullock for some years; no doubt her feelings for him were intensified when he was reported wounded in 1813. It was his second marriage; he had previously married Joanna Ginn at Gosport Holy Trinity on 30 April 1803, and had two children born in Gosport: Elizabeth Ann (bapt. 30 March 1804; she is the Eliza Ullock who appears in the Wimbledon parish register, as witness to a marriage, in 1817) and Thomas James (bapt. 20 May 1806). By 1815 his first wife was dead and his children needed a new mother, a role which Ruth Lancaster appears to have filled admirably. In 1816 Thomas William married one of his parishioners, Anne Walford of Banbury. Henry, for his part, married Henrietta Hunter Malins, at Lambeth St Mary, on 1 May 1823; she was the daughter of William Malins of Newbiggin, Surrey, and his wife Mary (*née* Hunter); her brother Richard became Vice-Chancellor of Lincoln's Inn and was knighted in 1867.
121. Trollope, *Dr. Wortle's School*, Chapter 1.
122. In Eyre-Matcham, *The Nelsons*, 261.

VI
Letters to Schopenhauer at Wimbledon

Introduction

Thanks to either a quirk of fate or a self-regarding whim on the part of his mother, none of the letters which Arthur Schopenhauer wrote in England in 1803 has survived. Given that he wrote to his father, mother and sister, and to at least two school friends in Hamburg, the loss is as surprising as it is regrettable. Judging by the return letters, it will have been his letters to his mother that contained his clearest — and bitterest — comments on Mr Lancaster's; those letters Johanna Schopenhauer almost certainly destroyed (cf. her remarks on her son's outspokenness). We are, however, fortunate in being able to produce a reasonably complete sequence of letters addressed *to* young Schopenhauer at this time. These letters are both interesting and revealing; they tell us a good deal both about Arthur Schopenhauer at the age of 15 and about his time at Wimbledon, and fill in the necessary background. The loss of his own letters is compensated not only by these return letters, but by an account of Mr Lancaster's academy written by his mother, an account which can only have been based on those missing letters. We also have Mr Lancaster's own account of his aims and methods.

It is impossible to read the letters addressed to Schopenhauer at Wimbledon by his parents without feeling sorry for him. His mother's letters are totally self-centred, his father's grotesquely fussy. There is an all too obvious contrast between the letters young Schopenhauer received from the Grégoires following his return from two years in Le Havre in 1799 and the letters he now receives from his own parents. It is the letters from the Grégoires which contain the affection. It is no wonder that he called those two years at Le Havre the happiest of his childhood. His letters from his parents will have done little to relieve his unhappiness in Wimbledon. Also included in this chapter are three letters which were written after the Wimbledon period, but which include interesting and relevant material. One or two letters which he received while at Wimbledon are omitted because they contain nothing of interest.

Letters

1. From Lorenz Meyer (23 May 1803)[1]

Hamburg, 23 May 1803

I never thought for a second, dear Schopenhauer, that you would so faithfully keep your promise to write to me. Perhaps you thought yourself that I held such an opinion of your *punctilio* and wrote to me to put me to shame for not taking seriously the promise which you made to me on the eve of your departure.[2] Be that as it may, your letter gave me greater pleasure than you will have imagined, in that I gather from it that the beauties of Westphalia, and even Amsterdam itself, have not quite erased me from your memory.

But what will come of the rest of your tour now that war seems certain? I fear you may find yourself answering this question in person, here in Hamburg, and that all too soon, unless your father changes his mind and goes on with the tour instead of returning home out of fear of the war.[3] My first thought on hearing that war was imminent was the hope that you might be over the Channel and in England by then; for judging by my own experience and feelings on the matter I should be sorrier to miss a trip to England than one to France. I am surprised that you like Holland so much.[4] I have always thought of Holland as a starchy, strait-laced country, with inhabitants to match. How much you enjoyed that Strassburg pie on your journey through Westphalia[5] I can imagine all the more clearly in that I have always enjoyed it myself in Hamburg. It's a pity I didn't ask you to visit my old tutor when you were in Amsterdam. His name is Meyer and he lives at a Mr Ferescarode's (op de Rosengragt, Amsterdam). So far as his means allowed he would have been sure to make you most welcome. I am still very fond of him, and know him to be very fond of me too. If you should return to Amsterdam, I hope very much that you will call on him.

There is not much news. There has been an exchange fraud

which was the talk of Hamburg. The ringleader in the affair, who had fled to Celle, was apprehended there, but hanged himself with his handkerchief. He worked here for a certain Herr Hildebrandt from whom he is supposed to have helped himself to 30,000 thalers. A tallow-chandler was also involved, but he is now in prison awaiting the appropriate punishment. At Herr Runge's[6] everything is the same as usual. Herr Hauptmann[7] is forever quarrelling with Fritz Meyer.[8] When Droop[9] left, to go to Herr Rixner's estate in the country, the Captain advised him to steer clear of the girls. Of course, he does need to take care, for his employer has 36 of them. What will become of Fr. Meyer,[10] who was supposed to be going to Bordeaux, I do not know, but I suppose he will be staying here, since there is a war coming. Yesterday I was in the garden and jumped over a very wide and pretty deep ditch. I got across, but the bank gave way and I fell on my back in the ditch, getting completely covered in water. How muddy my clothes got I need hardly say!!! No time now to tell you anything else; it is half past three and I must go to dine. Write soon to oblige

Your friend
[Lorenz] Meyer[11]

p.m. I have just been speaking to Rodde.[12] He sends greetings and this evening will probably bring a few lines for you.

The Prussians are said to have occupied Hanover in order to prevent the French from getting a foothold there. In Hanover they are preparing to defend themselves against the French with might and main.

Monsier Arthur Schopenhauer
en France ou en Angleterre

II. From J.S. (19 July 1803)[1]

New Castle,[2] 19 July 1803

Dear Arthur,

Upon our arrival here this morning we found your letters waiting.[3] I am glad that on the whole you are getting on well and that you are meeting with kindness and courtesy; as for the rest, you must discover how best to accommodate yourself. Among so many boys there are bound to be one or two like-minded ones; at all events, I hope that by now you are more settled; when you wrote your letter of 8 July you were still very much the new boy. You must be a little more forthcoming with people than you are in the habit of being. In all social intercourse someone has to make the first move, and why shouldn't you be just as capable of doing so as someone else who, though older than you, has not had the advantage which you have enjoyed from such an early age of living so much among foreigners, and therefore holds back out of shyness, because he lacks the courage to come forward? The formality must of course strike you as odd, but it is necessary for the sake of social propriety. Little as I like starchiness, I like even less the uncouthness that is concerned only with smug self-satisfaction. You have no mean leanings in the latter direction, as I have often noticed to my sorrow, and I am glad that you are now obliged to live with people of a different stamp, even if they do rather tend to the other extreme. I shall be very pleased if I see, on my return, that you have taken on something of this 'complimentary' manner, as you call it; that you may go too far in that direction I fear not.

Drawing, reading, playing your flute, fencing, and going for walks is a good deal of variety, you know. For years I knew hardly any other pleasures, and thrived on it. At your age you are not really ready for society: in order to enjoy to the full all the pleasures of life, one must first understand how to live, and you are as yet only at the preparatory stage.

Meanwhile, this month will soon be over and in *August* your father will allow you to go up to London once a week, on the understanding that you will go to the *Percivals*,[4] who have been so friendly and have repeatedly asked that you should do so; I do not like the thought of you eating on your own in an inn. You have money, and if it runs out your father has told you where to apply for more.[5] I imagine we shall be back in London in about six weeks. If you want to join us then and accompany us on the rest of our tour, I advise you to make sure that by the time we return your father will have cause to be satisfied with your handwriting, otherwise I cannot be responsible for the consequences. If I were in your place I should devote all my time and all my best endeavours to making sure of attaining this goal. You are sensible enough to realise how essential it is for your future livelihood to be able to write well, rapidly and legibly, and I simply cannot understand how with due care and plenty of practice you could find it so difficult to acquire a purely mechanical skill. One can do anything that one really wants to do, of that I am absolutely convinced from my own experience, so if your handwriting is not up to scratch it will be your own fault, and you will have to bear the consequences. It is our duty and our intention to do everything in our power to bring out the best in you, but we cannot be expected to choose the means according to whether or not they meet with your approval.

You seem to be unlucky with my presents: the [tie] pin has gone the same way as the pencil and the [pen] knife, but don't worry, when we are back in London you shall have another, even prettier[6] one; until then Miss Lancaster[7] will no doubt help you out with some ordinary pins. Our journey has so far gone very well, we have not stayed in any one place for long — you know that your father does not like meeting people — and so I have not had much company except my own, but the constant changes of scene are much to my liking and my diary[8] has made such progress that when we reach Edinburgh in a couple of days' time I shall have to have recourse to a second volume[.] In the past fourteen days I have seen many beautiful and remarkable things above and below ground: many fine mansions, parks and gardens, and — even more to my taste — much beautiful countryside, some of it so romantic and wild and yet so beautiful — you have no idea how beautiful it was; I should never have imagined that there were such rocks in England. Darbyshire [sic] is indescribably beautiful; we were in a little spa town there, by the name of Matlock, and spent over two days there because it really was so beautiful, almost like Karlsbad but infinitely finer. I could not have enough of climbing the high, picturesque rocks. From there we drove to Castleton, a Peak village, where I went down into the Peak cavern with Duguet[9] and a guide; it was an arduous affair, twice I had to lie down flat in a little boat in order to pass underneath the overhanging rocks on the subterranean stream. In another place the guide carried me pick-a-back; the climbing we had to do was also very arduous and not without danger; it was an hour before I saw daylight again. How you would have enjoyed it! I have also seen some magnificent ruins,[10] particularly an old abbey, dating from the twelfth century, Fountains Abbey. Tarant near Dresden is nothing in comparison. It was exactly how I had always imagined such ruins to be. Then we went by underground canal into the coal mines outside Manchester, a good half hour underground all the way, in the course of which your father caught a chill and was not at all well for a couple of days;[11] but he is getting better now.[12] Today I saw the great iron bridge at Sunderland.[13] In brief, I shall have plenty to tell you, but can write no more now. We have good news from Hamburg: Adele[14] is well, I am happy to say. I expect to find a letter from you waiting for us in Edinburgh. Goodbye, dear Arthur, I am often sorry for your sake that you are not with us, but at least you are spending your time more profitably, if not so agreeably. Take to heart everything that I have written and follow my advice. You will not regret it. Goodbye. Your father is expecting letters from you soon, but on proper paper.

J. Schopenhauer

Mr Arthur Schopenhauer
at the Rev: Mr Lancaster
Wimbledon commons,
Wimbledon

III. From Lorenz Meyer (22/23 July 1803)[1]

Hamburg, 22 July 1803

Dear Schopenhauer,

I was beginning to think you had forgotten all about me or had not received my last letter. At least fifty times I was on the point of writing to ask you to answer, but never got further than the resolution, and now, not wanting to neglect your reply, I am sitting down with your very welcome letter still fresh in my mind and am beginning to dash off an answer which will at least show you how to write much in a little space. Do you get the contrast? — You can imagine my surprise when I saw where you are and heard that your parents had gone to Scotland. The place where you are at present I know well, maybe even better than you know it yourself at this stage!!! To prove the truth of this let me tell you that just outside Wimbledon is West Hill, where the old and now half gaga [Mr J.A. Rücker] lives.[2] To get from there to Richmond Park one can go across Wimbledon Common, on the left of which, if I am not mistaken, a large boarding school was pointed out to me, which is, I believe, where you now find yourself. On Wimbledon Common (have I got the spelling right?) the cruel murderer Abershawe[3] is hanging in chains.[4] I remember very clearly riding with young H[enry] J[ohn] Rücker past the hill[5] where A. was hanging, and I remember that a narrow footpath led through scrub and thorns to the gibbet where he was hanging. I could not help remembering that the way to paradise is supposed to lie through thorns as one climbs a steep hill. This is a nice idea, but the reality is often different; as it is in this case . . .

Godeffroy's[6] letter went off to him this morning (with a note from me), by foot-post, since I did not have time to deliver it myself. So you have written to him several times and not to me?!!! I don't see why you should have done that, since you know that your letters afford me so much pleasure. In future send my letters direct, as you did this time, and leave me to send on the enclosures. You know that I am more reliable than, for instance, Godeffroy, who is capable of leaving a note lying around for a couple of weeks, albeit without intending any harm. Young Jacobi,[7] whom you mentioned in your letter, I seem to remember seeing, with Herr Lembke from Memel, in Bordeaux and Paris, not in London. Ask him, and if I'm not right, quiz him about where and under what circumstances he saw me. It may be that I am remembering him clearly enough but, as happens when travelling around, mixing up the servants. I should like to recall all the pleasant details of that very pleasant journey, so please excuse this request. If on one of your walks you should find yourself near glorious Westhill, try to get to speak to one of the Rückers, tell them that you know me, that you were at Herr Runge's, and — above all — greet them warmly from me and my father and tell them that I still remember the good times I enjoyed while staying with them. Don't forget to tell them that I am employed by Rücker & Westphalen and working at Herr Rücker's.[8] He is the brother of Mr Daniel Henry, for people are called by their Christian names [in England]; but [Mr Daniel Henry] is a stoutish middle-aged man. You can also tell the funny old gentleman with his highly polished water-closets,[9] and his chairs on which one is not allowed to sit, about me. Knowing this family of bachelors might be very convenient for you because you are living so close to them. Give John Henry my particularly warm greetings. Get to know these people. I am very glad that — leaving aside the boredom — you are eating, drinking and bathing well.[10] You can be sure that the grub at Herr Rücker's is even better than it can possibly be at your school.

I am just back from the post office, which has made me rather lose the thread of this letter. In a note I sent to him this morning I had asked Godeffroy to meet me there. He did not come. Perhaps he'll bring me an enclosure for you tomorrow evening, which I also asked him to do, since this letter will probably be delivered by one of my friends in order to save you the postage. I believe you have not yet written to Herr Runge. He would be very pleased to hear from you. At school he is the same as ever. The Capt.[11] is said to be getting more and more insufferable. The food was not improved by Mlle Smidt.[12] They get strawberries hardly ever, spiced beef sometimes, and eel soup very often. Nothing has been heard or seen of our friend Droop. The elder Simers had to undergo a severe punishment, viz. that of being tarred and feathered; the insufferable fellow had lied no less than seven times. Mme Runge[13] has not brought about any changes in the school meals, but she is bringing the school many [extra] holidays. People seem to be getting fed up with them now, for the day before every saint's day, etc., etc. (as the opportunities for slacking are called), is now a holiday. At midsummer there was not even an examination, and yet they had four and a half days off. Midsummer fell on a Friday. They were given Saturday off, Sunday and Monday were dog days. Bringing you up to date with events at school has saved me from having to tell you how surprised I was on turning over the previous sheet to find myself already at the end of it without even having told you any news. There are three items of news: a large fire which took place recently, Robertson,[14] the French, and a necessary evil brought about by the latter in the form of the blocking of the Elbe; but half past two is striking and I must dine. Today is Friday, so I'll finish this letter tomorrow! Adieu!

Saturday 23 July 1803

The big fire was [very] near to where you live,[15] on the Holländischer Brook, at a Herr Courvoisier's, who lives over the firm of Courvoisier & Hourriet. They dealt in clocks, fancy goods, and French stuff in general. The fire was caused by the fact that Courvoisier's men were packing on the top floor and smoking cigars. The fire accordingly began at the top of the building. It was still half daylight, at 7.30 p.m. on 1 July. Despite this, the fire burned so fiercely that it totally destroyed one house, almost entirely destroyed another (widow Haschen's) and partly destroyed basket-maker Quandt's house. There was an incredible amount of looting; people were arrested for it. Lots of things were ruined too; some clocks were thrown out of the window in order to save them, only to end up smashed to pieces. Two people were killed. One fireman was crushed when the windlass fell on his head; the other was burned to death.

And that is the end of that subject. Now for something more interesting. It concerns the famous Professor Robertson. At the time of your departure it was rumoured that he was going to go up in his balloon, but he kept putting it off. Finally the City Council allowed him to make an ascent. He had the most frightful weather. The experiment was to take place on the Artillery

Ground ['Sternschanze']. It was raining continuously. Entrance into the Artillery Ground cost 1 thaler. There were crowds of people there. Finally, after everyone had been soaked to the skin, he declared that he could not attempt the ascent. This occasioned many squibs, one of which I am sending you (it is no longer obtainable). It is [called] *The Wet Balloonist* [*Die klatrige Luftfahrt*].[16] Look after it, it is very rare. In order to redeem his honour, Robertson recently went up on the quiet, and, just as everyone had previously been against him, now everyone was for him. His ascent was fabulous and accompanied by a fine morning; he went up so high that I could not see him because, when he was pointed out to me, he was already at an immense height. This successful ascent gave rise to new leaflets singing his praises; here are two of them. *Die fixe Luftfahrt* I am sending you because of the double entendre we know about (NB. Sieveking).[17] All these leaflets are written in Low German. I hope you can understand them, because there are some very funny things in them. The news about the French I will miss out; it is too boring. —

Just one other thing, dear fellow. — If you want me to show my next letter to Godeffroy, write his in such a way that I can see it too. Godeffroy told me he couldn't show me his letter from you because it wasn't written like that. How much I hope that you will be as prompt in answering this letter as I was in answering yours, you can no doubt imagine. Always reckon on a lengthy reply from

Your
[Lorenz] Meyer

I hope this letter got too long for you. I did it on purpose in order to get an equally long one from you.

In future please address your letters c/o Rücker & Westphalen, because then I will always receive them a couple of hours — or maybe days — earlier.

Address: Mr Arthur Schopenhauer
        to the care of
            Md Wwe Anderson Drewe & Co.[18]
              Old Broad Street No. 40
                London
By Capt. Meyer

IV. From H.F.S. (26 July 1803)[1]

Edinburgh, 26 July 1803

Dear Son,

I must say that I am very surprised, and even worried, that we have only just received letters from you, whereas it was made clear to you that you were to write once a week. A week ago today your mother sent you a long letter which I beg you to take to heart; otherwise I shall be extremely annoyed, for writing is something you really must learn to do properly; the other things are unimportant by comparison. Mr Drewe will give you anything you may need; in August I am allowing you to spend one day a week in London, but no nights, and I urge you to behave yourself and to be careful at the riding school, and otherwise to write once a week, on decent paper, and John Wm Anderson,[2] Drewe & Co. will always send your letters off straight away, and now God be with you.

Schopenhauer

Mr Arthur Schopenhauer
to the Care of the Reverend Mr Lancaster at Wimbledon Commons
Wimbledon
[date stamp: 7 o'clock, Jy 29 1803 N.T.]

V. From J.S. (4 August 1803)[1]

Glasgow, 4 August 1803

Your letters of 25 July[2] we found here when we arrived the day before yesterday; in Edinburgh, where we spent six days, we received not a line from you. Presumably, dear Arthur, you did not want to write until you had received a reply to your first letter, but that was — to say the least — not very well considered, for your relationship with us is not such as to justify you in expecting to receive an answer to all your letters; on the other hand, *you* are under an obligation to give *us* an account of how you are spending your time and of everything that you are doing. Even if this were not the case, you should have borne in mind that we are touring and not staying long in any one place, so that if your letters are not at a given place before we get there, we shall either not receive them at all, or they will have to be forwarded, doubling the cost of the postage, and eventually we are likely to have the pleasure of opening them in your presence in London. For the rest I am not unhappy with what you write. Your father is very pleased to hear that you have asked for two extra writing lessons, and I am also of the opinion that this is the most sensible thing you could have done. It seems that you are not going to be able to spend your time in Wimbledon very agreeably, so at least try to spend it profitably. With two writing lessons a day, good intentions, and a great deal of practice in your own time, two months are bound to see you well on the way towards acquiring such a mechanical skill, provided you are determined to do so. There is another piece of advice about your writing, dear Arthur, which I must give you; this concerns not the outward appearance of your letters, but the more important part of them — the content. Make it a rule never — even when in a hurry — to send off a letter, or even the most trifling note, without looking through it, word for word and with great care. If you do not do this, you will, I warn you, often bitterly regret not having done so, and besides, this is the only way to perfect your style and rid it of mistakes. Expressions which civilized, well educated people should not allow to slip out even in the heat of the moment in conversation, expressions like 'infamous' bigotry,[3] will then no longer creep into your letters. It is true that one should write more or less as one speaks, but none the less one must, it seems to me, pay more attention to the choice and combination of phrases in a letter than in conversation. After all, one writes more slowly and deliberately than one speaks, and the person receiving a letter pays closer attention to it than to the words in a conversation. On the other hand I do realise that the place where you are at present cannot be exactly pleasant for you, profitable though it will no doubt be. I hope you are working hard at your drawing;[4] you will probably never again have so much time for it and such a good opportunity for learning. I am sure you will not neglect your flute[5] for the sake of drawing, but how is the singing going? When you sing 'God save the King', are you now able to make pretty cadenzas, like the wife of the gentleman[6] who teaches you? In Edinburgh I heard a certain Master Smith sing at a concert; he seemed to be about your age, and sang very prettily, but in a soprano voice, like a woman; can you do trills and arabesques too?

You are right to stick to your fellow countrymen since the others are no use to you. Eschenburg[7] struck me straight away as being rather Droop-like. Jacobi[8] I did not notice when I was at Mr L[ancaster's], but you really ought to spend less time reading his Schiller tragedies[9] and more time trying to read English. I should in fact like you to lay aside your poets altogether for some time and opt for a more serious form of reading. However attractive those writings may be, they are suitable only for leisure hours. You may have many of these, but at your age time is so valuable from the point of view of the future, that — if you have any sense — you will take maximum advantage of this spare time as well. I admit that spending one's time on works of artistic genius is very agreeable, but anyone who concerns himself continually with such things will eventually lose the ability to appreciate more serious things, and, believe me, Schiller himself would never have become what he is if he had read only poets in his youth; after all, as he says himself, life is earnest, art alone carefree, and now you need to enter into this earnest life, and it will certainly seem more than earnest to you, it will seem intolerable, if at your age you become accustomed to frittering away all your time on poetry. You are 15 now, you have read the best German and French authors, and to some extent the best English ones too, and yet outside school hours you have not read a single prose work, with the exception of a few novels — no history, nothing except what you had to read to keep Herr Runge happy. This won't do. You know that I have a sense of beauty, and I am glad that you have perhaps inherited it from me; but such a thing cannot act as our guide through the sort of world that actually exists; it must be preceded by some useful vocation, and I would rather see you become anything rather than a so-called *bel esprit*. These gentlemen[10] talk about poems, plays, musicians and painters as though life were only about going to the theatre and to concerts. They pride themselves (Lord knows how much) on amusing themselves and being able to throw around a few easily learned bogus words and fashionable phrases, and look down with scorn and contempt on the mere merchant who ultimately pays for their celebrated artists and probably has to provide their wise, self-important admirer with a corner of his office in order that, with all his enthusiasm for art, he is able to eat; unless, of course, his late father was so unpoetic as to earn money for his more enlightened son to spend on pictures and books. You will never be as bad as that, but at the end of your letter to me you did make me smile. The truth, you say, should burn through the Egyptian darkness in England with its torch.[11] How can you expect the truth to do any such thing? Darkness can be illuminated, but it cannot be induced to burn. In English that sort of thing is called 'bombast'; I don't know the German word for it. In the meantime you are obviously getting a generous portion of Christianity, and I can't altogether blame you if it strikes you as rather too much of a good thing, but I must be allowed to laugh a little too: do you remember how many arguments I had with you when you refused to do anything at all on Sundays and holidays, on the grounds that, so far as you were concerned, they were 'days of rest'? Now you are getting your days of rest with a vengeance.[12] In the meantime it is now August, and no doubt you will have been in London this week. Herr Paleske[13] or Herr Drewe will give you money if you need it; you are no spendthrift, so I need say no more. We have been in Scotland for a good fourteen days. I liked Edinburgh very much; we were there precisely at the time of the races and stayed in the city for six days, after which we went into the Highlands, where we spent a week travelling through the mountains, which are so sublime as to beggar description. I have continued to keep my diary faithfully right up to today and shall have much to tell you from it when we are together again.[14] I think I have now probably completed the best part of my journey through England and Scotland; I am unlikely to see anything more beautiful, more remarkable or more interesting than what we have already seen. Until three days ago the weather was also very kind to us, but since then it has been very bad; I've been here since the evening of the day before yesterday and have not yet been out of doors; that is why you are receiving such a long epistle. We met Herr Meyerhoff[15] here; you will probably remember him, he had just begun to work for your father when we left Danzig and escorted us to the gates of the city; he asked lots of questions about you and asked to be remembered to you. Young Rücker,[16] who used to be with Herr Jenisch, is here too; he was talking only yesterday of your birthday party in Rosenstrasse with the famous fireworks — his brothers were at the party and his father had just been made Praetor.[17]

Goodbye, dear Arthur, enjoy yourself and be good, and above all don't forget to drink my health as well as the others'.

Jeanette Schopenhauer.

Mr Arthur Schopenhauer.
at the Rev: Mr Lancaster's Wimbleton

VI. From H.F.S. (10 August 1803)[1]

I have received your letter of 1st instant, dear Arthur, and am glad that you are now determined to learn to write [properly]. This can only mean a great deal of practice; for a start I suggest that you copy out the letter which your mother wrote to you from

Glasgow, on which she spent only half an hour.[2] The quicker you learn to write a fluent, manly hand the sooner I shall be able to remove you from Mr Lancaster's; but do not imagine that I shall do so until you have learned to write properly, for a would-be[3] merchant simply must be able to write well and fluently. Your calculations about how long your letters take to reach us are uncalled-for; it is enough that you have been told to send a letter to Mr Anderson's office every week for forwarding to us, which you will in future have the goodness to do, in addition to getting Mr Drewe to pay you whatever you need.

Your mother expects, as I do, that you will not need reminding again to walk straight,[4] like other properly brought-up people, and sends her love

Adieu
Heinr. Floris Schopenhauer

Liverpool,[5] 10 August 1803
Mr Arthur Schopenhauer
to the care of the Rev. M. Lancaster
Commons
Wimbledon

VII. From Lorenz Meyer (23 August 1803)[1]

Hamburg, 23 August 1803

My dear *Schopenhauer!*

How much pleasure my correspondence with you affords me you will gather from the fact that, although I only received your letter of 8 August at 8.30 p.m. yesterday, I am already answering it. I am very glad to have the enclosure for Godeffroy, for with the aid of it I hope to get back my letter from you, which he still has. I wrote to him that if he cared to return it I would hand over your yesterday's letter to him. Without this little subterfuge I believe I should never get your first letter back.

Delighted as I was to receive your letter, I was sorry to gather that you are unhappy in your present position. If I knew that my parents were in Scotland, I should take the first mail coach and follow them. In a couple of days you would be there[2] and then you would be able to go everywhere your parents went. What do you think of this idea? I think this would be an *expedition* which would give you eternal pleasure!!—— !!—— *à la* Zigra![3]— ! — ? Among all the things which you tell me are not allowed on Sundays (such as dancing, running, fishing, singing, whistling, tippling, writing, reading worldly books, playing, shouting [your weakness], climbing, making a noise, etc., etc.)[4] I find no prohibition in respect of sleeping. That's what I should decide to do if I were not allowed to do anything else. The 60 unruly boobies of your *School* I can well imagine and should not need more than one day at the most [to sort them out]. I am glad that I can remember so clearly everything in your neighbourhood. Ask Jacobi how Herr Lembcke is and whether he is not by any chance in Hamburg; if this were to be the case, I should pay him a visit, for I like him well enough. If Jacobi should come to Hamburg, impress upon him not to visit my father . . . That you should go to Rückers [of West Hill], straight up to the house, just to convey greetings from me, is not what I meant when I wrote to you about them. I know that you are not like *certain people* (does that mean me?) who are at ease anywhere in the first quarter of an hour. However, my own view is that when travelling one often gets to know people in a couple of hours, and if one does not begin to make their acquaintance in the first quarter of an hour, nothing will come of it, for, since such friendships are not for ever, one does not need to spend so long getting acquainted.

There has been a frightful murder here,[5] a detailed description of which is enclosed. — Godeffroy has just returned all the missing letters.

Yours,
Meyer

[in the margin] Always send my letters to Rücker und Westphalen. Answer soon. Your mother may also like to see the enclosed. I hope that you will be indulgent and will not read this letter too critically.[6] On reading it through I notice a number of mistakes which I am allowing to stand. You can always reckon on a speedy reply to your letters.

M. Arthur Schopenhauer
to the Care of
Mssrs. Ww. Anderson Drewe & Co.
London.

VIII. From H.F.S. (25 August 1803)[1]

My dear Arthur,

Your mother is not very satisfied with your last letter, and since

I have absolutely no notepaper this evening I will just say in reply to yours of 14th instant that you need a great deal of practice if you are going to be able to write a fluent and manly hand; that means leaving out all the fancy flourishes; kindly note the capital letters which I have underlined and in future copy them. The swimming lessons seem to me both dangerous and pointless.[2] In drawing and singing you are bound to make some progress since you are already embarked upon them and you are due home in London on Michaelmas Day, 29 September.[3] I want you to acquire the best and clearest German hand and to send me a reply which will satisfy me.

Your father
Heinr. Floris Schopenhauer

Bristol[4] 25 August 1803

Mr A. Schopenhauer Esquire
to the care of the Rev. M. Lancaster at
Wimbledon
Commons
[date stamp: 10 o'clock Au. 27 1803. F.N.]

IX. From H.F.S. (2 September 1803)[1]

London, 2 Sept. 1803

My dear Arthur,

Two months ago today we left London and have since travelled 1,600 miles; now we are back again and shall be staying here at least until some time next month. You can come to us on Tuesday morning so that we can see you and take you to the races at Enfield.[2] When your time with the schoolmaster is over, bring me your report,[3] which everyone is sure to be given. Learning to hold the pen in such a way that one can move it just with the fingers, without moving the hand, and can therefore wield it lightly, is the whole secret of writing a good, fluent hand. Yes, you have been in Wimbledon almost ten weeks now, and by the end of the twelfth week I was hoping to see you writing properly and [therefore] to be able to have you back with us in our present lodgings:

Norfolk Street No. 43 — Strand
New Church

You are costing me a lot of money in postage with your letters of immoderate length;[4] bring them with you when you come on Tuesday and give me more pleasure than you have set out to do so far. Adieu

           Heinr. Floris Schopenhauer

To
Mr Arthur Schopenhauer
to the Care of the Reverend Mr Lancaster
Wimbledon
Common
[date stamp: 10 o'clock, Sp 3 1803 M.N.]

X. From H.F.S. (4 September 1803)[1]

My dear Arthur,

 This is just to say that I have read in the newspapers[2] that the races will take place in Enfield on 6th inst. Don't get yourself all exhausted and dirty by walking all the way, but come in on the first ordinary coach, which we shall meet. I repeat that you are to pay attention to what I said in my letter of the day before yesterday, so that we can arrange for you to be released from Mr Lancaster's; but before that the appointed [three] months must be over so that our money is not wasted, and by then your mother will have a piano here.

               Schopenhauer

Norfolkstr. N. 43,
4. Sep. 1803

M. Arthur Schopenhauer
to the care of the Rev. M. Lancaster
Wimbledon
[date stamp: 4 o'clock Sp. 5 1803 M.N.]

IX. From Charles Godeffroy (8 September 1803)[1]

            Hamburg, 8 Sept. 1803

Dear Arthur,

 Your letter of 8 August reached me safely, forgive me for leaving it unanswered for so long, but I'm rather busy at the moment, partly in the office, and partly at the chaplain's,[2] where I am now having pre-confirmation lessons.

 You would surely be delighted if I could serve up several of the latest news items, but I simply have none. I was glad to read in your letter that you are having such a good time in Wimbledon,³ which seems very understandable because, according to your letter, you are spending all your time on the *beaux-arts* and on gentlemanly pursuits. You must be able to ride very well already if you are having riding lessons in London, and you must be pretty expert at shooting too, particularly since you have such fine pistols.

Fourteen days ago I came across a French song which goes to the tune of the song about the sailor boy, 'Contre les chagrins de la vie', and is very nicely done. If it were not so long, I would send you a copy of it.⁴

I hope, dear Arthur, to see you in Hamburg again this winter, but your stay in England seems very long if you are going on to Montpellier. No doubt you are looking forward to Paris. I don't mind telling you that I would give anything to be with you in the French capital; my own journey there will now not take place because of the war. Forgive me if my letters are not as long as Lorentz Meyer's, but when you return I hope to make up for it verbally. Adieu, my friend; of silly old, or good old, Droop I have no news; farewell

Charles Godeffroy.

XII. From J.S. (13 September 1803)¹

Friday morning, 13 Sept. 1803

I expect you got back to Wimbledon in one piece, but you could have written to tell us that you did; write without delay, you know how your father manufactures worries when he has no real ones. With this letter you will receive a pair of inexpressibles [trousers] which I ask you to look after. We have little news. Not knowing where to go out to, I am remaining dutifully at home, declaiming the while that popular verb je m'ennuie, tu t'ennuies, etc., and to keep up my spirits am playing the sonatas, which I like better every day. Goodbye, Arthur, my greetings — in moderation — to the Lancasters, and make the most of the short time which you have left with them.

J. Schopenhauer

Mr Arthur Schopenhauer
at the Rev: Mr: Lancaster's Wimbledon
common

Letters to Schopenhauer at Wimbledon

XIII. From Lorenz Meyer (16 September 1803)[1]

Hamburg, 16 Sept. 1803

You see, dear Schopenhauer, that I am once again troubling you with a letter. That is only a manner of speaking, for I trust that this is not the case, although one could easily get the idea that it were, at least on one side, if one did not know you better than that, since you have not answered my last letter, which you will have received long ago. For my part, I never enjoyed corresponding with anybody as much as with you. — Here there is all sorts of news. I only wish I could remember it all. For a start: a certain Herr Heimann, who spent a long time in Paris, living an awfully loose, dissolute life, and who was known as crazy Heimann, has shot himself, or at least has tried to do so. A couple of years ago he inherited 300,000 thalers. He quickly got through it all, with the exception of 60,000 thalers, which he was persuaded to tie up in a ten-year investment.

As I say, he spent a long time living in a scandalous, dissolute way in Paris; he ran up enormous debts and let it be known that as soon as he had no money left he would shoot himself. His creditors pursued him more and more closely, not letting him out their sight, for fear that he might give them the slip. He therefore thought up a ruse to escape them. He suddenly had a set of mourning clothes made, had his — numerous — servants dressed in black too, and let it be known that an uncle of his had died and had left him an immense fortune; but in order to claim it he would have to travel to Hamburg. His creditors, who swallowed the story hook, line and sinker, let him go, and so he arrived safely in Hamburg. When people in Paris heard that the whole story had been a lie, they wanted to have him apprehended; however, he eluded the police, and for some time nothing was heard of him, until finally it was rumoured that he had shot himself in the Concert Hall. This turned out to be true. He wrote to a court official to say that he was going to shoot himself. When the official came to see him the deed was already done. But he was not dead and is now almost recovered. He is currently under hospital arrest. — Riesau is now fully recovered. Would you believe it, he spends most of his time playing piquet with his guard! It is barely credible. He has also requested a bottle of wine a day (every afternoon). He has asked for books, too, and has been given them.[2]

Herr Thormöhlen, my father's book-keeper, has been appointed to look after Riesau's books and business. Everything is in apple-pie order. He kept a meticulous record of everything right up to the day of the murder. — Recently a big theft of wood from the builder's yard was discovered, and more and more of those involved are being found and apprehended.

Herr Runge and the Capt. came to see us yesterday. I asked the latter about you, and he began to bemoan your fate in being cooped up in a school in England. I hastened to explain that you were a gentleman[3] and not a common schoolboy. Whether he understood this explanation, I cannot tell. Fritz Meyer is off to Bremen soon and has complained to me that you have not answered him. — There has been no post from England since Friday (today is Monday). I hope to receive a letter from you soon. — If the French invade England, what will you do then? — Four members of my family have fallen sick in a row, but, thank God, all except my second sister are now well again. Now there really is no more news. This letter is far from meeting with my approval, and I am in two minds about whether to tear it up in the morning. Write back soon to

Your

G.C.L. Meyer

Mr Arthur Schopenhauer
to the Care of Mrss W. Anderson Drewe & Co
London.

PS. Don't forget to bring me something nice from England.

XIV. From H.F.S. (17 September 1803)[1]

London, 17 Sept. 1803

My dear Arthur,

I see they go in for very large bills; I wonder whether you could not refuse to pay the fortnightly singing master[2] his guinea fee; meanwhile perhaps the piano lessons will help you to progress in singing on your own.

If there is no danger in sending them by post I will send you with this letter three pound sterling notes (Nos. 19361, 19362 and 19363) so that you can pay one and all and can see how generously I always treat you. Mr Lancaster, whose bill amounts to £25,[3] I will pay in cash or by order as he prefers; please greet him and his family from your mother and myself, and don't forget to bring all your things with you.

Schopenhauer

Mr Arthur Schopenhauer
of Hambr.
to the Care of the Rev. M. Lancaster
Wimbledon
Commons

XV. From Lorenz Meyer (30 September 1803)[1]

Hamburg 30 Sept 1803

Dear Schopenhauer,

In your last letter, which, if I am not mistaken, I received four days ago, on 26th inst. (I've looked it up and that is right) you announce that you are only staying in London until the beginning of next month. Lest my letter may not reach you in time, I am writing today; as I am very busy, this letter will hardly be a long one. — That, as a result of your stay in England, you find yourself hating the whole nation[2] I am sorry to hear, since I, on the contrary, found myself, as a result of my own rather shorter stay there, confirmed and strengthened (even against my will) in my preconceived good opinion of England and its island inhabitants. Of course, the fact that we found ourselves in such different situations there will be a major factor in our different impressions. You were living in a school, were not much better off than a common-or-garden boarder, went up to London once a week, and otherwise saw no one but your Mr Lancaster and boys whose company you did not relish. I, on the other hand, went everywhere with my father; we went to receptions, were politely received everywhere, and, so far as possible in so short a time, saw all the sights of the famous city of London. You really wanted to go to France,[3] had been frustrated in that wish, and were therefore in a bad humour. I, on the other hand, found all my wishes fulfilled and therefore enjoyed London to the full as the last stop on my journey. So you see that for so many reasons I was bound to like England, whereas it was out of the question that you could ever like it as much![4] —

[Two paragraphs omitted]

I hope to see you here soon.

Yours
Meyer

M. Arthur Schopenhauer
to the Care of Mrss W. Anderson
Drewe & Cie
London

Letters to Schopenhauer at Wimbledon

XVI. *From Charles Godeffroy (28 March 1804)*[1]

Hamburg, 28 March 1804

Dear Arthur

Forgive me, forgive me! — No, I should rather say pity me, dear friend, pity me, why I need not say; you will guess why.[2] When you were leaving I promised to answer all your letters promptly, and kept that promise until your last letter; but then it was impossible for me to write. The story that follows is my excuse.

As you know, I go in for physical experiments. At the beginning of January someone gave me a piece of phosphorus. I had already performed this experiment several times in the dark, but since I am unselfish and like to share things with others, I invited my sister[3] to come to my room one evening to share my enjoyment of the experiment. Having an audience, I wanted to do things particularly well and therefore rubbed my piece of phosphorus on the wall so fiercely that it caught fire. On top of that, I had been so careless as to pick the phosphorus up in my bare hand, instead of putting it on the end of a quill. The burning piece fell off on to my hand and before I could get rid of it my hand (the right one) was covered with burning phosphorus and was burning like mad. If I had known then what I know now, I would have put my hand straight into the water jug, which would have put the phosphorous out. Instead, in my panic I ran downstairs and rubbed my hand on a bare, whitewashed wall, rubbing my hand to pieces in the process, so that the skin hung down in ragged pieces. I suffered from this accursed burning for ages, and it's only in the last fortnight that I have been able to write again; so be indulgent with me and don't start thinking that my friendship for you has cooled.

Fritz Meyer's sister married a certain Herr Wass three weeks ago, and our friend Fritz has now been apprenticed to Herr Meyer, a baptised Jew.

You know, Arthur, that last year I was supposed to be going to Paris, which didn't come off,[4] although I was very keen that it should. Now I have another trip in view which in all probability will come off. Where to? I hear you asking. Well, guess! Where would you expect me to be going? To England, to England, of course, where I shall have more fun than you have had.[5] You probably know the British chaplain Knipe[6] (which is pronounced Neip); well, he is travelling to England in three or four weeks' time, and I am going with him.[7] Together we shall travel through the whole of England and perhaps even to Scotland. You will see that

I shall have no time to be bored,[8] for I shall not be staying anywhere for more than three weeks. I am looking forward very much to this, my first such journey, although I don't like the idea that we shall not see one another until later, for I shall hardly be back before September.

It is now two months since I heard from you, and I suspect that the fact that I haven't written to you probably explains it. However, I hope that our correspondence can now be as lively as it was before, if not livelier, and that it will not come unstuck like your correspondence with Lorenz.[9] The above-mentioned has been complaining bitterly about the rubbish which he says you have written to him, but I have not seen the letter in question and do not know how he replied.

I am seeing a good deal of our friend Etienne[10] at present. On Sundays we — he, Fritz (and sometimes Tanner and Waser too) and I usually go for a walk beyond the city gates, where we pass the time with pistol shooting,[11] or with fighting battles (with snowballs as our weapons).

The 27th of this month was a great day for me: I was confirmed, and am very glad to have it behind me.

As I write this I have no idea where it will reach you, but expect it will be in Paris, for, having enjoyed yourselves there so much, you will hardly be in any hurry to head for gloomy old Montpellier.[12] Adieu, dear friend; please answer, as I am sure you will;[13] adieu, adieu.

Believe me, I have forgotten nothing.

Your friend
[Charles] Godeffroy.

XVII. From Charles Godeffroy (20 August 1804)[1]

Kendale, 20 August 1804

Dear Arthur,

Your letter from Vienna I received — God knows why it took so long — on 17th inst., not in London, as you will see, but elsewhere in England, and indeed in Kendale, the largest town in Westmorland. My situation and circumstances, dear Arthur, are much changed recently; I am not returning to Hamburg, but am going to stay in Liverpool for two years. First, however, let me tell you about my journey, about which you wanted to know. On 25 May we set sail from Dockenhuden,[2] for Husum (where the packet-boats now arrive);³ after spending two long days there waiting for a favourable wind, we embarked on the packet on 28th, and arrived at Harwich after a journey of eight days. I experienced little or no seasickness. On the way from Harwich to London we slept in Witham, and arrived in London on [5 June].⁴ In that capital city we stayed four weeks. In that short time I saw an extraordinary number of things, including all the theatres (but I saw neither Mrs Siddons nor Cooke, just Kemble): the Opera, Drury Lane, Covent Garden, Haymarket, Astley's Circus, etc. I did not like Westminster Abbey; in St Paul's I even crawled around the dome; in the Tower I was particularly interested by the towers themselves, the remains of the Spanish Armada, and the armoury. London I admired rather than liked; it is too big to be likable. On 4 July we left London for Oxford, in which city we spent a week; we dined in college⁵ all the time, where yours truly found himself in the midst of a gaggle of professors, one of whom spoke very good German. Oxford was the last place at which we stayed; from there we came to Kendale via Birmingham and Manchester. Kendale is Knipe's⁶ home town; his sister, who is married and living here, provided us with rooms in her house. Ten days ago I made a tour of Cumberland, where we saw the highest mountains in England; I climbed the highest mountain in England, Skid[d]aw, which is 3,100 ft high. My father had asked Knipe to look out for a good position for me, and two days before his departure he found one for me in Liverpool. At the moment I am living at Knipe's sister's and am going to Liverpool in two days' time; Knipe left five days ago. The English nation I like well enough, but cannot help feeling that, if the truth be told, the Englishman has less substance than he likes to think. The English have an immensely high opinion of their Volunteers,⁷ but those whom I have seen on parade are less impressive than our Hamburg soldiers. A propos, Schopenhauer, if you have grown and stand as crookedly as a cross, crosses are as yet quite unknown to me (I stand as straight as an old tower). Neither Fritz nor Lorenz has had letters from me, but I'll write to them from Liverpool. Before I left Hamburg Fritz told me that he was beginning to play long solos. Adieu, dear Schopenhauer, enough of this scribbling for now; more from Liverpool.

Your old friend,
Charles Godeffroy

Letters to Schopenhauer at Wimbledon

XVIII. From H.F.S. (23 October 1804)[1]

Hamburg 23 Oct. 1804

My dear Son,
    Now that you have given me your written word to learn to write well and fluently, and to reckon perfectly, I will rely on you to do so, with one further request: that you will also manage to bring yourself to walk straight, as other people do, in order that you will not get round shoulders, which look horrible. Holding oneself well is equally important at one's writing desk and in everyday life; if, when dining out, one sees someone sitting with a bent back, one assumes him to be a shoemaker or a tailor in disguise. It is good that you have resolved to have yourself a suit of clothes made, but to it you need to add a winter waiscoat; Herr Kabrun[2] will provide the outlay. Be as respectful to this good man as you are grateful, and ask him to let you write the letters of exchange and invoices, in his counting house, so that these continue to look capable of being sent anywhere in the world. There are few houses where you would be so well placed to learn the merchant's trade as that of my dear old friend Kabrun in Danzig. Therefore pay attention and listen to what he says, which cannot but be very helpful to you when it comes to getting on in the world. It is not worth sending on your new flute, because half the time you are to spend in Danzig is already over; but do go on playing on your old one at one or other concert since this will act as a further recommendation to you in your native city. Your mother writes that you have suddenly turned into a young gentleman, and that people are telling her how nicely behaved you are; see that this niceness extends to your room and to your luggage, for that business in Braunau[3] really was very tiresome.
    If at the riding school, [through] expert tuition, or as a result of exercising with a good drill sergeant,[4] you are able to acquire better deportment, I will gladly pay for it, but you must also practise your French and English and again entreat Herr Kabrun to let you write letters in these languages as well as in German; he would be happy to assist you if necessary, and once you have acquired his business style, you will have acquired everything that you need; besides, I should prefer you not to return to Herr Jaenish's office here in the capacity of a learner, and now God be with you.

Schopenhauer

Hamburg, 23 Oct 1804

Arthur Schopenhauer
Dantzig

Notes

I

1. Source: *S-Jb*, 46 (1965) 133 ff.
2. On 11 May 1803, the eve of his departure for England and France, A.S. wrote in Lorenz Meyer's autograph book:

Wenn vor der Erinnerung Zauberstab
Vor deinen Blick einst ein Bild rollt herab,
Von dem was du lang nicht gesehen:
So wünsche ich dass auf dem bunten Bild,
Von so unterschied'nen Gestalten gefüllt,
Auch meine alsdann möge stehen.

3. Clearly the Schopenhauers' journey to England, and therefore A.S.'s term at Mr Lancaster's, very nearly never took place, thanks to the imminence of war and Schopenhauer *père*'s anxious disposition; according to A.S.'s diary, news of England's new declaration of war on France on 18 May reached the Schopenhauers while they were in the packet-boat on their way from Calais to Dover.
4. Maybe this had something to do with A.S.'s part-Dutch ancestry.
5. See A.S.'s diary for 6 May.
6. Dr Johann Heinrich Christian Runge (1768-1811) was, from 1797, headmaster of the best-regarded boys' academy in Hamburg (at Katharinenkirchhof 44), which A.S. attended from 1799 to 1803. Dr Runge, who had studied theology at Halle at a time when pietism was rife there, was a remarkable man; he sought to be a friend to his 40 pupils and mixed socially with their parents. In a later chapter his educational ideas are discussed and contrasted with those of Thomas Lancaster.
7. Carl Friedrich Hauptmann (1778-1839) was an usher at Dr Runge's academy. He taught geography, and must also have been partly responsible for *Moralunterricht* (as religion was called), for A.S.'s friend Charles Godeffroy calls him 'Sittenprediger Hauptmann'. For obvious reasons he was generally known as 'The Captain'. He was neither popular nor respected, partly because he lacked Dr Runge's *rapport* with his charges and partly, I suspect, because of his incompetence.
7. He too studied theology at Halle. He was to marry Dr Runge's sister in 1805 and subsequently left teaching.
8. Fritz (Georg Friedrich) Meyer (b. 1788, son of Domherr Johann Friedrich Lorenz Meyer) was a cousin of Lorenz Meyer; he later went to Bordeaux as a merchant and became Hamburg consul-general there. He died at Bordeaux in 1878.
9. Ferdinand Droop (b. 1785. son of Johann Friedrich Droop) was another contemporary of A.S. at Dr Runge's. In a letter to A.S. Charles Godeffroy writes of the 'dummen aber guten Droop'. What became of him is not known.
10. Fr. Meyer: Fritz Meyer, whose departure for Bordeaux was delayed by the war.

11. (Georg Christian) Lorenz Meyer (1787-1866, son of the wine importer Johann Valentin Meyer) was one of A.S.'s main friends at Dr Runge's. His letters, which A.S. criticised as being filled out with 'undigested' news items, make interesting reading and are an important source of information. He also kept a diary (excerpts from which were edited by Hildegard von Marchtaler in 1968). The unpublished diary of his stay in England in summer 1802 is no less important in the present context.

12. Rodde was another school friend. He is not mentioned in Lorenz Meyer's diary; shortly afterwards he went out of circulation.

II

1. Source: *S-Jb*, 52 (1971), 85 ff.
2. J.S. did not care for Newcastle. In her diary she wrote:

In Newcastle . . . we could find nothing to do except sleep. The city is quite large, has a few handsome streets and many narrow, winding ones; it is important for Great Britain, mainly because of the coal trade, but everything has the look and the smell of this trade, and for the person travelling for pleasure the city has little to offer.

Whether his former 'pet' knew that Richard Jameson was buried in Newcastle, having died there seven years previously, is not recorded.

3. She is probably referring to A.S.'s letters to his mother and father of 8 July. Even before he went to Mr Lancaster's he was in the habit of writing letters on Mondays.

4. Mr and Mrs Percival had a son of the same age as A.S. and at least two daughters; they lived at Sydenham. The son, who showed A.S. round London occasionally, may have been George, b. 12 April 1789 in London, son of Samuel and Mary Percival. The family features in A.S.'s diary.

5. That is, Mr Samuel Drewe of Wm Anderson Drewe and Co. (40 Old Broad Street) or his deputy (Mr Paleske?).

6. She uses the English word.

7. Miss Lancaster: Miss Eliza(beth) Lancaster, Thomas Lancaster's eldest daughter, who, following her mother's death in 1797, appears to have acted as housekeeper/matron.

8. J.S.'s diary was published in Leipzig in 1813 under the (misleading) title *Erinnerungen einer Reise durch England und Schottland in den Jahren 1803-1805* [sic]; there have been many subsequent editions. Though not a great travel diary, it is a fascinating document. It differs from most others in that J.S. and H.F.S. travelled throughout England, including the north (then little visited by foreign travellers).

9. Johannes Duguet and his wife Sophie were manservant and lady's maid to (H.F.S. and) J.S. from 1800 to 1814. Sophie Duguet appears in Adele Schopenhauer's novel *Anna* (Leipzig, 1845) under her real name. J.S. gives a fuller account of the Peak Cavern in her diary; with her account it is interesting to compare that to be found in *Moritz's Travels in England*.

10. In her diary she mentions Richmond Castle; they may also have taken in Easeby.

11. Because of the chill which H.F.S. had caught, they were obliged to break their journey for several days at Catterick Bridge, where they stayed at the ancient George and Dragon, the 'lonely Inn in a wide moorland place' of Dickens's 'The Holly-Tree'. In 1803 the George and Dragon was still the only house at Catterick Bridge, as it had been in 1442, when it first appears as a coaching inn, and as it was when Leland passed through in 1535 ('Katerikbridge selfe hath but one house as an yn'). J.S.'s account of the George and Dragon is particularly interesting because she goes into detail with which native diarists (and earlier German diarists) do not bother. Floris and Johanna Schopenhauer were kindly received by the landlord and his wife. Daniel Ferguson, who originally came from Moulin, Perthshire, and was landlord of the George and Dragon in its heyday, rode to Richmond to fetch the apothecary — no doubt Henry Blegborough (1735-1810), a prominent Richmond man who was mayor in 1779, 1788 and 1801 - and Mistress Elizabeth Ferguson was most assiduous in her attendance in H.F.S.'s sick room. The son of the house who produced 'half a library' to while away the time for the Schopenhauers was the Rev. Daniel Ferguson (bapt. Catterick 25 August 1780), who went up to Emmanuel College, Cambridge, as a sizar in 1798. His ordination papers show that he attended lectures by James Fawcett (1752-1831), Norrisian Professor of Divinity. He took his BA in 1802 and was ordained deacon at Winchester (for York) on 6 March 1803, his ordination title being the curacy of Carnaby (Yorkshire). In summer 1803 he was probably also Curate of Langton (County Durham), for J.S. says that he was curate of a parish near Catterick Bridge; he married in 1804, his wife coming from Killerby, near Langton. He was priested in 1805, one of his sponsors being the then rector of Alston, C. Alderson. He was rector of Broughton Sulney (Nottinghamshire) in 1807-8; from 1808 to 1859 he was rector — and patron — of Walkington. He became JP and DL of the East Riding. He died on 29 November 1859, aged 79 (*GM*, 1860/I, 189).

12. When this was written A.S.'s parents were spending the night at Durham, probably at the Queen's Head (1 North Bailey) or at the Red Lion (now Hatfield College). J.S. approved of Durham, which she described in her diary as 'one of the oldest, though not one of the largest towns in England . . . most picturesquely situated in a charming valley surrounded by cultivated hills'. Travelling half a generation later, Dr S.H. Spiker, librarian to the King of Prussia, gave a slightly fuller description:

> The streets of Durham are narrow and crooked; but its situation on the banks of the Wear, is in the highest degree picturesque . . . The banks, which fall in a gentle slope to the river on both sides, are covered with a luxuriant vegetation, and buildings of all descriptions rising amphitheatrically above each other.

(*Travels through England, Wales and Scotland in the year 1816*, 2 vols in 1, 1820, 129). Johanna Schopenhauer's description is reminiscent of Sylas Neville's comment that 'The Assembly rooms at the Red Lion where we dined command a delightful prospect of river, city and country' (*Diary*, 11 November

1772). Neville went on, 'My companion taken ill with a fit while we were at dinner'; let us hope the Schopenhauers fared better. Johanna Schopenhauer's description of Durham is a good deal more complimentary than Smollett's:

> The city of Durham appears like a confused heap of stones and brick, accumulated so as to cover a mountain, round which a river winds its brawling course. The streets are generally narrow, dark, and unpleasant, and many of them almost impassable in consequence of their declivity. The Cathedral is a huge, gloomy pile; but the clergy are well lodged.

(*The Expedition of Humphry Clinker*, Matt. Bramble's letter of 15 July.) Thomas Gray, writing in 1753, was much more impressed with Durham:

> Suffice it to tell you, that I have one of the most beautiful vales here in England to walk in, with prospects that change every ten steps, and open something new wherever I turn me, all rude and romantic; in short, the sweetest spot to break your neck or drown yourself in that ever was beheld.

(*Works*, ed. Gosse, II, 241.) More important, however, is the fact that, in view of her remark to her son about 'dear' Christianity, the absence from Johanna Schopenhauer's account of any comment on Durham's most visible and celebrated attraction — the Norman cathedral — is striking and smacks of hypocrisy.

13. Described in great detail in her diary, so A.S. would presumably have been told all about it.

14. Adele: A.S.'s sister (b. 1798).

III

1. Source: *S-Jb*, 46 (1965), 135 ff.
2. Lorenz Meyer spent from 18 May to 21 October 1802 travelling in France and England with his father; his journey is described in an unpublished diary in the Staatsarchiv in Hamburg. He is referring to the house at which he stayed the previous summer, West Hill House, Wandsworth, residence of John Anthony Rucker (1719-1804), who is the old man in question. Johann Anton Rücker was born in Hamburg but came to England in George II's time (dropping the *Umlaut* in his name in the process). He rapidly made good as a merchant. In 1765 he was a partner in the Merton Abbey calico printing works; by 1792, according to Lysons, he was the owner of one of the two calico printing manufactories at Mitcham. The textile printing industry was an advanced and flourishing one, in which there was money to be made; it clearly brought J.A. Rucker considerable wealth, for by 1792 he was in occupation of Putney Bowling Green, the site of a once fashionable place of entertainment for public breakfasts and evening assemblies, and a very handsome villa had lately

been built for him at Wandsworth near Lord Spencer's recently extended park. This house, which was built for him by a Mr Gibson of Hackney, was, from its elevated position, a conspicuous object in the neighbourhood; it was known first as West Hill House, and afterwards as Melrose Hall; it subsequently became the Royal Hospital for Incurables. On old Mr Rucker's death on 21 May 1804, aged 85, West Hill House passed to his nephew, Daniel Henry Rücker, who sold it in 1824.

When Lorenz Meyer stayed at West Hill House *c.* 1802 there were three generations of Ruckers living there: John Anthony Rucker, his nephew Daniel Henry Rücker (brother of Martin Albert Rücker, 1758-1824, partner and director of the firm of Rücker und Westphalen of Grosse Reichenstrasse 42, Hamburg, to whom Lorenz Meyer was indentured for seven years) and young Henry John Rücker (presumably born in 1788-90). Henry John was the son of Conrad Rücker of Hamburg and therefore a nephew of Daniel Henry; when Lorenz Meyer returned to Hamburg from Wandsworth in autumn 1802 he went to Conrad Rücker to tell him how his son was getting on. In his unpublished travel diary, written in French, he wrote of his stay at West Hill House:

Saturday 9 October [1802]. We took our seats in Mr Rücker's carriage at three o'clock and arrived at Westhill at four o'clock. The rain had stopt. Old Mr Rücker welcomed us. After dinner we played whyst. I shared a bedroom with Henry John, who made me a present of a fishing rod.

Sunday 10 October. After breakfast we attended a chapel two miles from Westhill. We heard the sermon; it was my first time. Having returned at one o'clock, H.J. Rücker and I mounted our horses and rode to Richmond Park. My little pony cantered all the time. We went no farther than Richmond. Coming back through the park we took the wrong route and on leaving the park found ourselves seven miles from Westhill. Crossing Wimbelton [*sic*] common we saw the famous Abershaw on his gibbet. We gallopt all the way, reaching Westhill at four o'clock. We dined there and in the evening John R. read a sermon to his uncle in English, to which we had to listen. At bedtime Henry John and I spent a long time talking about Hamburg. The weather was very good. That evening the moon had a large ring round it.

Monday 11 October. After breakfasting and playing billiards at Westhill we took our leave and were driven back to town.

Henry John Rücker also became a City merchant; in 1838 he had a counting house at the rear of Little Tower Street, approached from 14 Mincing Lane.

J.A. Rücker's nephew, Daniel Henry, reappears briefly in the present story when Lorenz Meyer writes to A.S. on 31 August 1804:

In two weeks' time Herr D.H. Rücker from London is giving a ball in the Schimmelmann Hotel in Rhainville; he is supposed to have let it be known that it is going to be the greatest ball that Hamburg has ever seen; let's hope that it will be!!

In his next letter, dated 26 October 1804, Lorenz Meyer reports, in less than enthusiastic terms:

> So far as the ball at Rhainville given by Herr Rücker is concerned, there is nothing much to report. It was splendid enough, but was almost entirely a family affair, as you would readily understand if you knew how large a family the Rückers are. There was no one to be seen except male and female cousins, uncles and aunts, mothers, fathers and children, all of them belonging to Rücker's family. I should think non-relatives formed less than an eighth of those present. Nor did I meet anyone who really enjoyed it.

Whether Schopenhauer ever got to know the Rückers of West Hill House is not known, although it is possible that he owed his presence at Mr Lancaster's to an enquiry made by his father of Daniel Henry Rücker's brother, a fellow Hamburg businessman and family friend.

3. In the late eighteenth century Louis Jeremiah (Jerry) Abershawe was the chief highwayman of the Wimbledon/Wandsworth district. He lived in Coombe Wood, but spent most of his time in the Bald-Faced Stag, from which he would sally forth to attack those crossing Wimbledon Common. He was eventually hanged on Kennington Common, and was then brought to be suspended in chains on Wimbledon Heath. Lorenz Meyer's account is particularly interesting because it represents first-hand evidence; the story is told at second hand in Hone's *Table Book* of 1827.

4. The practice of hanging executed bodies in irons was a common one. Executed highwaymen were exhibited beside the roads they had infested. Hugh Phillips's *The Thames about 1750* reproduces a political print in the British Museum showing the bodies of three hanged men exhibited in irons, together with a set of gibbet-irons from Rye.

5. The hill on which the gibbet stood is Jerry's Hill.

6. Charles (Karl) Godeffroy (1787–1848) was one of A.S.'s best friends at Dr Runge's. The son of a well-to-do family, he lived in the Weisses Haus at Dockenhuden, and was a shy, somewhat indolent young man. He later became Prussian Minister in St Petersburg. He married a daughter of A.S.'s one-time employer, Senator Martin Johann Jenisch, and later employed Dr Julius Frauenstädt as tutor.

7. The 'young Jacobi', who was evidently one of A.S.'s very few companions at Mr Lancaster's (he was the only boy who was there at the same time of whom we hear more than once), may be Karl, son of Andreas Ludolf Jacobi (1746–1825), lawyer and court counsellor of Hanover), and therefore a nephew of the Mlle Caroline Jacobi who was Fanny Burney's successor as second keeper of the robes to Queen Charlotte from 1791 to 1797, when she returned to Germany. He would also have been distantly related to the 'Mr Jacobi' (Baron Jacobi: Constans Philipp Wilhelm von Jacobi-Klöst) who was Prussian Minister in London from 1792 to 1816; Caroline Jacobi was a cousin of Baron Jacobi. Karl von Jacobi (1790–1875) became a Hanoverian general.

8. L.M.'s employer is Martin Albert Rücker (1758–1824).

9. Old Mr Rucker's concern is understandable. Water-closets only date from the mid-eighteenth century and were therefore a luxury at this time.

10. The Rev. Lancaster attached importance to Cleanliness, and those who chose to avail themselves of it were 'during the Summer Months, accommodated with the Use of a cold Bath, at a moderate Expense'. By the same token, Mr Lancaster stressed the quality of the school food and emphasised that the school had its own extensive vegetable garden.

11. The Capt.: 'Sittenprediger' Hauptmann.

12. Presumably Mlle Smidt is the school matron at Dr Runge's.

13. Dr Runge had evidently married recently.

14. 'Professor Robertson', who was by no means the first balloonist, has not been identified.

15. From Easter 1796 to 1806 the Schopenhauer family lived at Neue Wandrahm 92. The Holländischer Brook is near by.

16. *Klatrig* means 'wet' in every sense.

17. Presumably Meyer is referring to another classmate, Eduard (Heinrich) Sieveking (b. 1790, son of Heinrich Christian Sieveking), who settled in London as a merchant, founded the firm of Edward Henry Sieveking and died there in 1868. It is, however, possible that Meyer is referring to Wilhelm Sieveking (b. 1789, son of the celebrated Georg Heinrich Sieveking), who settled in Montpellier as a merchant and died there in 1837. It is even possible that he is referring to Georg Heinrich Sieveking, the 'Hamburger Rothschild', who had an estate at Neumühlen (near Altona) and a town house at Neue Wall 149; G.H. Sieveking was originally an enthusiastic supporter of the French Revolution, but prudence cooled his ardour; Meyer could therefore be referring to Herr Sieveking's idea not being very 'fix', although it is more likely that he is referring to an incident involving a classmate.

18. H.F.S. mentions (Sir) John William Anderson (Bart) in his letter of 26 July 1803, and the first person the Schopenhauers called on following their arrival in London on 26 May was his wife, Lady (Dorothy) Anderson. H.F.S. names the firm after the widow of its founder, William Anderson of Danzig. In fact the firm was known as Anderson Drewe and Co. from 1801 to 1806; the title was subsequently changed to J.W. Anderson Drewe & Co. (1808-10). In 1803 Sir John William Anderson, Bart, son of William Anderson, must have been in semi-retirement; the day-to-day running of the firm will have been in the hands of his partner, Samuel Drewe, who gave up his partnership about 1811 after becoming a governor of the Bank of England. Herr Paleske may have been involved in Anderson Drewe & Co., although (unlike the clerk Emanuel Harrington and another employee, Henry Walter) he is not mentioned in Sir John William Anderson's will. Anderson Drewe & Co. clearly acted as H.F.S.'s English bankers.

IV

1. Source: *S-Jb*, 36 (1955), 84.

2. John William Anderson: Sir John William Anderson, Bart, of Holcombe House, Mill Hill. He was the husband of the Lady Anderson on whom the Schopenhauers called immediately on arrival in London. Born in Danzig in October 1735-36, he was third son of William Anderson of

Danzig, merchant, who was born in Scotland about 1700. William Anderson set out to seek his fortune and settled in Danzig, where he must have taken to dining at the 'ordinary' run by the widow of one Major Thomas Sheldon, for he duly fell in love with her daughter Lucy, whom he married on 11 September 1721. William and Lucy Anderson lived in the Englisches Haus in the Brotbänkengasse (near the Trosieners and opposite Speicherinsel). William Anderson was not only a merchant but also butler to the English resident and steward of the English House, an open house for travellers from England. William and Lucy Anderson had a total of eight children: Elizabeth (bapt. 22 December 1722, m. Lieutenant-Colonel Gunther of Danzig), William (bapt. 11 April 1724, apparently died young, perhaps in 1749), Lucy (bapt. 6 May 1726; m. first Andrew Scott of the British Factory in 1746 and had a son Gilbert, and second Rev. Borgraf of Danzig), Andrew (merchant and burgess in Danzig; bapt. 30 December 1729, m. Christine Albrecht in 1755, d. 1772 without issue), Mary (bapt. 1 May 1732), Anna Concordia (bapt. 4 June 1733, died unmarried), John William (bapt. 11 October 1735) and Susanna Louisa (bapt. 15 December 1737, m. John Simpson, merchant in Berlin and formerly in Memel, and had a son, George). William Anderson died at Danzig, probably about 1737 (and in any case before 1746), and his wife in 1772-3, about the same time as their eldest son, Andrew. H.F.S. knew Lucy Anderson, but his main contact was naturally with John William, who was of his own generation. John William Anderson, for his part, settled in London as merchant and indeed Merchant Adventurer. He became a member of the Glovers' Company, which at that time owned a hall in Beech Lane, Cripplegate; this probably means that he exported gloves to Poland and Russia in exchange for timber, grain, hemp. etc. He was elected alderman of Aldersgate Ward in 1789, sheriff in 1791, and Lord Mayor in 1797. On 5 May 1798 he was created a baronet, and the same year was elected president of Christ's Hospital; he was also treasurer of the Honourable Artillery Company and a governor of the Royal Exchange Assurance. He was elected one of the MPs for the City of London in 1793 and re-elected in 1796 and 1800. He married, in 1762, Dorothy, daughter and co-heiress of Charles Simkins, of Devizes. They had no children. He died on 21 May 1813 and his wife on 30 November 1817; the baronetcy then became extinct. The Andersons lived at Holcombe House in Mill Hill village, a stuccoed villa designed in 1775 by John Johnson, a feature of the interior being the elaborate eighteenth-century plasterwork. There was a domed Grecian temple in the grounds. H.F.S. presumably first knew John William Anderson in Danzig. It is strange that he and his wife do not reappear in the diaries of J.S. and A.S. John Anderson (1674-1743) and his son, John Anderson (1717-90), who were both Burgomaster of Hamburg, were not related, although their names do underline the links between Britain and Hamburg in the eighteenth century.

V

1. Source: *S-Jb*, 52 (1971), 87 ff.

2. A.S. appears to have written to both his mother and his father on 25 July, by which time he was finding the Sundays at Mr Lancaster's extremely tedious. Since his letters have not survived, we know of them only from this one.

3. A.S.'s view of the 'infamous bigotry' which he encountered at Mr Lancaster's is discussed presently.

4. Drawing was an 'extra' at Mr Lancaster's; A.S.'s drawing master may have been the young John Whichelo (1784-1865).

5. On the contrary, A.S. — who was a very keen flute-player — no doubt sought solace in his treasured ivory flute (cf. Peacock's Sir Oran Haut-ton) when Mr Lancaster's regimen became too much for him; unfortunately he was not allowed to play it on Sundays.

6. The idea of A.S. harmonising prettily while singing 'God save the King' is a nice one; the identity of the peripatetic singing master is not known.

7. 'Eschenburg' may have been a son of the famous English scholar Johann Joachim Eshenburg (1743-1820) of Brunswick; nothing more is heard of him.

8. Jacobi: see letter III, n. 7.

9. Johanna Schopenhauer has a point: A.S. was meant to be reading English. Whether Mr Lancaster allowed him to read Schiller on Sundays is not recorded.

10. This was, of course, a time of extreme fashions — not to say poses — in literary as in other things.

11. This often quoted phrase, like the 'infamous bigotry', is known only from his letter.

12. See Chapters VII and VIII.

13. Paleske appears to have been Drewe's deputy or assistant.

14. Presumably A.S. was allowed to read the diary.

15. Nothing more is heard or known of Meyerhoff.

16. 'Young Rücker' is probably Henry John Rücker; 'Herr Jenisch' is the merchant Senator Martin Jenisch to whom A.S. was apprenticed in 1805 (see Paul T. Hoffmann, 'Schopenhauers Hamburger Lehrherr. Der Senator M.J. Jenisch', *Hamburger Fremdenblatt*, 4 October 1931).

17. Praetor: magistrate.

VI

1. Source: *S-Jb*, 36 (1955), 84 f.

2. It is a rather long letter to have been written in half an hour and, more importantly, is not a suitable model for A.S.; his mother's syntax is shocking.

3. A.S. was not so much planning a career as a merchant as being bribed and browbeaten into it. His father first offered him a tour of England and France (in return for agreeing to renounce his literary and scholarly ambitions), then shunted him off to Mr Lancaster's, or, better, agreed to his wife's proposal that this should be done.

4. Both his parents mention this, so it does seem that young A.S. was

inclined to slouch. and when he got to Mr Lancaster's, he will have found the Rev. Lancaster no less concerned to get his charges to walk upright in token of their uprightness.

5. In August 1804 A.S.'s friend Charles Godeffroy was to find himself working in Liverpool ('an Englishman from Liverpool' was among those at one of G.H. Sieveking's famous parties at Neumühlen at about the same time); his stay with this down-to-earth family gave him the self-confidence which he had been unable to develop during his unhappy childhood.

VII

1. Source: *S-Jb*, 46 (1965), 137 ff.
2. Not true; the journey would have taken about a week, depending on the means of transport.
3. The allusion is lost, but Zigra is mentioned in Meyer's letter of 10 February 1804 as a well known practical joker of the time in Hamburg.
4. Clearly the list of forbidden activities comes from A.S.
5. Religious mania led the probationer clergyman Riesau/Rüsau to murder his whole family. Lorenz Meyer refers to Riesau in later letters and in his diary.
6. It sounds as though A.S. got his own back on his friends for his parents' critical reaction to his letters; this applied particularly to Lorenz Meyer's letters. Charles Godeffroy's much more carelessly written letters do not appear to have come in for the same reaction; but then A.S.'s relations with these two friends were clearly different — he was for ever fighting with Charles Godeffroy at Dr Runge's, but shared with him a desire not to end up in a counting house; both boys' fathers were strongly opposed to intellectualism, which they associated with poverty.

VIII

1. Source: *S-Jb*, 36 (1955), 85.
2. An example of H.F.S.'s fussiness.
3. According to Dorothy Wordsworth, 29 September is 'The grand festival of Hamburghers, dedicated to St. Michael, observed with greater solemnity than Sunday, but little of festivity' (in her Hamburgh Journal of 1798).
4. Bristol is described at some length, and in very positive terms, in J.S.'s diary.

IX

1. Source: *S-Jb*, 36 (1955), 85f.
2. The Schopenhauers were evidently fond of going to the races at Enfield, where they knew William Mellish (MP for Middlesex from

1806; d. 1839), who owned an estate at Bush Hill Park which A.S. described in his diary as 'very fine'. There is no reason to think they knew the Meyers of Forty Hill (Enfield), although they may have done.

3. No report has been preserved, but we gather from Mr Lancaster's *Plan of Education* that a half-yearly report was sent out, for the inspection of parents and friends. A 'Specimen of the Synopsis' was not included in the *Plan of Education*, but one is preserved in the British Library; it is headed 'Synopsis of the Business done by Master   in the Prosecution of his Studies at WIMBLEDON SCHOOL, commencing   '. From left to right the columns read: Dates (179), Read (two columns), Construed (five columns), Parsed (one column), Translated (two columns: English and Original), Scanned (one column); Committed to Memory (thirteen columns in all), subdivided into Languages (four columns, one each for Latin, English, French and Greek), Grammars (four columns, one each for the same languages), F[rench] V[erbs] (one column), Spelling (two columns: English and French), Geography (one column), Abrid[gements?] (one column); Written (nine columns in all), subdivided into Copy Books (one column each for Latin, English and French), Dictates (*ditto*); Composed (two columns, one each for Themes and Verses); Worked (four columns in all, one for Sums and three for Problems, which have one column each for Geography, Glob[e] and Maps); the two final columns are headed 'Repeated', and are subdivided into L[atin] G[rammar] and R[ules of] A[ccidence].

4. A.S. had either mended his ways or, more likely, had taken to sending the results of his writing lessons to his parents.

X

1. Source: *S-Jb*, 36 (1955), 86.
2. H.F.S. was, like his son after him, a reader of *The Times*.

XI

1. Source: *S-Jb*, 51 (1970), 34 f.
2. Whether or not this is a reference to the chaplain to the British embassy at Hamburg, whom Charles Godeffry knew well, is not clear. See letter XVI, n. 6, below.
3. It is interesting to see that A.S., in letters written to his two friends on the same day, gave totally different accounts of his life at Wimbledon.
4. An example of Godeffroy's laziness?

XII

1. Source: *S-Jb*, 52 (1971), 89.

XIII

1. Source: *S-Jb*, 46 (1965), 138 f.
2. According to Lorenz Meyer's letter to A.S. of 30 March 1804, Riesau was broken on the wheel. The execution, which took place on 19 March, is described in detail in L.M.'s unpublished diary.
3. A.S. was a parlour boarder.

XIV

1. Source: *S-Jb*, 36 (1955), 87.
2. The original has *Sänger*, which I take to mean singing master.
3. Mr Lancaster's academy was intended for the sons of the well-to-do; his fees *were* high.

XV

1. Source: *S-Jb*, 46 (1965), 140.
2. This letter is the only source of A.S.'s often quoted comment; his own letter has not survived.
3. Where A.S.'s best friend (Anthime Grégoire) lived. At the age of nine A.S. spent two years (1797–99) with Anthime's family at Le Havre. When he eventually returned to Hamburg he had forgotten his own language and was to all intents and purposes a little Frenchman.
4. Lorenz Meyer's analysis is surely right.

XVI

1. Source: *S-Jb*, 51 (1970), 36 ff.
2. Whether A.S. guessed why, there is no way of telling, but Lorenz Meyer also wrote to him on 30 March 1804 about the accident in question.
3. Charlotte Godeffroy, who presently married one Richard Parish (of Hamburg).
4. Because of the war with France.
5. Evidently A.S. had written to Charles Godeffroy in rather different terms from the letter of 8 September 1803, or Godeffroy had heard from Lorenz Meyer that A.S. was not enjoying himself.
6. In Kendal Charles Godeffroy stayed with John Knipe's sister Margaret and her husband, James Barrow.
7. It was to be months rather than weeks before the journey came off.
8. This must reflect a comment by A.S. about being bored.
9. See Lorenz Meyer's letter to A.S. of 30 March 1804 (*S-Jb*, 1970, 143).
10. Etienne has not been identified.
11. A pastime which A.S. must have indulged in, too. (We have Charles

Godeffroy's word for it that A.S. had a fine pair of pistols.)
12. Why Montpellier is 'gloomy' is not clear.
13. He did, though not until 29 April.

XVII

1. Source: *S-Jb*, 51 (1970), 38 ff.
2. Dockenhuden is where Charles Godeffroy lived.
3. Having been re-routed because of the war. In 1805 Crabb Robinson travelled home from Husum to Yarmouth, his passage costing £7.
4. The original has the 25th [*scil.* May], an obvious slip.
5. The college will have been John Knipe's college, Queen's, and it may well be that while they were there Knipe enquired about the chances of a college preferment, for that is what he obtained a year later, when he was appointed rector of Charlton-upon-Otmoor.
6. Charles Godeffroy stayed with Mr and Mrs James Barrow in Kendal. John Knipe, like his sister Margaret, came from Ambleside.
7. Mr Lancaster was a Volunteer.

XVIII

1. Source: *S-Jb*, 36 (1955), 87f.
2. Jakob Kabrun (1759–1814) was a respected Danzig merchant, friend of H.F.S. and benefactor of the English chapel. A.S. seems to have liked his first 'principal', for he was to send him an inscribed copy of his first publication. What has not been known is that Jakob Kabrun was of Scottish extraction or origin (James Cockburn). Like Floris Schopenhauer, Jakob Kabrun owned a collecton of pictures. He had a son, Karl, who was in Danzig from 1805 to 1835.
3. A.S.'s untidiness (as regards his luggage) was the cause of an incident at Braunau (Bohemia) when the family were on their way home from Vienna in 1805.
4. It sounds as though A.S., as parlour boarder, escaped the attention of the 'Sergeant of the Guards' who was in attendance at Mr Lancaster's establishment!

VII
Wimbledon School

Mr Lancaster's and Other Academies

On Monday 27 June 1803 the Schopenhauers and their friends the Percivals dined with Mr Lancaster in order to discuss young Arthur's proposed attendance as a parlour boarder at what was popularly known as the Rev. Mr Lancaster's academy but was in fact called Wimbledon School. Three days later, on the evening of Thursday 30 June, Arthur Schopenhauer drove out to Wimbledon, on his own, to begin what can perhaps best be described as his incarceration, for all too soon Mr Lancaster's came to symbolise the prison of the world.

In a long, rambling, self-justifying letter to her son dated 28 April 1807 Johanna Schopenhauer wrote, 'Everything that I have done for you has been good for you . . . that you went to Mr. Lancaster's was my doing.'[1] Leaving aside the fact that this particular experience was, in some ways, disastrously bad for him, it is interesting to find Johanna claiming — in retrospect — to have been responsible for sending her son to Mr Lancaster's. Whether her claim was strictly true does not matter. He was sent to Mr Lancaster's for several reasons. In the first place he was sent there — presumably at his father's insistence — to perfect his English. This is what he later wrote in his *curriculum vitae*:

Postquam Londini sesquimensem commorati eramus, parentes in interiorem Angliam Scotiamque iter continuaverunt, ego autem apud ecclesiasticum quendam, prope Londinium habitantem relictus sum, ut Anglicam linguam perdiscerem, quod probe feci, tribus ibi peractis mensibus. [*SW*, ed. Deussen, XIV, 284]

At the same time Floris Schopenhauer's letters to his son suggest that he was also sent there to improve his handwriting, while Johanna no doubt wished to get her son off her hands in order to enjoy her English tour the more.

Why the boarding school was Mr Lancaster's is less certain. The presence of the Percivals on 27 June suggests that they were at least of assistance, and it is possible that their son was (or had been) at Mr Lancaster's. It may therefore have been the Percivals who recommended Mr Lancaster's as a suitable example of the ubiquitous academy, or it may already have been recommended to the Schopenhauers before they left Hamburg, either by one of the Rückers or by the Rev. John Knipe. We have seen that Arthur Schopenhauer's Hamburg schoolfriend, Lorenz Meyer, was employed by Martin Albert Rücker, whose brother (Daniel Henry Rücker) lived just down the road from Mr Lancaster. Daniel Henry Rücker was naturally a frequent visitor to Hamburg; after staying with him in Wandsworth in 1802 Lorenz Meyer reported back to his employer, who was a business associate of Floris Schopenhauer. The Schopenhauers no doubt also knew the Rev. John Knipe, who had been at Queen's with Parson Lancaster's cousin and will therefore have heard about the school at which his college friend was apparently to have been employed. We may therefore be confident that it was the Percivals or the Rückers or John Knipe who put the Schopenhauers on to Mr Lancaster's academy. That it was situated so close to the Wandsworth in which Voltaire had been so kindly received may well have clinched the matter in Floris Schopenahuer's peculiarly obsessive mind.

They will already have had a tolerably good idea of what an English 'academy' was like, from the work of two of Johanna Schopenhauer's most obvious and estimable predecessors as travel diarist: C.P. Moritz and the Rev. G.F.A. Wendeborn. In his *Travels through several parts of England in 1782* Moritz gave an excellent description of the typical late eighteenth-century academy. If we are to be able to assess Johanna Schopenhauer's description of Mr Lancaster's, Moritz's account is as important for us as it must have been for her:

> I have seen the regulation of one seminary of learning, here called *an Academy*. Of these places of education, there is prodigious number in London; though, notwithstanding their pompous names, they are in reality nothing more than small schools set up by private persons, for children and young people.

Wimbledon School

One of the Englishmen, who were my travelling companions, made me acquainted with a *Dr. G*****, who lives near *P——*, and keeps an academy for the education of twelve young people, which number is here, as well as at our *Mr. Kumpe*'s, never exceeded, and the same plan has been adopted and followed by many others, both here, and elsewhere.

At the entrance I perceived over the door of the house a large board, and written on it, *Dr. G****'s Academy*. Dr. G. received me with great courtesy as a foreigner, and shewed me his school-room, which was furnished just in the same manner, as the classes in our public schools are, with benches and a professor's chair, or pulpit.

The usher, at *Dr. G****'s*, is a young clergyman, who, seated also in a chair, or desk, instructs the boys in the Greek and Latin Grammars.

Such an under-teacher is called an usher; and by what I can learn, is a commonly tormented being, exactly answering the exquisite description given of him in the Vicar of Wakefield. We went in, during the hours of attendance, and he was just hearing the boys decline their Latin, which he did in the old job-trot way; and I own it had an odd sound to my ears, when instead of pronouncing, for example *viri veeree*, I heard them say *viri, of the man*, exactly according to the English pronunciation, and *viro, to the man*. The case was just the same afterwards with the Greek.

Mr. G**** invited us to dinner, when I became acquainted with his wife; a very genteel young woman, whose behaviour to the children was such, that she might be said to contribute more to their education than any one else. The children drank nothing but water. For every Boarder, Dr. G. receives yearly no more than thirty pounds sterling; which, however, he complained of as being too little. — From forty to fifty pounds is the most that is generally paid in these academies.

I told him of our improvements in the manner of education; and also spoke to him of the apparent great worth of character of his usher. He listened very attentively, but seemed to have thought little himself on this subject. Before and after dinner the Lord's Prayer was repeated in French, which is done in several places, as if they were eager not to waste, without some improvement, even this opportunity also, to practise the French, and thus at once accomplish two points. I afterwards told him my opinion of this species of prayer, which, however, he did not take amiss.

After dinner the boys had leave to play in a very small yard, which in most schools, or academies, in the City of London, is the *ne plus ultra* of their play-ground in their hours of recreation. But Mr. G**** has another garden at the end of the town, where he sometimes takes them to walk.

After dinner Mr. G**** himself instructed the children in writing, arithmetic, and French, all which seemed to be well taught here; especially writing, in which the young people in England far surpass, I believe, all others. This may, perhaps, be owing to their having occasion to learn only one sort of letters. As the Midsummer holidays were now approaching (at which time the children, in all the academies, go home for four weeks) every one was obliged with the utmost care to copy a written model, in order to shew it to their parents, because this article is most particularly examined, as every body can tell what is, or is not good writing. The boys knew all the rules of syntax by heart.

All these academies are in general called boarding-schools. Some few retain the old name of schools only; though it is possible, that, in real merit, they may excel the so much-boasted of academies.

It is in general the clergy, who have small incomes, who set up these schools both in town and country; and grown up people, who are foreigners, are also admitted here to learn the English language. Mr. G**** charged for board, lodging, and instruction in the English, two guineas a week. He, however, who is desirous of perfecting himself in the English, will do better to go some distance into the country, and board himself with any clergyman, who takes scholars, where he will hear nothing but English spoken, and may at every opportunity be taught by young and old.[2]

In the original German edition of his book Moritz named the master of the academy in question as Mr Green of Paddington. His account is important not merely because he is describing a school of much the same kind as existed behind the elegant Jacobean façade of Thomas Lancaster's house, but because as a foreigner he takes nothing for granted and therefore gives a fuller account than most contemporary English writers bother to do. Moritz's comment on handwriting will not have been lost on Floris Schopenhauer.

Wimbledon School

Dr Wendeborn, for his part, included in his *A View of England* (1791) a fuller and more critical account of the contemporary academy, which is important because it takes a critical view of English education, which Johanna Schopenhauer may well have discussed with Dr Wendeborn before she left Hamburg. It is a view which she came to share. Here, then, is an abridged version of Dr Wendeborn's account:

> Besides these Grammar-schools, a number of a more private nature, for both sexes, are to be met with, which go under the denomination of Boarding-schools, or, by a more refined name, that of Academies. There is hardly a small town, or even a large village in England, where the traveller is not presented with the sight of a large black board, on which is inscribed in golden letters, 'A Boarding-school' or 'An Academy'. Some of these houses, by their outward appearance, do not promise much . . . Every person, man or woman, is at liberty to set up a boarding-school, if they have any hope of meeting with success; though there are many, even within my own knowledge, who are in all respects very well qualified for the education of children; yet there are others who are quite the contrary. A tradesman, who, perhaps, has failed in business, either from misfortune or his own fault, or a woman, who never had a proper education herself, or whose moral character cannot very well bear a strict enquiry, will set up boarding-schools, and sometimes meet with more encouragement than those who are more deserving. They keep ushers, teachers, and masters to assist them, who are frequently as unqualified for the business they are employed in, as those by whom they were hired at a salary as low as possible. I confess, I have often wondered, how unconcerned many English parents seem to be about the education of their children. Many a rich man, when he has a horse to be broken in, or a dog to be trained, will carefully enquire whether the person he entrusts them with, is properly qualified for the business; but, this is not always the case with parents, when they place their children to be educated. Clergymen, who are not provided with a sufficient income to support themselves or their family, will now and then set up a boarding-school, and such are mostly the best of the kind, though they also admit of exceptions . . .
>
> The generality of children, who are educated in these

schools, do not make any great progress in their learning. The frequent holidays, which sometimes continue for several weeks, and are given, during the course of the year, for the benefit of those who keep such schools, do not contribute towards their improvement, either in learning or manners. They go home, during such a vacation, to their parents, where they indulge themselves in every thing else but what they are to learn at school: for very few fathers or mothers give themselves the trouble to prevent them from returning worse to school than they came from thence; though some, perhaps, will discharge even this duty towards the education of their children.

It ought to be said, in favour of the generality of English boarding-schools for boys, that they are more calculated to make them useful for society, than to fill their head and their memory with such things as are very useless to those who afterwards follow no learned professions. Good school-masters are more intent to make those, whom they instruct, develope their capacities, and render them in time prudent and skilful to discharge the duties of life and society, than to make them shine with a little learning, that is forgotten almost as soon as they leave the school. Rousseau, in his treatise on education, very justly censures those school-masters, who chiefly teach their boys those things, which render them in the course of life more vain than useful; but I wish he had left out an anecdote, with which he concludes the first volume of his Emilius, and the truth of which I have had an opportunity of examining. An English gentleman, after three years absence, returned to his own country. Being desirous to know what progress in learning his little boy, nine years of age, had made during his absence, he repaired to the school where he was placed, in an afternoon, and walking with his son, accompanied by the school-master, on the play-ground, he asked the boy, Where stands the kite of which you see the shade here on the ground? The boy, knowing that his school-fellows as well as himself, used to play with their kites on the other side of the wall, where the highway runs along, answered immediately, 'Over the road.' The father, thinking his son, only nine years old, answered his question from optical principles, embraced his child with parental warmth, finished his examination immediately, and rewarded the school-master most bountifully the day following, by settling an annuity upon him. Full of his usual fire, honest Rousseau exclaims upon this occasion, 'Quel homme que ce père-là, et quel fils lui étoit promis! La question est précisément de l'âge: la réponse est bien simple; mais voyez quelle netteté de judiciaire enfantine elle suppose! C'est ainsi que l'élève d'Aristote apprivoisoit ce coursier célèbre, qu'aucun écuyer n'avoit pu dompter!' A person unacquainted with the merits and talents of Rousseau, both [of] which are so estimable, might here ask, Where is the deep and sharp-sighted philosopher? and find it difficult to avoid laughter. The young modern Alexander, whom he extols so highly, has never acquired any celebrity.

The mode of education in England has its singularities, in schools for boys as well as for girls. This may be considered as the foundation of those characteristic traits, by which the English distinguish themselves from other nations. When in England the Romish was the established religion, and its government had more resemblance to such arbitrary power as is prevalent in many other countries, the education, under the direction of priests, who were either foreigners, or Englishmen educated abroad, was more similar to that in other countries, and consequently the character of the nation more like that of its neighbours. But, at present, if a child born in England, was from its early years educated in a foreign country, and sent back to England at the age of eighteen, let it be boy or girl, it would be spoiled for life, and find itself if not wretched, at least very uncomfortable in its native country. An Englishman, educated from his early days in France, Germany, Italy or in Switzerland, will always, even against his will, betray something of the foreigner; he will find, that many of his countrymen, from prejudice, will look upon him in such a light, that he cannot gain their confidence and esteem so easily as if he had been bred among them; and, if I may express myself so paradoxically, being left more to nature, had been more transformed, by the art of English education, into an Englishman. I need not mention, that if a German boy, at three years of age, were to be carried over to England, and educated among English boys, he would become in time a complete Englishman. He would, if he returned to his own country, at the age of manhood, express as much aversion and indignation against German manners, and the German way of life, as ever a true John Bull would shew, if he were at once, out of the midst of England, transported into

Westphalia. That the English extol their manners, their way of life, their pleasures, above those of any other country, and, from a ridiculous national pride, despise and laugh at them as infinitely inferior to theirs, is owing to the education which they receive. So much does an Englishman's national character, his way of thinking, nay his whole happiness, depend on the manner in which he is educated!³

If the Schopenhauers knew this account, and had perhaps even discussed it with Dr Wendeborn, why were they not put off by it? There are two answers. One is that their sentimental view of England, which was fundamental to their view of life, caused them to close their eyes to the realities, some of which are spelled out by Dr Wendeborn. The other point is that the shortcomings of the English academy as described in *A View of England* might have seemed irrelevant, for Floris and Johanna Schopenhauer were not choosing a new school for their son, but merely an establishment at which he would spend a term — in the privileged capacity of a parlour boarder — mainly to perfect his English. If this is how they looked at it, the final chapter of this book shows them to have made a fundamental mistake, for rarely, if ever, can a single term at a given school have had so traumatic and so decisive an effect. On the other hand the truth of Dr Wendeborn's words is borne out in a most striking way, for Arthur Schopenhauer, at the age not of three but of fifteen, carried back to Germany precisely that 'aversion and indignation against German manners' of which Dr Wendeborn writes.

When they visited his establishment for the first and only time on 27 June the Schopenhauers will have been as impressed by its elegance and eligibility as Thomas Lancaster intended parents to be. No doubt Mr Lancaster put himself out for his obviously affluent guests; after all, no less a person than Frederick the Great had been struck by the splendour of Floris Schopenhauer's carriage. At dinner the conversation will inevitably have turned to the names of the great and the good associated with Wimbledon in general and Thomas Lancaster's house in particular. One whose name was no doubt mentioned was William Wilberforce (1759–1833), who until 1786 lived in another old house near by and must have discussed his grand scheme for the abolition of slavery with William Grenville in the house that Grenville sold to Thomas Lancaster. That Mr Lancaster did mention Wilberforce, either on this occasion, or in a sermon or other homily in the course of the next three months, can hardly be doubted in view of the terms in which Schopenhauer wrote many years later:

> This book [*Slavery and the internal slave-trade in the United States of North America*, 1841] constitutes one of the gravest indictments of human nature ever made. No one will lay it aside without horror, and few will do so without tears. For whatever its readers may have heard, imagined, or dreamt about the unhappy state of the slaves or about human hard-heartedness and cruelty in general, will pale into insignificance when he reads how those devils in human form, those bigoted, church-going, strictly sabbatarian scoundrels, especially the Anglican parsons among them, treat their innocent black brethren who through injustice and violence have fallen into their devil's claws. [*P&P*, 'On Ethics,' sect. 115]

That dig at the Anglican clergy clearly belongs together with many others which have in Thomas Lancaster their ultimate archetype and butt.

More especially Mr Lancaster will have mentioned Earl Spencer and the other government men of his acquaintance, quickly getting on to the subject at once closest to his heart and of most interest to his guests: Lord Nelson and Lady Hamilton. After dinner he will have shown his guests his 'large and commodious house' with its 'spacious and lofty' apartments fitted up in a style suitable for the 'young nobleman and gentlemen' for whom the school was intended; since it was June, they were no doubt also shown the 'extensive' gardens. When they were leaving, well satisfied with what they had seen, they were most likely given a copy of the 'Sketch' of Mr Lancaster's *Plan of Education* (and details of his impressively high terms) for which 'Noblemen and Gentlemen' were invited to apply — if, that is, they had not already procured a copy from one of the several addresses in town at which they were available, most of these[4] being close to their hotel.

His parents having been duly impressed with Mr Lancaster and his establishment, to say nothing of being impatient to set out on their tour of England, Arthur Schopenhauer was packed off to Wimbledon School three days later. What he found and experienced there came as a very nasty shock indeed, for Mr Lancaster's turned out to be totally different from the equivalent establishment in Hamburg which he had been attending. As the extent of his unhappiness — and the reasons for it — became clear his mother became less impressed with Mr Lancaster (cf. her letter of 13 September, in which she tells her son to greet the Lancasters, but not too cordially), while his father, predictably (and rightly) took exception to the size of the bill with which he was eventually presented.

Wimbledon School was a private boarding school at which some sixty boys between the ages of 6 and 16 received an ordinary English boarding-school education, with music, fencing, dancing and drawing as extras; it was, in other words, a typical 'academy' of the time. Why it came as such a shock to young Schopenhauer, and why his experience of it proved to be so traumatic, can be understood only if we bear in mind the sort of education to which he was used.

Dr Runge and Parson Lancaster

From June 1797 to August 1799 — that is, from the age of nine to the age of eleven — young Schopenhauer was in France. Most of the time he was staying with the family of a business friend of his father's, M. Grégoire de Blésimaire, at Le Havre.[5] If such a long absence from home at such an early age seems rather extraordinary, we should remember that Schopenhauer's father had said, 'Mein Sohn soll im Buche der Welt lesen,'[6] and that he himself later wrote that those years in Le Havre were the best part of his childhood. This was surely true. The son of the family, Anthime Grégoire, became the best friend he ever had, while Anthime's parents, who lacked Johanna Schopenhauer's selfishness and Heinrich Floris Schopenhauer's fussiness, provided a relaxed atmosphere in which he could begin to grow up. As a result of those two years he forgot his own language and turned into a typical French boy, right down to the *sensibilité* (to the sufferings and joys of other people) which M. Grégoire (in a letter dated 27 vendémiaire: 19 October 1799) urged him to retain. At about the same time Anthime's mother, in a letter which was far more affectionate than any he received from his own, also commented on his *sensibilité*. While at Le Havre he was taught, together with Anthime, by the family tutor, M. Durand, who was responsible for introducing him to French literature. The boys read 'La Henriade' with their tutor, but they naturally also read 'lighter' things: Schopenhauer recommended Anthime to read an adventure story, and was in turn advised to read Molière's comedies, which would 'make him die with laughing'. Maybe it was a foregone conclusion that someone who read 'La Henriade' at the age of ten would come to share Voltaire's detestation of religious fanaticism; it is certainly a fact that Arthur Schopenhauer came to do so.

When he returned to Hamburg in 1799 he was sent to the most appropriate school, that of Dr Runge.[7] This is important in the present context, because in reacting against Mr Lancaster's academy in summer 1803 Schopenhauer will inevitably have compared it with the school which he had attended for the past four years and which he clearly enjoyed. In his *curriculum vitae* he wrote:

> Under the guidance of this most excellent man and of the other teachers in his institution I learned what a merchant needs to know and what an educated person ought to know. Latin, however, was not taken seriously; there was only one lesson a week, and that only for form's sake. This teaching I enjoyed for almost four years.

The headmaster of the academy was Dr Johann Hinrich Christian Runge (1768-1811). After studying theology at Halle he did what most graduates in his position did: he failed to obtain a preferment, and therefore went in for teaching. He was, however, a born teacher, and soon made good. It was in 1797 that he opened his own school at Katharinenkirchhof 44; the modest building belonged to the Katharinenkirche. The school was much the same size as comparable English schools, for it took 40 pupils, taught in two classes. The ushers were Hans Christian Friedrich Westphal and Johann Carl Friedrich Hauptmann. Herr Westphal, who was responsible for the commercial subjects of arithmetic, algebra and book-keeping (most of the boys' fathers were merchants, although many of the boys did not wish to follow in their father's footsteps; Charles Godeffroy for one regarded the usual *comptoir* as 'im Grunde ein Greuel'), seems to have been a colourless, ineffectual character — even Lorenz Meyer, who was destined for a commercial career, does not mention him in his diary. Herr Hauptmann, generally known as 'The Captain or 'Capt.', taught geography and *Moralunterricht*; he was unpopular with the boys, partly because he did not know how to handle them, and partly because he was too much the *Sittenprediger*. French and (for the older boys) English were taught by part-time or by occasional teachers. Lorenz Meyer mentions three French teachers (M. Gremion, M. Guerrier and M. Faymereau). I do not know who taught English, although there were plenty of obvious candidates around, including Hannibal Evans

Lloyd, and Mr Remnant of the English library. Fencing was taught by Herr Labroue.

As to Schopenhauer and his 14 or 15-year-old fellow pupils, what strikes one most (from their diaries) is that they are a droll mixture of child and grown-up. They seem to like nothing better than playing blind-man's-buff. Schopenhauer is forever fighting, and comes to school with a red face after an experiment with gunpowder had gone wrong, and Charles Godeffroy gives himself a nasty burn while conducting an experiment with phosphorus. After school, however, they are transformed into perfect little gentlemen; they spend their evenings at balls and masquerades, they play whist, they drink, and so on.

When Schopenhauer entered the academy in 1799 Dr Runge was still only 32 (in 1803 the Rev. Lancaster was 53), although he had been teaching for some ten years and was about to publish a series of booklets which would enshrine the results of his experience. In 1800 he published his *Pädagogische Haustafel oder notwendige Verhaltungsmassregeln für Eltern zur pflichtmässigen Erziehung ihrer Kinder* (Hamburg, 1800). Dr Runge is a thoughtful and humane person. He knows that the beginning of education is the parents' treatment of their child. He urges parents to treat their children firmly but reasonably, avoiding inconsistency and arbitrary authoritarianism. The emphasis is on what we should call psychology. Dr Runge is always concerned with reality; he is opposed to hypocrisy. I doubt whether Schopenhauer at the age of ten will have read the booklet, but he will have seen for himself that Dr Runge avoided the irrational authoritarianism of his own father (and, later, of the Rev. Thomas Lancaster). I cannot help thinking that Mr Lancaster will have been the very embodiment of the unenlightened and hypocritical approach which the excellent Dr Runge eschews.

In 1804 Runge published another booklet, *Leitfaden zum Religions-Unterricht für meine reiferen Schüler* (Hamburg, 1804), in which his pietistic, rationalistic view of religion is succinctly expressed. It is a far cry from the old-fashioned, unenlightened religiosity of Mr Lancaster, which mostly took the form of a series of interdictions.

The third and last of Dr Runge's publications is the most immediately relevant: his *Bericht über meine Schulanstalt an die Eltern meiner Schüler* (Hamburg, 1808). It is this booklet that describes in some detail the teaching which Schopenhauer received in 1799–1803. The school is split into lower and upper school. In the lower school the subjects taught are: Latin (two hours a week), French (two hours), German (two hours), *Denkübungen* (two hours), geography and topography (six hours), history (four hours), natural history (two hours) and religion (four hours). In the upper school topography is replaced by English (two hours), and *Denkübungen* by mathematics (two hours). Judging by Lorenz Meyer's diary, the 'upper school' probably meant those of 14 or older. Lorenz Meyer appears to have had his last *Denkübung* just after his fourteenth birthday. In the upper school, at least, religion seems to have gone under the name of ethics (*Moral*). Schopenhauer's ethics classes in 1802 (when he was 14) included the following topics:

1. On there being no such thing as a 'necessary' lie.
2. On our duty to spare others' feelings.
3. On the need to avoid tempting people.
4. On the need to avoid backbiting.
5. On our duty to improve the lot of other people.
6. On the need for patience and tolerance.
7. On gossiping.
8. On helping others in business.
9. On obliging other people (also: on kindness, compassion, generosity and charitableness).
10. On the need to forgive one's enemies.
11. On friendship.
12. On our duties towards our brothers and sisters and towards servants.

At this stage ethics seems to have been taught by Dr Runge himself. Although it is not easy to make valid comparisons, one is safe in saying that at Dr Runge's morality was taught positively, as moral philosophy proper, whereas at Mr Lancaster's religion was taught negatively, as a matter of interdictions and sanctions. There is no reason to think that Mr Lancaster would have been prepared to argue any point of Christian doctrine or even to discuss morality except in a dogmatically Christian context. For him morality without religion was 'mere Pagan Virtue' and therefore no virtue at all.

All this might be thought to suggest that German education was ahead of English at the time. This was in fact the case, although it is not my concern to argue the point; after all, if Schopenhauer's English headmaster had been Dr George Chapman, his impression (and ours) would have been different. What matters is that Dr Runge was a far more enlightened person and schoolmaster than Mr Lancaster. There were plenty of exceptional schoolmasters in

England at the time; unfortunately Schopenhauer was not sent to one of them. Dr Runge had, moreover, enjoyed a better education than Thomas Lancaster. Appleby Grammar School was a good school, but someone who had completed his schooling there was not 'educated' in the way in which someone who had attended first the Johanneum in Hamburg, then the Akademisches Gymnasium there, and then the University of Halle, was educated. Even if he had gone on to Queen's College, Oxford, Thomas Lancaster would still have compared badly with the product of a more cosmopolitan background, and indeed of the European Enlightenment. When all is said and done, there would remain a world of difference between the old-fashioned 'Georgian' parson and the genuinely enlightened man. Dr Runge was a remarkable man; he sought to be a friend to his pupils, and believed in parents and teachers working together, which is one of the reasons why he mixed socially with his pupils' parents. He believed, too, in what he called 'Privat-Fleiss', and actually taught his boys how to study. He was a more charismatic figure than Mr Lancaster, who merely gave homilies on 'that Pest of Youth — Idleness'.

The two headmasters differed both in their views of education and in their methods. For Dr Runge education was a matter of persuasion and reason, precept and example; he sought to turn out soundly educated, morally good people. Thomas Lancaster sought to turn out good young Christians, if necessary by force. In *Frank Mildmay* Captain Marryat wrote that 'Some tutors attempt the *suaviter in modo*, my schoolmaster preferred the *fortiter in re*.'[8] Runge believed in the *suaviter in modo*, while Lancaster was of the *fortiter in re* persuasion. By this I do not mean to imply that Lancaster flogged Christian doctrine into his pupils in a literal sense, although he may well have done so. What I mean is that his approach was evidently 'You must believe this, and if you don't I will punish you.' That young Arthur Schopenhauer, who was in many ways a remarkably sophisticated 15-year-old, reacted against this very sharply was hardly surprising. All that is surprising is the virulence of his reaction, to which we shall return.

There is no reason to suppose that the Rev. Thomas Lancaster was a particularly enlightened or, in purely academic terms, a particularly successful schoolmaster (unlike, for instance, Richard Yates at Appleby Grammar School, or Joseph Wilson at Barton School, or Richard Jameson's friend George Chapman at Dumfries and elsewhere, or even his own friend, John Farrer, at Witton-le-Wear), although the lack of positive evidence may possibly be misleading.

Nor is there any evidence that he possessed the charisma of these men or, more important, of Dr Runge. The evidence suggests that the Rev. Lancaster was no less old-fashioned as pedagogue than as cleric, although there are one or two intriguing details which make one wonder whether this is the whole truth. I am thinking of his 'poetic effusions' and more especially of his practice of beginning Latin verse composition with the composition of nonsense verse. Such details suggest that to rhyme Lancaster with grammaticaster may be less than just. There is, however, no reason to suppose that his intellectual powers were of a particularly high order (if they had been, he would presumably have gone to Queen's), or that he had thought particularly deeply about education. He was certainly no innovator. What kind of education he purveyed we shall see presently. The fact that his school prospered was most likely due to the magnificence of his establishment and its good tone — calculated to appeal to the *ton* — than to any academic excellence, which parents would, after all, have sought elsewhere. Almost by definition his school, with its appeal to the nobility and the gentry, was catering for non-academic youths unable to get into the public schools of the day; it is only being remembered now because a rather troublesome foreign boy attended it for a period of three months; Mr Lancaster would not have been flattered had he known that this would be the case.

Mr Lancaster's Plan of Education, 1: Theory

There is no lack of evidence as to Parson Lancaster's ideas on education and the sort of school he ran. His *Plan of Education* (1794, 2nd edn 1797) provides one sort of evidence, while on the other hand we have Johanna Schopenhauer's clearly partial account of the school (tantamount to Arthur Schopenhauer's own account), supplemented by the even more partial evidence of her son's writings. There is also unique additional evidence to be gleaned from the letters Schopenhauer received while at Wimbledon, which reveal some of the main points he made in his own missing letters. Before we examine these various forms of evidence, it will be convenient to consider the staff who put them into effect.

In his *Plan of Education* Lancaster insisted on a proportion of one teacher to every ten pupils. By 1803, when the school had about 60 pupils, he employed four ushers and a resident drawing master, as well as a similar number of part-time teachers. Johanna

Schopenhauer made it clear that

> The reverend gentleman in Wimbledon did not concern himself with the actual teaching; unseen by the pupils he spent the day in his study, where he instructed in English a number of young foreigners, who resided in his house not as ordinary pupils, but as parlour boarders. Only at midday, at the end of the teaching day, did he appear at his desk in the schoolroom to receive the masters' reports. Four resident teachers, who took it in turn to be duty master for a week at a time, gave the necessary instruction, all four of them doing so together in the same big room.[9]

Since all the boys were taught together, irrespective of age, the four ushers will each have been responsible for teaching one of the four 'divisions', or subjects, classics, French, English and commercial studies.

The ushers' identities are unimportant, for Arthur Schopenhauer will have had relatively little to do with the ushers, although, despite his privileged position as parlour boarder, he must have fallen foul of one or other of them in his capacity of duty master — if, that is, his propensity for fighting was as much in evidence as it had been at Dr Runge's. Any such incidents apart, the important people as regards Schopenhauer's term at Wimbledon are his headmaster and, to a lesser extent, the Rev. Herbert Randolph, vicar of Wimbledon.

Whoever the ushers were, Schopenhauer will inevitably have been reminded by them of *The Vicar of Wakefield*, a favourite novel in the Schopenhauer household, from which he would have known that an usher's life was a dog's life. The vicar's eldest son, George, who was 'bred at Oxford', being intended for one of the learned professions, returns home after three years of vagabondage and tells his father:

> My first scheme, you know, Sir, was to be usher at an academy; and I asked his advice on the affair. Our cousin received the proposal with a true sardonic grin. 'Ay,' cried he, 'this is indeed a very pretty career that has been chalked out for you. I have been an usher at a boarding-school myself; and may I die by an anodyne necklace, but I had rather be an under-turnkey in Newgate. I was up early and late: I was browbeat by the master, hated for my ugly face by the

mistress, worried by the boys within, and never permitted to stir out to meet civility abroad. But are you sure you are fit for a school? Let me examine you a little. Have you been bred apprentice to the business?' — 'No.' — 'Then you won't do for a school. Can you dress the boys' hair?' — 'No.' — 'Then you won't do for a school. Have you had the smallpox?' — 'No.' — 'Then you won't do for a school. Can you lie three in a bed?' — 'No.' — 'Then you will never do for a school. Have you got a good stomach?' — 'Yes.' — 'Then you will by no means do for a school.' No, Sir: if you are for a genteel, easy profession . . . avoid a school by any means'.[10]

The long and short of it is, as Goldsmith wrote, that 'there was no great degree of gentility affixed to the character of an usher'.

In addition to four full-time resident assistants Mr Lancaster also employed several part-timers to teach the 'military exercise' and most of the optional extras (dancing, fencing and music). According to Johanna Schopenhauer the part-time assistants came down from London several times a week to teach these subjects, in each of which the boys received two hours' tuition a week. We gather from his *Plan of Education* that Mr Lancaster attached importance to 'the military exercise' (or 'Prussian exercise'), 'which conduces much to make a Boy erect and firm in his Gesture and Motion', and that 'A Sergeant of the Guards attends twice a Week, to instruct such as are directed to cultivate this Branch of Education.' Whether Arthur Schopenhauer enjoyed the attentions of the drill sergeant is not known, but he enjoyed gymnastics and was told by his father to cultivate an erect posture and not to slouch. Mr Lancaster attached importance to physical as well as moral uprightness. Dancing, in which Schopenhauer was skilled, was taught by a Mr Galliard, who attended twice a week. Who taught fencing and music is not known.

Mr Lancaster employed a resident drawing master ('a Gentleman of acknowledged Abilities and polished Manners is engaged to reside here, for the sole Purpose of instructing *daily* such [pupils] as learn Drawing'). John (C.J.M.) Whichelo (1784-1865) is said to have been drawing master at one time. Whether he had been enlisted by summer 1803 (when Thomas Baxter was in Merton filling a sketchbook with drawings of the Nelson circle) is not known, but it is certainly possible that he taught young Schopenhauer the rudiments of drawing. That Schopenhauer took drawing we know from his mother's letters to him. Whichelo, who practised in London, produced not a few drawings of Wimbledon and many more of the surrounding area; his water colours include one of Wimbledon Common.[11] He painted a portrait of Nelson in September 1805, immediately before the admiral left Merton for the last time. (This portrait, which was given to Admiral Sir William Parker, is reproduced in the Folio Society edition of Southey's *Life of Nelson*.) Thereafter Whichelo, who became marine and landscape painter to the Prince Regent, is said to have gone in for Nelsonian subjects; his drawings include one of 'HMS *Victory* in the Battle of Trafalgar'. The portrait of Nelson marked the beginning of Whichelo's public career as a painter; he was an occasional exhibitor at the Royal Academy from 1810 onwards, and in 1823 became an associate of the Old Water Colour Society. Another possible candidate for the position of drawing master is Robert Bremmel Schnebberlie, who exhibited topographical drawings at the Royal Academy from 1803 to 1821 and produced a pen-and-ink sketch of 'Rev. Mr. Lancaster's Academy' in 1810. Schnebbelie, who engaged in drawing for the *Gentleman's Magazine* and other periodicals, became the typical starving artist. He was found dead, apparently from want, in 1849.

Miss Lancaster probably acted both as hostess to her father's visitors (including the Schopenhauers) and as the 'steady Matron' to whom he refers in his *Plan*; there may have been an assistant matron in the person of Mrs Ann Farrer. Mr Lancaster also employed, among others, a gardener and a dairyman who may be identical with the school servants George Higgins and Thomas Hammon who joined in the subscription for the Wimbledon Infantry Volunteers. Given that Arthur Schopenhauer was taught mainly by him, Mr Lancaster's ideas and methods are more important than his staff. His *Plan of Education* is essential reading. What follows is intended as an introductory commentary.

This work, *A Plan of Education*, published at Mr Lancaster's expense by one of the most eminent booksellers of the time, Cumberland-born George Robinson of Addison's Head, 25 Paternoster Row, belongs to a well established eighteenth-century genre, that of the 'plan of education'. Such 'plans' are of two kinds: the solid and detailed contribution to the educational debate of the time, an early example of which is Locke's *Some Thoughts Concerning Education* (1693), and the less substantial work which is often no more than a public relations exercise, an extended and often pretentious prospectus for a particular school. Naturally some 'plans of education' (e.g. Vicesimus Knox's *Liberal Education* and William Milns's *The Well-Bred Scholar*) straddle the two genres.

That Parson Lancaster's *Plan*, for its part, belongs to the second category is clearly shown by its baroque title:

> *A Plan of Education*, for a limited number of Young Gentlemen, humbly submitted to the consideration of those parents, who regard the health, comfort and virtue of their children, as points essentially to be attended to in the course of their education, By a Clergyman of the Established Church.

Indeed, without doubting his sincerity, Thomas Lancaster's *Plan of Education* is, by this token, an excellent example of the species described by his colleague William Barrow in *An Essay on Education* (1802):

> He that opens an Academy, it is supposed, must do something to prove his fitness for the office, which he undertakes; and to attract notice and pupils . . . To obtain credit or celebrity . . . by [the publication of an academic work] requires a considerable degree of learning, or of judgment; more indeed than he who undertakes to become the instructor of others, is sometimes found himself to possess . . . To publish an Essay on Education is an easier and safer expedient. It is not difficult for an Adventurer . . . to detail a specious system of moral and literary instruction, which it is neither intended nor possible to reduce to practice; to censure the errors and misconduct of other schools, and to insinuate the superior management of his own; to inculcate with apparent candour general rules and principles, which are in fact merely a recommendation of his own peculiar plan; to declaim on the folly and cruelty of the rod, and the superior advantages of lenity and tenderness; to pretend to treat his pupils with the kindness and confidence of friendship, and to train the infant mind to science and to virtue without toil and discipline. To profess these things is easy; and too many parents have been induced to give credit to such professions by their wishes to find them true.[12]

Mr Lancaster's title, intended to appeal to the Polite parents of not very bright children, also signals his awareness of the existence of works such as James Elphinston's *Plan of Education at the*

Academy of Kensington (1764), Thomas Sheridan's *A Plan of Education for the Young Nobility and Gentry of Great Britain* (1769), Vicesimus Knox's *Liberal Education, or, A Practical Treatise on the Methods of acquiring Useful and Polite Learning* (1781) and William Milns's *The Well-Bred Scholar* (1794). He probably also knew of the writings of men like John Locke and Joseph Priestly, although we must remember that he is himself essentially a village schoolmaster gone up in the world. He knew Samuel Parr. In trying to see his *Plan of Education* in context, it will be useful to make comparisons not only with some of the works just named, but also with William Barrow's *An Essay on Education* (1802) and with the *Treatise on Education* (4th edn 1790) of Richard Jameson's friend, George Chapman. William Barrow (1754–1836), who became archdeacon of Nottingham, came from Sedbergh — close to Thomas Lancaster's home ground — and was master of an academy in Soho Square, London. He and Lancaster were later acquainted from committee meetings of the Society of Schoolmasters.

Thomas Lancaster wrote that his *Plan of Education* 'neither claims the Merit of Originality, nor can reasonably incur the Censure of Plagiarism, though it should appear that he has availed himself of what others have written'. No doubt he is referring to two works which had appeared since he began teaching in 1768: Thomas Sheridan's *A Plan of Education* (1769) and Vicesimus Knox's *Liberal Education* (10th edn 1789).

Thomas Sheridan (1719–88), whose father was a Dublin schoolmaster and close friend of Swift, progressed from acting (in the 1740s to the 1760s) in Dublin and London to lecturing on elocution and writing on education and allied subjects. His *General Dictionary of the English Language* came out in 1780, and his edition of Swift's works in 1784. His son, Richard Brinsley Sheridan, was an MP in the Whig interest from 1782. Thomas Sheridan's *A Plan of Education for the Young Nobility and Gentry of Great Britain* was, surely, the source of Thomas Lancaster's title. It was probably also a source of inspiration so far as his basic aim was concerned. Sheridan eschews a narrow academic aim, writing that 'The sole end proposed at present is to make good Latin and Greek Scholars, and minute philosophers; whereas the true ends of education in all Christian countries, ought to be to make good men, and good cizitens.'[13] For Thomas Lancaster, writing in the Jacobinical '90s, the word 'citizen' would have had far too democratical a ring; he therefore lays the emphasis, as Thomas Sheridan had done, on the creation of good Christians, and indeed of 'Christian gentlemen'. Sheridan may well have given him his starting point; besides, did not Sheridan lay all the emphasis on the three things closest to Thomas Lancaster's schoolmasterly/clerical heart — religion, morality and the English language? Above all, did he not stress that his plan was chiefly calculated for the education of gentlemen? To justify this emphasis Sheridan quoted Locke's hundred-year-old view, which Thomas Lancaster also evidently shared and accepted: the view that 'the Gentleman's calling is that which is chiefly to be taken care of; for if those of that rank are by their education once set right, they will quickly bring all the rest into order'.[14] Nothing will have won deeper approval from Parson Lancaster than Sheridan's reference to 'our Religion. The Gentleman's Religion'. There are, naturally, things in Thomas Sheridan's *Plan of Education* of which Mr Lancaster could not possibly have approved, notably the division of the school into vocationally oriented classes, and the abolition of the rod; but such points of disagreement are incidental. What matters is that Sheridan gave him the emphasis and the basis of his own *Plan of Education*, while Vicesimus Knox was useful on the more practical details. As we shall see presently, there are also other, more detailed, parallels between Sheridan's and Lancaster's plans of education.

Vicesimus Knox (1752-1821) was headmaster of Tonbridge School from 1778 to 1821. A staunch Whig and no less staunch upholder of the classical *status quo* in education, he was a popular and influential writer. His *Liberal Education*, which quickly made its mark in the 1780s, when Mr Lancaster was founding his academies, may be taken as a useful yardstick for assessing establishments like Wimbledon School:

> The aims and methods of schools of good, but not of the first, standing, may be inferred from Knox's *Liberal Education*. The author, who was master of Tunbridge school from 1778 to 1812, and a very popular writer for some forty years, was always a staunch upholder of 'the established manner' in education. The basis of all sound instruction was to be found in Latin and Greek alone; but, when the foundation had been laid, it was desirable to include modern studies in the superstructure. The school was primarily concerned with the grammar of the two languages and the writing of verse and of prose in both; the list of authors to be read was but a short one. To these indispensable studies there might be added, as opportunity offered, the elements of geography and history,

French, some mathematics and such accomplishments as music, drawing and fencing. These last received only a tepid encouragement from Knox, who was more warmly in favour of dancing and 'the learning of the military exercise, which is now very common'. Boys were expected to read English and easy Latin books in their leisure time; it was a general rule of practice with Knox that as much self-initiated effort as possible should be exacted from the pupil. He set his face against all such debilitating aids as translations, 'keys', 'introductions' and the like.

That the established curriculum was not universally satisfactory is evident from the pains Knox took to show the inadequacy of the instruction given in many private schools, commonly termed 'academies', which prepared boys for 'business' and 'the office'. Though these academies professed to teach many things, of which Latin or, more frequently, French was one, Knox asserted that their success was confined to reading, writing and summing. Forty years later he repeated this opinion; but the public demand in the interval had brought about a great increase in the number and efficiency of schools of this kind, the monopoly of the grammar school and the severely classical course being seriously impaired in consequence.[15]

One of Knox's main themes was, therefore, the inadequacy of the education offered by the private 'academies', which, notwithstanding the pretentiousness of their syllabuses, did in reality do little more than teach the three Rs. The popularity of his book evidently commended it to Thomas Lancaster, who was then full of ambition for the success of his new school and knew that in order to attract attention and pupils he would have to publish some suitable work. On the title page of his *Plan of Education* he has three classical tags, two of which appear on opposite pages of Knox's book,[16] and a number of his texts are ones recommended by Knox. In saying this I do not mean to imply that Lancaster's *Plan* derives from Knox's much more substantial work, for it does not. The classical tags in question ('Omne tulit Punctum, qui miscuit utile dulci' — Horace; 'Studio fallente laborem' — Horace; 'Possunt, quia posse videntur' — Virgil) reflect the philosophy of the academy: 'Our fundamental Maxim . . . is, "That they are expected to do their best." ' 'The Author's Aim . . . has been to mix the *useful* and the *pleasant*.'

In availing himself of what others had written Thomas Lancaster evidently leant most heavily on Knox's *Liberal Education*, but he also seems to have read William Milns's *The Well-Bred Scholar*, which came out in 1794, just as he was preparing his *Plan* for the press, for his choice of Latin texts in particular corresponds so closely with Milns's as to suggest that he quarried in *The Well-Bred Scholar*, the title of which would have been likely to catch his eye. It is possible, however, that the parallels point to no more than a highly conservative classical tradition.

In many ways the most interesting, because most extreme, comparison is that with George Chapman's *A Treatise on Education*. Lancaster and Chapman were obviously opposites. Lancaster, who completed his education at Appleby Grammar School, is, on the evidence of his *Plan*, a pompous, bombastic, self-important character. Chapman, who held an LLD from Aberdeen, is a much plainer, more thoughtful sort of person, more sensitive and, I suspect, more sincere. His *Treatise on Education* is written in the same kind of clear, plain, unpretentious English as Richard Jameson's letter to the Bishop of Durham's secretary. His book dispenses both with the mass of classical tags that seem almost *de rigueur* in the South British example of the genre, and with Parson Lancaster's stilted, old-fashioned style, in which almost every word is capitalised. Chapman's work is in every way superior, more thorough, more thoughtful, more detailed. It is an advanced and sensitive work deeply concerned with the philosophy and methodology of education. Lancaster, unlike Chapman, is concerned to impress his readers, who will have been very different from Chapman's readers.

In making comparisons between Chapman's *Treatise* and Lancaster's *Plan* we must, however, remember that they are different kinds of work addressed to different audiences by two schoolmasters providing very different kinds of education. Whereas Chapman was providing a straight classical education, Lancaster was combining 'liberal' and commercial education under the umbrella of what he will no doubt have described as 'polite' education. Lancaster's priorities — health, learning, discipline, religion and morals — are what we should expect in a work of the kind described by William Barrow. Chapman, by contrast, is concerned only with education proper. His *Treatise* is a product of the Scottish Enlightenment, informed by the same spirit of liberal humanism as John Stevenson's lectures, Richard Jameson's informal lessons to Johanna Schopenhauer and — further afield — Dr Runge's classes with her son. The opening paragraph of the *Treatise* is worthy of a Herder:

> Man is eminently distinguished among the inhabitants of this globe. He derives this distinction from the structure and aspect of his body, and still more from the powers and affections of his mind.

How different is the opening of Parson Lancaster's *Plan*:

> Education, in its true Extent, may be understood to comprehend the Application of all the Arts and Sciences which are necessary to render a Child, by that Time he shall become a Man, able to sustain a respectable Character and Occupation in civilized and polished Society.

Taken by itself, Lancaster's opening may simply sound typical of its time. The comparison with Chapman, however, shows that Lancaster has a far narrower aim and view of education. Lancaster is, of course, addressing potential customers; Chapman writes as an educational reformer. Parson Lancaster's pomposity must have been pretty obvious to his pupils; it is clearly revealed when he writes in these terms:

> With a Mind unbiassed, and disposed to Reflexion, I have frequently meditated on the best Methods of executing the Functions of the Profession in which Divine Providence has placed me . . . And in the Plan I have traced out, I have at least *endeavoured* to deserve well of my Generation.

The most significant single difference between the two men, however, is the fact that George Chapman is offering his pupils an *education* in a sense in which Thomas Lancaster is not. He is clearly teaching his pupils to think for themselves, while Thomas Lancaster, proceeding largely by rote, is arguably *discouraging* thought. This fundamental point is important, because Schopenhauer's view of education was formed in reaction against the kind of 'education' purveyed at Wimbledon School.

Thomas Lancaster's syllabus provides evidence as to the nature of his school. We see from his *Plan of Education* that his scheme of things included reading, elocution, writing and shorthand, English, Latin, French, Greek, Arithmetic, 'merchants' accompts' and mathematics, geography, history and biography, and the extras. Compared with the typical syllabus of the time,[17] the range of subjects is quite good, except on the 'science' and 'military' sides. His syllabus puts the emphasis squarely on classical, technical and commercial education, and in doing so is typical of the time. The absence of 'science' (astronomy and natural science [physics]) and 'military subjects' (navigation, fortifications and surveying) shows that he did not prepare pupils for the army or navy, while the fact that his school was mentioned in 'Mathematical publications'[18] shows that he believed himself to be doing justice to mathematical subjects. If his syllabus shows that he was basically offering an elementary education for potential merchants and men of the world, his *Plan of Education* as such shows nothing more clearly than his pretensions. In some ways his blank 'synopsis' or report form is a better guide to what was taught than is the *Plan*, which expatiates upon several subjects that were clearly peripheral. The synopsis reveals both the elementary nature of the education offered and the mechanical, catechetical nature of the instruction, which struck Schopenhauer as crude.

The curriculum fell into four 'divisions': Classics, English, French and Commerce. Each division was taught by a different master. Thomas Lancaster's own subject was English, although Johanna Schopenhauer says that he only taught English to his foreign parlour boarders. The boys were divided into 'sets' (presumably by age) for teaching purposes, these sets involving problem-solving, memorising a speech or extract, dictation, and composition.

It is, however, a basic feature of Mr Lancaster's *Plan* that it is expressed, for the most part, in vague, general terms. The tone is grandiloquent, sententious, at times sanctimonious. He goes into less detail about the textbooks used, and the teaching of the various subjects, than do most other similar works. This applies across the board and most obviously to the teaching of the main academic subjects: Latin, French and English. Thus whereas William Barrow prescribes the Eton Latin Grammar, and George Chapman lists a number of similar works (Thomas Ruddiman's *The Rudiments of the Latin Tongue*, 24th edn, 1782; John Mair's *An Introduction to Latin Syntax*, 6th edn, 1770; Hugh Christie's *A new and easy introduction to the making of Latin*, Edinburgh, 1760; etc.), Mr Lancaster mentions only William Turner's *Exercises to the accidence* (13th edn, 1774). His pupils naturally read fewer classical texts than do, say, George Chapman's budding classicists.

The same goes for French. William Barrow recommends J. Palairet's *A New Royal French Grammar* (16th edn, 1796) and L. Chambaud's *The Elements of the French Language* (1762), but Mr

Lancaster is quite unspecific. At Wimbledon School, we are told, a quarter of the timetable is devoted to 'the Study of this FASHIONABLE LANGUAGE', and 'all the young Gentlemen are STRICTLY REQUIRED TO SPEAK IT DAILY from the Time of Morning, till that of Evening Prayers'. This sounds particularly enlightened, but it is not, for our headmaster shows absolutely no awareness of the problems involved in the study of the French language at school, a subject to which William Barrow devotes a whole chapter.[19] In the course of it he inveighs against the way in which 'fashionable academies' require their pupils constantly to speak French, a practice which, he argues, serves only to prevent them from speaking at all (perhaps that was the point!) Thomas Lancaster seems blithely unaware that there is a problem here. This is all the more surprising in that he claims to be familiar with what other educationalists have written, and evidently knew Vicesimus Knox's *Liberal Education*. In a section devoted to 'Learning French at school' Knox quotes with approval the remarks on this subject by L. Chambaud in the preface to *The Elements of the French Language*, a firmly established textbook of the time:

> It is a great abuse introduced in most schools, to force beginners to speak nothing but French among themselves. They must of necessity either speak wrong ... or condemn themselves to silence. The first cannot but be very detrimental to them; since they thereby accustom themselves to a barbarous broken French, which is no language at all, and cannot be unlearned without infinite pains. The second is still worse, for it hinders them from disclosing freely their thoughts, and straightens in some measure their understanding; but, above all, gives them the utmost aversion to the language, their books, and their master: to prevent which, too much care cannot be employed.[20]

One would expect a thoughtful schoolmaster to respond in some way to this powerful argument. That Mr Lancaster does not do so shows his constitutional conservatism (it was Locke, back in 1693, who first advocated 'talking [French] into Children in constant Conversation') or, most likely, his determination to give the public what it wants, whatever the educational arguments. His point of view is understandable, for fashionable academies like his own regarded French as an important part of the polite education they offered, because it was the key to the good breeding of which the French were the very model.[21] It would have been interesting indeed to hear Arthur Schopenhauer's comments on his fellow pupils' attainments in French, which must have been woefully inferior to his own.

When he went to Mr Lancaster's, Schopenhauer will already have been better educated than his new headmaster in French, and maybe in Latin, and perhaps even in some aspects of English literature. Mr Lancaster taught English, and it was to perfect his English that young Schopenhauer was sent to him. So far as the teaching of his own subject is concerned, Mr Lancaster is singularly uninspired by comparison with some other more outstanding schoolmasters of the time. He does not give the subject the emphasis which it is given by George Turnbull (*Observations upon Liberal Education in all its Branches* (1742), or by Thomas Sheridan, George Chapman and William Barrow. He writes, 'As soon as a Boy can read an easy Book, he will most probably request Permission to learn to write: and I can see no Reason why his Request should not be granted, as soon as made,' which is reminiscent of Thomas Sheridan's 'When they can read English with tolerable fluency, and spell common words with accuracy, then let them learn to write.' But he does not say how his pupils actually learn their own language once they have learned to read and write; he merely speaks of putting 'an easy ENGLISH GRAMMAR' into their hands. The comparison with Chapman and Barrow is again revealing. Barrow, for instance, recommends the use of J. Ash's *The Easiest Introduction to Dr. Lowth's English Grammar* (new edn, 1768), R. Harrison's *Institutes of English Grammar* (2nd edn, 1784) and, eventually, R. Lowth's *A Short Introduction to English Grammar* (new edn, 1789). Chapman prefers Anne Fisher's *A Practical New Grammar* (28th edn, 1795). Thomas Lancaster again gives the impression of complacency.

It is, however, when it comes to English literature or *belles-lettres* that he is seen in the most uninspired and uninspiring light, for he 'also occasionally points out the Excellencies of the various Writers, whose Works have adorned and enriched our language'. This sounds like yet another echo of Thomas Sheridan, who drew his pupils' attention to 'the purest and most elegant passages, extracted from the best English writers'.[22] No doubt Thomas Lancaster was no worse than the majority of contemporary schoolmasters in this respect, but two points remain: that he none the less falls far short of the likes of George Chapman, and that his attitude cannot have endeared him to Arthur Schopenhauer, who had a deep love of poetry. With his senior pupils Chapman discussed Joseph Trapp's *Lectures on Poetry* (1742), John Newbery's

The art of poetry on a new plan (1762), *The Poetical Preceptor* (1777), Charles Rollin's *The method of teaching and studying the Belles Lettres* (7th edn, 1770), Lord Kames's *Elements of Criticism* (5th edn, 1774) and the work of Thomson, Pope, Milton and other poets. This is not so very different from what Richard Jameson was offered by John Stevenson. The contrast again speaks for itself.

Mr Lancaster does not, of course, mention the teaching of English as a foreign language, although it must be supposed to have been as mechanical as the other teaching. It is a fair assumption that Schopenhauer will have had an easy English Grammar put into his hands and that he will have been required to commit parts of it to memory. The grammar was most likely Mr Fisher's *English Grammar* (Rev. J. Wilson, 1792) or Anne Fisher's *A Practical New Grammar*. He would also have been given a dictionary for use, probably *Newbery's Spelling-Dictionary of the English Language* (new edn, 1791). *Entick's New Spelling Dictionary* (new edn, 1788), being designed for persons of inferior social station (including 'Foreigners'!), would hardly have been considered suitable by Mr Lancaster, although Dr Chapman used it. It may be that what Schopenhauer learned by rote during the week was tested on Saturdays. Letter-writing, as a part of the curriculum, may also have been involved, although his letters would not have been suitable for inspection by Mr Lancaster if they had been written in English. They were, however, written in German. He may even have been encouraged to write simple verse in English. We know that he translated pieces by English poets into German, and vice versa.

There remains the question of his actual reading in English, on which Mr Lancaster's *Plan* throws no light. It is likely that he read whatever he could get his hands on, meaning some of the English poets (notably Milton and Shakespeare), books to do with geography and history (biography), and homiletic works. Parson Lancaster probably shared Thomas Sheridan's guarded attitude to the English poets:

> let them read a few, a very few of our English poets. Milton's Paradise lost, his Comus, Samson Agonistes, Lycidas, and L'Allegro & Penseroso can not be too often repeated. A few of Shakespeare's Tragedies might be read, but . . . let our whole tribe of rhimers, whatever name or reputation they may have acquired, be kept far from their sight.[23]

Whatever about the English poets, Schopenhauer's reading is

unlikely to have included the novelists, some of whose works he already knew, for Thomas Lancaster probably shared, albeit for different reasons, Schopenhauer's own later view that young people ought not to read novels. Mr Lancaster (who, unlike several of his Wimbledon friends, did not even subscribe to as prudish a novel as Fanny Burney's *Camilla* when it came out in 1796) would have spoken of their corrupting effect. His pupil argued that through novels a false view of life may be foisted on naive young readers, thus arousing expectations which can never be fulfilled in reality. There is no evidence that the English dictations Schopenhauer was given to write were 'moral' ones, but it is certain that they were. Thomas Sheridan wrote in his *Plan of Education* that 'the boys shall study their own language in books of religion and morality';[24] there is absolutely no reason to suppose that Thomas Lancaster did not agree, or that he did not extend the practice to his foreign parlour boarders.

The two final sections of Thomas Lancaster's *Plan* deal with discipline, religion and morals. So far as discipline is concerned, it is obvious that his system of punishment is more authoritarian than the 'jury system' practised at nearby Cheam School by William Gilpin (1757-1848), whom Thomas Lancaster very likely knew. Gilpin's wife, Betsey, was the daughter of the Rev. James Farish, vicar of Stanwix, near Carlisle, a clerical contemporary and 'neighbour' of Thomas Lancaster's father. Mr Lancaster may well have known her as a child.

Parson Lancaster begins the final section of his *Plan of Education* by explaining that the religion he seeks to inculcate has nothing joyless about it. The impression which Schopenhauer gained of Church of England religiosity was completely contrary to this statement. In particular he was appalled by his experience of the English Sunday in general and the English boarding-school Sunday in particular. Mr Lancaster wrote that

> Such Parts of every Sunday as are not occupied in attending public Worship, may be profitably filled up by reading the Holy Scriptures and other Books which deliver religious Instruction in a sobre and rational Manner.

We shall see what these 'other Books' were when we consider Schopenhauer's experience of Sundays at Mr Lancaster's, which was at the heart of his professed 'hatred' of England.

It is possible, if unlikely, that Schopenhauer would have taken slightly more kindly to what he was offered by way of 'religion' had Parson Lancaster's own lack of enlightenment, and therefore of education, not been so apparent to him. Certainly he would have been more likely to respect a headmaster who was prepared to reason with his pupils, as Dr Runge did. That said, the fact remains that to Mr Lancaster young Arthur Schopenhauer will have personified 'the blasphemous Atheist, who could pretend to *live without God in the World*'. If his headmaster realised this, he would have done his best to remonstrate with his parlour boarder, the sharpness of whose reaction ('infamous bigotry') thus becomes more explicable; when he used the phrase, he may well just have come from a wigging from Mr Lancaster on the subject of his horrible atheism.

Mr Lancaster's presentation is as pompous as his ideas are conservative and his teaching methods crude. His methods have, of course, no connection with the 'Lancasterian' system; in other words, he and his academy have no connection with the contemporary educational and social reformer Joseph Lancaster and his famous monitorial system. That Schopenhauer knew of this system is shown by one of his 'Counsels and Maxims':

> The younger a man is, the more in every respect he has to learn. Now nature has relegated him to a system of mutual instruction which he receives when associating with people like himself and in respect of which human society may be called a large-scale Bell-Lancaster educational establishment.[*P&P*, I, 429]

If Schopenhauer thus regarded this system of mutual instruction as a natural system of education, Thomas Lancaster will inevitably have taken the Tory view of the Lancasterian undenominational system, regarding it as an attack on the Anglican establishment.

Mr Lancaster's Plan of Education, 2: Practice

It is when one proceeds to consider how Thomas Lancaster's plan of education worked out in practice that its shortcomings are most clearly revealed. We are fortunate, and Mr Lancaster perhaps unfortunate, in that Johanna Schopenhauer left a detailed and highly critical account of Wimbledon School, which was obviously based on her son's experience of it and is indeed tantamount to his own account of the school.

In the general part of her *Reise durch England und Schottland* Johanna refers indirectly to her son's experience at Wimbledon School when she writes of the typical English boarding-school education (in terms reminiscent of Dr Wendeborn's account) as 'an extremely pedantic form of education [in which] a thousand ostensibly respectable prejudices and a senseless and heartless bigotry rob the Englishman at an early age of any chance of achieving an independent view of life'.[25]

Later in the same work she gives a detailed account of Mr Lancaster's academy which is of the greatest interest and importance, since the material could have come only from her son, whose jaundiced view of Mr Lancaster and all his works informs it. This, then, is the only known account of Mr Lancaster's school by a pupil or parent. It is headed 'Boys' Boarding School':

Generally it is country parsons, who rent or buy large, elegant premises not far from the church in which they officiate, who also go in for running a boarding school in tandem with their official duties, in doing which the reverend gentlemen do uncommonly well for themselves.

We had occasion to become intimately acquainted with the Rev. Mr Lancaster's academy in Wimbledon, eight miles from London. It is considered to be one of the best; even Lord Nelson had two of his nephews educated there. Basically they are all much the same; it is only the number of pupils and the quality of the furnishings that distinguish one from another.

The reverend gentleman in Wimbledon did not concern himself with the actual teaching; unseen by the pupils, he spent the day in his study, where he instructed in English a number of young foreigners, who resided in his house, not as ordinary pupils but as parlour boarders. Only at noon, at the end of the teaching day, did he appear at his desk in the schoolroom to receive the masters' reports. Four resident ushers, who took it in turn to be duty master for a week at a time, gave the necessary instruction, all four of them doing so together in the same big room. Each stands at his little desk, and the boys file from one to another. This goes on for four hours non-stop, from eight to twelve.

School begins and ends with prayers in strict conformity with the Book of Common Prayer, in accordance with which prayers must be offered up for the King and other members of the royal family, for those big with child, for those suckling infants, and so on.

The boys receive instruction in the ancient languages, in geography, history, writing, arithmetic and French. Anyone wishing to take fencing, music, dancing or drawing has to pay extra, the appropriate teachers coming down from London several times a week. For all the other worthwhile things which our children learn in Germany no one has a thought.

The boys eat together — and pretty badly at that — under the supervision of the duty master, are taken by him for walks on the Common at set times, play under his supervision in the playground, and are made to take their daily dip in a great tub, even in winter, when the ice has first to be broken.

Everything — teaching, punishment and everything to do with the children — is done mechanically in accordance with given rules, regardless of age, character and ability. How could it be otherwise when there are 60 of them, between the ages of 6 and 16; the duty master changes each week, each in turn thanking God that he is relieved of the burden of the next three weeks and can recover from the exigencies and short rations of his duty week at the extremely well provisioned table of the reverend gentleman, together with the parlour boarders and any other company. No teacher gets to know the children well, since each one has them in his care only for some twelve weeks in the year at wide intervals.

The parlour boarders, on the other hand, have a fine old time, for they bring in the reverend gentleman three times as many guineas as the ordinary boarders. Only a few of the pupils, whose parents can afford it, are suffered to join them. These pupils attend normal lessons, but they eat at the well provisioned table, and are allowed to roam garden and orchard to their hearts' content, while their fellow pupils have to keep to the dreary playground and receive a terrible beating if they stray into these forbidden preserves. Thus the children are taught, from a tender age, that to the rich all things are permitted, and that money is therefore the highest goal for which they should aim.

If a boy steps out of line, does not learn his lesson, or gets up to mischief in the playground, then as a punishment he is given a page of Greek or Latin to learn by heart. If he does not know it by the appointed time the teacher writes his name on a piece of paper and places it on Mr Lancaster's desk. In the evening those thus accused are called into the headmaster's study, all together, no matter how many. The Head addresses them as 'Sir' or 'Gentlemen' and asks, without any further consideration of their supposed misdemeanour, whether they knew their lines or not. Naturally they have to say that they didn't know them. Without further ado he asks them what they deserve. They answer that they deserve to be beaten, whereupon the reverend gentleman at once proceeds to carry out the punishment with his own fair hand, often on seven or eight offenders in a row, regardless of whether the boy in question is only six or seven, and in the most humiliating way.

If two boys have been squabbling or fighting, one is made to accuse the other; but even if his grievance is clearly justified, he will receive no satisfaction so long as the accused denies the charge. The accuser has to produce witnesses; even if he and his witnesses are clearly lying, the accused boy is punished unless he can produce other witnesses to prove his innocence. Everything is done in accordance with the conventions of English law; no one thinks of trying to fathom the children's characters, of inculcating into them a feeling for right and wrong in a higher sense, or a love of knowledge as such.

We refrain from all comment on such a method of education; everyone will make them for himself and will feel what an advantage we Germans have in this respect too over these proud island dwellers, and will sense what the outcome of this early maltreatment is likely to be.

On Sunday mornings the boys are assembled in the schoolroom. Mr Lancaster is vicar not of Wimbledon but of Merton, a village half an hour away; but by way of practice for himself he makes the boys listen, first thing in the morning, to the sermon which he will preach at Merton at noon. This he combines with the form of service prescribed by the Church of England, so that the whole thing lasts a good hour. At eleven o'clock they are paraded in twos on the playground, in their Sunday suits, and are then marched off, accompanied by all four ushers, to Wimbledon Church, where with sermon, service and hymn-singing they are obliged to stay for two hours. In the afternoon they are marched off to church again, and at eight o'clock in the evening another lengthy service is held in the schoolroom, complete — again — with prayers for the King and the royal family; in between all these devotional exercises they are required to read their Bibles.

They are allowed to go for a walk accompanied by a teacher, but any sort of game or any expression of joy is prohibited and is indeed severely punished.[26]

This account is both clear and self-explanatory. That Arthur Schopenhauer reacted strongly against 'English bigotry' and the type of 'education' of which this is the product is hardly surprising. These are matters which call for discussion, but first we need to consider the personal antipathy between Arthur Schopenhauer and his English headmaster, for young Arthur Schopenhauer was, of course, the sort of pupil that headmasters have nightmares about. He not only walked with a slouch, was untidy and given to fighting, but was sarcastic and outspoken to the point of being loud-mouthed at times. To make matters much worse, he was highly intelligent and highly articulate. He was not only the proverbial 'little horror', but was more intelligent, better educated and more sophisticated than his English headmaster.

One wonders whether his parlour boarder baited the 'Northern bear' beyond endurance, for the fact is that Schopenhauer spent his morning (together with Jacobi, Eschenburg and maybe other foreign boys) being taught English by Mr Lancaster in his study. He had extra writing lessons, which he presumably took with the writing master, who will have been unimpressed with his fancy flourishes. Otherwise his time was devoted to drawing, reading (especially Schiller and other poets, including Milton and Peter Pindar), playing the flute, singing, fencing, taking swimming lessons, going for walks (a 'rural walk daily' and occasional walks on the Common were part of Wimbledon School routine), and so on. To one of his friends he boasted that his time was largely devoted to 'the *beaux arts*' and to 'gentlemanly pursuits'. In fact it was because he found life unutterably dreary that he was obliged, like Thomas Love Peacock's Sir Oran Haut-ton, to console himself with his flute and with gymnastics. Throughout the last two months he went up to London once a week to deliver his weekly letter to 40 Old Broad Street for forwarding to his parents and to collect his pocket money from Mr Drewe. He also took riding lessons while in London. Whether he was able to practise with his rather splendid pistols is not recorded. Lorenz Meyer, evidently quoting from a missing letter, spoke of his friend being a 'gentleman and not a common schoolboy', but if Schopenhauer boasted to his friends of the fine idle time he was having he did not disguise the fact that he was unhappy. He found very irksome indeed the whole new manner of life at Mr Lancaster's, with its formality or 'complimentary manner', as he called it.[27] The mechanical style of instruction, the regimentation and prohibitions, the long Sunday services, and the regulation march on the Common (taken by the drill sergeant?), were the burden of complaining letters on the dreariness of his existence, letters which mostly received a dusty answer from a mother who not only showed a singular lack of affection for her son but who had — she *later* admitted — been responsible for sending him to Mr Lancaster's.

Young Schopenhauer inevitably found it difficult to make friends, eventually settling for a sort of friendship with Karl Jacobi. The English boys no doubt regarded him as stand-offish. In fact he had little in common with them; one of them stole his tie pin, and maybe his pencil and penknife. He remained unsettled and grew more deeply unhappy as term progressed. As a parlour boarder he was underemployed and therefore often bored, but the boredom which he experienced went far beyond what most boys suffer when they do not know what to do with themselves, and became the very prototype of that *ennui* which his later philosophy proclaims to be man's necessary condition and curse.

If Mr Lancaster must have regarded his sophisticated, cosmopolitan, rowdy, trilingual young German as 'one of those things which are sent to try us', his pupil's reaction was, characteristically, a good deal sharper. There can be not the slightest doubt that Schopenhauer regarded his headmaster as belonging to 'that old-fashioned, truism-dealing, commonplace, narrow-minded set of Pedants' (*his* English!) which, he says, reached its height in England at precisely the time when Thomas Lancaster began teaching. Nor is there any reason to suppose that he was not basically right in this view. Trelawney's words in his *Adventures of a Younger Son* may, I think, be applied to Mr Lancaster: 'The master . . . was one of those pedagogues of what is called the old school. He had implicit faith in his divining rod, which he kept in continual exercise, applying it on all doubtful occasions.'[28] Indeed, we have already noted that Mr Lancaster belonged to the *fortiter in re* class of pedagogues as described by Captain Marryat:

> I was sent to school to learn Latin and Greek, which there are various ways of teaching. Some tutors attempt the *suaviter in modo*, my schoolmaster preferred the *fortiter in re*; and, as the boatswain said, by the 'instigation' of a large knotted stick, he drove knowledge into our skulls as a caulker drives

oakum into the seams of a ship. Under such tuition, we made astonishing progress.[29]

Johanna Schopenhauer's account makes it clear that 'the master's blessing' was wont to descend on his charges' heads, or backsides, at regular intervals.

Arthur Schopenhauer evidently regarded his English headmaster as crude, vulgar, ignorant and narrow-minded to a degree, that is, as a bigot, a canting hypocrite and a prime example of what was — alas! — known as *Engländerei*. If he had read Mr Lancaster's *Plan of Education* he would not have been disposed to agree that his headmaster had 'a Mind unbiassed and disposed to Reflexion'. There was never a chance that he would take to Parson Lancaster. He was, after all, sent to Mr Lancaster's to help him prepare for a career he despised, and no doubt felt cheated in being sent there at all instead of accompanying his parents on the tour which he had been promised by his father. He will therefore have been predisposed to dislike Mr Lancaster; but what he found will have horrified him. Not only were his fellow boarders naive and probably boorish compared with himself; so too was Thomas Lancaster. There was never any way in which the north-country clergyman and former schoolmaster-cum-peasant of Maughanby could begin to impress the young sophisticate and cosmopolitan. Schopenhauer will inevitably have compared Mr Lancaster with his own headmaster, Dr Runge. Runge was twenty years younger than Lancaster and was, as we have seen, a thoroughly enlightened product of the *Aufklärung*. Schopenhauer's abomination of Thomas Lancaster's 'religion' was the result not only of having it rammed down his throat, but of the comparison he will have made with Dr Runge. Schopenhauer was not opposed to religion as such or even to Christianity as such, for he is one of the most religious of all philosophers, and 'religion' is one of the key words in his work; but he was passionately opposed to the canting humbug, philistinism and prudishness by which he found himself faced.

Pulpit Terrorism

Schopenhauer's strongest and most forcefully expressed views on Mr Lancaster and his academy have as their subject or starting point the Sundays which he so detested and which he regarded — for the rest of his life — as part and parcel of a greater evil, English bigotry. Let us therefore consider first Sundays at Wimbledon School and then the 'artificial' or unnatural system of education practised there, diametrically opposed as it was to the kind of education which Schopenhauer had hitherto experienced and which he was to advocate in his work.

Mr Lancaster's views on religion and morals, and on how Sundays should be spent, are to be found in his *Plan of Education* under the heading 'Religion and Morals', these being the two articles in question:

> I have joined these two Articles together, because the latter ought to bear the same Relation to the former, as the Effect bears to its Cause. For as the first, without the last, is detestable Hypocrisy and Fanaticism; so the last, without the first, is mere Pagan Virtue. But before I proceed further I beg Leave to explain that the RELIGION I mean to inculcate has Nothing *morose, melancholy,* or *austere* in it. In a just Medium between the blasphemous Atheist, who would pretend to *live without God in the World*; and the weak Votary of Enthusiasm and Superstition, who would wish us to consider 'every innocent Enjoyment as an Offence to the Deity', I would have my Pupil's Mind well convinced of the Existence of God — completely instructed in his Nature and Attributes — and accustomed to think of him with Cheerfulness. He should be taught to regard the Supreme Being as the Author of all his Enjoyments, and consequently to look up to him with Gratitude and Love. He should be frequently reminded, that the Eye of this beneficial Creator and Ruler of the Universe is always over him — that he is *particularly pleased* with those who are *obedient* to his Laws, which are revealed to us in the Holy Scriptures — and that he is *terrible* only to such as *despise* and *disobey* his Commandments. All the Perfections of the divine Nature may be illustrated to the Pupil, in such a Way, as to make *each* a suitable Foundation in his *Mind*, for the Superstructure of some *Virtue* in his *Conduct*.
>
> Such Parts of every *Sunday* as are not occupied in attending public Worship, may be profitably filled up by reading the Holy Scriptures and other Books which deliver religious Instruction in a sober and rational Manner. And a Portion of this Day ought generally to be assigned to the Business of storing young Minds with the Doctrines of *Christianity*, so far at least as an able and judicious Illustration of our excellent

Church Catechism will authorize us to proceed. There are many valuable Works on this subject, by some of our best Divines, as Bishop *Williams*, Mr. *Lewis*, Archibishop *Wake*, and Archbishop *Secker*; some of which are very proper to be committed to Memory, and others to be attentively perused.

In Aid to the good Impressions which we endeavour to make on the Minds of our Pupils, by spending the *Lord's Day* in an improving Manner; it is thought necessary and proper to begin and end *every* Day with Prayers selected from the Service of the Church. This contributes to preserve a Sense of the Presence and Blessings of God, and is conducive to the Order and Regularity of Business.

Religion, thus attended to, affords a suitable and firm Foundation for the Practice of *good Morals and gentlemanly Behaviour* on all Occasions. And if my Pupil duly remembers that he is a *Gentleman* and a *Christian*, I shall have great Hopes of his acting up to the Respectability and Value of those Characters.

The terms in which Mr Lancaster used to address his pupils on the subject of the 'Sabbath' (for Schopenhauer a cant word typical of the 'Jewish sabbatarianism' of the English) may be inferred from his *Sermon* of 1814, in which he urged his congregation to:

Religiously reserve the Sabbath for the uses, to which God hath commanded you to consecrate it; as, I presume, you would not be understood to tell your Creator and Judge, that you know better than he does, how you ought to employ it. Zealously and attentively frequent public worship, at your parish-church, both morning and evening; and persevere in that and all other duties of the day, till you can conscientiously 'call the Sabbath a delight'.[30]

The boys of Nelson House School (as it then was) will have heard these words at early morning prayers; no doubt the words which Schopenhauer heard on the subject eleven years previously were much the same.

After an early morning address in such terms, young Schopenhauer was marched off to church. 'How I hated this day!' says Arthur Clennan in Dickens's *Little Dorrit* as he thinks of the Sundays of his boyhood, 'when, like a military deserter, he was marched to chapel by a piquet of teachers three times a day, morally handcuffed to another boy', and of 'the resentful Sunday of a little later, when he sat glowering and glooming through the tardy length of the day, with a sullen sense of injury in his heart'.[31] Schopenhauer felt no differently, and expressed himself in no uncertain terms on the subject. That he did so many years after his Wimbledon experience only shows the strength of his indignation. This is what he wrote in his essay 'On Religion', published almost half a century after his Wimbledon trauma:

> Look at England . . . where by an audacious piece of priestcraft, the Christian Sunday, established by Constantine the Great in opposition to the Jewish Sabbath, is falsely identified with it, even as regards the name, and this in order that Jehovah's commands for the Sabbath, that is, the day on which the Almighty had to rest from his six days' labours (so that it is essentially the last day of the week), may be applied to the Christian Sunday, the dies solis, this first day that gloriously opens the week, this day of devotion and joy. As a result of this fraud, *Sabbath-breaking* or *the desecration of the Sabbath*, that is to say, the slightest occupation, whether by way of business or pleasure, all games, music, knitting, worldly books, is in England looked upon as a grave sin. Surely the man in the street is bound to believe what his spiritual mentors impress upon him: that provided he follows *a strict observance of the holy Sabbath and a regular attendance on divine service*, in other words, provided on Sundays he invariably idles away his time and does not fail to sit in church for two hours to hear the same old litany for the thousandth time and to rattle it off parrot fashion, he can reckon on indulgence with regard to the odd peccadillo which he occasionally permits himself. Those devils in human form, the slave-owners and slave traders in the Free States of North America (which should be called the Slave States), are, as a rule, orthodox, pious Anglicans who would consider it a grave sin to work on Sundays, and who, placing their confidence in this and in their regular attendance at church, hope for eternal happiness. [*P&P* 'On Religion'; Schopenhauer's English, which may well derive verbatim from the Rev. Thomas Lancaster, is italicised]

Presumably the English phrase 'a regular attendance on divine service' is Mr Lancaster's. Be that as it may, the lengthy sermon was one of the principal horrors of the English Sunday. We need to remember that Schopenhauer was not used to sermons at all, let alone by such determinedly old-fashioned clerics as the Rev. Thomas Lancaster and the Rev. Herbert Randolph. At Dr Runge's the boys had discussions with their headmaster on 'ethics', arriving together at rational and humane precepts which were acceptable not only because they were as rational as they were humane, but also because they were the outcome of free discussion. By contrast the idea of 'doing God's will' (a cant concept defined by Thomas Lancaster in his *Plan of Education* in terms which will have been familiar to Arthur Schopenhauer), because one would be eternally damned if one did not, simply did not measure up. By comparison with Dr Runge's civilised procedure, Mr Lancaster's is crude; it also backfired quite spectacularly. At issue, basically, is the contrast between the European Enlightenment and what Schopenhauer called the 'Egyptian darkness' of church-ridden late Georgian England.

It would be easy to come to the conclusion that Schopenhauer is going too far and that his criticism is therefore not sound, but it would be quite mistaken to do so, for he is only voicing what was a commonly held view of English sabbatarianism. What upsets him is partly the hypocrisy so memorably described by Peter Pindar in his elegy 'The Sorrows of Sunday', which ends:

Life with the down of cygnets may be clad!
   Ah! why not make her path a pleasant track?
'No!' cries the PULPIT TERRORIST, (how mad!)
   'No! let the world be one huge hedgehog's back.'

Vice (did his rigid mummery succeed)
   Too soon would smile amid the *sacred walls*;
VENUS, in tabernacles make her bed;
   And PAPHOS find herself amid SAINT PAUL'S.

Avaunt HYPOCRISY, the solemn jade,
   Who, wilful, into ditches leads the blind:
Makes, of her canting art, a thriving trade,
   And fattens on the follies of mankind!

Look at ARCHBISHOPS, BISHOPS, on a Fast,
   Denying hackney-coachmen e'en their beer;
Yet, lo! their BUTCHERS knock, with *flesh repast*;
   With *turbots*, lo! the FISHMONGERS appear!

The POTBOYS howl with porter for their bellies;
  The BAKERS knock, with custards, tarts and pies;
CONFECTIONERS, with rare ice creams and jellies;
  The FRUITERERS, lo! with richest pine supplies!

In *secret*, thus, they eat, and booze, and nod;
  In *public*, call indulgence a *d—mn'd evil*;
Order their simple flocks to *walk* with *God*,
  And *ride themselves* an airing with the *Devil*.[32]

This must have been the poem by Peter Pindar that most struck young Schopenhauer; indeed, it may even account for his acquisition of Pindar's *Works*. How Schopenhauer must have relished that 'PULPIT TERRORIST, (how mad!)', exposed as he was on Sundays to *two* archetypal 'pulpit terrorists'.

In the long passage from 'On Religion' just quoted Schopenhauer is, in effect, echoing the view expressed by J.W. von Archenholz in his *A Picture of England* of 1789:

> The clergy and the laity who wish to pass for good christians, seem to think that abstaining from all work and worldly affairs on a Sunday entitles them to such denomination. This Judaical and popular custom is supported by a statute which was enacted when puritanism was in full vigour, and which has not a little contributed to that gloomy taciturnity which forms such a conspicuous feature in an Englishman's character.
>
> The above law prohibits the amusements of music and dancing on the only day when the tradesman or mechanic has time to divert himself.
>
> We cannot but deplore the weakness of human nature on beholding great and enlightened men becoming the zealous partizans of ridiculous and even pernicious customs. The learned Dr. Johnson was so attached to this in particular, that, on his death-bed, he conjured Sir Joshua Reynolds to grant him one request: — The English Apelles promised his assent — and found it to be — 'That he would not paint *on a Sunday.*'[33]

Assuming that Schopenhauer was familiar with Archenholz's work before he came to England, he was at least forewarned, although the Sundays which he spent with his parents before being packed off to Wimbledon will have lulled him into a state of unpreparedness for what was to come. The wording of his remarks in 'On Religion' is so close to Archenholz that one wonders whether he may not have been recalling Archenholz's words when he came to write from bitter personal experience, particularly since Archenholz's implied criticism of Samuel Johnson also points forward to Schopenhauer's extremely outspoken comments on the good doctor. Archenholz goes on to describe how the English spend their Sundays if they can:

> Sunday is very strictly observed in England; and as all kinds of work, even music, are prohibited, that day is therefore usually destined to the pleasures of the country. All the citizens who have country-houses, repair to them on Saturday afternoon, to make preparations for their friends on the following day. The prodigious number of ale-houses and taverns situated near the capital, is then full of persons of both sexes; and, contrary to the general usage, an *ordinary* is kept for their reception. All the great roads around London are also crowded with carriages, horses, and foot-passengers; and I may fairly assert, that three-fourths of the inhabitants of the capital keep the *Sabbath* in this manner.[34]

Unfortunately for him the delights of the English country were taboo for Schopenhauer, who was thus exposed to the full blast of what he called English sabbatarian superstition, the horrors of which are spelt out in his mother's travel diary:

> On the Continent Sunday is . . . not only a day of rest, but a day of joy . . . There are few people who do not look forward to Sunday each time it comes round . . . if only because it gives them a chance to go to the theatre after working every evening during the week.
> In London things are very different. Music and dancing are prohibited, people are not even allowed to think of going to the theatre, all shops and exhibitions are bolted and barred. The unbelievable pedantry with which people watch over the observance of the Sabbath exceeds even that of the Jews, who only forbid work, not pleasure.
> Some of the foremost families in the kingdom were recently denounced in the churches of the city — virtually by name — as Sabbath-breakers and dreadful sinners, and had

contumely piled upon them in all the papers because they held musical evenings on Sundays, and because it occasionally happened that the company which they gathered around them on Saturday evenings stayed on dancing and playing cards until after midnight, thereby breaking the Sabbath before it had properly begun.

'Is it true that in Germany people play cards on a Sunday?' we heard one woman ask. 'Sunday is the favourite day for playing cards, for then one does not have other things to do,' was the reply. 'Good Lord!' a second woman sighed; 'but,' she added sanctimoniously, 'they can't be blamed for it; they are not taught any better,' whereupon she looked at us heathens pityingly. 'But at least they don't play for money, do they?' asked a third. 'Of course they do, often for large sums of money.' They all shuddered. 'God bless us all,' said a fourth woman. 'I once played cards on a Sunday (though not for money, of course), and I have never been able to forgive myself.' Only a couple of minutes earlier all four had been bewailing the fact that, since it was Sunday, they could not play a rubber of whist; they were out in the country, in appalling weather, and were bored stiff, while their husbands for their part were sitting there motionless as statues, as though glued to their bottles.

The typical Englishman divides his Sunday between public devotions, private devotions, and drinking; his wife spends such time as her devotions leave free in gossiping with one of her cronies and running down her dear neighbour, for there's no law against doing that on Sundays. The children are particularly hard done by, since special Sunday schools have been built into which they are shepherded on Sunday evenings after already, in the course of the day, having had to listen to the mumbo-jumbo of the Book of Common Prayer, twice in church and once at home.

But it is still worse for the foreigner unaccustomed to such things! You open the piano, and your landlady comes curtseying into the room and begs you not to forget that it is Sunday. You take up a book, and a visitor, seeing that you had abandoned yourself to a worldly book, treats you to a well-meant speech on the subject. Annoyed, you sit down at the window and without thinking take up your knitting, whereupon the populace assembles in front of the house and with its scolding brings down upon you a second visit from the landlady, who, in her sabbatarian zeal, expresses herself somewhat less mildly than she did the first time. If you go about your business away from the window, the servants express their horror — if not in words, then at least by looks — every time they enter the room. If you wish to play a game of whist with your fellow countrymen in the privacy of your room, then your own servant is entitled to report you to the nearest magistrate, and you will not go unpenalised.

What is one to do on this day which comes round fifty-two times a year? One goes for walks, if the time of the year and the weather permit, and tries to forget that all tolls cost twice as much on Sundays, for the greater glory of God. In winter, or when the weather is bad, one simply possesses one's soul in patience; there's nothing else to do.[35]

This remarkable description makes it all the more surprising that she was not more sympathetic about the Sundays at Wimbledon which her son so detested. We need to remember that on Sundays the 15-year-old foreigner was subjected to an early sermon by the Rev. Lancaster, after which he was marched off to Wimbledon St Mary's (the old church, not the present Victorian one) for the eleven o'clock service, which lasted up to two hours in those days. At St Mary's he will have had the honour of listening to sermons by the Rev. Herbert Randolph. Son of Dr Thomas Randolph (1701-83, one-time President of Corpus Christi College, Vice-Chancellor of Oxford and Lady Margaret Professor of Divinity) and brother of Dr John Randolph (Bishop of London, 1809-13), the Rev. Herbert Randolph (1748-1819) was vicar of Wimbledon from 1777. He was an old-fashioned conservative cleric; in his report on the parish written on 28 December 1806, in preparation for the archbishop's visitation, he showed himself in an intolerant light, referring disparagingly to the Toleration Act (of 1689!).[36] That the Rev. Herbert Randolph is partly responsible for Schopenhauer's abomination of English religious intolerance cannot be doubted. So far as young Schopenhauer was concerned, the presence of ecclesiastical bandsmen (assuming them to have been present), so memorably described in Hardy's *Under the Greenwood Tree* will hardly have compensated for the length and nature of the sermon:

> On Sundays people were expected to attend the service in Church . . . the singing was accompanied by violin and wind instruments . . . till orchestras were displaced by the barrel

organ, the harmonium and eventually the organ . . . The sermon was a great feature of the service, the preacher having an hourglass beside him to determine the length of his discourse. It is on record that he has been required to turn it over and continue till the sand ran through a second time.[37]

If Arthur Schopenhauer had been brought up in such a hard school, he might have reacted less strongly, although I doubt it. Whether the Rev. Thomas Lancaster or the Rev. Herbert Randolph used the hourglass is not recorded. Nor did Schopenhauer find any relief from the lengthy sermon in hearty hymn-singing, of which he remarked in his travel diary, on 21 May 1803, that Protestant hymn-singing — or braying, as he calls it — gave him sore ears. In referring to braying he is using one of his favourite metaphors, for in the annotations in not a few of his books the ass's head is used emblematically to denote the assininity of English bigotry.

After the lengthy service at St Mary's there remained the horrors of an English boarding-school Sunday, to say nothing of being marched off to St Mary's again in the afternoon, and school prayers in the evening. Such time on Sunday as was not occupied in attending public worship was spent, in accordance with Mr Lancaster's *Plan*, in reading the Bible and 'other Books which deliver religious Instruction in a sobre and rational manner'. These books, which Mr Lancaster's pupils were expected to commit to memory, or at least to peruse attentively, and which evidently caused the young Schopenhauer much misery, included John Williams, *A Brief Exposition of the Church Catechism* (1689); William Wake, *Principles of the Christian Religion in a Commentary on the Church Catechism* (11th edn, 1786); Thomas Secker, *Lectures on the Catechism of the Church of England* (7th edn, 1791); John Lewis, *The Church Catechism explain'd* (32nd edn, 1772).

Otherwise, Sundays at Wimbledon School were a matter of prohibitions. It is clear from Lorenz Meyer's letter of 23 August 1803 that Schopenhauer had written to him listing all the things he was forbidden to do on Sundays, which included dancing, running, fishing, singing, whistling, tippling, writing, reading worldly books, playing, shouting, climbing, making a noise, etc. Young Arthur understandably felt that there wasn't much left that was worth doing. Meyer noticed that sleeping was not included in the list, and said that that was what he would do (treating Sundays as a cat treats rainy days!). Schopenhauer, who was the one exposed to such 'infamous' prohibitions, felt that it was no laughing matter. So far as Sundays at Wimbledon School were concerned, words may fail the modern reader, but they did not fail Arthur Schopenhauer. The subjective origin of some of his maxims is obvious. When he writes in 'What a Man is' that 'It is difficult to keep quiet when one has nothing to do' it is reasonable to suppose that this goes back to the experience of a repressed 15-year-old known to his friends for his noisiness. Similarly the statements that 'Complete inactivity quickly becomes intolerable, since it gives rise to the most appalling boredom' ('Counsels and Maxims') and that 'youths view with alarm the prospect of hours of inactivity' ('On the Different Periods of Life') doubtless reflect his experience at Wimbledon. But so, less obviously, does his whole view of boredom as one of the poles of human existence, the very sign of the vanity and worthlessness of existence. It is accordingly no exaggeration to say that the cornerstone of his whole philosophy was cut at Wimbledon.

Education or Brainwashing?

The rod which Mr Lancaster wielded so readily was the badge of office of the pedagogue of the old school, who purveyed, in Johanna Schopenhauer's view, 'an extremely pedantic form of education, in which a thousand ostensibly respectable prejudices and a bigotry the most senseless and heartless rob the Englishman at an early age of any chance of achieving an independent view of life'.[38] Reporting his travels in 1790, George Forster had said much the same thing: 'Their education robs Englishmen of any chance of developing their emotional and spiritual lives.'[39] Arthur Schopenhauer's view was much the same.

This damning criticism brings us to the fundamental inadequacy of Thomas Lancaster's whole approach to education, for the essentially mechanical, catechetical nature of the instruction in his school reveals that his aim was not to educate his pupils in the real sense of teaching them to think for themselves, but to turn out readymade 'Christian gentlemen' ('if my Pupil duly remembers that he is a Gentleman and a Christian, I shall have great Hopes of his acting up to the Respectability and Value of those Characters'). I would argue that this aim falls short of education. The 'weekly Recital of the principal Parts of the English Grammar in the *catechetical* Form', in which Schopenhauer apparently took part, has much to be said for it; but when the same method is applied in the moral sphere, education is left behind and what is left is brainwashing. For all his undoubted good intentions, Thomas Lancaster's plan of education involves inculcating prejudice. This is the root criticism by German travellers of contemporary English education. Was it, one wonders, his dissatisfaction with Thomas Lancaster's brand of education that caused Schopenhauer to interest himself in the work of Joseph Lancaster, whose *Improvements in Education* was published in 1803?

It is brainwashing that is the subject of one of the comments in English in Schopenhauer's notebooks:

> There is not so gross an absurdity that I would not make all men firmly believe it, if only I were allowed to impress their minds with it, while they are under six years of age, by repeating it constantly to them with an awfull earnest. [*HN*, IV/1, 54]

In his experience the person who was most given to reiterating gross absurdities with 'an awfull earnest' was, of course, the Rev. Thomas Lancaster. Passages in *Parerga und Paralipomena* make it clear that it is the early imprinting of religious dogma to which Schopenhauer objects:

> the power of religious dogma, when imprinted early, is accordingly such as to stifle conscience and ultimately all compassion and every humane feeling. But if you want to see with your own eyes . . . the effect of religious brainwashing at an early age, consider the English. Look at this nation, favoured by nature before all others and better endowed than any with reason, intelligence, independence of mind and strength of character; then see how they are debased beyond all others, indeed, how positively contemptible they become through their stupid ecclesiastical superstition, which appears beside their other abilities like a fixed idea or monomania. For this they have to thank the fact that education is in the hands of the clergy, who take good care to impress all the articles of faith on their minds, at a tender age, in such a way as to induce a kind of partial paralysis of the brain. This in turn expresses itself throughout their lives in the form of that idiotic bigotry which makes them degrade themselves, so that one can't make head or tail of them [*P&P*, 'On Religion']

This is evidently something on which he feels particularly strongly, for he returns to the subject later in the same essay

> Only . . . by preparations carried out well in advance can faith be made to flourish, in other words, by preparing a good soil in which it will thrive; such a soil is ignorance. Therefore in England, from the earliest times down to our own, care has been taken that two-thirds of the nation are unable to read; and so to this day there prevails in that country a blind faith such as one looks for in vain elsewhere. But now there too the government is taking education out of the hands of the clergy, which means that it will soon be all over with that faith of theirs. [Ibid.]

Although Schopenhauer was pleased to write that 'when anyone in England wishes to describe something as very obscure, nay, totally unintelligble, he says *it is like German metaphysics*' ('On Philosophy at our Universities'; Schopenhauer's English italicised), it was nonetheless his considered opinion that the English were shockingly ignorant in philosophical matters and indeed showed a complete lack of culture with regard to all speculative philosophy or metaphysics. The blame for this he inevitably lays at the door of 'the parsons, the Anglican parsons, those craftiest of all obscurantists' (*P&P*, 'On Philosophy and Natural Science', sect. 93). He added that things would not improve so long as the education of the supposedly 'cultured' classes was carried out by 'the orthodox oxen of Oxford'.

He went further, however, in seeing the abolition of Latin as an intellectual and philosophical lingua franca as partly responsible for this state of affairs:

> The abolition of Latin as the universal language of scholars and the rise of the petty provincialism of national literatures have been a disaster for the stock of human knowledge in Europe . . . This is why the English nation, so intelligent and discerning, is still degraded by the most scandalous bigotry and priestly tutelage. [*P&P*, 'On Learning and the Learned']

Although Latin loomed so large in his own education at Appleby Grammar School and in his early teaching at Maughanby, Thomas Lancaster would certainly not have agreed, not because he and his German pupil differed on the usefulness of a classical education, but because they had *totally* different ideas on what constitutes education as such.

This point can be made most clearly by quoting Schopenhauer's distinction between 'natural' and 'artificial' education in his essay 'On Education':

> Given the nature of the human mind, concepts should be deduced from intuitive perceptions, and should accordingly precede them . . . This is the natural mode of education.
> With the artificial mode of education, on the other hand, the head is crammed full of concepts by being lectured and taught and through reading before one has anything like an extended acquaintance with the world of intuitive perception . . . The result is that such education perverts the mind . . . for instead of developing in a boy the capacity to discern, judge, and think for himself, his teachers merely seek to cram his head full of second-hand ideas . . . Thus, while it is still quite poor in intuitive perceptions, concepts and value judgments — or rather prejudices — are impressed upon the child's mind . . . And so it comes about that men go through life with their heads full of absurd notions, whims, fancies, maggots, and prejudices that ultimately become fixed ideas . . . it is incredible how much harm is done by early implanted chimeras and the prejudices to which they give rise.
> Precisely because early imprinted errors are generally ineradicable, and the power of judgement the last thing to reach maturity, children up to the age of 16 should be spared all theories and doctrines, which may be grossly mistaken. Thus they should be spared all philosophy, religion, and general views of life of any kind whatsoever . . .

The autobiographical relevance does not need stressing. It amounts to an argued condemnation of the whole 'artificial' education purveyed by such a one as Mr Lancaster. The idea that boys up to the age of 16 (Schopenhauer, we remember, was virtually that age while at Mr Lancaster's) should be spared *all* dogma, and therefore *all* religion, could not be more clearly expressed. The Rev. Thomas Lancaster would have been shocked by his former pupil's argument, but in another sense he would barely have understood it, for it represents the polar opposite of everything he had always taken for granted. That is precisely Schopenhauer's point.

Notes

1. In A.S., *SW*, ed Deussen, XIV, 135 (also in *Arthur Schopenhauers Briefwechsel*, ed. M. Brahn, Leipzig, 1911, 16).
2. C.P. Moritz, *Travels through Several Parts of England in 1782*, 1795, 79–83 (also in *Moritz's Travels in England*, 77–80).
3. F.A. Wendeborn, *A View of England*, II (1791), 131–8.
4. No. 19 Thavies Inn, Holborn; No. 10 Henrietta Street, Covent Garden; No. 11 Little Street, Leicester Square; Mr Hodgson's, No. 50 Strand. Their hotel was in Bridge Street, Blackfriars.
5. On his stay at Le Havre, see A. Hübscher, 'Jugendjahre in Hamburg', *S-Jb*, LI (1970), 6–9.
6. Ibid., 6.
7. I have gratefully made use of the accounts of Dr Runge and his school by Paul Hoffmann (*Jahrbuch der Schopenhauer Gesellschaft*, 19, 1932, 226–9) and Hildegard von Marchtaler (*S-Jb*, 49, 1968, 95–7).
8. Marryat, *Frank Mildmay* (1829), Chapter 1.
9. Her full account of Mr Lancaster's appears later in the chapter. Any firm evidence as to the identity of the four ushers in 1803 is lacking. They probably included Richard Farrer. Richard Brant is a possible candidate and Joshua Ruddock a less likely one. Richard Farrer (? son of Richard Farrer of Market Harborough, cleric; matric. BNC, 1793; BA, 1797, MA, 1800) married Ann Elizabeth Dunn at Wimbledon in 1797, in the presence of five Lancaster family witnesses and of one Jn Carvalhoe (French master?); both Richard Farrer and his wife were described as of Wimbledon; it may be that Farrer had replaced the Oxonian assistant classics master for whom Mr Lancaster advertised in 1790. Richard Brant, who lived in Charterhouse Square before he moved to Wimbledon, was a fellow member of the Society of Schoolmasters; he had a son, William Crawley, who went up to Oriel in 1808, following in Thomas William Lancaster's footsteps. The Rev. Joshua Ruddock moved to Wimbledon from Parson's Green; son of Joshua Ruddock of London, he attended St Paul's School before going up to Trinity College, Cambridge, in 1789, aged 18; he took his BA in 1784 and his MA in 1787; in 1800 he was in Parson's Green, assisting the Rev. Thomas Bowen's widow to run Fulham Park House School; in 1804 he became vicar of Hitchin; he resided at The Keir, Wimbledon Common; in 1827 his wife was running a prep. school in Wimbledon. I must emphasise that there is no evidence that any of these men were employed by Thomas Lancaster, although he cannot but have known them all.
10. Goldsmith, *The Vicar of Wakefield* (1766), Chapter XX.
11. Mr W. Myson tells me that he has seen a painting of Wimbledon Common by Whichelo in the Christchurch Art Gallery in New Zealand. For a list of some works by Whichelo, see *A Catalogue of the Remaining Works of the late John J. Whichelo*; these works were sold by Messrs Christie Manson and Woods on 10 April 1866. (I am grateful to Christie's for a copy of this catalogue.)
12. Barrow, *Essay on Education*, I, iv.
13. Thomas Sheridan, *Plan of Education* (1769), 42, 53.

14. Ibid., 52.
15. *The Cambridge History of English Literature*, ed. Sir A.W. Ward and A.R. Waller XIV (Cambridge, 1932), 388 f.
16. V. Knox, *Liberal Education* (10th edn, 1789), I, 270 f.
17. See N. Hans, *New Trends in Education in the Eighteenth Century* (1951), Chapter III, 'Private academies'.
18. Ibid., 246.
19. Barrow, *Essay on Education*, II, 102-28.
20. Knox, *Liberal Education* (9th edn, 1788), I, 186 ff.
21. See Lord Chesterfield's *Letters to his Son* (1774), letter No. LXIX, Strachey edn (1901).
22. Thomas Sheridan, *Plan of Education*, 55.
23. Ibid., 101.
24. Ibid., 55.
25. J.S., *SS*, XVI (1834), 118.
26. Ibid., 257-63; my translation.
27. After leaving England he wrote in his travel diary (12 November 1803) of the 'stiff and boring English dinners' through which he had had to sit.
28. Trelawney, *Adventures of a Younger Son*, Chapter 1.
29. Marryat, *Frank Mildmay*, Chapter 1.
30. Thomas Lancaster, *Sermon* (1814), 23.
31. Dickens, *Little Dorrit*, Chapter 3.
32. Peter Pindar, *Works*, IV, 129-34.
33. J.W. von Archenholz, *A Picture of England*, I (1789), 170 f.
34. Ibid., I, 170 f.; II, 120.
35. J.S. *Reise* (repr. Stuttgart, 1965), 196-9 (the section is entitled 'Sonntag').
36. Lambeth Palace Library MS VP II/2/2b, 159-62.
37. Hudson, *Barton Records*, 61.
38. J.S., *SS*, XVI (1834), 118.
39. *George Forster's sämmtliche Schriften*, III (Leipzig, 1843), 264.

VIII
After-Effects

English Language

Although Schopenhauer *père* believed passionately in the educative value of travel, we need to remember that this particular grand tour was intended as a bribe, accepting which would commit his son to the mercantile career he did not relish. In agreeing to send Arthur to Mr Lancaster's — for it was Johanna Schopenhauer who was instrumental in sending him there — Floris Schopenhauer was breaking the terms of his pact with his son. That said, Schopenhauer was sent to Mr Lancaster's for several different reasons. His mother wished to get him off her hands in order to be able to enjoy *her* grand tour the more, and also hoped that he would be tamed and would learn to take life seriously, while his father hoped that he would learn to write the plain, manly hand necessary to the would-be merchant. Above all, however, he was sent to Mr Lancaster's to perfect his English. And perfect it there he did: it was above all to the Rev. Thomas Lancaster that he owed the remarkable command of English of which he was so proud and which never left him. He wrote most fully on the subject in a letter to Francis Haywood dated 21 December 1829, in which he stresses his debt to his English school:

> As to my knowledge of the English language I owe it chiefly to having received part of my education in England — where I was even for a while a parlour boarder at the Revd Mr. Lancasters in Wimbleton, in 1803, — further to a good deal of English reading ever since, & lastly to having lived very much in English company on the continent. My English accent is such as to have made me very frequently been

mistaken by Englishmen for their countryman at first acquaintance, though I confess that usually in the course of half an hour they would be undeceived . . .
  I do not doubt but that my English writing be deficient in several respects, that it may sometimes have a foreign taint, that even some faults against grammar or against orthography may occur; the latter of which must be accounted for by my having a hundred times more occasion to read or speak English than to write it, and a part of my deficiency would quite disappear if I were able to dictate instead of writing myself. Yet for all that I know well enough the exact meaning and import of every English term or phrase & have a pretty store of them at [my] command. [*SW*, XIV, 411 f.; *Ges. Br.*, 1978, 119 f.; the letter is written in English]

There is no reason to doubt the truth of this statement; being written in English, it bears itself out, and in any case we have Charles Eastlake's unsolicited word for it that Schopenhauer spoke 'perfect' English. In a letter to Frauenstädt of 29 June 1855 Schopenhauer reports being visited by an American graduate student from Boston, named Young, with whom he spoke English for two and a half hours. Young, he said, 'is amazed how very English I am'.[1] In 1857 he wrote, 'I understand English as well as German: as a rule any Englishman takes me for his fellow countryman for the first quarter of an hour' (*SW*, XV, 590).
  The quality of his English may be judged by what he himself wrote on the subject, and from the fact that many of his records, not a few of his annotations, and some of his longest letters, were written in English. More immediate evidence of his linguistic competence is his first extant poem, evidently written during his time at Wimbledon School, which took the form of a translation of Milton's 'On Time', the original of which is as follows:

Fly envious Time, till thou run out thy race,
Call on the lazy leaden-stepping hours,
Whose speed is but the heavy plummet's pace;
And glut thyself with what thy womb devours,
Which is no more than what is false and vain,
And merely mortal dross,
So little is our loss,
So little is our gain.
For when as each thing bad thou hast entombed,

And last of all thy greedy self consumed,
Then long eternity shall greet our bliss
With an individual kiss;
And joy shall overtake us as a flood,
When every thing that is sincerely good
And perfectly divine,
With truth, and peace, and love shall ever shine
About the supreme throne
Of him, to whose happy-making sight alone,
When once our heavenly-guided soul shall climb,
Then all his earthly grossness quit,
Attired with stars, we shall for ever sit,
  Triumphing over death, and Chance, and thee
O Time.

This is the 15-year-old schoolboy's translation:

Flieh' neidsche Zeit, bis du dein Ziel erreichet,
Beschleunige der Stunden schweren Gang,
Des Eile nur dem Schritt des Senkbleys gleichet,
Es sättige dich was dein Rachen schlang,
Das Eitle, Falsche, denn nur das wird dein,
Nur Erdentand und Staub;
So wenig ist dein Raub,
Und der Verlust so klein.
Wirst endlich alles Böse du begraben,
Zuletzt die eigne Gier verzehret haben,
Dann nahet Ewigkeit mit hohem Gruss
Und bringt den untheilbaren Kuss;
Und einer Fluth gleich wird die Freude steigen,
Das Göttliche hell scheinen
Und Wahrheit, Friede, Liebe sich vereinen
Um dessen Thron zu schweben,
Zu dem wir uns im Himmelsflug erheben,
Ihn anzuschaun durch alle Ewigkeit
Tief unter uns die dunkle Erdenbahn,
Ruhn ewig wir, in Sternen angethan,
Erhaben über Zufall, Tod und dich, o Zeit.
[*SW*, ed. Deussen, XVI, 1942, 43]

He used to translate into English too. The margins of his editions of the German poets contained many renderings into English, an example being these lines from the Prologue to Goethe's *Faust*:

> I like to see the old one now and then,
> And do t' avoid a rupture all I can;
> In a great Lord, forsooth, it's very civil,
> To speak humanely even to the devil.

In his article on Schopenhauer in the *Fortnightly Review* Francis Hueffer referred to 'a long and elaborate letter on Goethe's theory of colour, writen by him to Sir C. Eastlake, in perfectly grammatical and all but idiomatic English'.[2] Charles Lock Eastlake's translation of Goethe's *Theory of Colours* came out in 1840 and is mentioned in the essay 'On the Theory of Colours' in *Parerga und Paralipomena* as 'so excellent a translation . . . that it was a perfect reproduction of the original; indeed it can be read and understood more easily than the original'. It is therefore not surprising that Schopenhauer wrote to Eastlake the following year.

Charles Eastlake had, many years previously, been one of the English dinner companions whom Schopenhauer sought out. This is revealed in his reply:

> You say you used to be in Berlin, and your perfect knowledge of English leads me to think that we met some twenty years ago. At dinner in the inn at which I was staying I used to meet daily a gentleman of your name, who spoke perfect English. He was a speculative philosopher and, as he told me, author of a work entitled *Die Welt als Wille und Vorstellung*. So we are perhaps not unknown to one another. I gave you my name at the time and told you that I was a painter. [*SW*, XIV, 532 f.]

Schopenhauer was in Berlin from spring 1820 to spring 1822 and from 1825 to 1831. The occasion in question happened in 1828, when Eastlake was in Berlin being shown the Solly collection by Gustav Friedrich Waagen:

> Taking meals at the *Gasthof* in Berlin was a melancholy and contentious individual of forty . . . This was Johanna Schopenhauer's son Arthur. He and Eastlake discovered their common interest in the Laocoön and talked at length about the views of Lessing, Winckelmann and Goethe.[3]

Schopenhauer had apparently forgotten about this by 1841. The correspondence was not continued. Nor did Eastlake translate Schopenhauer's treatise on colour.

If his knowledge of English had not been so good, Schopenhauer would not have proposed to himself first to translate Hume into German, then to translate Kant into English. It was in 1824 that he set on foot a negotiation for translating Hume into German. There was, of course, as Helen Zimmern noted, an elective affinity in mind and misfortune between the two philosophers; Hume's first efforts, like Schopenhauer's, had been condemned to obscurity. 'Out of every page of David Hume's, there is more to be learnt than out of the philosophical works of Hegel, Herbart, and Schleiermacher, all put together,' he wrote in the third edition of *Die Welt als Wille und Vorstellung*, where he singled out for particular praise the first of the *Four Dissertations* of 1757 (*The Natural History of Religion*) and the *Dialogues concerning Natural Religion* of 1779. He possessed the second edition (1779) of the latter, as well as the *Essays and Treatises on several subjects* (new edition, 2 vols, 1777), the *Essays, moral and political* (3rd edn, 1748) and the *Essays on suicide and the immortality of the soul* (new edn, 1799). He attached particular importance to the *Dialogues concerning Natural Religion* because he saw them as furnishing cogent arguments for the miserable condition of the world and the untenability of all optimistic ideas.

The plan to translate Hume was the subject of a letter to the publisher Brockhaus written on 25 November 1824. The relevant part of the letter is as follows:

I take the liberty to make a proposition to you.

In my view the present parlous state of philosophy in Germany makes the publication of two of Hume's works most opportune. They are:

1. His *Natural History of Religion*. This little work, which I consider the more important of the two, has been translated into German only once, in 1759 (shortly after it appeared in England in 1755), together with three other dissertations on divers subjects. The translation in question is not only badly written and out-of-date; it is also full of mistakes.

2. His *Dialogues concerning Natural Religion*. These were translated in 1781 and published together with a dissertation by Plattner on atheism. I have not seen this book, which is presumably out of print.

These two works belong together, although the second

one only appeared after Hume's death because he was apprehensive as to its reception by his bigoted fellow countrymen. It would therefore be appropriate to bring them together in a new translation, which could be entitled *David Hume's Religionsphilosophie* and would amount to about 250 octavo pages. The intention of both works is, firstly, to show that the belief in gods, whether many or one, and the worship of them, originates in the fear of unknown powers, which in turn results from the fact that mankind has to endure many great afflictions without knowing the reason why; then, secondly, to demonstrate the total inadequacy of all so-called proofs of the existence of God. The presentation of both themes gives them a cloak of respectability. The treatment is absolutely masterly: shrewd and to the point, and written withal not only intelligibly, but attractively, with wit and humour on every page. For precisely this reason, and because both subject and treatment belong to the realm of popular philosophy, I believe that such a book would not meet with the chilly reception which the public currently accords to philosophical works. It would, I imagine, find many readers among the general public, and would be found all the more interesting for presenting an opposition point of view. At the present time it would, more especially, act as a foil to the recent German translation of Benj. Constant, *La Réligion*.

So far as my credentials as a translator are concerned, let me say that having, early in life, acquired a thorough knowledge of English from the clergyman of a parish not far from London, my knowledge of English has remained fluent, so much so that all the Englishmen with whom I have been much in company (particularly in recent years in Italy) said they had never heard a foreigner speak their language so perfectly; on two occasions they even mistook me for an Englishman for a while. My German style you can judge from my writings. Those opposed to my views have never failed to concede that my powers of expression and the liveliness of my style are first-class. I can therefore undertake to produce translations which would attain a perfection far removed from the shoddy work usually turned out, which, with constant recourse to the dictionary, reproduces but incompetently the meaning of the original, often missing it altogether, and does not begin to convey its spirit.

I therefore proffer my services as translator of English

prose, in the field not only of philosophy, but of the natural sciences, history, politics and novels, and can honestly promise that my work will come up to all expectations, for few can be as well equipped for the task as I am. [*Ges. Br.*, 1978, 366 f.]

Although the idea of translating Hume's writings on natural religion into German as an introduction to his own philosophy and, more generally, as a counterblast to the philosophical systems and religious ideas then current in Germany was never realised, Schopenhauer did go so far as to write (in German) a 'Preface to [the proposed] Translation of Hume's Works':

> I scarcely venture to lay before the enlightened philosophical public of our day this new German rendering of Hume's popular philosophical writings, because this public stands upon an eminence from which it not only looks down upon the once famous French philosophers — such as D'Alembert, Diderot, Voltaire, Rousseau — with evident contempt, as narrow and obstinate, but ranks the English philosophers of recent centuries little higher.
>
> Neither can there be any doubt that Hume would have spared himself the trouble of setting forth, in lengthy discussions and dialogues, sceptical arguments against the chief truths of natural religion, and then of conducting their defence; wearily weighing reasons and counter-reasons, and thus constructing a firm foundation for the belief in these truths — he would have spared himself this trouble, if the brilliant philosophical discovery of our day had already been made in his time. I mean the important discovery that understanding comes from perceiving, and especially from perceiving revelations of the transcendent and god-like, which dispenses with the necessity of all reflection and reasoning on such subjects. Therefore I acknowledge that I lay this translation before my philosophic contemporaries not as a book for instruction, but as a means for better measuring their own greatness and the loftiness of their own standpoint, that they may the more perfectly appreciate the same.

> Zu sehen wie vor uns ein Mann gedacht,
> Und wie wir's denn zuletzt so herrlich weit gebracht.

The same holds good with regard to his diction. Had Hume had the good fortune to live till our present philosophic period, he would have improved his style; he would doubtless have cast aside that terseness, lucidity, precision, and attractive liveliness which are natural to him, and endeavoured to spread a mysterious obscurity over his writings. By means of heavy involved periods, out-of-the-way expressions, and made-up words, he would first have puzzled his readers, and then, as they continued their perusal, would have made them wonder how it was possible to read so much without gleaning one single idea. This must make them feel that the less the text makes them think, the more the author must have thought. Therefore in this respect, too, the philosophic reader of our time will have the satisfaction of looking back with gratified pride on this Coryphaeus of a past period.

As to what has called me to this little work, it is merely this, that since my stay in England as a boy the English language has come very easily to me, and I have a great deal of spare time since I consider myself excused from working out my own thoughts for communication, for experience has verified what I foresaw and predicted — that they would find no readers among my contemporaries.[4]

However amusing, and however revealing, the irony here is unlikely to have done much to help the project come to fruition. At one stage one thinks of Hoffmann's literary tomcat, Murr, who goes so far as to inscribe a deep work of which he understands not a word. This brings us back to metaphysics in general and German metaphysics in particular.

'Must I plunge into metaphysics? Alas, I cannot see in the dark; nature has not furnished me with the optics of a cat.'[5] Thomas Gray's attitude, voiced in 1736, is typical of the 'English' distrust of metaphysics, in which German metaphysics commonly pass as the *non plus ultra*, for 'when anyone in England wishes to describe something as very obscure or indeed as totally unintelligible, he says *it is like German metaphysics*' (*P&P*, 'On Philosophy at the Universities'; Schopenhauer's English italicised). By the time these words appeared in 1851, the idea of the unintelligibility or so-called mysticism of German metaphysics — particularly of the Kantian variety — had become fairly widely accepted in England. The idea was first voiced by Hazlitt, who wrote in the *Edinburgh Review* in August 1817, 'As for the great German oracle Kant, we must take the liberty to say, that his system appears to us the most wilful and monstrous absurdity that ever was invented.'[6] It may well be that Thomas Love Peacock, who took the *Edinburgh Review*, was inspired by these words to make Kantian metaphysics one of his targets in *Nightmare Abbey* (1818) and, subsequently, in *Crotchet Castle* (1831). One of the visitors at Mr Glowry's table in *Nightmare Abbey* is Mr Flosky (based on Coleridge), who 'lived in the midst of that visionary world in which nothing is but what is not', and who accordingly 'plunged into the central opacity of Kantian metaphysics, and lay *perdu* several years in transcendental darkness, till the common daylight of common sense became intolerable to his eyes'.[7] Peacock returns to this target in *Crotchet Castle*, where we find the following characteristic dialogue:

> *Mr. Skionar.* I cannot agree with you, Mr. MacQuedy, that you have found the true road of metaphysics, which the Athenians only sought. The Germans have found it, sir: the sublime Kant and his disciples.
> *Mr. MacQuedy.* I have read the sublime Kant, sir, with an anxious desire to understand him; and I confess I have not succeeded.
> *Rev. Dr Folliott.* He wants the two great requisites of head and tail.[8]

By 1831, of course, Carlyle had put his finger on the problem of German 'mysticism' as perceived by men like Hazlitt, Peacock, Shelley and Byron; in his review article on 'The State of German Literature', which appeared in 1827, he wrote:

> We come now to the second grand objection against German literature, its *Mysticism* . . . Mysticism is a word in the mouths of all: yet, of the hundred, perhaps not one has ever asked himself what this opprobrious epithet properly signified in his mind; or where the boundary between true science and this Land of Chimeras was to be laid down. Examined strictly, *mystical*, in most cases, will turn out to be merely synonymous with *not understood* . . . The chief mystics in Germany, it would appear, are the Transcendental Philosophers, Kant, Fichte, and Schelling! With these is the chosen seat of mysticism, these are its 'tenebrific constellation', from which it 'doth ray out darkness' over the earth. Among a certain class of thinkers,

does a frantic exaggeration in sentiment, a crude fever-dream in opinion, anywhere break forth, it is directly labelled as Kantism; and the moon-struck speculator is, for the time, silenced and put to shame by this epithet. For often, in such circles, Kant's Philosophy is not only an absurdity, but a wickedness and a horror; the pious and peaceful sage of Königsberg passes for a sort of Necromancer and Black-artist in Metaphysics; his doctrine is a region of boundless baleful gloom, too cunningly broken here and there by splendours of unholy fire, spectres and tempting demons people it, and, hovering over fathomless abysses, hang gay and gorgeous air-castles, into which the hapless traveller is seduced to enter, and so sinks to rise no more.[9]

Carlyle emphasises not only that Kant thus suffers from being not understood, but also that 'among all the metaphysical writers of the eighteenth century . . . there is not one that so ill meets the conditions of a mystic as this same Immanuel Kant'.

The fact that such important parts of the British debate about the 'central opacity of Kantian metaphysics' took place in the *Edinburgh Review* means both that we need look no further for Peacock's inspiration on this score, and that Schopenhauer may well have been moved by this same debate to conceive, in 1829, the plan of damping down this *ignis fatuus* by translating Kant into English. Although the plan came to nothing, Kant was presently relieved in that his place as butt was taken by Hegel. In 1846 G.H. Lewes wrote that Hegel's perfect philosophy leads only to 'clouds of mysticism' and 'bogs of absurdity',[10] which is another story. What all this means is that Schopenhauer's own lucidity, which he owed to England, came as something of a relief.

Whether prompted by the *Edinburgh Review* or not, in 1829 Schopenhauer conceived the plan of translating into English the main works of his favourite philosopher, Kant. He had long since come to the conclusion that British ignorance of Kant's philosophy was a 'downright disgrace', as the following quotation from *The World as Will and Idea* makes abundantly clear:

> Their ignorance of the Kantian philosophy, which has now, after seventy years, become a downright disgrace to Englishmen of learning, is principally responsible for the whole wretched position of the English; and this ignorance in turn depends, in large measure, upon the nefarious influence

of the wretched English clergy, who . . . inspired by the basest obscurantism . . . resolutely oppose all real education, all scientific research, and indeed all advancement of human knowledge as such; and by means of their connections and their scandalous, inexcusable wealth, which merely increases the misery of the people, their influence extends even to university teachers and authors, who accordingly (*pace* Th. Brown, *On Cause and Effect*) resort to every kind of suppression and perversion of the truth in order not to go against that 'cold superstition' (as Pückler very happily designates their religion) or the current arguments in its favour. [*WWI*, Book 2, Chapter XXVI]

Schopenhauer's plan to translate Kant is the subject of three long and interesting letters written in English. The first is the letter to Francis Haywood of 21 December 1829, part of which we have already had occasion to read. The most important remaining parts of the letter are as follows:

Sir,   though so perfectly a stranger to you, that I am not even acquainted with your name, I take the liberty to address you, hoping to be excused on consideration of its being a concern of a merely litterary nature, that makes me so bold. What **prompts me to do so is a passage in your very sensible analysis** of Damirons 'Histoire de la philosophie en France' in the Foreign Review and Continental Miscellany of July 1829, where speaking of Kant's Critic of pure reason you say 'We are sensible of the difficulties which the original presents and of the singularity of its terminology, and we should hail as a fortunate circumstance, particularly at the present moment, the translation of this and other of Kant's more important works.'

I am glad to see that you desire the transplantation of Kant's works into England, as I myself nourish the thought of it this many a year. Kant's sublime works were certainly not made for one century nor for one country alone: they will once spread over all Europe. But it is especially in England that I hope they will thrive well and even perhaps bear better fruit than they did in their own country, where their fate has been a thorough neglect for the first years after appearing, to which succeeded universal admiration, which however was soon turn'd off from them to a most unworthy object, the nonsensical philosophy of Fichte, who even now is generally held a philosopher and by some even put on a level with Kant, merely upon traditional authority, as nobody reads his philosophical works, which were never reprinted. He was soon overset by Schelling whose many extravagancies and absurdities are however redeem'd by some merit. But neither is he yet read any more, as the edition of his collected works never went beyond the first volume, that appear'd 1809. I will not mention the numberless monstrous and mad compositions which were call'd forth by Kant's works as 'the sun, being a god, breeds maggots kissing carrion' — but so much did by and by degenerate our German philosophy that we now see a mere swaggerer and charlatan, without a shadow of merit, I mean Hegel, with a compound of bombastical nonsense and positions bordering on madness, humbugh about a part of the German public, though but the more silly and untaught part, to be sure, yet by personal means and connections he contrived to get a philosopher's name and fame. The more enlightened part of the learned public certainly takes him for what he is, while this also holds no other philosopher in esteem but Kant, who alone therefore is universally read even now, a proof of which is the 7th edition of the 'Critic' having appeared last year, 48 years after the first, while all his successors in public favour after a short glare perished for ever.

The course of my experience has convinc'd me of the truth of Lord Bacon's opinion, that in warm climates people are generally more sensible and intelligent than in cold ones, but that the eminent geniusses of cold countries surpass by far even the most distinguished of warm regions. Germany has in the last century brought forth two of the very first rate talents, Kant and Goethe, yet the generality of the nation is extremely dull and their want of judgement is but the more set off by their learning. It is therefore very wrong to judge of nations by the great men born among them, i.e. of the rule by the exceptions. Without intending any flattery I sincerely believe the English nation to be the most intelligent in Europe & accordingly we find the climate of England knowing neither our chilling cold nor our scorching heat, but being truly temperate.

I therefore am of the opinion that the transplantation of Kant's works into England will prove highly beneficial for

Kant's glory & for the improvement of the English: most certainly it will exercise a deep influence, first on the learned alone, but by their medium, in the course of time, on the whole nation. Very often have I ventured to affirm that if Kant had written in English or in Latin, never would Parliament have been disputing 4 years about the emancipation of the Catholics & the mob in Ireland would not have fought about it.

Taking it for granted that in your above mention'd passage you expressed your true sentiment & therefore share my wish of transplanting Kant's Works to England, I come to make you a proposal for carrying it into effect, desiring that you on the other hand, will lend me your aid for procuring the means viz: a publisher. For it is myself whom I am going to offer as a translator, believing (as I am going to state more at large) that, all things well poised, there will hardly be found a man more proper for the task than myself; but as I have no litterary acquaintance whatever in England, I hope that you, Sir, will not shun some trouble, in order to forward an enterprise for which you expressed your anxious wishes . . .

English books, no doubt, ought to be written by Englishmen. But our case is of a particular nature: it is the reverse of all ordinary cases, in this, that the greater difficulty lies in the understanding of the text, not in the rendering of its purport. Now, though there are a few Englishmen, that know Germany very well indeed, still I entertain very great doubts whether any one of them knows it in so eminent a degree as to understand perfectly & without any mistake even merely the verbal sense of Kant's writings: yet granting even this to be the case still it would be very far from enabling such a one to be Kant's translator. A merely verbal translator would very often be excessively incorrect and write things either without any sense at all or with a quite false one of his own making. In order to translate Kant it is absolutely required to have penetrated his meaning to the very bottom, nay even to be deeply imbued with his doctrine, & this is impossible without having made a profound study of his philosophy during many years: for it is universally allowed that even few Germans truly understand Kant and no one ever penetrated his meaning at first reading: it is only by & by that the student gets into the train of his ideas and reaches the genuine sense of his positions, as his meditations are the profoundest that ever entered into man's mind: & if his style is obscure, it is chiefly so by the immense depth of his thoughts. But in compensation of this, whoever got into the right understanding of Kant's discoveries, finds his mind quite altered, he now views all things in another light, he smiles on your disputes about spirit & matter, knowing that there is no such thing as spirit, but no such thing as matter neither; they are erroneous notions; likewise on your queries about a future state or the beginning of the world, knowing time to be ideal, not real, & so on. Locke's, Hume's and Reid's disquisitions on the human mind (not to mention the most shallow Dougald Stewart or the equally shallow French Ideologists) bear to Kant's the proportion of juvenile prolusions, or that of elementary Geometry to the analysis infinitorum.

If however any Englishman, that has made during life metaphysics his only pursuit, knows German so perfectly as to have been enabled to make a proper & continued study of Kant's works & can give public evidence of his having truly understood their import, such a one no doubt, will be fittest to translate them & most willingly do I resign the task to him. But if it should happen, that such a man were not to be met with, then I am apt to think that I alone am the proper man: because I doubt very much that any of our german metaphysicians knows English so well as I do: moreover very few or perhaps none of those yet alive have so firmly & strictly adhered to Kant as I did & have made like me his works the main point of their erudition. These are the reasons why I feel in myself the vocation to be his apostle in England, & dare claim the honour of it.

I do not doubt but that my English writing be deficient in several respects . . . Yet for all that I know well enough the exact meaning and import of every English term or phrase & have a pretty store of them at command: moreover my just mentioned deficiencies may be very well supplied by any philosophically learned Englishman (yourself, Sir, for instance) who would take upon himself the task of correcting my manuscript, clearing it from all grammatical faults or improprieties of speech & improving the style & elegance of expression. He ought however to confine himself entirely to the linguistical and stylistical part of the business, carefully avoiding whatever alterations might in the least affect the sense: nor would I for my own sake ever venture to see my English printed without its having previously undergone such a purification. Still I am very well aware that even so the work will hardly attain that degree of elegance & pleasing conciseness which it might acquire if originally penned by an Englishman. But there is nothing perfect under the sun, & by the above stated view of the case you conceive, that every individual qualified in one respect for being Kant's English translator will always be found deficient in another; but then, what is, in a work of this nature, a little deficiency in point of elegance & style compared to one in point of correctness & accuracy? I would accordingly venture to say, that my deficiency seems very inconsiderable if compared to that of an English translator who without having previously penetrated Kant's opinions in general, now sits staring at a passage he does not know what to make of, till he gets rid of it by putting in its stead some commonplace thought of his own store, though express'd in very choice English. On the whole therefore, I believe that the way I propose is the only one to bring forth to light a creditable English translation of Kant: nay I might even presume to say that the possibility of it is a rare chance not to be foregone, as, for all I know, a century may pass ere there shall again meet in the same head so much Kantian philosophy with so much English as happen to dwell together in this grey one of mine: wherefore I consider myself in a manner as in duty bound to offer my services to the English public, verily more for the advancement of knowledge & truth than for my own emolument: if my proffer be rejected, neither the fault nor the greater loss shall be mine.

In translating I would adhere as closely as possible to Kant's words, yet a thoroughly verbal translation would not be to the purpose, as our language has a far greater grammatical perfection & richer store of words than the English, of which advantages Kant avail'd himself to the utmost extent, being pleased moreover to deliver his abstruse cogitations in intricate & perplexedly twisted periods of an immense length; all the which would never agree with the English Idiom: therefore his periods must be resolv'd in shorter ones and the style generally simplified. I hope to effect this to my own satisfaction & by pursuing this plan to render Kant even more intelligible in English than he is in German: for I am naturally fond of clearness and precision, & Kant by the by was not.

Moreover I have a great subsidy in this that bearing always the whole of his doctrine in mind, I can explain what he says in one place by what he said in many others. I therefore would add an introductory preface & some short explanatory notes, wherever any particular obscurity occurs or reference to his other writings is made — but chiefly elucidating terms that might be used in some rather uncommon signification: for never will there be a Kant without some cant. It's odd enough that Sterne made a prophetical pun saying in Tristram Shandy 'of all the cants which are canted in this canting world the cant of criticism' (the common name in Germany for Kant's philosophy) 'is the most tormenting'. I observe that Kant chang'd the original C of his name in a K.

Just to make the experiment I have translated a short passage which I shall annex to this letter as a specimen. It is taken from the 'Prolegomena to all future Metaphysics' & of a nature to be in some measure understood even out of context, giving moreover a hint at the proportion his philosophy bears to Locke's and the like . . .

It is, Sir, from your zeal for the propagation of truth and knowledge that I hope you will take upon you the trouble of finding a publisher for Kant's works in English, provided that I have succeeded in satisfying you that I am particularly fit to be his translator. At any rate I hope for your indulgence as to the liberty I have taken & beg you will believe me to be your most obedient servant

Berlin, 21th december 1829.   Arthur Schopenhauer

Annex

Prolegomena, p. 63:

Whatsoever is to be manifested to us as an object, must be manifested to our perception. But all our perceptions are effected by the means of our senses: for the understanding does not perceive intuitively, it only reflects. Now as by what has been hitherto proved, the senses never nor even in any respect whatever, manifest to our cognizance the things as they are in themselves, but merely their appearances, which are no more than the ideas of our sensitive faculty, it follows 'that we must deem all the bodies, along with the space wherein they subsist, to be nothing more than mere ideas in our minds and that consequently they exist nowhere else but only in our thoughts'. Now is not this clear idealism?

Idealism consists in maintaining that there exist no other but thinking beings and that all things besides, which we deem to perceive are merely the ideas of those thinking beings without any really outward object corresponding to them. Now on the contrary what I say is this: things subsisting extrinsically of us are manifested to us as objects of our senses; but nothing do we know of what they may be in themselves, our knowledge of them extending no further than to their appearances i.e. to the ideas, which they produce in us by affecting our senses. Accordingly I certainly allow bodies extrinsical of us to exist i.e. things which, though entirely unknown to us as to what they may be in themselves, yet come into our notice by means of the ideas, which we acquire from their influence on our sensitive faculty: to these things we apply the name of bodies, meaning by this term merely the appearance of an object unknown to us indeed, but not the less real. May this be called Idealism? Why, it is the very reverse of it.

That we may, without detracting from the real existence of outward things, assert that a good many of their qualities do not belong to those things in themselves, but only to their appearance[,] and accordingly have no existence of their own and independent of our ideas of them, this is a truth that has been generally received and allowed long before Locke's time; but more especially since it. Of this kind are warmth, colour, taste &c. Now not the slightest argument can be alleged to shew it as inadmissible, that I, upon weighty reasons, reckon to the mere appearance besides the above mentioned also all the remaining qualities of bodies, those, I say, which are called primary ones, as extension, place and space in general with all its dependencies, such as impenetrability or materiality, form and the like. As little, therefore, as he may be styled an Idealist, who maintains the colours to be no qualities adhering to the objects themselves, but only to our organ of sight as modifications thereof; as little is my doctrine liable to be called idealistical, merely because I find, that still more, *nay all the qualities constituting the perception of a body* appertain merely to its appearance. For by this I do not, as real Idealism does, evert the existence of the appearing things, but only shew that we can never through the medium of senses know them so, as they are in themselves.

I should be glad to know, how my positions ought to be

constituted in order to contain no Idealism. No doubt I ought to say that the idea of space is not only perfectly congruous to the relation in which our senses stand to the objects (for that is what I have said) but also that it is perfectly resembling those objects; a position to which I cannot attach any sense, no more than to this that the sensation of red in my eye bears a resemblance to the quality of the Cinnober that occasions it. [*Ges. Br.*, 1978, 118-23]

Francis Haywood's reply, when it came, was extremely disappointing:

Liverpool 18 January 1830.
Dear Sir,
    The Publishers of the Foreign Review have forwarded the letter to me, which you were so obliging as to write to the author of the article on Damiron. I am the writer of the article in question, and as such reply to your letter. It would give me very sincere pleasure to have the means of introducing Kant to the knowledge of English readers. The Latin translation has always seemed to me insufficient for this, and some time ago, I myself began a translation of the Critik der reinen Vernunft. The difficulty of the task and the necessity of attending to other matters prevented me from making great progress, but I should have still continued the undertaking, had I not been given to understand, that Sacchi in Pavia was about to publish an Italian translation of the same work, and I have always thought that were there either a French or Italian translation of Kant, it would nearly supersede the necessity of an English one. Your letter has made me again think upon the subject. Conjointly with yourself perhaps I might have courage to appear before the world as Kant's translator. My own knowledge of German is limited, but still from having some information upon the doctrines of Kant, I might be better enabled to translate his works than those who have a better knowledge of the language but a less knowledge of the author. Now what I would propose to you is this, that we should jointly undertake the translation of the Critik der reinen Vernunft, that I should send you chapters or books as they were translated, that you should correct them and return them to me, that we should have the work printed by some first rate publisher, either selling him the work or

retaining it in our own hands, you not being called upon for one penny advance, in case we printed it ourselves, but my paying all charges and dividing with you half the profits, or if this would not be agreeable to you, I would take all the arrangements upon myself, send you the translation for correction and approval and pay so much for the same, it being understood that whether I published anonymously, or in my own name, I should state that the work appeared under your sanction, the proofs having all been corrected and examined by yourself.

You will let me know which of these plans suits you best, or whether there is any other mode by which the matter can be rendered agreeable to you. All the expence of postage &c. you will please charge to me in this business.

I translated, and added a preface and notes to Bretschneider's reply to H.J. Rose last year, which I will send you by the first opportunity that I can. Believe me to remain yours very sincerely

Francis Haywood.[11]

Schopenhauer made clear his disappointment, and the reasons for it, in a letter to Messrs Black, Young & Young, written from Berlin in January 1830:

You have had the kindness of forwarding to Mr. Fr. Haywood in Liverpool the letter directed to the author of Damiron's analysis which I took the liberty to send you 21 Dec. for which I beg you will accept my thanks. Perhaps you will remember that I intimated to you at the same time that the letter concerned a literary undertaking likely to fall under your own department. And in fact I did not think otherwise but that Mr. Haywood would communicate my plan & my letter to you. But by his answer I understand that this has not been the case & also that Mr. H. is not altogether the man I had been led to imagine by his aforesaid analysis. To remedy the mistake I made in all this, the simplest means offering itself to me is to send you a copy of my letter to Mr. H., upon the perusal of which you may deliberate & resolve whether you will lend your aid to the proposed enterprise. This is no other but an English translation of Kant's Works to be made by me, A German philosopher. As you, gentlemen, are of the commercial profession I cannot expect that you should have very distinct & correct notions of Kant, his philosophy, its high worth & importance & the quite peculiar difficulty attending its translation. This is the reason why I preferred to apply first to some man of science, who might expound the case to you. But then you certainly will not be wanting some learned friend to whom you may communicate my plan & my letter who will be an able judge of the matter. I even would for this purpose recommend the very sensible & clever gentleman who wrote the analysis of Novalis & that of Jean Paul's Works in your Review, if only I was sure that not he too, like Mr. H., will have more in view his private advantage than the good of literature & the genuine perfection of the work in intended contemplation. On this account I even think it proper to subjoin Mr. H.'s answer to my letter, chiefly that you may satisfy yourself of his neither questioning the utility of my plan nor my ability for its execution. I think I may fairly do so, without derogating from the laws of equity or goodfaith as the letter contains nothing like a secret or that might in any way prejudice Mr. H. However I beg that you will never mention to him or any body else my having communicated also his answer to you, & I trust that you will not betray my confidence in this point.

I have been utterly astonished at Mr. H's offering himself for a translator, as by what he says on Kant in his analysis of Damiron I plainly see that he has but a very incorrect & mere hear-say knowledge of the Kantian philosophy, for all he may say to the contrary in his letter: and as to his knowledge of German I wonder he has not given me a specimen of it by answering me in my own language. A very satisfactory reason might be found to his taking no notice whatever of what I, who should know best, had said about the necessary precedence of the translation of Kant's Prolegomena to that of his Crit. of p. r., but intending on the contrary to begin by the latter: to wit, that there is a Latin (though by no means commendable) translation of this Critic, upon which an English sham translation might easily be made and sent me, in order to receive, as a return, a genuine and correct one, understood to be the improved copy of the first.

Though this be but a surmise, yet at any rate Mr. H. belongs precisely to that sort of translators from which I might preserve Kant, being fully convinced that he can never be translated, like any other author, by a man merely, though ever so well, understanding German, but only by a man quite versed in his philosophy, thoroughly imbibed with it, in short a man whose hair is grown gray in that study, like myself. Now for all I know a century may pass ere there shall again meet in the same head so much Kantian philosophy with so much English as happen to dwell together in mine. I therefore offer my service to the English public verily more for the advancement of knowledge and truth than for my own advantage: if my proffer is rejected neither the fault nor the greater loss will be mine.

As to Mr. H. I think I may save myself the trouble and postage of answering his letter, as he may understand by himself that my views & his are far from agreeing. He indeed might object that he only desired my help as I did his; but then his want bears to mine the proportion of a house quite defective in the foundations to one wanting a little finishing in the ornaments of the top.

If you should approve of my plan but by any particular and outward circumstance be prevented from undertaking the business, I would of course be obliged to you if you would recommend & give it over to some other respectable publisher.

I therefore now lay the matter entirely in your hands & have the honour to be etc.

Arthur Schopenhauer.

[*Ges. Br.*, 1978, 123 f.]

Schopenhauer had evidently set his heart on translating his favourite philosopher into his favourite language, but there is more to it than that, for he is surely right both in his statement that 'for all I know a century may pass ere there shall again meet in the same head so much Kantian philosophy with so much English as happen to dwell together in mine', and in his doubts about Francis Haywood's competence. It is a matter of fact that Haywood's less than successful translation of Kant's *Critick of pure reason* (1838) was followed, logically enough, by an even less rewarding commentary, *An analysis of Kant's Critick of pure reason* (1844). Schopenhauer was, above all, right about his own excellent qualifications as potential co-translator; the minor mistakes in his English are neither here nor there. It is a great pity that his project did not get off the ground, for if anyone was capable of fully understanding Kant and of translating him lucidly it was Arthur Schopenhauer. Practically every word he wrote shows that. Knowing this himself, he refused to take no for an answer, as we see from his letter to the poet Thomas Campbell, written in January 1831:

> Sir, Having understood by the public papers that an association for the encourgement of Literature has been formed in London which has its object to purchase the copyrights of meritorious works lacking a publisher and that you, Sir, are one of the chief promoters and Directors of this laudable institute, I take the liberty of laying before you a case that seems to fall within the aforesaid category.
>
> It concerns an English translation of Kant's principal works, which I have been contemplating these many years, but could not effectuate for want of a publisher or literary acquaintance in England. A year ago I made my proposal to an eminent English bookseller, but was refused.
>
> Whatever may be your own notions about German philosophy, you certainly will allow that merely to judge by the deep and lasting influence which Kant's writings are exercising these fifty years on German literature and German opinions in general, as well as by the wide spread and unaltered fame of that philosopher, he must have been a most extraordinary genius, and that consequently his writings are well worth a nearer acquaintance than by vague reports and second-hand information. I for my part, who have spent all my life in metaphysical studies believe him to be the greatest philosopher that ever lived and think him and Goethe the only first-rate geniuses that Germany ever produced. Moreover as his philosophy sprung forth from Locke's and Hume's speculations, or at least sets out from them, it is quite apt to fix the attention of English readers: as also, in another respect, because it throws a light upon some tenets of the Hindoo and Buddhaistic faith, now generally known in England. And generally on account of its intrinsic value I do not doubt that being transplanted to England it would by and by exercise a deep influence on the literature and the opinions in general of that nation, so that the transfer of Kantian philosophy to England might even by time come to be considered as an event of historical importance. In this view I have been confirmed by several passages in your foreign reviews, expressing a longing for an able translation of Kant's works, together with a sense of the immense difficulty of the task.
>
> All this, I suppose, you will easily admit. But another

question is, how I, being German, should venture to offer myself for making an English translation, a proposal that at first sight may seem strange, yet I verily believe, that, all things well poised, there hardly can be found a man more proper for that task than myself. To make you understand why this should be the case I am in the necessity of acquainting with a little myself . . .

I beg, Sir, you will excuse the liberty I took and the length of this letter. If you are pleased to honour me with an answer, it will reach me by post without any nearer direction.

I am, Sir, with the peculiar esteem due to your genius and merits, your most humble and obedient servant.

Arthur Schopenhauer

[*Ges. Br.*, 1978, 126 f.]

It is strange that this letter, delivered by hand by an English acquaintance of Schopenhauer's, a Mr Capes, who was to testify to the quality of the philosopher's English, appears to have gone unanswered. One would have thought that a letter from Germany on the subject of Kant would have attracted Campbell's attention, for he had himself studied Kant in Germany, spoke German, knew Klopstock, was intimately acquainted with Schlegel and had met Goethe. Indeed, Goethe, after a long conversation with Campbell in Weimar, formed a high opinion of him: 'I consider Campbell as more *classical* than my favourite Byron, and far above any modern English poet whose works have fallen in my way.'[12] Campbell himself was less polite about his friend Schlegel, whom he described as 'exceedingly learned and ingenious, but a visionary in German philosophy, and by far too mystical'.[13] This too is surprising, for Campbell was apt to 'plunge over head and ears into Teutonic metaphysics', particularly the metaphysics of Kant.[14] Indeed, during his first extended visit to Germany in 1800, he spent *twelve successive weeks* in the study of Kant's philosophy'.[15] He spent much of this first visit in Altona; presumably he was not entertained by the anglophile Schopenhauers. He came even closer to crossing Arthur Schopenhauer's path in October 1825, when he stayed at the Hotel St Petersburg, nearly opposite the university in which Schopenhauer was then lecturing, and which he — Campbell — visited, recording, 'I have got every piece of information respecting the University, and every book that I wished for . . . Among the few professors whom I have found, I have met with great civility.'[16] Perhaps Schopenhauer had also met Thomas Campbell without remembering him; there would have been no more obvious person to entertain a visiting English notability, for by this time Schopenhauer himself was living 'ganz auf englischem Fuss', his life style being very much that of an anglophile eccentric.

English Ways

Schopenhauer himself remarked that he 'lived very much in English company on the continent' (*SW*, XIV, 411). This applies not only to his travels, e.g. in Italy in 1823, when he lived almost entirely in the company of Englishmen, but also to his ordinary day-to-day routine. Thus in his student days at Göttingen (1809-11) he dined regularly with the American William Astor (1792-1875), who went on to increase from $20 million to $50 million the fortune accumulated by his father John Jacob Astor (born in Heidelberg in 1763 as Johann Jakob Astor). All his life he had a predisposition for the company of Englishmen (and Americans). In his later years in particular he was very much a creature of habit, living a somewhat eccentric, withdrawn, solitary life, to comments about which he was sensitive. And the extraordinary thing about this life was that it was as 'English' as he could contrive to make it. He had a portrait of Shakespeare in his study, and preferred English articles for domestic purposes. He had a cold sponge bath every morning (the Rev. Lancaster must have been responsible for that!), kept his accounts in English and annotated his books in English. He read English books, reviews and newspapers; in his later writings he takes to quoting incidents from *The Times* with considerable frequency. A confirmed bachelor *malgré soi*, he noted (in English) in 1831, 'Matrimony = war and want! Single blessedness = peace and plenty' (*SW*, XVI, 80), and there are said to have been among his papers notes — in English — on the subject of love and marriage, dating from 1819-22 and 1825-31, couched in a forcible plainness of speech which rendered them unfit for publication. In one of the fragments from the manuscript, which was destroyed, he revealed his non-bachelor's cloven hoof when he quoted Byron: 'The more I see of men, the less I like them; if I could but say so of women too, all would be well.'[17] Shortly afterwards he quoted, from Bacon's 'Essay of marriage and single life', the words:

> He that hath wife and children, hath given hostages to Fortune, for they are impediments to great enterprises, either of

virtue or mischief. Certainly the best works and of greatest merit for the public have proceeded from the unmarried or childless man, which both in affection and means have married and endowed the public. [SW, XVI, 77, 79]

An interesting document written in English, on the cover of an account book, in 1832, is a summary of the respective attractions of Frankfurt am Main and Mannheim:

Frankfort:
Healthy climate
Fine country
Comforts of large cities
Changes of large cities
Better reading room
The Nat. Museum
Better plays, operas, concerts
More Englishmen
Better coffeehouses
No bad weather
The Senkenberg library
No inundations
Less noticed
The gaiety of the place and all about it
You are more at large and not so beset with company given by chance, not by choice and more at liberty to cut and to shun whom you dislike
An able dentist and less bad physicians
Not such intolerable heat in summer
The physical Museum

Manheim:
Fine Weather (intolerable heat)
Silence and no throng (throng at the play and dinner)
More consideration
Better foreign bookseller
The Harmony and its library
The Heidelberg library
A truly sociable establishment
Better baths in summer
Sparest much in books
Less danger of thieves
In later years a servant to keep
Nothing is περιμάχητογ (the play)
A nicer table in later years
A very good supper-place

[SW, XVI, 1942, 153 f.]

At the time, it should be said, he was hestitating between Frankfurt and Mannheim as the place in which to live. Having drawn up this list, he did the logical thing and settled among the 'Shopkeepers and Moneymakers' (his words) of Frankfurt, where his routine in later years included dining at the Englischer Hof (of course!) at one o'clock; Wallace reported that:

> It was noticed that for some time he had each day put down on the table a gold coin, which he afterwards replaced in his pocket, but it was not easy to guess the import of the action. It turned out that it was in consequence of a wager he had made to himself to pay the sum over to the poor-box the first day the officers there talked of anything besides horses, dogs, and women. Schopenhauer's idea was probably not original: a book of sketches of travel (*Bilder aus Helvetien*, &c.) by the poet Matthisson, published in 1816, tells the same story of an Englishman at Innsbruck in 1799.[18]

The story is interesting because it shows Schopenhauer acting the Englishman, something he was prone to do. Having dined, he would take his daily constitutional. If someone walking in the opposite direction veered to the left when passing him, he was liable to remark, in a voice loud enough to be heard, 'Why don't the blockheads turn to the right? An Englishman always turns to the right.'[19] After his walk he would repair to the reading room and *The Times*.

On the continent the English attitude towards animals, particularly dogs, is proverbial. Certainly it is true that Schopenhauer 'counted it among the glories of Englishmen that they had organized a society such as that of [the] "Prevention of Cruelty to Animals", and was himself an energetic promoter of similar schemes in Germany'.[20] His life and works alike testify to his love of animals, particularly dogs. In addition to a Tibetan gilt-bronze Buddha on a marble stand in one corner of the room, his study contained Hagemann's bust of Kant, an oil portrait of Goethe, and some sixteen canine portraits which may reflect his reading, in 1829, of Thomas Brown's newly published *Biographical Sketches and Authentic Anecdotes of Dogs* (*SW*, XVI, 147). From his student days at Göttingen onwards he had a succession of poodles. As Francis Hueffer wrote:

> The only companions of his solitude were his poodle and his books. With the former he lived on terms of intimacy, observing with keen interest its canine individuality; only in cases of exceptional ill-behaviour the opprobrious epithet of 'man' was applied to it.[21]

His favourite poodle, in the 1840s, was Atma, whose name nicely combined his owner's attachment to Buddhism with a swipe at the Hegelian *Weltgeist*. His last dog, Butz, was known to the children of the neighbourhood in Frankfurt am Main, who would see him looking out of the window, as 'young Schopenhauer'. Curiously enough, Arthur Schopenhauer's relationship with his dog(s) is prefigured when his mother writes of her impressions of Frederick the Great's palace of Sans-Souci:

> Near the palace . . . I observed several small grave-stones . . . They marked the tombs of the beautiful greyhounds which had once been the four-footed favourites of the ruler of millions, and whom he, in bitter feelings of discontent, had frequently declared to be 'his only real friends'. How gloomily and heavily must his contempt for mankind have pressed down his haughty soul, when he expressed a wish to be buried here in the midst of his dogs. Many a man might look with envy on the treatment these creatures received: they led a luxurious life and slept on soft beds. They enjoyed unbounded freedom in the king's rooms, as the sofas and chairs testified . . . The page who waited on them . . . even addressed them in the third person plural.[22]

English Literature

The supposedly English virtues of Schopenhauer's work are the product both of a remarkable command of colloquial English, and of a wide knowledge of English literature, some of it acquired before he went to Mr Lancaster's, but much of it facilitated by the improved command of English which he owed to the 'parson terrorist' of Wimbledon. We have seen that his childhood was spent in a house whose shelves included much English literature, especially novels. Paradoxicaly his own knowledge of English literature was weakest in the field of the novel, although he did have some very firm favourites among the English novelists, notably Sterne, Goldsmith and Scott. His library of English literature included the complete works of Burns, Byron, Gay, Goldsmith, Gray, Milton, Peter Pindar, Pope, Scott and Shakespeare, as well as most of Smollett and Sterne. Writers represented in his library by individual works included James Beresford, Boswell, Dickens, Isaac D'Israeli, Dryden, Fielding, Samuel Johnson, Ben Jonson, Lady Mary

Wortley Montagu, Thomas Paine, Percy, Shelley, William Shenstone and Swift.

The English philosophers (Bacon, Berkeley, Hobbes, Hume, Locke, Priestly, Adam Smith and others) naturally loom large both in his library and in his survey of the History of Philosophy, his favourite unquestionably being 'the great David Hume' (*P&P*, 'Fragments of a History of Philosophy'), with whom he identified for a variety of reasons, among them the fact that 'Even as clear and popular a writer as David Hume was fifty years old before people began to pay any attention to him, although his works had been produced many years earlier' (*P&P*, 'On Philosophy at the Universities'). Philosophical works in English in his library included Berkeley's *Works* (2 vols, 1843); most of Hume; Locke's *On the Conduct of the Understanding* (new edn, 1799), *An Essay concerning Human Understanding* (1753) and *Two Treatises of Government* (1772); James Beattie's *Essays on the Nature and Immutability of Truth* (1744); Burke's *A Philosophical Enquiry into the Origin of our Ideas of the Sublime and Beautiful* (1792); Joseph Priestley's *Disquisitions relating to Matter and Spirit* (1782); Thomas Reid's *An Inquiry into the Human Mind* (1764); Shaftesbury's *Characteristics* (1790); and Adam Smith's *Essays on Philosophical Subjects* (1799) and *The Theory of Moral Sentiments* (1793; in his copy he noted, 'His is therefore a very gentlemanly system of morals, placing us on the footing of good company' (*HN*, V, 165 f.).

His library of English philosophy and literature was very much a working library. References to his favourite English philosophers are omnipresent in his works; this is a subject which is sufficiently well known. So far as English literature is concerned, there are references in *Die Welt als Wille und Vorstellung* to Burns, Byron, Johnson, Paine, Scott, Shakespeare, Shenstone, Southey, Swift and Wordsworth. In *Parerga und Paralipomena* he refers to James Beresford, Bulwer Lytton, Byron, Goldsmith, Johnson, Jonson, Milton, Pope, Richardson, Scott, Shakespeare, Shenstone, Sterne and Swift. In addition to his beloved Sterne, it is the writers who feature in both his main works that concern us here: Byron, Johnson, Scott, Shakespeare, Shenstone and Swift.

It is surprising that Schopenhauer failed to present himself to Byron in Venice in November 1818. He was, after all, carrying a letter of introduction to the man who was not only one of his favourite poets but also his sister's idol. Whether he was also carrying T. Martyn's *The gentleman's guide in his tour through Italy* (1787) is not recorded. Robert von Hornstein recalled Schopenhauer relating how he came to spurn the opportunity to meet Byron:

> I was carrying a letter of recommendation to Byron from Goethe . . . I was continually on the point of calling on him with Goethe's letter, when one day I gave up the intention. I was walking in the Lido with my inamorata, when she exclaimed in the greatest excitement: 'Ecco il poëta inglese!' Byron rushed past me on horseback, and for the rest of the day my lady could not forget the impression he had made on her. I thereupon decided not to deliver Goethe's letter. I was afraid of becoming jealous of him. How greatly I have regretted it ever since! [SW, XVI, 258]

Byron for his part was shortly to find himself enslaved by the charms of the Countess Guiccioli. Schopenhauer sighed with him: 'The more I see of men, the less I like them; if I could but say so of women too, all would be well.'[23] In his copy of Byron's *Works* (Frankfurt, 1826) he marked the lines from 'Stanzas to . . . ' which he quoted and, in his own words, 'did his best' to translate in a letter to Frauenstädt dated 2 March 1849:

> In the desert a fountain is springing,
> In the wide waste there still is a tree
> And a bird in the solitude singing,
> That speaks to my spirit of thee.

> In der Wüste ist doch eine Quelle
> In der weiten Oede — ein Baum,
> Und ein Vöglein, singend so helle,
> Belebet den einsamen Raum.   [SW, XIV, 636]

His admiration of Byron clearly goes beyond his admiration of individual works such as 'his immortal masterpiece, "Cain"', just as it goes beyond his sympathy for a fellow iconoclast and pessimist. The fact is that Schopenhauer felt a real sense of kinship with Byron, whom he sees as having given beautiful expression to a philosophy similar to his own. This is why, in one of his most important and characteristic chapters, that on 'The Vanity and Suffering of Life' (*WWI*, III, 382   401), he quotes these lines from the fourth canto of Byron's 'Grotto of Egeria':

> Our life is a false nature, — 'tis not in
> The harmony of things, this hard decree,
> This uneradicable taint of sin,
> This boundless Upas, this all-blasting tree
> Whose root is earth, whose leaves and branches be
> The skies, which rain their plagues on men like dew —
> Disease, death, bondage — all the woes we see —
> And worse, the woes we see not — which throb through
> The immedicable soul, with heart-aches ever new.

Byron here expresses Schopenhauer's most fundamental belief, that life is at bottom something which ought not to be. This explains why he is quoted at this crucial point, and why Schopenhauer admired him so greatly.

Both *Die Welt als Wille und Vorstellung* and *Parerga und Paralipomena* contain a wide range of references to Shakespeare, whom Schopenhauer describes as a genius whose intuitive, experiential wisdom makes him one of the greatest minds the world has seen; he is one of the two great dramatic poets of modern times, 'much greater than Sophocles'. These are the judgements of one who knew his Shakespeare uncommonly well from a very early age; he probably knew him well even before he went to Wimbledon, and no doubt also read him while there. Shakespeare is part of an extensive tissue of literary quotation which is one of the unique features of Schopenhauer's philosophy, which is not only singularly lucid but also extraordinarily literate. Shakespeare is appropriated and incorporated into that philosophy, for what are the lines 'We are such stuff / As dreams are made on' but an expression of the 'world as idea'? Shakespeare is praised for the 'perfect metaphysical insight' of these lines from Schopenhauer's best-loved Shakespearean play, *Hamlet*:

> we fools of nature
> So horridly to shake our disposition,
> With thoughts beyond the reaches of our souls.

There are indeed, Schopenhauer agrees, 'more things in heaven and earth than are dreamt of in your philosophy'. He agreed, too, with Shakespeare's conception of fate and character — agreed, that is, that 'What is decreed must be' (*Twelfth Night*). Like Shakespeare, Schopenhauer sees man as a strolling player in the theatre of life.

After Shakespeare and Byron one of Schopenhauer's favourite

English poets was the poet-turned-landscape-gardener and contemporary of Dr Johnson, William Shenstone (1714-63). He possessed Shenstone's *Essays on Men and Manners* (London: J. Cundee, 1802) and *The Poetical Works* (Cooke's edition. *c.* 1800). No doubt it was the good sense and graceful style of the *Essays* which appealed to him; his copy of the work was heavily annotated, and he frequently quoted from it the maxim 'Liberty is a better cordial than Tokay'. This slightly surprising taste for Shenstone's work is, I think, partly explicable by the date of publication of Schopenhauer's copies of the works, which suggests that he bought both the *Essays* and the *Poetical Works* in 1803 and that they therefore acquired sentimental value for him. It seems likely that in 1803 he spent at the London booksellers some of the pocket money which he collected from Mr Drewe. We know from his mother's letters that he was already very keen on poetry at this time. While some of the editions of English poets in his library date from a later period (Byron, *The Works*, 1826; Gay, *The Poetical Works*, 1811; 'Ossian', 1805), it is a fact that most of his editions of the English poets date from 1803 or earlier (Burns, *The Works*, 3 vols, 1800; Goldsmith, *The Poetical Works*, 1796; Gray, *The Poetical Works*, n.d. [1798?]; Milton, *The Poetical Works*, 2 vols, 1731; Percy, *Reliques*, 3 vols, 1803; Pindar, *The Works*, 4 vols, 1794-6; Pope, *The Works in nine volumes*, 5 vols only, 1803; John Roach, *Beauties of the modern Poets*, 3 vols, 1793; Shenstone). It seems likely that Schopenhauer bought most of these editions in 1803. This in turn means both that his knowledge of the English poets was remarkable for a 15-year-old, and that his knowledge of English literature was, on the whole, more static than has been realised.

Schopenhauer's attachment to *Tristam Shandy* went back to his childhood and was inherited from his mother; but if Johanna Schopenhauer was so attached to *Tristram Shandy* for its sentimentality and because she identified Yorick with the childhood mentor of whom she was so fond, her son will have had other reasons for his predilection. The fact that he did not think so highly of Sterne's *Sentimental Journey* (in *P&P* he said that to think that life is a romance which breaks off in the middle, like the *Sentimental Journey*, is aesthetically and morally unacceptable) shows that the appeal of *Tristram Shandy* was not simply its sentimentality. In 'On the Metaphysics of the Beautiful' (*P&P*) he implies that *Tristram Shandy* is the acme of the novel; but what appeals to him is not Sterne's technical originality so much as the originality of his mind and attitudes. He was given to quoting Sterne's 'an ounce of a man's own wit is worth a ton of other people's', which speaks for itself, but there is more to it than that, for he also wrote — in English, in the margin of his copy of Boswell's *Life of Samuel Johnson* — that 'The man Sterne is worth 1000 Pedants and commonplace-fellows like Dr. J.' This brings us to the real point, which is that, in the context of *The Life and Opinions of Tristram Shandy*, originality amounts not only to unorthodoxy, but to opposition to orthodoxy and therefore to bigotry. The very fact that Schopenhauer contrasted Sterne and Johnson shows that he — rightly — thought of them as opposites. Since he regarded Dr Johnson as a bigoted ass, it follows that Sterne's utter open-mindedness was much to his taste. Not only are the two longest chapters in the novel (Trim's sermon and Slawkenbergius's tale) concerned with the bigotry of the orthodox clergy, but, even more significantly, the whole novel, which breathes tolerance, is implicitly concerned with the same thing. And the bigotry of the orthodox (Anglican) clergy was as much Schopenhauer's hobby-horse as the arts of fortification were Uncle Toby's. He was obsessed by it, as his vitriolic comments on Samuel Johnson — and on the Anglican clergy — show. Lichtenberg condemned Sterne as a 'scandalum ecclesiae'; no doubt it was precisely this that Schopenhauer appreciated. He also shared, to a marked degree, Sterne's delight in ridiculing pedantry.

It is, of course, impossible to separate the originality of Sterne's method from the originality of his perceptions, which is why the Shandean method was adopted by those who had anti-orthodox ideas to express. This applies as much to Schopenhauer's own *magnum opus* as it does to the novels of Wieland and Nicolai. The continual literary allusions and quotations from Schopenhauer's miscellaneous reading (often in English) in *Die Welt als Wille und Vorstellung* not only serve to underline the non-academic nature of his philosophy; they are also 'Shandean' digressions which underline the idiosyncrasy of his (or anyone else's) mind. *Tristram Shandy*, let us remember, was written in accordance with Locke's view of the association of ideas as an irrational process, something in which Schopenhauer was interested. The whimsy of the novel, which appealed more strongly to Schopenhauer than it did to most of his fellow countrymen, reflects the wayward ways of the human mind. After *Tristram Shandy* itself *Die Welt als Wille und Vorstellung* is the most Shandean of works.

Although the primary appeal of *Tristram Shandy* to Arthur Schopenhauer was not, therefore, what has been called its 'shameless sentimentality', Sterne's power of sentimentality will not have been without its appeal. Neither will the fact that Sterne is the most patently English of all English humorists. Nor again will the 'bewitching enormity of human eccentricity' in this most English of novels have been without its appeal to one whose parts were not only exceptionally good but also more eccentric than most. The risibility of so much in the novel will have been very much to Schopenhauer's taste, despite its total lack of the sarcastic and sardonic, in which he was wont to indulge himself from an early age.

And so we come back to what Wieland called the 'sheer paganism'[24] of the novel, which is not only marked by a defiance of fate, but which also contains the starting point of Schopenhauer's philosophy:

> When I reflect . . . upon Man; and take a view of that dark side of him which represents his life as open to so many causes of trouble — when I consider . . . how oft we eat the bread of affliction, and that we are born to it, as to the portion of our inheritance . . . When one runs over the catalogue of all the cross-reckonings and sorrowful Items with which the heart of man is overcharged, 'tis wonderful by what hidden resources the mind is enabled to stand out, and bear itself up, as it does, against the impositions laid upon our nature. [Book IV, Chapter 6]

Schopenhauer's other early favourite among English novelists was Goldsmith, whose *Vicar of Wakefield* he later described as one of the few exceptional novels which do not foist on to naive youth a false view of life. Otherwise *The Vicar of Wakefield* appealed to him for the same reasons that it appealed so strongly to writers of the previous generation. In a letter to Hamann dated from Riga on 5 September 1767 Herder, who knew and loved it, described *The Vicar of Wakefield* as 'magic, full of knowledge of the world, criticism, artistry and such gentle humour that on a third reading I am still finding things in it which I missed on previous readings'.[25] He went on to read it for a fourth time, describing it to Karoline Flachsland, in January 1771, as 'one of the most beautiful books in any language'.[26] For Goethe, who no doubt discussed it with Johanna Schopenhauer, whose favouite novel it was, it was remarkable above all, for its good-humoured irony.

Both *Tristram Shandy* and *The Vicar of Wakefield* are novels which held their greatest appeal for German writers of Johanna Schopenhauer's generation. They are novels, the taste for which

Arthur Schopenhauer inherited from his parents. With Walter Scott it was different, for he was introduced into Germany, by Tieck, only in 1818. Schopenhauer got to know his work in the 1820s and came to regard him — with so many Germans of the Romantic generation — as *the* great British novelist. He calls him 'the incomparable Sir Walter Scott' (*P&P*) and refers to *The Tales of My Landlord*, the first three series of which (I: *The Black Dwarf, Old Mortality*; II: *The Heart of Midlothian, Rob Roy*; III: *The Bride of Lammermoor, The Legend of Montrose*) he possessed, as 'the most interesting fictional work I know', adding, 'this novel depicts the most varied scenes with remarkable veracity and introduces divers characters which are true to life and precisely drawn' (see *HN*, III, 67). In other words, he saw Scott's works as Shakespearean. Given his enthusiasm for Shakespeare, he could say no more. In the present context, however, the real significance of Schopenhauer's delighted discovery of Scott is that the Waverley novels helped to keep his Anglophilia burning bright.

No more than a suggestive curiosity among his English books was James Beresford's *The Miseries of Human Life*, the eleventh edition (1826) of which he possessed, and to which he refers in *Parerga und Paralipomena*; he does not seem to have known the early German translation (*Menschliches Elend*, Bayreuth, 1810). James Beresford (1764-1840), fellow of Merton College, Oxford, was also responsible for an edition of *Popular Tales of the Germans* (2 vols, 1791). Schopenhauer does not appear to have reacted strongly to *The Miseries of Human Life*, which he may well have considered flippant; he was possibly misled into buying it by the title. Be that as it may, it was appropriate that the last book he read, on the eve of his death, was Isaac D'Israeli's *Curiosities of Literature* (Vol. I, 1834), and his last word on life was a note which he wrote — in English — in his copy of the book, and which read, 'Death shows that life is not worth our while & we leave our pursuits and their success behind us, as the toys and the dresses of our childhood, for others to play with' (*HN*, V, 458).

Of the writers who might be thought most likely to appeal to him — Swift, Fielding and Peacock — there is either relatively little sign, or no sign at all, in Schopenhauer's library and writings. It is true that he possessed both *A Tale of a Tub* (1734) and *Travels into Several Remote Nations of the World by Lemuel Gulliver* (2 vols, Paris, 1804), but there is no sign, in terms of annotations, of any particular reaction to them. Of Fielding's works he possessed only *The History of Tom Jones* (1791). Of Peacock, with whom he had a good deal in common, he seems to have known nothing, probably because he was a contemporary of Peacock and his knowledge of English literature was essentially static.

In comparing young Arthur Schopenhauer to Sir Oran Haut-ton in the last chapter I was thinking not only of the remark made by one of his father's employees at his birth ('Wenn er dem Papa ähnlich wird, muss er ein schöner Pavian werden'), and not only of his penchant for flute-playing and gymnastics, but also of how much Schopenhauer and Peacock have in common. They were both keen readers of Buffon and great admirers of the orang-utan, so that with the evidence of Peacock's *Melincourt* we may compare the following story:

> Schopenhauer was highly amused at the fair held in Frankfurt in 1857, when a live orang-outang, then a rarity in Europe, was exhibited. He went almost daily to see 'the probable ancestor of our race', regretting that he had been forced to defer making his personal acquaintance so long. He urged all his friends not to let this opportunity slip by. He was especially struck with its expression, which had not the maliciousness of a monkey's, and by the head, whose frontal bone and *os verticus* were decidedly better formed than those of the lowest human races; neither did it betray the animal in its gestures. He thought the longing of the Will after cognition was personified in this strange and melancholy beast, and compared his mien to that of the prophet gazing over into the Promised Land.[27]

Leaving aside their fascination with the orang-utan, which was very much the reverse side of their attitude towards man, they have many attitudes in common. Thus they were both very outspoken on the subject of their least favourite philosophers, and if these philosophers were not the same, their real objection was to the 'central opacity' which one (Peacock) associated with Kant and the other (Schopenhauer) with Hegel. Both were given to quoting Byron's 'Our life is a false nature', and there is no reason to think that Peacock was less in earnest than Schopenhauer when he did so. Like Peacock, Schopenhauer ignored fashion and continued to dress in the formal manner customary in his early years; he always wore tails and white tie for dinner. Both men were brilliant — and largely self-taught — classicists, as well as great ironists. And so on. I should perhaps add that although Schopenhauer apparently did not know

Peacock's work, Peacock must have known of Schopenhauer's, for he was a subscriber to the *Westminster Review*; but this is not to say that he read it, for he embodied the English view of the German metaphysics which he held in such slight regard. Like Peacock, Schopenhauer read both the *Westminster Review* and the *Edinburgh Review* (of which he had a lower opinion than Peacock). He also regularly read the *Quarterly Review*, the *Athenaeum* and *The Times*. This reading was an essential part of his daily routine, in the English manner, as were his *idées fixes*, one of which concerned Dr Johnson.

With his high seriousness and High Toryism, Samuel Johnson was a man after Thomas Lancaster's heart. Was not the worthy doctor a loyal churchman, an ex-schoolmaster and a great man? Was he not a friend of Burke, whose views on the French Revolution Thomas Lancaster so emphatically shared? Was he not the very model of the Christian gentleman, and therefore the very opposite of the godless David Hume? William Agutter's famous sermon of 1786 contrasting the deathbeds of the godly doctor and the ungodly philosopher must have powerfully impressed Parson Lancaster when his young cousin gave him an account of it shortly before his tragic death. One can imagine Dr Johnson's devoutness being held up to the boys of the Rev. Lancaster's academy as a shining example worthy of emulation. Indeed, it is by no means unlikely that Schopenhauer's intemperate dislike of Dr Johnson, *and* his unqualified approval of Hume, had such an origin; at all events, Johnson was clearly associated in his mind with those aspects of Hanoverian Anglicanism which he learnt to detest at Wimbledon. He possessed the 1848 edition of Boswell's *Life of Samuel Johnson*, but he knew Johnson's work well before 1848, as *Die Welt als Wille und Vorstellung* shows, and the attitudes which he expresses in the extraordinary annotations in his copy of Boswell's *Johnson* are those which became fixed in his mind following his experiences at Wimbledon.

Schopenhauer's basic view of Samuel Johnson is summed up in a note opposite the half-title page of his *Life of Samuel Johnson*. The annotation reads, 'This Dr. Johnson is a true pattern of that old-fashioned, truism-dealing, commonplace, narrow-minded set of Pedants, which, 80 years ago, had reach'd its height in Engld.' Beneath this is a postscript: 'Above all, mind, that bigotry is an infallible sign of a narrow-limited [*sic*] understanding. And Johnson was as bigoted as an old woman.' It seems likely that the annotations, of which this is the first, were written, like the references to Dr Johnson in Schopenhauer's letters, in the last year of his life. What is abundantly clear is that the set of pedants in question included Thomas Lancaster, whose beginnings as a schoolmaster dated from precisely eighty years previously. The category was probably designed with the Rev. Lancaster in mind. I have no doubt at all that Thomas Lancaster was in Schopenhauer's mind when he inscribed that note. The language is that which a clever, precocious schoolboy might use to deride a conservative, clerical schoolmaster a good deal less quick-witted than himself, quite apart from showing how well the English which he learnt at Wimbledon has lasted. The intemperate nature of the philosopher's language is readily — and only — explicable in terms of having had Dr Johnson's example rammed down his throat by that other Hanoverian pedant, Thomas Lancaster.

This annotation is typical of many which appear in the same volume (see *HN*, V, 451 ff.). In subsequent marginal jottings Dr Johnson is described as 'a philistine', 'an ass', 'a bigoted rascal', a 'pedant and commonplace-fellow', 'a bigotted priest-ridden, narrow-minded fellow', 'a vile scribbler', 'vulgar', 'an arch-Anglican ass', and so on. The doctor's work is dismissed a 'mere mechanical drudgery'. At one point Schopenhauer sides with Joseph Priestley against Johnson, no doubt because Priestley was a radical and a staunch opponent of the Established Church of England, although Schopenhauer's approval of Priestley's *Disquisition on Matter and Spirit* (1777) will have been not unconnected with the work's indebtedness to Kant. Priestley will have been anathema to Thomas Lancaster, who knew him.

The only complimentary reference to Samuel Johnson comes when Schopenhauer remarks, in 'What a Man has' (in *P&P*) that Dr Johnson 'agrees with my opinion' that:

> A woman of fortune being used to the handling of money, spends it judiciously; but a woman who gets the command of money for the first time upon her marriage, has such a gusto in spending it, that she throws it away with great profusion.[28]

Among the English books in Schopenhauer's library there were some surprising titles. I am thinking, in particular, of the *Works* of Peter Pindar (4 vols, 1794-6; he lacked the subsequent fifth volume) and several works by Thomas Paine (*The Age of Reason*, Paris, 1794; *Letter addressed to the People on the Advantages of the French Revolution*, 1795; *The Rights of Man*, 2 parts, 1795). While young Schopenhauer went in for sarcasm, and was no respecter of persons, let alone parsons, the rather repetitive works of a satirist, many of whose targets cannot have been all that well known to his young German reader, are not an obvious choice. Nor, given his near-total lack of interest in politics, are the works of the radical pamphleteer. Assuming that Schopenhauer bought these works in England in 1803 (which need not be the case, for his father could have bought them in 1797, which would account for the absence of the fifth volume of Pindar, which was published in 1801), we need to account for his interest in the work of these popular but second-rate writers.

Peter Pindar is mentioned twice in Johanna Schopenhauer's travel diary, where he is called 'the celebrated English poet'. Evidently the Schopenhauer family knew his satires directed against the King. Pindar's verse was evidently to Arthur Schopenhauer's taste, for it chimed in with his own penchant for satire and the telling phrase: in particular he will have greatly relished Pindar's vitriolic anticlerical satires such as 'The Parson Dealer'. At Mr Lancaster's academy young Schopenhauer was exposed not only to his headmaster's Sunday sermons but to his daily homilies. Given that Parson Lancaster cultivated the great and the good, or, rather, those whose goodness consisted in their greatness, and given that Wimbledon was valiant in plot and pot, it is inevitable that his homilies will have included frequent references to Pitt, Dundas, Jenkinson & co. In order to get his own back, is it not likely that Schopenhauer, on one of his weekly visits to London, bought the works of the satirist whose principal butts were Parson Lancaster's political heroes and indeed clergymen like Parson Lancaster himself, who, as we have seen, may well have been discomfited at this time by meeting 'Peter Pindar' at Merton Place? I have no doubt that such was the case, since even the most casual glance through the volumes at John Walker's (44 Paternoster Row) would have shown him that 'Pindar' was amusingly outspoken on precisely those things which were making life so intolerable for him: the English clergy and the 'prim, and starch, and silent'[29] English Sunday. What the Rev. Lancaster called 'a strict observance of the holy Sabbath' Schopenhauer came to deride as English 'Jewish Sabbatarianism'. In 1803, when he was being subjected to regular misery for the first time in his life, it must have brought relief to find Pindar writing:

> Thus did the royal mandate, through the town,
> Knock nearly all the Sunday concerts down!
> Great act! ere long 'twill be a sin and a shame

For cats to warble out an am'rous flame!
Dogs shall be whipp'd for making love on Sunday,
Who very well may put it off to Monday.[30]

Indeed, Peter Pindar's attacks on his own bugbears would have been enough by themselves to account for the way in which he evidently relished Pindar's work.

Much the same goes for Tom Paine. Wimbledon in the years after the French Revolution attracted not only Tories but Jacobins, not only King's Friends but also the King's enemies. Of the latter none was more notorious than that frequent visitor to Wimbledon, Tom Paine. His very name will have been anathema to Parson Lancaster, in whose sermons and homilies alike Paine must have figured as the veritable Antichrist. Did young Arthur Schopenhauer respond by going out and buying Paine's works? It is likely that he did, and certain that his interest in Paine had to do with the latter's atheism as such.

Two of Schopenhauer's favourite philosophers were anathema to Thomas James Mathias and, no doubt, to Thomas Lancaster: Voltaire and Hume. In *The Pursuits of Literature* Mathias recorded his view that 'All the minor powers of infidelity, anarchy, sedition, rebellion and democracy' derive from Voltaire,[31] while Hume is described as having 'set up . . . a slop-shop of morality in the suburbs of Atheism'.[32] Despite Voltaire being Heinrich Floris Schopenhauer's favourite philosopher, it is probably fanciful to imagine his son reading Voltaire and Hume while at Mr Lancaster's, although his interest in them may have been spurred by Mr Lancaster's disapproval of them. No doubt the phrase 'infame Bigotterie', to which Johanna Schopenhauer objected, reflected his father's adulation of Voltaire, for Arthur Schopenhauer shared his father's veneration for 'the great Voltaire' and especially for his 'immortal *Candide*', while what he loathed was precisely what Voltaire called 'l'infâme'. For him, Voltaire and Hume together overthrew the theodicies which had propped up theism (see *WWI*, III, 404).

English Bigotry

In assessing the impressions that Arthur Schopenhauer carried away from Wimbledon in 1803, we must remember that he was at the time a highly impressionable, hypersensitive 15-year-old. Having previously spent the happiest part of his childhood at Le Havre, he was bound to react against England, particularly in view of his father's hyper-sentimental attitude towards the country and the fact that he felt cheated in being sent off to an academy while his parents enjoyed the tour he had been promised. What he found at the Rev. Mr Lancaster's none the less horrified him. It was not the alien routines and mechanical style of instruction that irked him most. Within a matter of hours he seems to have taken a violent dislike to his English headmaster and everything he stood for. His first Sunday at Wimbledon School was the last straw; the intolerable routine of the late Georgian boarding-school Sunday, for which nothing had prepared him and everything had made him unprepared, was for him the sign of what he immediately called 'infamous bigotry'. He scorned the cant and hypocrisy that he associated with his headmaster, and was appalled by the fact that the kind of 'education' to which he found himself subjected was not so much education as brainwashing. It was this brainwashing, he came to feel, that explained the bigotry.

Schopenhauer's intemperately expressed dislike of English ecclesiastical superstition, and the narrow-mindedness and the Church-ridden nature of the country's institutions (particularly its educational system), was to be repeated throughout his work for the rest for his life. He carried away from Wimbledon an unfavourable impression not only of the English boarding-school system but of the English national character as such, of which he considered the former to be symptomatic. As W. Wallace remarked, 'Like most foreigners . . . he was struck by a prevalent tone of cant and hypocrisy, and by the predominance of ecclesiastical interests in ordinary life.'[33] That is a considerable understatement, as is best shown by some notably pithy annotations in English which adorn the pages of not a few of the works of English literature in his library. Particularly striking examples include a note in his copy of James Boswell, *Life of Samuel Johnson*(1848), to the effect that 'This Dr. Johnson is a true pattern of that old-fashioned, truism-dealing, commonplace, narrow-minded set of Pedants, which, 80 years ago, had reach'd its height in Engld. Above all, mind, that bigotry is an infallible sign of a narrow limited understanding. And Johnson was as bigoted as an old woman.' There are many similar annotations (*HN*, V, 451 ff.). His copy of R.C. Dallas, *Recollections of the Life of Lord Byron* (1824), is similarly adorned with a note reading, 'Vile & degrading English bigotry' (ibid., 455). And so on.

His view of the English clergy corresponds exactly with the view expressed in his edition of Peter Pindar's *Works*, most obviously in the poem 'The Parson 'Dealer':

What pity 'tis, in this our goodly land,
Amongst the apostolic band,
  So ill divided are the loaves and fishes!
Archbishops, Bishops, Deans, and Deacons,
With ruddy faces blazing just like beacons,
  Shall daily cram upon a dozen dishes;
Whilst half th' inferior Cassocks think it well,
Of beef and pudding ev'n to get the *smell*.

A plodding Hostler willing to be Master,
And rise in this good world a little faster,
  Left broom and manger at the Old Blue Boar;
Meaning by *pars'ning* to support a table,
Lo, of Divines he kept a liv'ry stable;
  A pretty stud, indeed — about a score.

Of diff'rent colours were his Gospel hacks;
Some few were whites, indeed — but many blacks:
  That is, some tolerable — many sad;
And verily, to give the Devil his due,
The man did decency pursue,
  Which shows he was not *quite* so bad.

For, lo! to dying persons of nobility,
He sent his parsons of *gentility*,
  To give the necessary pray'r:
To parting people of a *mean* condition,
Wanting a soul physician,
  He suited them with blackguards to a hair.

To such as were of mild disorders dying,
  Viz. of the doctor, gouts, or stones, or gravels,
He sent *good* priests — of manners edifying —
  To comfort sinners on their travels:

But to *low* people in infectious fever,
  Or any other dangerous one in vogue,
Such was his honesty, the man for ever
  Most scrupulously sent a *rogue*.

It happen'd, on a day when FATE was raging,
Crimp-like, for other regions, troops engaging,
   When clergyman were busy all as bees,
A poor old dying woman sent
To this same parson-monger, compliment,
   Begging a clergyman her soul to ease.

Unluckily but *one* was in the stall,
And *he* the very best of all —
   What should be done?
Necessitas non habet legs —
So to the priest he goes, and begs
   That he would visit the old crone.

'Sir,' quoth the parson, 'I agreed
'To go to *gentlefolks* in time of need,
   'But not to ev'ry poor old lousy soul.' —
'True,' cry'd the patron; 'to be sure 'tis true:
'But, parson, do oblige me — prithee do —
   'Let's put her decently into the hole:

'All my black tribe, you know, are now abroad —
'I'd do it, if I could, *myself*, by G-d;'
   'Then what a dickens can I do or say?'
'Go, mumble, man, about a pray'r and half;
'Tell the old b——ch her soul is safe;
   'Then take your fee, and come away!!!'[34]

Much of what Schopenhauer was to criticise so virulently in the English clergy is criticised by Pindar. It is therefore hardly surprising that Pindar's work was relished by Schopenhauer, whose own comments on the English clergy, so strikingly similar, can only reflect his first-hand experience of them in the person of the Rev. Thomas Lancaster. When he writes of the 'crude and narrow-minded English *reverend*' (*P&P*, 'On Ethics', sect. 116; Schopenhauer's English italicised) he must have had Thomas Lancaster in mind. His view is static because he always thinks of the same person, an old-fashioned cleric belonging to the period of the 'fat slumbers' (Gibbon) of the Church of England. His comments are too frequently repeated and too outspokenly expressed to be ignored. What follows is but a sample:

After-Effects

There is no Church that dreads the light more than the Church of England, for no other has such great pecuniary interests at stake, its income amounting to £5 million sterling, which is said to be £40,000 more than the income of the whole of the remaining Christian clergy of both hemispheres put together. On the other hand, there is no nation which it is so painful to see methodically stupefied by the most degrading blind faith as the English, who surpass all others in point of intelligence. The root of the trouble is that there is no Ministry of education, so that this has remained in the hands of the parsons, who have taken care that two-thirds of the nation shall not be able to read and write; indeed, from time to time they had even had the confounded impertinence to yelp at the natural sciences. It is, therefore, a duty to humanity to smuggle into England, through every conceivable channel, light, open-mindedness and scientific knowledge, in order to put paid to the handiwork of those best-fed of all priests. When educated Englishmen display on the continent their Jewish Sabbatarian superstition and other forms of asinine bigotry they should be treated with undisguised contempt, *until they be shamed into common sense*, for such things are a scandal to Europe and should no longer be tolerated. Therefore one ought never, in the ordinary way, to make the least concession to English ecclesiastical superstition, but promptly stand up to it in the most caustic and trenchant manner wherever it raises its ugly head. For the effrontery of these Anglican parsons and their slavish followers is quite incredible, even at the present time; it should therefore be confined to its island, and whenever it ventures to show itself on the continent it should at once be made to play the role of the owl by day. [*P&P* 'Sketch of a History of Ideal and Real'; Schopenhauer's English italicised]

It is high time that missions of reason, enlightenment and anticlericalism were dispatched to [this island of prejudice and priestly imposture] with v. Bohlen's and Strauss's biblical criticism in one hand and the *Critique of Pure Reason* in the other, in order to put a spoke in the wheel of those self-styled *reverend* parsons, the most arrogant and impudent in the world, and accordingly to put an end to the scandal. Meanwhile we may put our trust in steamships and railways, which are just as favourable to the exchange of ideas as to that of goods, whereby they greatly imperil the vulgar bigotry which is nurtured in England with such cunning solicitude and sways even the upper classes . . . That by the crudest bigotry those parsons totally degrade the most intelligent of nations, which is in almost every respect the first in Europe, and thus make it an object of *contempt*, is something that should no longer be tolerated, particularly when one bears in mind the means by which they have attained that end, to wit: by arranging the education of the masses entrusted to them in such a way that two-thirds of the English nation are unable to read . . . Moreover, the real source of that scandalous obscurantism by which the English people are thus deceived is the law of primogeniture, that is, the law that makes it necessary for the aristocracy (in the widest sense) to provide for younger sons. If these are not fit for the navy or army, the *Church Establishment* (characteristic term) with its five million a year affords them a charitable institution. For the young country gentleman *a living* (another very characteristic expression) is thus procured, either through favour or for money. Such livings are very often offered for sale in the newspapers and even by public auction, although for decency's sake they do not sell the actual living, just the right of bestowing it once (*the patronage*). But as this transaction must be completed before the actual vacation of the living, appropriate padding is added to the effect that the present incumbent, for instance, is 77 years of age, and the fine opportunities for hunting and fishing that attach to the living, and the well-appointed vicarage, are invariably emphasised. It is the most shameless simony in the world. From this it is easy to see why in good (meaning genteel) English society all ridicule of the Church and its cold superstition is regarded as being in bad taste . . . in accordance with the maxim 'quand le bon ton arrive, le bon sens se retire'. For this reason, the influence of the parsons in England is so great that, to the lasting disgrace of the English nation, Thorwaldsen's statue of Byron, her greatest poet after the incomparable Shakespeare, was not allowed to be placed in Westminster Abbey, her national Pantheon, alongside her other great men. This was simply because Byron had been honest enough not to make any concessions to Anglican parsondom, but went his own way unhampered by them, whereas the mediocre Wordsworth, the frequent target of his ridicule, had his statue duly installed in Westminster Abbey in 1854.

> By such infamy the English show themselves to be a *stultified and priest-ridden nation*. Europe very rightly laughs at them . . . Voltaire, on the other hand, whose writings were a hundred times more hostile to the Church than Byron's, reposes in glory in the French Pantheon, the Church of Sainte-Geneviève. He had the good fortune to belong to a nation that does not allow itself to be led by the nose and ruled by parsons. The effects of this priestly imposture and bigotry are inevitably demoralizing. It is bound to be demoralizing when parsons tell the people a pack of lies to the effect that half the virtues consist in spending Sundays in idleness and rattling off automatic responses in church, and that one of the greatest vices, paving the way for all the others, is *Sabbath-breaking*, that is, failing to spend Sundays in idleness. Thus in those papers that go in for giving accounts of criminals under sentence of death, they explain that their whole career of crime arose from that same shocking vice of *Sabbath-breaking*. [P&P, 'Essay on Spirit Seeing'; Schopenhauer's English italicised][35]

In view of the outspokenness of Schopenhauer's comments on English simony, it is amusing to note that his father at one stage thought of purchasing him a benefice, only dropping the idea because of the cost!

It needs to be emphasised that all Schopenhauer's later comments on English superstition, bigotry, prejudice, narrow-mindedness and ignorance are elaborations on what he experienced and wrote at the age of 15. Even at that age he was not accustomed to mincing his words; 'infamous bigotry' says it all. In reading his comments we must look beyond his intemperate expression to the basic facts. The first of these facts is that by common consent there was a good deal wrong with the Church of England of George III's time, and especially with the 'hunting' branch of the clergy. It is this that we see embedded in Schopenhauer's works like a fly in amber. His comments are by no means without parallel or without historical justification, while his very outspokenness is arguably a Georgian characteristic.

We also need to remember that, although Schopenhauer later occasionally met English clergymen on their travels in Germany, the only English clergyman whom he knew well was the Rev. Thomas Lancaster. Even the Rev. Herbert Randolph he knew only as a 'pulpit terrorist'. The very fact that his comments on the English clergy, which were repeated *ad nauseam*, showing his

After-Effects

obsession with the subject, remained unchanged — most of his knowledge and criticism of things English remained static, for he never visited the country again; it is only his reading that develops — confirms that the Rev. Lancaster was his model and his real butt. There is a characteristic annotation in which he imagines Mr Lancaster getting the boot. At the end of Chapter LII of Dickens's *Pickwick Papers* there is an incident which Schopenhauer evidently found satisfying, when Mr Weller the elder is driven beyond endurance by the impudence of the Rev. Stiggins:

> when Stiggins stopped for breath, he darted upon him, and snatching the tumbler from his hand, threw the remainder of the rum-and-water in his face, and the glass itself into the grate. Then, seizing the reverend gentleman firmly by the collar, he suddenly fell to kicking him most furiously, accompanying every application of his top-boot to Mr. Stiggins's person, with sundry violent and incoherent anathemas upon his limbs, eyes, and body.
> 'Sammy,' said Mr. Weller, 'put my hat on tight for me.'
> Sam dutifully adjusted the hat with the long hatband more firmly on his father's head, and the old gentleman, resuming his kicking with greater agility than before, tumbled with Mr. Stiggins through the bar, and through the passage, out at the front door, and so into the street — the kicking continuing the whole way, and increasing in vehemence, rather than diminishing, every time the top-boot was lifted.
> It was a beautiful and exhilarating sight to see the red-nosed man writhing in Mr. Weller's grasp,. and his whole frame quivering with anguish as kick followed kick in rapid succession; it was a still more exciting spectacle to behold Mr. Weller, after a powerful struggle, immersing Mr.Stiggins's head in a horse-trough full of water, and holding it there, until he was half suffocated.
> 'There!' said Mr. Weller, throwing all his energy into one most complicated kick, as he at length permitted Mr. Stiggins to withdraw his head from the trough, 'send any vun o' them lazy shepherds here, and I'll pound him to a jelly first, and drown him artervards! Sammy, help me in, and fill me a small glass of brandy. I'm out o'breath, my boy.'

In the margin of his 1842 Tauchnitz edition of *The Pickwick Papers* Schopenhauer wrote, in English, 'The author sheweth here allegorically how the English nation ought to treat that set of hypocrits, imposters and money-graspers, the clergy of the established humbug, that devours annually £3,500,000!' In writing this, 40 years after his term at Wimbledon School, he is showing how he would have liked to treat his English headmaster.

Schopenhauer was by no means the first continental writer to record his distaste for English religiosity and its concomitant vices, although this distaste has never been so intemperately expressed by a writer who remained, in many respects, as pronounced an anglophile as one is likely to meet. Voltaire's 'Ecrasons l'infâme', let us remember, referred not only to Catholicism but to the intolerant fanaticism embodied in any dogmatic, State-sponsored religion, including the anglicanism which he knew from his stay in Wandsworth. Tolerance, on the other hand, was not only an ideal for Voltaire, idolised as he was by Schopenhauer's father; it also loomed large in the ethics taught by Dr Runge. Young Schopenhauer, brought up on freedom and tolerance, was deeply shocked by what he experienced at Mr Lancaster's; Heine referred to 'jenes . . . kirchengängerische England'[36] with exasperation similar to Schopenhauer's. That Schopenhauer at the age of 60 was still as appalled as he had been at 15 by the readiness of the English not only to combine political freedom with moral slavery, but to pride themselves on their superiority while doing so, is hardly surprising.

Schopenhauer and England: Conclusions

From his term at Mr Lancaster's Arthur Schopenhauer gained an anglophobia which was limited to those specific aspects of English life which had made him so miserable there. His statement that he had come to hate the whole nation as a result of his experiences at Wimbledon was a characteristic exaggeration. He continued to detest some aspects of the English national character and of English life, his continual references to them reminding one of nothing so much as Uncle Toby's hobby-horse in *Tristram Shandy*. Schopenhauer's hobby-horses remained with him throughout his life. In due course his basic admiration for England reasserted itself and he retained an old-fashioned anglophilia that was more typical of his parents' generation of sentimental travellers than of his own generation. If, in 1803, it was what he later called the 'vile and degrading English bigotry' (*HN*, V, 455) that was foremost in his mind, this came to be tempered with an equally sincere belief that the English nation was 'the most intelligent in Europe' (*SW*, XIV, 409). This Janus-headed view persists, as can be seen from the *Parerga und Paralipomena* of 1851, and it is precisely his admiration for what he sees as the Englishman's independent-mindedness that leads him again and again to denounce the way in which English education and the English clergy seem to him to be undermining this independent-mindedness, thus reducing the most intelligent of nations to a figure of fun.

If Schopenhauer had merely left Wimbledon with a series of 'maggots', or even with a new view of England and its religion, his three months there would have been of relatively little interest. As it is, I can think of no other writer to have been so profoundly influenced by the experiences of a single term. Indeed, is the work of any other major philosopher so much the product of such rapidly acquired youthful likes and dislikes? What we have just been seeing was only the most immediate and most obvious after-effect. More important is the fact that he conceived a view of education that was completely contrary to that practised by his English headmaster. But there is something yet more important, for a man's view of education is a fundamental part of his view of life, and the attitudes in which Schopenhauer became fixed to such an extraordinary degree following his traumatic experience are important because they include the basic components of the philosophy that was eventually to become famous. His philosophy, when he came to formulate it, shows the pervasive influence of his English reading, is riddled with allusions to his three months in Wimbledon, and is indeed in many ways an 'English' philosophy written in an 'English' style. Above all, it is a philosophy designed as a refutation not only of the by then rampant Hegelianism but of 'Christianity' as understood and practised by the Rev. Thomas Lancaster, who is the invisible *bête noire* behind it. Schopenhauer's knowledge of French and English, and therefore of Voltaire, Locke, Hume and the early writers on Buddhism, gave him the weapons wherewith to set about destroying 'l'infâme'; ironically, the sharpest of those weapons was the one he owed to Thomas Lancaster: his excellent command of English.

It was this command of English, drummed into him by Thomas Lancaster, which enabled him to create a philosophy which was a deliberate negation of everything Mr Lancaster believed in, for it was above all to the Rev. Thomas Lancaster that he owed his intemperate dislike both of Christianity *à l'anglaise*, and of Christianity *tout court*. This is something he did not have when he went there; Dr Runge's humanistic teaching did not incline him to think thus. It is therefore quite certain that his reaction against Thomas Lancaster changed radically his attitude to religion, and that his subsequent work would have been quite different but for his Wimbledon experience, the significance of which can therefore scarcely be exaggerated.

However, Schopenhauer not only set about destroying the infamous, which he, like Voltaire, identified with the fanaticism of dogmatic Christianity; he also found a substitute for it. One of those best qualified to view his philosophy in the round has told us that his work can 'most simply be viewed as the attempt to transport to Europe the philosophy of the Upanishads and of Theravadin Buddhism, and to present this as the natural consequence of a true interpretation of the philosophy of Kant'.[37] What needs to be stressed here is that the motive force behind his work thus defined was the need to counter those 'absurd and revolting superstitions' which were exemplified for him in the joyless, dreary religion of his English headmaster.

By perfecting his pupil's English that same headmaster gave him no less than the key to his philosophy. Not the least of the reasons why English was his favourite language was the fact that it opened up for him the glories of Sanskrit literature. Much of his reading of and on the Upanishads, on Buddhism and on oriental thought generally, was done in English, and most of the rest in French (in which he was no less fluent). Apart from a run of *Asiatic Researches* dating from 1806 to 1812, his library contained many such works in English. Those of which he thought most highly were Robert Spence Hardy's *A Manual of Buddhism* (1853) and *Eastern Monachism* (1850); indeed he said that he learned more about Buddhism from Hardy than from anyone else. With Brian Haughton Hodgson's *Sketch of Buddhism* (1828), on the other hand, he was not impressed; he wrote in his copy of 'the author's propensity to distort the Buddhistic doctrines to the tenets of his own miserable belief', and at one point wrote in the margin, 'O you ass.' He also possessed, among other books, Edward Upham's *The History and Doctrine of Buddhism* (1829) and William Ward's *A View of the History, Literature, and Religion of the Hindoos* (3rd edn, 2 vols, 1817). The whole subject merits a separate study.

Had Schopenhauer not had such an expert knowledge of English his work would have been very different. Not only the whole basic structure of his philosophy is indebted to England and his English school; so too is much of the incidental detail which gives that philosophy its unmistakable and unforgettable flavour. One could not easily overestimate the importance of England for his philosophy, and that means, above all else, the importance of the linguistic skill and the attitudes that were implanted at the Rev. Mr Lancaster's academy. One of the 'English' qualities which he most admired was independence of mind. It is a quality which his own work embodies and exemplifies to a remarkable degree, for he took as his working motto Polonius' advice to Laertes:

This above all, — to thine own self be true;
And it must follow, as the night the day,
Thou canst not then be false to any man.

It was advice which he followed to the letter. Intellectual honesty was something which he prized very highly. He once summed up the whole aim of his life as being 'To desire as little as possible and to know as much as possible' (*SW*, XVI, 64), which is also an expression of the Buddhism about which he was much more serious than he sometimes allowed himself to seem, reading the Oupnekhat daily as other men read their Bible.

Not only is its independence of mind a supposedly English quality (to say nothing of the extravagant obstinacy into which independent-mindedness may degenerate), so too are the style, tone and concrete nature of his work. He said that his journey of 1803 was so valuable because it brought him concrete experiences instead of the usual vague ideas of puberty. He detested vagueness as much as he detested cant and sententiousness. One of his greatest strengths as a philosopher is his style, his blessed lucidity. This was excellently described by Francis Hueffer in 1876:

> Schopenhauer instinctively abhorred obscurity or timid duplicity of any kind. His intellect is piercing, and his language lucid and forcible to a degree attained by few German writers, philosophic or otherwise . . . It is . . . one of Schopenhauer's greatest merits to have divested philosophical science of the cant of the schoolroom, and he might have justly applied to himself those admirable words occurring in a letter from Bolingbroke to Swift, in which the palm is awarded to those philosophers 'who strip metaphysics of all their bombast, keep within the bounds of every well-constituted eye, and never

bewilder themselves whilst they pretend to guide to reason of others.'[38]

It need hardly be said that this lucidity, far from being the normal inheritance of a German philosopher of the time, is a deliberately acquired virtue. Nietzsche, who learned so much from Schopenhauer himself, was to write, 'Is it his hard matter-of-fact sense, his inclination to lucidity and common sense, which often make him seem so English and so un-German?'[39] If this clarity owes most to his acquired matter-of-factness and to his determination to avoid at all cost the 'tumours and turgidities' (Nietzsche)[40] of Hegelianism, it may well also reflect his determination to avoid the cant which he associated with the sermons he had had to endure at Wimbledon.

Given that Schopenhauer was such an egregious anglophile, it is appropriate that it was in England that his reputation was first established. The earliest positive judgement — indeed, the earliest judgement on his philosophy in English, appeared in the context of an article entitled 'Last Judgment on Hegel's Philosophy' in *The Pilot* of May 1841, in which Schopenhauer was described as the greatest philosopher of the age — 'which is saying a good deal less than the good fellow thinks it is', Schopenhauer added in the rough draft of a letter to his publisher on 17 May 1841 (*SW*, XVI, 345), by which he meant that 'There is no philosophy in the period between Kant and myself, only academic charlatanism.'[41]

Greatest philosopher of the age or not, Schopenhauer did not benefit from this early review, because *The Pilot* was too obscure to attract notice. It was only when his cause was espoused by John Oxenford in a review article entitled 'Iconclasm in German Philosophy', which appeared in the *Westminster Review* of April 1853, that his reputation began to be made both in England and Germany.

What mattered in Oxenford's article was his recognition of Schopenhauer's importance; it is this that is emphasised from beginning to end:

> Few indeed, we venture to assert, will be those of our English readers who are familiar with the name of Arthur Schopenhauer. Fewer still will there be who are aware that the mysterious being owning that name has been working for something like forty years to subvert the whole system of German philosophy . . . And even still fewer will there be who are aware that Arthur Schopenhauer is one of the most

ingenious and readable authors in the world, skilful in the art of theory building, universal in attainments, inexhaustible in the power of illustration, terribly logical and unflinching in the pursuit of consequences, and . . . a formidable hitter of adversaries . . . this most eccentric of philosophers . . . while Schopenhauer's teaching is the most genial, the most ingenious, and . . . the most amusing that can be imagined, the doctrine taught is the most disheartening, the most repulsive, the most opposed to the aspirations of the present world, that the most ardent of Job's Comforters could concoct . . . we shall be greatly surprised if our brief outline of this genial, eccentric, audacious, and, let us add, terrible writer, does not tempt some of our readers to procure for themselves a set of works, every page of which abounds with novel and startling suggestions. We only wish we could see among the philosophers of modern Germany a writer of equal power, comprehensiveness, ingenuity and erudition, ranged on a side more in harmony with our own feelings and convictions, than that adopted by this misanthropic sage of Frankfort.[42]

Schopenhauer attached particular importance to Oxenford's description of his style as 'that odd mixture of sarcasm, invective, and common sense argument, which constitutes the polemic style of Schopenhauer, and, at the same time, allows that private pique, which is never wholly forgotten, to appear in the form of bitter irony'.[43] This remains an excellent description of the philosopher's *tone*. The article may have been merely descriptive, as Oxenford claimed, but on the whole Schopenhauer was delighted with it. Oxenford's enthusiasm was well calculated to set the 'sage of Frankfort' (who objected to the epithet 'misanthropic': *SW*, XV, 210) on the road to fame. That it did so was attested by Schopenhauer himself, when he said that he was discovered by 'the *Westminster*, etc'. (ibid., 427). By the time he wrote that, however, he had discovered and come to appreciate an *earlier* review article which had appeared in the *Westminster Review* a year earlier, in April 1852. His first reaction was that the April 1852 article was weak by comparison; he also assumed that it was by Mrs Sinnett, translator of Fichte's *The Destination of Man* (1846), who was responsible to George Eliot for most of the German reviews in the *Westminster Review* at this time. He soon changed his mind, however, and came to approve of the April 1852 article, which he now assumed to be Oxenford's work, and which therefore becomes an intrinsic part of John Oxenford's discovery of the German Swift:

> German philosophy has never come in contact with a more savage adversary than Arthur Schopenhauer; nor, if he meets the attention which his acuteness and erudition deserve, with one more decidedly dangerous. If he has been insulted by the silence of the Hegelians, Herbartites, &c., he is, at any rate, resolved to avenge his wrongs by his own loudness; and his book is chiefly interesting as a complete 'show up' of the German philosophers since the time of Kant. His scurrility . . . is worthy to be compared with that of Swift . . . his hits are so very hard, and are backed by such an amount of strong sense, that if they once come before the notice of the public it will be difficult to ignore them. It has usually been the custom with German philosophers for each to have a language of his own . . . Schopenhauer, however, writes so that he who runs may read . . . and may be as formidable an enemy to the church philosophical . . . as Voltaire was to the Church of Rome.[44]

On reflection Schopenhauer could not fail to be flattered by the comparison with Swift, for it is he, rather than Hagedorn or Lichtenberg, who deserves the title of 'the German Swift'. He is linked with Swift not just by the misanthropy which he was at pains to disclaim, and not just by the acuity and acerbity of his style; nor is it Swift's 'Digression in praise of Digressions' that matters, digressive though Schopenhauer's method is. It is no coincidence that the work of Swift's that meant most to him was *A Tale of a Tub*, his 1734 edition of which included numerous underlinings. The main parallel between *A Tale of a Tub* and Schopenhauer's two main works is the fact that both authors address themselves to what they see as numerous and gross corruptions in religion and learning.

When Schopenhauer later had ideas of having his work translated into English, he regarded the translations in Oxenford's article(s) as the ideal model. On 22 October 1857 he wrote to the young German scholar David Asher:

> Since you are *thoroughly* anglicized, you would be well qualified to translate my works . . . As an ideal model I would commend to you the few pages which John Oxenford translated, in the *Westminster Review* for April 1853, in such a way that

I was *quite amazed*: he reproduced not just the meaning, but the style, my mannerisms and gestures, astonishingly well — it was just like looking in the mirror! I should be very glad to look through your version before you send it off, *to prevent all possibility of a mistake & to see that all be right . . . Think of it.* [*SW*, XV, 590; Schopenhauer's English italicised]

Asher did think of it, and evidently thought better of it, although Schopenhauer returned to the subject a year later, in a letter written on 3 January 1859:

You write English astoundingly well, faith you do, and I am glad of it, for your sake, as it is your trade, and for my sake, because I see in you the future rare and unparalleled translator of my works, it's for that you have come into the world. Believe me, it's so. But don't now you think that I shall go on writing in English. No such thing: you may though, if you choose: no objection. But with me it would only be an affectation, moreover a task, and a bore to boot. [Ibid., 676; the letter is written in English]

Perhaps it was as well that this strange project never got off the ground, even if it did mean that Schopenhauer was not to see an English translation of his work, and that it was to be almost thirty years before one appeared.

Before that, however, Francis Hueffer planned to publish a translation of *Die Welt als Wille und Vorstellung*, as we gather from a letter which Swinburne wrote to Andrew Chatto on 26 June 1874:

I hope it is true that you are about to publish a translation of Schopenhauer by Dr. Hüffer, whose consummate mastery of English will make him the fittest man to introduce to English students the great thinker and man in person, whose fame has excited such deep interest and attention in England as well as in France.[45]

Chatto and Windus agreed to publish such a work. The firm's letter books contain two letters on the subject. The first, addressed to 'Dr. Franz Heaffer [*sic*], 5 Fair Lawn Merton SW' and dated 27 June 1874, states, 'We are disposed to run the risk of bringing out an edition of Schopenhauer's "The World as Will and Imagination", with a memoir of his life and writings by yourself.' Hueffer's translation, entitled *The World as Will and Imagination*, was accordingly advertised by Chatto and Windus as 'in preparation' from 1874 to 1876. In 1876, as the other letter reveals, the plan was dropped: 'The agreement between us respecting "Schopenhauer" is cancelled by mutual agreement.' It appears that Francis Hueffer and Andrew Chatto had agreed that Hueffer had more pressing projects in hand; the letter is merely a formal confirmation of their agreement.[46] What remained were two interesting articles which deserve to be remembered.[47] It is a pity from the point of view of the present story that the English translation of Schopenhauer's *Magnum opus* was not prepared in Merton.

It was therefore not until 1883-6 that a translation of Schopenhauer's best-known work appeared: *The World as Will and Idea*, by R.B. Haldane and J. Kemp. It was followed fairly swiftly by other translations, notably a series of selections from the *Parerga und Paralipomena*, by T.B. Saunders, which appeared from 1891 onwards. Given the very considerable impact of Schopenhauer's disciple, Nietzsche, when his works began to appear from 1896 onwards, we should expect to find Schopenhauer having most impact on English writers in the 1880s and early 1890s. And so he did; but that is another story.

Notes

1. In *Arthur Schopenhauers Briefwechsel*, ed. Brahn, 285.
2. See *Fortnightly Review*, XXVI (1876), 774. A.S.'s letter to Eastlake in his *Ges. Br.* (1978), 191 ff.
3. David Robertson, *Sir Charles Eastlake and the Victorian Art World* (Princeton, N.J., 1978), 32.
4. The translation is Helen Zimmern's.
5. *Works of Thomas Gray*, ed. Gosse, II, (1903) 4.
6. *Edinburgh Review*, August 1817.
7. Thomas Love Peacock, *Nightmare Abbey* (1818), Chapter 1.
8. Peacock, *Crotchet Castle* (1831), Chapter 2.
9. *Edinburgh Review*, October 1827, 304-51.
10. G.H. Lewes, *Biographical History of Philosophy*, IV (1846), 208 f.
11. In W. Gwinner, *Schopenhauer's Leben* (Leipzig, 1878), 95 f.
12. See *Life and Letters of Thomas Campbell*, ed. Beattie, III, (1849) 441. For details of Campbell's extended visits to Germany, see ibid., I, 271-356; II, 353-92.
13. Ibid., II, 262.
14. See Cyrus Redding, *Literary Reminiscences and Memoirs of Thomas Campbell*, II (1860), 230 f; also I, 173.
15. *Life and Letters of Thomas Campbell*, ed. Beattie, I, 342; Campbell's

own italics.
16. Ibid., II, 446 f.
17. *Letters and Journals of Lord Byron*, ed. T. Moore, I (Brussels, 1830), 499.
18. Wallace, *Arthur Schopenhauer*, 171.
19. Ibid., 176.
20. Helen Zimmern, *Arthur Schopenhauer: his Life and his Philosophy* (1876), 155.
21. Francis Hueffer, 'Arthur Schopenhauer', *Fornightly Review* (1876), 784.
22. J.S., *My Youthful Life*, II, 33 f.
23. See n. 16 above.
24. Wieland, *Briefe*, II, 286 f.
25. Herder, *Briefe*, ed. W. Dobbek and G. Arnold, I (Weimar, 1977), 83.
26. Ibid., I, 304.
27. Zimmern, *Arthur Schopenhauer*, 243 f.
28. Boswell's *Johnson*, under 1776.
29. Peter Pindar, *Works*, II, 166.
30. Ibid., II, 67.
31. *The Pursuits of Literature* (6th edn, 1798), xvii.
32. Ibid., 320.
33. Wallace, *Arthur Schopenhauer*, 43.
34. Peter Pindar, *Works*, II, 306 ff.
35. Cf. Marryat, *Peter Simple*, Chapter XXXVIII: 'The law of primogeniture is beset with evils and injustice.'
36. For Heine's view of England, see, especially, his 'Englische Fragmente'. Although there are close parallels between Schopenhauer's and Heine's views, notably of English religiosity, it needs to be remembered that Heine, unlike Schopenhauer, did not speak English, nor did he know England so well.
37. Claud Sutton, *The German Tradition in Philosophy* (1974), 79.
38. *Fortnightly Review* (1876), 780 f.
39. Nietzsche, *Die fröhliche Wissenschaft*, Book II, sect. 99.
40. Ibid.
41. Zimmern, *Arthur Schopenhauer*, 150.
42. *Westminster Review*, April 1853, 388 f., 394, 407.
43. Ibid., April 1853, 401.
44. Ibid., April 1852, 678.
45. Swinburne, *Letters*, ed. C.Y. Lang, II (1959), 299 f.
46. I am grateful to Chatto and Windus for clearing up this point.
47. Francis Hueffer's articles: 'Arthur Schopenhauer', *Fortnightly Review*, December 1876, 773-92; 'The Literary Aspects of Schopenhauer's Work', *New Quarterly Magazine*, VIII (January-July 1877), 352-78.

Select Bibliogrpahy

Anon., *A Particular Description of the City of Dantzick* (1734).
Anon., *Memoirs of Emma Lady Hamilton* (1891)
Anon., *Sketch of the Life of the late George Chapman* (Edinburgh, 1808).
Anon., *The Picture of London for 1803.*
Anon., *The Pursuits of Literature: a Satiric Poem* (1794).
Archenholz, J.W. von, *A Picture of England* (2 vols in 1, 1789 and 1791; new edn 1797).
Barrow, W., *An Essay in Education* (2 vols, 1802).
Bayne-Powell, R., *English Country Life in the Eighteenth Century* (1935).
—— *Eighteenth-century London Life* (1937).
Benson, P. (ed.), *My dearest Betsy: a self-portrait of William Gilpin, 1757-1848* (1981).
Bewick, T., *A Memoir* (Newcastle, 1862).
Boswell, J., 'Journal of My Jaunt, Harvest, 1762', in *Boswell Papers (Isham Collection)* ed. G. Scott, I: *Early Papers* (n.p., 1928).
—— *Boswell's London Journal, 1762-1763*, ed. F.A. Pottle (1950).
Bower, A., *The History of the University of Edinburgh* (2 vols., 1817).
Burney, F., *The Journals and Letters of Fanny Burney*, ed. Joyce Hemlow, XII (Oxford, 1984).
Cambridge History of English Literature, The, ed. Sir A.W. Ward and A.R. Waller (Cambridge, 1932); IX, Chapter 15; XIV, Chapter 14: on education.
Campbell, T., *Life and Letters of Thomas Campbell*, ed. W. Beattie (2 vols, 1849).
Carlyle, A., *Autobiography of the Rev. Dr. Alexander Carlyle* (1860).
Chodowiecki, D., *Von Berlin nach Danzig. Eine Künstlerfahrt im Jahre 1773*, Berlin [1883].
Clark, A.W.H., *Monumental Inscriptions in the Church and Churchyard of St. Mary's, Wimbledon* (1934).
Clark, E.G., *George Parker Bidder, the Calculating Boy* (1983).
Cowper, S., *Letters of Spencer Cowper*, ed. E. Hughes (1956).
Dalzel, A., *History of the University of Edinburgh* (2 vols, 1862).
Dictionary of National Biography.
Dunsby, F.S.N., *Danzig, Marienburg, Oliva, Zoppot* (Danzig [1913]).
Dunsby, M., 'Die Englische Kirche in Danzig', *Mitteilungen des Westpreussischen Geschichtsvereins*, Heft 31 (1932), 1-12.
Edwards, E., *Lives of the Founders of the British Museum* (1870).
Erskine, D., *Lord Dun's Friendly and Familiar Advices* (Edinburgh, 1754).
Eyre Matcham, M., *The Nelsons of Burnham Thorpe* (1911).
Farington Diary, The, ed. J. Greig (8 vols, 1922-8).
Farrer, J., *Memoir of the late Rev. John Farrer* (Newcastle-upon-Tyne, 1844).
Feret, C.J., *Fulham Old and New* (3 vols, 1900).
Fiedler, Hans, 'Danzig und England', *Zeitschrift des Westpreussischen Geschichtsvereins*, Heft 68 (Danzig, 1928), 61-125.
Foster, J., *Alumni Oxonienses* (8 vols, 1887-91).

Select Bibliography

Furness, W., *History of Penrith* (Penrith, 1894).
Garbutt, G., *A Historical and Descriptive View of. . . Sunderland* (Sunderland, 1819).
Gérin, W., *Horatia Nelson* (1970).
Goldsmith, O., *The Vicar of Wakefield* (2 vols, 1766).
—— *The Collected Letters of Oliver Goldsmith*, ed. K.C. Balderston (Cambridge, 1928).
Gordon, P.L., *Personal Memoirs* (2 vols, 1830).
Graham, H.G., *The Social Life of Scotland in the 18th Century* (1928).
Grant, A., *The Story of the University of Edinburgh* (2 vols, 1884).
Green, J.R., *A Short History of the English People* (1874).
Gwinner, W., *Schopenhauer's Leben* (Leipzig, 1878).
Hans, N., *New Trends in Education in the Eighteenth Century* (1951).
Hardwick, Mollie, *Emma, Lady Hamilton* (1969).
Harrison, James, *Life of Lord Nelson* (2 vols, 1806).
Herder, J.G., *Briefe*, ed. W. Dobbek and G. Arnold, I, (Weimar, 1977).
Herrmann, F., 'Who was [Edward] Solly?', *Connoisseur*, 164 (1967), 229-34; 165 (1967), 13-18, 153-61; 166 (1967), 10-18.
Hinchcliffe, E., *Appleby Grammar School* (Appleby, 1974).
Hodgkin, R.H., *Six Centuries of an Oxford College* (1949).
Hoffmann, Paul, 'Schopenhauer und Hamburg', *Jahrbuch der Schopenhauer-Gesellschaft*, 19 (1932), 207-51.
Holcroft, T., *Anna St. Ives* (1792).
—— *Travels from Hamburg* (2 vols, 1804).
—— *Memoirs of Thomas Holcroft* (1926).
Holdgate, M., *A History of Appleby* (Appleby, 1970).
Horn, D.B., *British Public Opinion and the First Partition of Poland* (1945).
—— *A Short History of the University of Edinburgh 1556-1889* (Edinburgh, 1967).
Hudson, E., *Barton Records* (Penrith, 1951).
Hübscher, A., 'Der Philosoph lernt schreiben. Unbekannte Briefe von Schopenhauers Vater an seinen Sohn', *Schopenhauer-Jahrbuch*, 36 (1955), 82-8.
—— 'Ein vergessener Schulfreund Schopenhauers', *Schopenhauer-Jahrbuch*, 46 (1965), 130-52.
—— 'Jugendjahre in Hamburg', *Schopenhauer-Jahrbuch*, 51 (1970), 3-21.
—— 'Zwei Hamburger Jugendfreunde', *Schopenhauer-Jahrbuch*, 51 (1970), 32-40.
—— 'Unbekannte Briefe von Johanna Schopenhauer an ihren Sohn', *Schopenhauer-Jahrbuch* 52 (1971), 80-110.
Hueffer, F., 'Arthur Schopenhauer', *Fortnightly Review*, December 1876, 773-92.
—— 'The Literary Aspects of Schopenhauer's Work', *New Quarterly Magazine*, VIII (January-July 1877), 357-78.
Hunter, W., *Biggar and the House of Fleming*, 2nd edn (Edinburgh, 1867).
Jackson, T.G., 'Eagle House, Wimbledon, *Surrey Archaeological Collections*, X (1890-1), 150-65.
—— 'Eagle House, Wimbledon', *The Wimbledon and Merton Annual* (1903), 9-25.
Jacob, V., *The Lairds of Dun* (1931).

Select Bibliography

Jagger, J.E., *Lord Nelson's Home and Life at Merton* (Merton Park, 1926).
Klessmann, R., *The Berlin Gallery* (1971).
Knight, Ellis C., *The Autobiography of Miss [Cornelia] Knight*, ed. R. Fulford (1960).
Knox, V., *Liberal Education* (1781; 9th edn, 1788; 10th edn, 1789).
Lancaster, T., *A Sermon preached in St. John's Chapel, Sunderland* (Sunderland, 1784) [Sunderland Reference Library; not in BL or Bodleian].
—— *A Sermon preached at Hanworth in the County of Middlesex, on Thursday, April 23, 1789* (1789).
—— *A Plan of Education* (1794; 2nd edn, 1797).
—— *A Sermon preached at Merton, Surrey, on Thursday, the 13th of January, 1814* (1814).
La Roche, Sophie von, *Sophie in London, 1786*, ed. C. Williams (1933).
Leip, Hans, *Die Lady und der Admiral* (Hamburg, 1933).
Lysons, D., *The Environs of London* (4 vols, 1792-6).
McDowall, W., *History of the Burgh of Dumfries* (Dumfries, 1867).
Mackenzie, E., *A descriptive and historical account of the town and county of Newcastle upon Tyne* (Newcastle-upon-Tyne, 1827).
Mackenzie, H., *Anecdotes and Egotisms of Henry Mackenzie, 1745-1831*, ed. H.W. Thompson (1927).
Magrath, J.R., *The Queen's College* (2 vols, 1921).
Marchtaler, H. von, 'Lorenz Meyers Tagebücher', *Schopenhauer-Jahrbuch*, 49 (1968), 95-111.
Marples, M., *Romantics at School* (1967).
Marshall, J., *Travels . . . in the Years 1768, 1769 and 1770*, III (1772).
Matheson, C., *The Life of Henry Dundas* (1933).
Maxwell, J.S., *The Centenary Book of St. John's, Dumfries* (Dumfries, 1968).
Moritz, C.P., *Travels, chiefly on foot, through several parts of England* (1795).
—— *Moritz's Travels in England*, ed. P.E. Matheson (1924).
Morley, E.J. (ed.), *Crabb Robinson in Germany 1800-1805* (1929).
Mossner, E.C., *The Life of David Hume* (1954).
Nelson, *The Dispatches and Letters of Vice Admiral Lord Viscount Nelson*, ed. Sir N.H. Nicolas (7 vols, 1844-6).
—— *The Letters of Lord Nelson to Lady Hamilton* (2 vols, 1814).
—— *Nelson's Letters to his Wife*, ed. G.P.B. Naish (1958).
Neville, S., *The Diary of Sylas Neville, 1767-1788*, ed. B. Cozens-Hardy (1950).
Nicolson, J., and Burn, R., *The History and Antiquities of the Counties of Westmorland and Cumberland* (2 vols, 1777; repr. 1976).
Nimmert, B., 'Danzigs Verhältnis zu [England und Schottland]', *Zeitschrift des Westpreussischen Geschichtsvereins*, Heft 53 (Danzig, 1911), 169-74.
Oman, C., *Nelson* (1950).
Oxenford, J., 'Iconoclasm in German Philosophy', *Westminster Review*, April, 1853, 388-407.
Papritz, J., 'Dietrich Lilie und das Englische Haus', *Zeitschrift des Westpreussischen Geschichtsvereins*, Heft 68 (Danzig, 1928), 127-84.
Patterson, M.W., *Sir Francis Burdett and his Times* (1931).
Pettigrew, T.J., *Memoirs of the Life of Lord Nelson* (2 vols, 1849).
Phillips, H.J., *The Thames about 1750* (1951).
Pindar, P., *The Works of Peter Pindar, Esqr.* (5 vols, 1794-1801).

Select Bibliography

Pocock, R., *Tours in Scotland*, ed. D.W. Kemp (Edinburgh, 1887).
—— 'Northern Journeys of Bishop Richard Pococke', in *North Country Diaries (Second Series)*, ed. J.C. Hodgson, *Publications of the Surtees Society*, CXXIV (1914), 199-252.
Porter, J., *Thaddeus of Warsaw* (4 vols, 1803).
Pottle, F.A., *James Boswell: the Earlier Years, 1740-1769* (1966).
Price, L.M., *The Reception of English Literature in Germany* (1968).
Prior, J., *The Life of Oliver Goldsmith*, M.B. (2 vols, 1837).
Pückler-Muskau, Prince, *Tour in Germany, Holland and England*, III (1832).
Raistrick, A., *Two Centuries of Industrial Welfare: the London (Quaker) Lead Company* (1938).
Ramsay of Ochtertyre, J., *Scotland and Scotsmen in the Eighteenth Century* (2 vols, 1888).
Rathbone, P., *Paradise Merton: the Story of Nelson and the Hamiltons at Merton Place* (1973).
Redding, C., *Literary Reminiscences and Memoirs of Thomas Campbell*, II (1860).
Richardson, M.A., *The Local Historian's Table Book*, Historical Division (5 vols, Newcastle-upon-Tyne, 1841-6).
Ritson, V., 'A Chapel of Ease: The Early Records of St. John's Church, Sunderland', *Antiquities of Sunderland*, IX (1908), 126-61.
Robinson, F.J.G., 'Trends in Education in Northern England during the Eighteenth Century: a Biographical Study', PhD, Newcastle-upon-Tyne, 3 vols (1972).
Schopenhauer, A., *Sämtliche Werke*, ed. P. Deussen (16 vols, Munich, 1911-42).
—— *Der handschriftliche Nachlass*, ed. A. Hübscher (5 vols, Frankfurt a.M., 1966-75).
—— *Gesammelte Briefe*, ed. A. Hübscher (Bonn, 1978).
—— *Arthur Schopenhauers Briefwechsel und andere Dokumente*, ed. M. Brahn (Leipzig, 1911).
—— *Reisetagebücher aus den Jahren 1803-1804*, ed. Carlotte von Gwinner (Leipzig, 1923).
—— *The World as Will and Idea*, trans. R.B. Haldane and J. Kemp (3 vols, 1883-6).
Schopenhauer, J., *Sämmtliche Schriften* (24 vols, Leipzig and Frankfurt a.M., 1830-1).
—— *Reise durch England und Schottland in den Jahren 1803-1805* [sic] (Leipzig, 1813; new edn 1830, repr. Stuttgart, 1965).
—— *My Youthful Life* (2 vols, 1847).
Scott, W., *The Heart of Midlothian* (1818).
Sebag-Montefiore, C., *A History of the Volunteer Forces* (1908).
Shelley, Frances Lady, *The Diary of Frances Lady Shelley, 1787-1817*, ed. R. Edgcumbe (2 vols, 1912).
Sheridan, Thomas, *A Plan of Education* (1769)
Sichel, Walter, *Emma Lady Hamilton* (1905)
Smollett, T., *The Expedition of Humphry Clinker* (1771).
Solly, H., *These Eighty Years* (2 vols, 1893).
Somerville, T. *My own Life and Times, 1741-1814* (Edinburgh [1861]).
Stephens, A., *Memoirs of John Horne Tooke* (2 vols, 1813).
Sterne, L., *The Life and Opinions of Tristram Shandy* (9 vols, 1760-7).

Select Bibliography

Stuart, D.M., *Dearest Bess: the Life and Times of Lady Elizabeth Foster* (1955).
Summers, J.W., *The History and Antiquities of Sunderland* (Sunderland, 1858).
Sutton, C., *The German Tradition in Philosophy* (1974).
Swift, F.B., 'Maughanby School', *CWAAS*, LIV (1954), 236-47.
Swift, J., *Swift's Writings on Religion and the Church*, ed. T. Scott (2 vols, 1898).
Sykes, J., *Local Records* (2 vols, Newcastle-upon-Tyne, 1833).
Third Year's Report of the Literary and Philosophical Society of Newcastle-upon-Tyne (1796).
Todd, T.O., *The History of the Phoenix Lodge* (Sunderland, 1906).
Tours, Hugh, *The Life and Letters of Emma Hamilton* (1963).
Thornbury, W., and Walford, E., *Old and New London* (6 vols, 1873-8).
Trelawney, E.J., *Adventures of a Younger Son* (1831).
Trench, Mrs Melesina, *Journal kept during a visit to Germany, 1799, 1800* (1861).
Victoria County History of Surrey, ed. H.E. Malden (4 vols, 1902-14).
Wallace, W., *Life of Arthur Schopenhauer* (1890).
Warner, R., *A Tour through the Northern Counties of England* (2 vols, Bath, 1802).
Wendeborn, G.F.A., *A View of England towards the Close of the Eighteenth Century* (1791).
Wieland, C.M., *Auswahl denkwürdiger Briefe*, ed. L. Wieland (2 vols, Vienna, 1815).
Woodforde, J., *The Diary of a Country Parson, 1758-1802* (5 vols, 1924-31).
Wordsworth, D., *Journals of Dorothy Wordsworth*, ed. E. de Selincourt (2 vols, 1941).
Wordsworth, W. and D., *The Letters of William and Dorothy Wordsworth, 1787-1805*, ed. E. de Selincourt, 2nd edn, rev. C.L. Shaver (Oxford, 1967).
Wraxall, N., *A Tour through some of the Northern Parts of Europe* (1775).
Wynne Diaries, The, ed. A. Fremantle (3 vols 1935-40).
Zimmern, H., *Arthur Schopenhauer: his Life and his Philosophy* (1876).

Index

Abershawe, Jerry 238, 263
academies 275-8
  see also Wimbledon School
Agutter, Rev. William 163, 357
Alcock, Samuel and Barbara 85-6
Alston 140-6
Anderson, John William and Dorothy 3-7, 11, 72, 242, 264-5
Anderson, Lady 97, 120
Anderson, William and Lucy 2, 68, 72, 264-5
Anne, Queen of Great Britain and Ireland 2, 68
Apostool, Mynheer 114-15
Appleby, Westmoreland 144-5, 150
Archenholz, Johann Wilhelm von 24-5, 311-12
art galleries 98, 107, 121-2, 131
Asher, David 374-5
Astley's 98, 120-1
Astor, John Jacob 345
Astor, William 345
Axe, Mr 202

Bacon, Francis 333, 345-6
Barlow, Joel 184
Barnby, Captain 109, 132
Barrow, William 161, 221, 289, 293, 295, 297
Bathurst, Lord 23
Baxter, Thomas 287
Beck, Rev. Alexander 68
Beckford, William 205
Beilby, Ralph 87
Bell, George, Provost 63
Bell, Robert 170
Bell, Thomas and Janet 174
Beresford, James 355
Betenson, Richard 170
Bethmann's 3
Bewick, Thomas 86-7
Bickerton, Rev. William 72

Biggar, 29-31
bigotry 306-16, 357-70
Billington, Mrs (singer) 98-9
Bolton, Mr and Mrs Thomas 204
Bolton, Thomas, Jr 204-5, 217
Bonaparte, Napoleon 193-4
Bond, Rev. Charles Frederick 175-6, 223-4
Bond, Henry 224
Boquet, Rev. Jean Robert 68, 80, 84
Bosville, 'Col' William 184
Boswell, James 12, 33, 40, 47-9, 54, 60-1, 64-6, 188, 357
Bowen, Rev. Thomas 165
Bower, A. 41
Bracken, Allan 15
Brant, Richard 222, 320
British Museum 115-16, 138
Bromley 112, 134-5
Brown, Rev. Jakob 68
Brown, James (bookseller) 57, 83
Brown, Sir William 2
Brownlow, Bishop 223-4
Buckinghamshire, Countess of 182
Buckland, Rev. John 224
Burdett, Sir Francis 176, 184
Burke, Edmund 176, 181, 188, 357
Burnet, Rev. Alexander 72, 78
Burnet, Rev. Thomas 68
Burnett, Sir Robert 182, 202
Burney, Ann *see* Lancaster, Ann (Rev. Thomas Lancaster's wife)
Burney, Charles 161-2, 187, 221
Burney, Charles Parr 218-19, 222
Burney, Fanny 218-19, 299
Burney, John (brother of Ann)

383

Index

and Sarah 217-20
Burney, William and Elizabeth 151-2
Burton, Billy 162
Bush, Sir William 182
Byron, George Gordon, Lord 1, 345, 349-51, 356, 365

Campbell, Thomas 19, 343-5
Canning, George 182
Capes, Mr 344
Carlyle, Alexander 33, 37-8, 45-8, 61, 63, 141, 174, 330-1
Carruthers, William 57
Castle, John 183
Cator, John 218, 232
Catterick Bridge 260
Chambaud, L. 295-6
Chancery 218-20
Chapman, Dr George 47, 59-64, 80, 88, 284, 290, 293-8
Charles I, King of England, Scotland and Ireland 64
Charles Edward (Stuart), Prince 60, 65
Chatfield, Allen 183
Chatterly, Ralph 17
Chatto & Windus, publishers 375-6
Chodowiecki, Daniel 68, 92
Churchill, Charles 65, 177
Clarke, James 141
Collingwood, Vice-Admiral Lord 213
Collinson, Septimus 145, 221-2
Concordia, Jungfer 72, 78
Cooke, Mr (actor) 113-15, 138
Corry, Sir Trevor 4, 73
Court, Mr (David?) 113, 135
Cowper, Spencer 153
Coxon, Rev. John 153, 157, 168
Cramp, Sally 7, 78, 81
Crosbie, Andrew 63-4
Curzon, Nathaniel 21

Dalzel, A. 38, 50
Danzig 1-13

English Chapel 2, 67-71
English House 2, 67-8
  Jameson as Chaplain 66-84
Davidson, Alexander 72
Denbigh, Kathleen 211
Derwentwater, Earl of 143
Dessein's Hotel 10
diary, Arthur Schopenhauer 95-118
Dickens, Charles 308, 367-8
D'Israeli, Isaac 355
Domville, Dame Maria 219
Douglas, Sir John, of Kellhead 56, 60, 65
Douglas, Captain William 60, 65
Douglas, Lord William 204, 207
Douglas, Sir William 2
Drawing Room 102
Drewe, Samuel 98, 113, 120, 242, 245, 304
Drummond, Colin 41, 46
Dumfries 56-61, 63-4
Dun, David Erskine, Lord 50-3, 55-6
Dundas, Henry 176-81, 188, 190, 192, 202
Dunsby, Martha 70
Durham 260-1
Durno, Sir James 11, 96, 99-100, 102-3, 108-9, 111-12, 124
Du Rosel, M. 165

Eastlake, Sir Charles 323, 325-6
Edinburgh University 32-50
education
  academies 275-8
  Arthur Schopenhauer on 319
  Dr Runge's, Hamburg 281-4
  Lancaster's Plan 285-300
  theories of 289-93
  Wimbledon (q.v.) 279-80, 284-5, 301-6, 316-19
Egerton, Rev. Henry 153, 161
Ekins, Dr Jeffery 153, 168
Ellenborough, Lord 209-10, 220
Elliott, Sir Gilbert 33
Ellison, Rev. John 149

Index

Enfield 113, 135
England
  and Arthur Schopenhauer's parents 1-26
  bigotry 360-8
  influence on Arthur Schopenhauer 368-76
  language 322-45, 370-1
  literature 348-60
  philosophy 323-9, 349
  ways 345-8
English Diary, Arthur Schopenhauer 95-118
Erskine, David, Lord Dun 50-3, 55-6
Erskine, John 53-4
Erskine, John (son) 54-5
Erskine, John Francis, Earl of Mar 54
Erskine, Thomas 184
Exeter 'Change 102, 126-7

Falkener, Everard 12
Farish, Rev. James 299
Farrer, Mrs Ann 288, 320
Farrer, Rev. John 145, 149-50, 221, 284
Farrer, Richard 320
Ferguson, Daniel 260
Feuerbach, Anselm 8
Feyerabendt, Johann Jakob 71
Fichte, Johann Gottlieb 333, 373
Fielding, Henry 355
Fitz-James (ventriloquist) 101-2
Fleming, Rev. Richard 51, 55
Fluelin, James 68
Forbes, Robert 49
Forster, George 316
Forty-five, The 32, 143
Foster, J. 200-1
Fowke, Captain Francis 182, 191, 193
Frankfurt 346
Frederick II (the Great), King of Prussia 5, 9-12, 68, 348
Fremantle, Captain Thomas 3, 74

Galliard, Mr (teacher) 287

Gardiner, Dr William 11, 72
Gebrüder Schopenhauer 6-7
Gellert, Christian Fürchtegott 81
George III, King of Great Britain 5, 110, 164-5, 189, 193, 199, 224-5
Gérin, Winifred 210
Gibbon, Edward 147
Gibsone, Alexander 11
Gibsone, Archibald 11
Gilchrist, Dr Evan 63
Gilpin, William 151, 299
Girdwood, John 31
girls' boarding school 122-4
Gleim, Herr 118
Godeffroy, Charles 21, 238-9, 249-50, 254-6, 263, 281
Goethe, Johann Wolfgang von 77, 325, 333, 344, 354
Goldsmid, Abraham 182, 202
Goldsmid, Benjamin 116, 138-9, 182, 202, 212
Goldsmith, Oliver 33, 35-6, 286-7, 354
Gordon, Collector 64
Gordon, Francis (ambassador) 67
Gordon, P.L. 31, 185
Graham, H.G. 58
Grant, Rev. James 48-50
Gray, Thomas 329
Greenwich Hospital 108
Grégoire family 233, 280
Grenville, William 170-1, 176, 190, 278
Grierson, Sir William 56, 60
Grischow, Karl Gottfried 68
Guild, Dr William 67
Guildford, Dowager Countess of 176, 220
Gurlay, Captain Robert 67
Gwinner, W. 208

Hagedorn, Friedrich von 15, 374
Haldane, R.B. 376
Halfhide, Mr (calico printer) 183, 202
Hall, Rev. Thomas 153-4, 158, 167

Index

Hamann, Johann Georg 77, 354
Hamburg 13-26
  Arthur Schopenhauer's education 281-5
  English House 14-16
  English visitors 16-19
  Nelson's visit 19-22, 209
Hamilton, Fatima Emma Charlotte Nelson 207
Hamilton, James, 4th Lord Bargeny 41
Hamilton, Lady Emma 20-3, 24, 182, 201-7, 210-12, 222
Hamilton, Sir William 201
Hamilton, William, of Bangour 41
Hammon, Thomas 191, 288
Hammond, Rev. Samuel 68
hanging, public 101, 125
Hardy, Thomas 194, 314-15
Harris family 99, 117, 122
Harrison, James 204
Hauptmann, Johann Carl Friedrich 235, 258, 281
Hay, Andrew 30
Hay, Rev. Peter 72
Haywood, Francis 322, 332, 339-40, 342
Hazlitt, William 81, 329-30
Hearne, Thomas 164
Hegel, Georg Wilhelm Friedrich 331, 333, 356, 372
Heine, Heinrich 368, 377
Hellier, Isaac, Jr 223
Hennings, Mr 116
Herder, Johann Gottfried von 77, 354
Herschel, Sir William 109-10
Hess, Herr von 111, 113
Hewit, Rev. John 165
Higgins, George 191, 288
Hodgkin, Benjamin 153
Hodgkin, R.H. 164
Holcroft, Thomas 10, 14, 17, 183-4, 187
Home, John 33
Hornby, Rev. Thomas 85-6
Horne Tooke, John 176, 180, 183-5, 188

Hornstein, Robert von 349-50
Horsley, Samuel, Bishop of Rochester 177, 181, 188
Howie, Rev. Alexander 56-7
Hueffer, Francis 325, 347, 371-2, 375-6
Hume, David 41, 45-6, 48, 326-9, 349, 360
Hunter, Prof. Robert 33-4, 37-40
Hutcheson, Professor 141
Huttwalker 116, 139

Ivatt, Richard 170

Jackson, Thomas Graham 171-2, 208
Jacob, Violet 53
Jacobi, Johann Georg 77
Jacobi, Karl 239, 247, 305
Jacobins 143, 186-7, 189
Jameson, Rev. Richard 2, 7-8, 11-12, 29-89
  and J.S. 7, 29, 36, 47, 74-84
  background 29-32
  Danzig Chaplain 66-84
  Episcopal minister 56-66
  last years 84-9
  private tutor 50-6
  student 32-50, 298
Jansz, Christoffel 3
Jeffrey, Lord 174
Jenkinson, Charles, Baron Hawkesbury 179-81
Jenkinson, Charles Cecil Cope 181
Jenkinson, Robert, Lord Hawkesbury 180
Jenkinson, Robert Banks, 2nd Earl of Liverpool 165, 180-1, 189, 226
Jepson, Rev. Graham 161
John, Dr Johann Wilhelm 7
Johnson, Dr Samuel 163, 188, 311-12. 353, 357-8, 361
Johnston, John, of Grange 48-9, 60, 65
Jourdan, Mr 98, 100, 107

Kabrun, Jakob 73, 83, 257, 270

Index

Kade, David 68
Kames, Lord 61, 63
Kant, Immanuel 329-37, 339-44, 356, 370
Kemble, Charles 111-12, 114-15
Kemp, J. 376
Kenworthy, Joshua 66
Kew 109, 113, 129
Klopstock, Friedrich Gottlieb 15, 20, 23, 344
Klopstock, Viktor 17
Knight, Cornelia 19, 204
Knipe, Rev. John 14-16, 23, 27, 254, 256, 272, 281
Knole Park 112, 135
Knox, Vicesimus 289-93, 296
Kramer, Hans 67

Laborie, M. and Mme (dancers) 99
Lancaster, Ann (wife of Rev. Thomas Lancaster) 151-2, 191, 216
Lancaster, Ann (daughter) 157, 216-17, 222
Lancaster, Eliza (daughter) 157, 175, 216-17, 224, 237, 288
Lancaster, Henry (son) 176, 212-17, 221
Lancaster, Joseph 317
Lancaster, Ruth (daughter) 157, 203-4, 214, 216-17
Lancaster, Ruth (mother) 142
Lancaster, Samuel and Sarah 217
Lancaster, Rev. Thomas (of Wimbledon School) 110, 140-66, 170-226
   and Dr Runge 280-5, 306
   and Lord Nelson 215-26
   and the Schopenhauers 175, 278-80
   at Parson's Green 159-66
   at Wimbledon 170-226
     anti-Jacobins and Volunteers 186-200
     house 170-6
     later life 215-26
     Lord Nelson 200-15
     'Symposiackls' 177-86
   background 1, 6, 140-6
   bigotry 306-16, 357-70
   parson 152-8
   pedantry 316-19
   Plan of Education 285-300
   village schoolmaster 146-52
   Wimbledon School (*q.v.*) 271-319
Lancaster, Thomas (cousin of Rev. Thomas Lancaster) 163
Lancaster, Thomas (father) 140-2, 144
Lancaster, Thomas Pierce (nephew) 217
Lancaster, Rev. Thomas William (son) 164, 176, 216-17, 220, 222
Lancaster, Timothy (son) 157, 162
Lancaster, Rev. William 159, 161, 163-4
Langhorne, John 149
La Roche, Sophie von 24
Lattimer, John and Sarah 151-2, 217
Leechman, Prof. William 141
Leighton family, Newcastle 84-5
Leip, Hans 20-2
Leslie, Thomas 69
Lessing, Gotthold Ephraim 15, 77
letters to Arthur Schopenhauer at Wimbledon 233-57
   from Godeffroy 249-50, 254-6
   from Heinrich Floris Schopenhauer 242, 245-6, 247-9, 252, 257
   from Johanna Schopenhauer 235-8, 242-5, 250
   from Meyer 234-5, 238-41, 246-7, 251-2, 253
   replies 233
Lever, Sir Ashton 103-5, 127-8
Lewes, G.H. 331
Lichtenberg, Carl Gustav 353, 374
Lilie, Dietrich 67-8, 92
literature, English, and Arthur Schopenhauer 348-60

Index

Livingstone, Rev. Robert 29, 33
Lloyd, Hannibal Evans 23
Locke, John 42, 83, 288, 291, 353
London
    Arthur Schopenhauer's visit 97-139
    Parson's Green 159-66
    Tower of 107-8
    see also Wimbledon; Wimbledon School
Lowthian, Richard 60
Lushington, Sir Stephen 182
Lysons, Daniel 176

Macaulay, Thomas Babington 147
MacCann, Anthony 19
McCarthy, Charles 165
Mackenzie, E. 88
Mackenzie, Henry 39-40, 176
Mackintosh, Sir James 184
Macpherson, James 66
Mallabar, George 66, 69, 71-2, 85
Mannheim 346
Marryat, Captain Frederick 212, 214, 284, 305-6
Maryland Point 113-14, 135
Matcham, Mr and Mrs George 204
Matcham, George, Jr 204-5, 217, 221, 226
Mathias, Thomas 177-8, 183, 360
Mathiessen, E.A. 111, 113-14, 134
Matthews, Mr (actor) 100, 125
Maughanby 146-8
Maxwell, Sir William 61
Maxwell, William and George 61
Mayplet, Rev. Edward 146
Mellish, William 113, 135
Merlin, John Joseph 105, 128
Merton 175-6, 200-11, 223-4
metaphysics 329-31 *see also* Kant
Meyer, Lorenz 234-5, 238-41, 246-7, 251-3, 259, 272, 281, 283, 304, 315

Milns, William 289-90, 293
Milton, John 15, 323-4
Milward, Richard 208
Monument 103
Moritz, Carl Philipp 24, 272-4
Munden, Mr (actor) 111, 113
Murray, James, of Broughton 32-3, 65
Murray, Dr William 15
Murray, Mr (Danzig merchant) 4-5, 11
museums 102-5, 115-16, 127-8, 138-9
Myers, Rev. J.D. 224

Navy 212-15
Nelson, Rev. Edmund 204
Nelson, Horatio, Lord
    and Danzig 84
    and Rev. Thomas Lancaster 215-26
    and the Schopenhauers 20-2, 208-9
    at Merton 200-15
    funeral 221
    portrait 288
    visit to Hamburg 15, 19-22, 24
Nelson, Rev. and Mrs William, and family 204-5, 217
Nelson-Ward, Horatia 210-11, 215
Newcastle-upon-Tyne 84-8
Newton, Mr (calico printer) 183, 202
Nicholson, J., and Burn, R. 144-5
Nicolas, Sir Harris 203
Nicolson, Bishop 146-7
Nietzsche, Friedrich Wilhelm 372, 376
North, Lord 176, 220

Oatlands 110, 134
Oman, Carola 204
opera 98-9, 122
Oxenford, John 372-4

Paine, Thomas 184, 188, 358, 360

Index

Paleske, Herr 109-10, 116, 245
Parker, Admiral Sir William 288
Parker, Chief Baron 143
Parr, Samuel 187, 221, 290
Parrott, Dr John and Charlotte 182-3, 202
Parson's Green 159-66
Paterson, Benjamin 182
Peacock, Thomas Love 304, 330, 355-7
Pennant, Thomas 144
Pepys, Samuel 160
Percival family 96, 99-100, 103, 107-8, 110, 114, 116, 124, 239, 259, 272
Perisot, Mlle (dancer) 99
Perry, James 180, 183, 188-9, 202
Philips, James 31, 33
Pindar, Peter (John Wolcot), 134, 177-82, 193, 204-5, 310-11, 358-60, 362-3
Pitt, William (the Younger) 156, 170-1, 176-81, 188, 190, 193
Playfair, John 37
Pococke, Richard, Bishop 53, 61, 144
Polonius 371
Polter, Professor 141
Porson, Prof. Richard 184-6
Pottle, F.A. 48
Price, Dr Richard 186
Priestley, Joseph 358
Pryce, Dame Elizabeth 218
Pückler-Muskau, Prince 174

Quasheebaw 207

Railton, Rev. Joseph 149, 167
Ramsay, John, of Ochtertyre 44-5, 52-3, 59
Randolph, Rev. Herbert 183-4, 216, 222, 286, 310, 314-15, 366
Randolph, Dr John 314
Randolph, Dr Thomas 314
Rathbone, Philip 203
Reid, Robert 182
Reid, Thomas 38, 41

religion:
  bigotry 306-16, 361-70
  brainwashing 316-19
  pulpit terrorism 306-16
  Sunday observance 192-3, 307-9, 311-16
Remnant, Mr (English library, Hamburg) 18, 23, 282
Richardson, Samuel 81-2, 160
Richmond (Surrey) 106, 129
Ritchie, Rev. William 50-1
Robertson, William 45
Robinson, Crabb 18-19
Robinson, George (bookseller) 288
Robinson, John (ambassador) 68-9
Robinson, Mr (merchant?) 96, 98
Rogers, Samuel 184
Romaine, Rev. William 158-9
Rosebery, Lord 193
Rosenberg, Barbara 68
Ross, Jacob, Anna Louise, and Elizabeth 68
Rousseau, Jean-Jacques 151
Rücker family 24, 182, 238-9, 245, 247, 261-3, 272
Ruddock, Rev. Joshua 222, 320
Runge, Dr Johann Hinrich Christian, school at Hamburg 235, 239, 244, 252, 281-5, 300, 306, 310, 370

Saint James's Park 99-100
Saint Paul's Cathedral 116-17
Saker, Thomas 206
Salthill 109-10, 133
Sanskrit literature 370-1
Saunders, T.B. 376
Savage, Rev. George 224
Schlegel, Friedrich von 344
Schmidt, Herr and Frau 109-10
Schnebbelie, R.B. 172, 288
Schopenhauer, Andreas (Arthur Schopenhauer's grandfather) 3
Schopenhauer, Arthur
  and England 368-76
  and English bigotry 357, 360-70

Index

and English language
  322-45, 370-1
and English literature 348-60
and English philosophy
  323-9, 349
and English religion 312-14,
  361-9
and English ways 345-8
and Hume 326-9
and Johnson 163, 357-8, 361
and Kant 331-45
and Nelson 20-2, 208
and religion 317-18
and Sanskrit literature 370-1
and Smith 33
and the Volunteers 117,
  196-200
and Wimbledon School (*q.v.*)
  271-319
background and parents 1-26
education 280-5
English diary 95-118
grand tour 25, 95-6, 322
letters to 233-57
lifestyle 345
on education 319
on marriage 345-6
on religion 303, 309, 317-19
pets 347-8
philosophy 13
publications 372, 375-6
style 371-5
translations by 323-9, 331-45
Schopenhauer, Heinrich Floris
  (Arthur Schopenhauer's
  father) 1-14, 19-25
  and Jameson 72-3, 83
  and Voltaire 3-4, 12, 83, 360
  and Wimbledon School 175,
    205, 278-80, 322
  business 3-4, 6-7, 22-3, 95-6
  in Danzig 1-13
  in England 6, 9-10, 95-6
  in Hamburg 13-26
  letters to Arthur
    Schopenhauer 242, 245-9,
    252, 257, 272
  marriage 7-9
Schopenhauer, Johanna (Arthur
  Schopenhauer's mother)

and dogs 348
and England 7-10
  and Jameson 2, 7, 29,
    36, 47, 74-84
  and Nelson 19-22, 208-9
  and religion 312-14
  and Wimbledon School 174,
    271, 278-80, 286, 295,
    300-4, 306, 316, 322
birth of Arthur
  Schopenhauer 9-11
childhood 8, 70, 73-4, 77-8
education and reading 78-82,
  352, 354
in Hamburg 22-5
letters to Arthur
  Schopenhauer 235-8,
  242-5, 250
marriage 8-9
travel diary 96
Schopenhauer, Karl Gottfried
  (Heinrich's brother) 6, 23
Schwalbe, Herr 114-16, 118
Scott, Rev. A.J. 200
Scott, Andrew and Lucy 11, 68
Scott, Claude 11, 23, 112,
  134-5
Scott, John (teacher) 32-3
Scott, Sir Walter 36, 56, 355
Scott, William 184
Shakespeare, William 105, 113,
  351
Sheldon, Major Thomas 72
Sheldon's Ordinary 2, 71
Shelley, Frances, Lady 206
Shenstone, William 352
Sheridan, Richard Brinsley
  137-8, 229, 290
Sheridan, Thomas 290-1, 297-9
Shield, William 183
Siddons, Mrs Sarah 112-14
Sievwright, Rev. Norman 51,
  55
Simpson, Lady Ann 161
Sinnett, Mrs (translater) 373
Sloman, William, and Robert
  24
Smith, Adam 33
Smollett, Tobias 46, 52, 141
Soermans, Hendrik 3

Index

Solly, Edward 23, 107, 130-1
Solly, Mrs Elizabeth 108, 131
Solly, Isaac (I) 3, 6, 11, 126, 219
Solly, Isaac (II) 102, 107, 126
Somerville, Thomas 37, 39
Sommer, Michael 70
Southey, Robert 212-13, 288
Spence, Robert 87
Spencer, George John, 2nd Earl 176, 180, 182, 188, 191, 202, 221-2
Spencer, Lady 206
Stephens, A. 184
Sterne, Laurence 10, 36, 75-7, 352-4
Stevenson, Prof. John 33-5, 37, 39, 41-7, 50, 90-1, 298
Stewart, Charles, of Shambellie 56-7, 60
Stewart, Prof. Dugald 38
Stewart, Prof. Matthew 7, 33-4, 37-8
Stewart, Col. William, 2, 67
Stirling, James 37
Storace, Signor (singer) 117
Story, John 57, 60
Stuart, Prof. George 34, 38
Suckling, Col. and Mrs William 207-8, 211
Suffolk, Lord 4-5
Suirmand, Master 113-14
Sundays 192-3, 303, 307-9, 311-16
Sunderland 152-8
Swift, Jonathan 142, 355, 374
Swinburne, Algernon Charles 375
'Symposiacks' of Wimbledon 177-86

Talbert, William 64
Temple, William 40, 48
textbooks, school 295-8
Thackeray, William Makepeace 159
theatre, and Arthur Schopenhauer 98, 100-3, 109, 111-17, 122, 125, 127
Thornhill, John 153-4, 167-8

Thoytt, Mr (mill owner) 202
Thrale, Henry 218-19
Tieck, Ludwig 81, 355
Tooke, John Horne 176, 180, 183-5, 188
translations by Arthur Schopenhauer 323-45
  Goethe 325
  Hume 326-9
  Kant 331-45
  Milton 323-4
Trelawney, Edward John 214, 305
Trollope, Anthony 224
Trosiener, Christian Heinrich and Elisabeth (Johanna Schopenhauer's parents) 72-3
Trosiener, Johanna *see* Schopenhauer, Johanna
Tucker, Rev. Johnnie 66, 72
Tunbridge Wells 112, 135
Turnbull, George 297

Ullock, Ruth (daughter of Rev. Thomas Lancaster) 157, 203-4, 214, 216-17
Ullock, Tom 214-15, 232

van der Hufen, Mynheer 96, 114
Vauxhall 109, 132-3
Victoria, Queen of Great Britain and Ireland 215
Vipond, Ann (niece of Rev. Thomas Lancaster) 217
Voltaire 3-4, 12, 83, 272, 280-1, 360, 366, 368
Volunteers 117, 189-200

Waagen, Gustav Friedrich 325
Wallace, W. 347, 361
Walpole, Horace 188
Waring, (Rev. John?) 165
Watt, James 181
Waugh, John, chancellor of Carlyle 145-6
Waugh, Rev. John 54
Wendeborn, Dr Gebhard Friedrich August 24, 66, 275-8

Index

Wesley, John 144
West, B. 214
Westminster Abbey 105-6
Westphal, Hans Christian Friedrich 281
Whichelo, C.J.M. 266, 287-8
Wieland, C.M. 77, 354
Wieler, Mr (merchant) 111
Wilberforce, William 278-9
Wilson, Rev. Joseph, Barton School 140-1, 284
Wilson, Rev. Joseph, Dumfries 64
Wimbledon 170-226
  anti-Jacobins and volunteers 186-200
  Nelson 200-15
  'Symposiacks' 177-86
Wimbledon School 271-319
  and other academies 271-80
  and the Schopenhauers 174-5, 205, 271, 278-80, 286, 295, 300-4, 306, 316, 322
  bigotry 306-16
  house 170-6
  Plan of Education 285-300
  practice 300-6
  religion 299-300, 303, 306-16
  staff 285-8
  textbooks 295-8
Windham, William 181
Windsor 110
Wolcot, John *see* Pindar, Peter
Wolf, Dr Nathanael Matthäus von 7-8, 26, 83
Woodforde, Parson 165
Wordsworth, William and Dorothy 14, 17-18
Wraxall, Nathaniel 6-7
Wynne, Eugenia 16-17

Yates, Richard 145, 149-50, 284
Young, Thomas 15

Zenobio, Count 184
Zimmern, Helen 326

For Product Safety Concerns and Information please contact our EU representative GPSR@taylorandfrancis.com
Taylor & Francis Verlag GmbH, Kaufingerstraße 24, 80331 München, Germany

www.ingramcontent.com/pod-product-compliance
Lightning Source LLC
Chambersburg PA
CBHW071237300426
44116CB00008B/1068